Technology-Rich
Learning Environments
A Future Perspective

Technology-Rich
Learning Environments
A Future Perspective

Myint Swe Khine
National Institute of Education
Nanyang Technological University, Singapore

Darrell Fisher
Science and Mathematics Education Centre
Curtin University of Technology, Australia

World Scientific
New Jersey • London • Singapore • Hong Kong

Published by

World Scientific Publishing Co. Pte. Ltd.
5 Toh Tuck Link, Singapore 596224
USA office: 27 Warren Street, Suite 401-402, Hackensack, NJ 07601
UK office: 57 Shelton Street, Covent Garden, London WC2H 9HE

British Library Cataloguing-in-Publication Data
A catalogue record for this book is available from the British Library.

TECHNOLOGY-RICH LEARNING ENVIRONMENTS
A Future Perspective

Copyright © 2003 by World Scientific Publishing Co. Pte. Ltd.

All rights reserved. This book, or parts thereof, may not be reproduced in any form or by any means, electronic or mechanical, including photocopying, recording or any information storage and retrieval system now known or to be invented, without written permission from the publisher.

For photocopying of material in this volume, please pay a copying fee through the Copyright Clearance Center, Inc., 222 Rosewood Drive, Danvers, MA 01923, USA. In this case permission to photocopy is not required from the publisher.

ISBN-13 978-981-238-435-5
ISBN-10 981-238-435-9
ISBN-13 78-981-238-436-2 pbk)
ISBN-10 981-238-436-7 (pbk)

Foreword

Leo Tan Wee Hin
National Institute of Education
Nanyang Technological University
Singapore

Over the last few decades, an expanding literature has emerged providing rich insights and information on the learning environments of classrooms, particularly in schools. Students' and teachers' perceptions of these environments have led to changes which have contributed to improved student achievement. A robust knowledge base exists that has proved valuable in teacher preparation and professional development courses and policy making that continues to aim for enhanced student achievement.

At the National Institute of Education in Singapore, we have identified three core areas to form the research agenda at the Centre for Research in Pedagogy and Practice over the next five years. These areas are Mathematics and Science Literacy, Language Literacy (both English and Mother Tongue), and Information and Communication Technology. We regard these areas as the keys to developing a society that will both continue to prosper in this era of globalisation as well as develop a cohesive society in the decades ahead. It is interesting to note that the third of these areas is a focus of this book.

This book is one of the first that links ICT with studies of learning environments and represents an exciting advance in that it brings into one volume work by some of the leaders in the field of studies of technology-rich learning environments. The influence of new technology is deservedly given an important place in these studies and will contribute to new models for classroom environment studies into the future.

The co-editors, Myint Swe Khine and Darrell Fisher are to be congratulated for their initiative in taking a future perspective on learning environment studies and in preparing this book.

Preface

Barry J. Fraser
Science and Mathematics Education Centre
Curtin University of Technology
Australia

Because students spend approximately 20,000 hours in classrooms by the time that they graduate from university, students' reactions to their teaching-learning experiences are of considerable importance. However, educators often rely exclusively on assessing achievement and pay scant attention to the quality of the learning environment. Teachers should not feel that it is a waste of valuable time to put energy into improving their learning environments because the research convincingly shows that attention to the learning environment is likely to pay off in terms of improving student outcomes (Fraser, 2001).

The field of learning environments has undergone remarkable growth, diversification and internationalisation during the past 30 years. A striking feature of this field is the availability of a variety of economical, valid and widely-applicable questionnaires that have been developed and used for assessing students' perceptions of leaning environment. Although earlier work often used questionnaires to assess learning environments, the productive combination of qualitative and quantitative methods is a hallmark of the field today.

Not only has learning environments research expanded remarkably over the past few decades on the international scene, but also Asian researchers have made important and distinct contributions particularly over the previous decade. Asian researchers have cross-validated the main contemporary learning environment questionnaires that originated in the West and have undertaken careful translations and adaptations for use in the Chinese, Korean, Malay and Indonesian languages. Asian studies have replicated Western research in establishing consistent associations between the learning environment and student outcomes, in using learning environment assessments in evaluation education programs, and in identifying determinants of learning environments. Goh and Khine's (2002) important book provides a unique focus on the distinctive contributions to the field of learning environments made by Asian researchers.

Currently, there is considerable optimism internationally that the integration of information communications technology (ICT) into the learning environment will provide teachers with the means to manage efficiently the diverse educational provisions needed to optimise each individual student's outcomes. In many educational settings, ICT is becoming more commonplace and, in some cases, the integration of ICT into the learning environment is becoming a major thrust. However, it is important that our optimism about the efficacy of technology-rich learning environments is accompanied by systematic research and evaluation.

Fortunately, past research on learning environments provides numerous research traditions, conceptual models and research methods that are relevant to the study of technology-rich learning environments. This book shows how we can draw on the rich resource of diverse, valid, economical and widely-applicable assessment instruments that are available in the field of learning environments as a starting point for developing questionnaires suited to technology-rich learning environments. Also, the book shows how we can draw on past evaluations of educational innovations from the field of learning environments to investigate success in creating effective ICT-rich learning environments. Hopefully this book will encourage and guide important future research into technology-rich learning environments.

References

Fraser, B.J. (2002). Twenty thousand hours. *Learning Environments Research: An International Journal, 4*, 1-5.

Goh, S.C., & Khine, M.S. (Eds.). (2002). *Studies in educational learning environments: An international perspective*. Singapore: World Scientific.

From The Editors

The field of learning environments has continued to thrive in educational research and what has been noteworthy in the last few years, is the increasing number of studies in technology-rich environments. This has been in keeping with developments in computer-assisted instruction, online learning, web-based learning, using the Internet in education, etc. This book on technology-rich educational learning environments was conceptualised as a collection of learning environment studies where researchers and educators could share the results of their work with others. These studies have been conducted in various parts of the world as indicated by the contributors who come from twelve different countries. This gives the book an international outlook. It is also hoped that the book, in bringing together current research with a future perspective will provide valuable information and ideas for future research in this area.

We would like to express our thanks to all the contributors for responding to our invitation to write about their work and for making this book a reality. The book is our joint achievement. We would also like to express our thanks to Professor Leo Tan, Director of National Institute of Education, Nanyang Technological University, Singapore, and to Professor Barry Fraser, Director of the national Key Centre for School Science and Mathematics, Curtin University of Technology, Australia, for their unstinting support throughout the period of development of this book. Indeed, we extend our thanks to everyone who has assisted in the publication of the book.

In the first chapter, Chang and Fisher describe a new questionnaire that assesses student perceptions of four core aspects of the Web-based learning environment, namely, Access, Interaction, Response, and Results. The development and validation of the WEBLEI is a significant outcome of this study as the questionnaire is available for web-based learning situations and future research. Khine, in the second chapter describes the development of a CD-ROM that integrates observations, discussions and contextualised examples to help trainee teachers effectively apply the theories and principles of classroom management and understand the philosophies governing good classroom management. Aldridge and Fraser, in Chapter 3, report on a study that involved the validation of a widely-applicable and distinctive questionnaire for assessing students' perceptions of their actual and preferred classroom learning environments in technology-rich, outcomes-focused learning settings. The TROFLEI was then used to investigate associations between students' perceptions of the learning environment and student outcomes.

Margianti's study described in Chapter 4 was conducted in university classes in Indonesia. Relationships between attitudes and achievement of university students in computer classrooms were investigated with a large sample of computer students in 50 university classes. Trinidad's Chapter 5 looks at methods used with Hong Kong educators to develop e-learning projects that use interactive computer-based learning resources; linked with networked communities of peers and experts; and online collaborations in and beyond the classroom while accessing online information. While in Chapter 6, Rickards examines effective teaching in technology-rich classrooms and how this is typically based on the individual teacher's level of competence with the technologies at hand and the ability to manage such classes. Zandvliet also focuses on the teacher in the next chapter and gives a broad, descriptive look into one Canadian province's emerging Internet classrooms and what may or may not be working for classroom teachers.

In Chapter 8, Clayton explores the concepts and procedures used in the development of an online learning environment perceptual measure in a tertiary institution. This overview is followed by a description of the scales and items, the web based delivery and storage procedures used in the creation of the OLLES. In the following chapter, Newby uses the CLEI to report the results of a study, also in a tertiary institution, that investigated differences between students' perceptions of aspects of the learning environment of open and closed computer laboratories, and also the differences in student outcomes from courses that adopt these approaches. Kesner, Frailich and Hofstein, in Chapter 10, describe the development of an Internet site that was developed to serve as a resource to complement the teaching materials for secondary school chemistry students and teachers in Israel. The site can be used to enrich and vary chemistry studies, mainly with relevant everyday life contexts and industrial applications. In Chapter 11, Muirhead considers the influence of computers and information technology links on the delivery of maritime education and training, and examines how these features can be used to open up future avenues of learning. The potential of marine simulation, satellite communications and distance learning methods to deliver training and education to seafarers on ships, using the global links of the Internet and the Worldwide web is discussed.

In The Netherlands, as in many countries, classrooms have become more and more culturally diverse. Van Tartwijk, Wubbels, den Brok, de Jong, and Veldman (Chapter 12) describe the development and use of a website to provide student teachers with both practical and theoretical information on communication processes in multicultural classrooms in The Netherlands. Workshops were organised in which student teachers and the teachers in schools used the electronic learning environment Blackboard for discussion. Lang and Wong in Chapter 13 provide an understanding of how e-learning is incorporated into the existing mode of teaching science in Singapore secondary schools. In order to do this, a classroom learning environment instrument (ELCEQ) was administered to obtain the students' perceptions of their e-learning classroom learning environments. Harper (Chapter 14) also focuses on the students as stakeholders in schools and looks at the Generation Y model. While promoting the effective use of technology in schools, Generation Y develops student leadership, and fosters a collaborative, constructivist learning community between student and teacher allowing students to act as responsible partners with their teachers in building new curriculum materials and new teaching and learning practices. Similarly, in the next chapter, Fulford and Eichelberger continue the idea of empowering stakeholders and describe how 'The System of Reciprocity has been employed by the Educational Technology Department, University of Hawaii, to create a mutually beneficial situation for its students, faculty, the department, the college and the university.

In Chapter 16, She and Fisher describe a web-based, multimedia, flash science learning program that focuses on helping students develop an understanding of water pressure through online e-learning environment in Taiwan. The study examines the learning environment created during implementation of this program in science classes and its impact on students' cognitive and affective learning outcomes. Chapter 17 is a description of one of the first uses of a learning environment questionnaire in Japan. Hirata and Fisher describe students' and teachers' perceptions of actual and preferred classroom environments in a

Japanese junior-high school and consider the potential of such measures in Japanese schools. The chapter finally discusses their potential to improve teaching and learning in Japanese classrooms using new educational technologies. In the final chapter, Hung and Chee describe issues related to balancing individual and social perspectives in technology-rich learning environment. In this regard, they propose four models of e-learning, which are web-based, and subsequently discuss design principles which can be generalized. They indicate how technology-rich learning environments require these design principles in order to facilitate the learning process.

Myint Swe Khine
Nanyang Technological University
Singapore

Darrell Fisher
Curtin University of Technology
Australia

About the Contributors

Jill M. Aldridge is a Post Doctoral Research Fellow at the Science and Mathematics Education Centre of Curtin University of Technology, Western Australia. Her research is in the field of teaching and learning. Currently her focus is on the integration of ICT into classrooms and whether this leads to a more individualised and outcomes-focused learning environment.

Perry den Brok is Associate Professor in a teacher training and educational research group of the Institute of Education (IVLOS) at Utrecht University (The Netherlands). His research is in the field of teaching and teacher education. Currently his focus is on multicultural and intercultural studies on classroom environments, and factors that explain differences in student perceptions of teaching.

Vanessa Chang is a Lecturer in Information Systems with the School of Information Systems, Curtin Business School at Curtin University of Technology, Perth, Australia. Her main areas of teaching are Systems Analysis and Design, Agile Systems Developments and IT Management. Her research interest is in the area of on-line learning environment. Her current PhD research is in web-based or on-line learning.

John Clayton is an Online Curriculum Designer for the Centre for Learning Technologies at the Waikato Institute of Technology, Hamilton, New Zealand. He is currently undertaking study for a Doctor of Science Education at Curtin University, Perth. Since 1999 he has been involved in developing and implementing a number of web-based courses from automotive systems to nursing. His current research interests are in teaching and learning in the online environment, particularly the most effective and efficient way to measure students' and teachers' perceptions of this digital world.

Ariana Eichelberger oversees work on the USA Department of Education *Preparing Tomorrow's Teacher's to Use Technology* (PT3) grant entitled *Learning Enhancement through Innovations* (LEI Aloha). As Outreach Manager for the LEI Aloha technology integration project in the Department of Educational Technology at the University of Hawaii at Manoa, she works with faculty throughout the University system to promote effective use of technology in the training of future teachers. Ariana's areas of expertise are instructional design, mentoring, and personnel training and management.

Darrell Fisher is a Professor of Science Education and Deputy Director of the Science and Mathematics Education Centre at Curtin University of Technology, Perth, Australia. His major research interests include classroom and school environments, and curriculum issues related to science, particularly curriculum evaluation. He has published and presented on these topics throughout the world. He is a Fellow of the Australian College of Education and the Regional Editor for Asia and Australia of *Learning Environments Research: An International Journal.* He is a world leader in learning environment research

Marcel Frailich has been a high school chemistry teacher for 20 years. She earned a B.Sc. and M.Sc. in chemistry. Currently she is a graduate student in the department of Science Teaching, the Weizmann Institute of Science. Her area of study is "Evaluation of the Educational Effectiveness of Using a web site in the Teaching and Learning of High School Chemistry in Israel". She was actively involved in the development of the site currently in the phase of implementation. In recent years she was also involved in continuous professional development of chemistry teacher in her region.

Barry J. Fraser is Professor and Director of the Science and Mathematics Education Centre at Curtin University of Technology in Perth, Australia. He is co-editor of the 72-chapter *International Handbook of Science Education* published by Kluwer, and Editor-in-Chief of the Kluwer journal *Learning Environments Research: An International Journal.* He is a fellow of the American Association for the Advancement of Science, International Academy of Education, Academy of the Social Sciences in Australia and Australian College of Education. He is the 2003 recipient of the Outstanding Contributions to

Science Education through Research Award from the National Association for Research in Science Teaching in the USA. He is an eminent scholar in learning environment research.

Catherine P. Fulford, is a Professor in the Department of Educational Technology at the University of Hawaii at Manoa. She conducts research in distance education and technology integration, and, teaches courses in instructional and visual design. Dr. Fulford is co-principal investigator of the Learning Enhancement through Innovations (LEI) Aloha project and has received numerous grants including United States Department of Education *Preparing Tomorrow's Teacher's to Use Technology* (PT3) Catalyst and Implementation grants.

Dennis Harper is founder and director of Generation YES and has been a leader in the field of computing and education for over 35 years in the USA and abroad. In 1996, Generation YES received a federal grant to expand its innovative "Gen www.Y" program and has done so with dramatic success. Over 600 schools nationwide have adopted this unique model for teacher professional development program in technology. At its core, Gen Y is a student-centered model in which students partner with teachers to develop technology-infused lessons.

Sonomi Hirata is in the Department of Early Childhood Education, Hakuoh University Women's College in Japan. She is also a part-time instructor in Psychology at Tokyo University of Agriculture and in the Jichi Medical School. She received her PhD from Waseda University. She has taught courses in teacher-training; Educational Psychology and Consultation in Education, and in other subjects in psychology. Her research interests include the relation between classroom climates and pupils' maladjustment behaviors and constructing psychological measures for evaluating learning environments.

Avi Hofstein holds a PhD in science education (chemistry) from the Weizmann Institute of Science. He is Head of both the Chemistry Group and the *Science for All* programs in the Science Teaching Department, The Weizmann Institute of Science, Israel. He has been involved in all facets of the curricular process in chemistry namely development, implementation, evaluation. He has conducted research in many areas of science education. In recent years, he has been involved in the development of leadership amongst chemistry teachers to promote reform in the way chemistry is taught in Israel.

David Hung is an Associate Professor at the National Institute of Education (NIE), Nanyang Technological University, Singapore. He is currently a contributing editor of *Educational Technology* and an associate editor of the *International Journal of Learning Technology*. Dr. Hung teaches and supervises undergraduate and graduate students and serves as a consultant and trainer to projects involving education and training, initiated by the Ministries of Education and Defence. Besides doing research in cognitive and learning sciences, he has been actively involved in online learning efforts at the NIE and in Singapore

Hsiao-Ching She is Professor in a science education group of the Institute of Education at National Chiao-Tung University. Her research is in the field of science teaching and learning. Her previous focus was on teacher-student communication behaviour and students' knowledge and construction in science classroom learning environments. Currently, her focus is on conceptual change involving higher hierarchical levels of science concepts, web-based science learning, and promoting science learning in heterogeneous classes.

Yvonne de Jong is a consultant in higher education at the Institute of Education (IVLOS) at Utrecht University (the Netherlands). Her work is in the field of ICT and education. She focuses on the use of electronic learning environments in higher education.

Miri Kesner is staff member of the science teaching department in The Weizmann Institute of Science. She started her career as a chemistry teacher in secondary schools after a BSc in chemistry and a teaching license from Tel-Aviv University. She holds a MSc and PhD in Science Education from The Weizmann Institute of Science. Her main activities include: curriculum development, implementation of educational programs, industrial chemistry, integrating ICT into chemistry studies, teachers professional development. and research in chemistry education.

Myint Swe Khine is Associate Professor at the National Institute of Education, Nanyang Technological University, Singapore, where he teaches courses in classroom management, IT integration and instructional design at both undergraduate and postgraduate levels. One of his academic qualifications includes a Doctor of Science Education from Curtin University of Technology, Australia. He has been a teacher educator for more than 20 years. He is the co-editor of the book *Studies in educational learning environment: An international perspective* published by World Scientific.

Eko Sri Margianti is Professor and President of the Gunadarma University Jakarta, Indonesia. She is the Secretary-General of the Indonesian Computer Society, the Chairperson of Funding and Development of Indonesia Private Association, Vice-President of Private Indonesia Tertiary Study of Computer Association, Board Member of SEARCC IT Professional Council in South East Asia and Chairperson of Computer Education Foundation in Jakarta, Indonesia. She completed her doctoral degree in learning environments at Curtin University of Technology in Australia.

Peter Muirhead has wide experience in the maritime industry having spent 17 years at sea. In 1979, he helped establish the new tertiary-level Australian Maritime College. He has over 25 years experience in the development and use of marine simulators and other technological methods. His present Chair is Inmarsat Professor of Maritime Education and Training at the World Maritime University, Malmö, Sweden. He is the author of many papers and research documents, as well as contributing to several books, dealing with various aspects of maritime education and training.

Michael Newby is in the Department of Information Systems and Decision Sciences at California State University, Fullerton. He received his BSc in Mathematics from the University of London, UK, his M.Sc. in Mathematics from the University of Bradford, UK and his PhD from Curtin University. He has published in journals such as the Journal of Educational Computing Research and the Journal of Information Systems Education and in proceedings of international conferences. His research interests include computer learning environments, and improving student learning in programming courses.

Quek Choon Lang is an Assistant Professor in the Instructional Science Academic Group at the National Institute of Education, Nanyang

Technological University. Her research interests include classroom learning environments, gifted education, information technology and interdisciplinary curriculum studies.

Tan Seng Chee is from the Instructional Science Academic Group of the National Institute of Education (NIE), Nanyang Technological University. He worked as a high school teacher for several years and headed the school's IT department. He completed his PhD in Instructional Systems from the Pennsylvania State University, under the supervision of Professor David Jonassen. His research interests include computer-supported collaborative learning and using computers to promote thinking. He currently heads a major research grant in computer-supported collaborative learning environments.

Tony Rickards is currently a Science Education lecturer in the Science and Mathematics Education Centre, Curtin University of Technology. Prior to this he worked at the Graduate School of Education, University of Western Australia, and the University of Southern Queensland, where he was founding Director of ITEL; an Information Technology Enhanced Learning research centre. He has had over 20 years of teaching experience in computer education at all levels in Australia. His current research, publications and professional involvement centre on teacher-student interpersonal behaviour in science, mathematics and particularly technology-rich learning environments.

Jan van Tartwijk works as Associate Professor and consultant for the Institute of Education (IVLOS) at Utrecht University and also for the Department of Educational Development & Research of Maastricht University. In his work he focuses on technology-rich learning environments, the use of electronic portfolios in education, and the interpersonal significance of (nonverbal) teacher behaviour in the multicultural classroom.

Sue Trinidad's work involves developing e-learning units that combine technology with innovative teaching, learning and assessment approaches. Her teaching and research interests include using technology effectively in education, technology planning and implementation and developing pedagogically and andragogically-sound online learning environments. She teaches technology education to post-service teachers at the Centre for Information Technology in Education (CITE),

University of Hong Kong. She has published and presented in the area of technology use and technology implementation.

Ietje Veldman is Director of Teacher Education at ICLON Graduate School of Education of Leiden University. After a career in Geography Education and curriculum development for Environmental Education she became a teacher educator. Her current interest is, among others, multicultural education.

Angela F.L. Wong is an Associate Professor in the Instructional Science Academic Group, National Institute of Education, Nanyang Technological University, Singapore. She is also the Associate Dean in charge of the Practicum component for all initial teacher-training programmes. She currently lectures in teaching methodology and instructional technology. Her areas of research interests include learning environments, science education and Practicum-related issues in teacher education.

Theo Wubbels is Professor of Education and works for the Institute of Educational Studies of the Faculty of Social Sciences at Utrecht University. Through involvement in the development of student counseling in secondary education he became a teacher educator and then a researcher. Since then his research and teaching topics have been, among others, social and interpersonal relationships in education, the study of learning environments with quantitative and qualitative methods, international studies of learning environments, and reflection in teacher education.

David Zandvliet is an Assistant Professor in the Faculty of Education at Simon Fraser University. His research interests lie in the areas of science, technology and environmental education with a focus on students' perceptions of their learning environment as it is described in a range of educational settings. He is also Director of the Faculty's Centre for Educational Technology.

Contents

Foreword v

Preface vii

From the Editors ix

About the Contributors xiii

Chapter 1
The validation and application of a new learning
environment instrument for online learning in
higher education 1
Vanessa Chang and Darrell Fisher

Chapter 2
Creating a technology-rich constructivist learning
environment in a classroom management module 21
Myint Swe Khine

Chapter 3
Effectiveness of a technology-rich and
outcomes-focused learning environment 41
Jill Aldridge and Barry Fraser

Chapter 4
The relationship between attitudes and achievement
of university students in computer classrooms
in Indonesia 71
Eko Sri Margianti

Chapter 5
Working with technology-rich learning environments:
Strategies for success 97
Sue Trinidad

Chapter 6
Technology-rich learning environments and the role
of effective teaching   115
  Tony Rickards

Chapter 7
Learning environments in new contexts:
Web-capable classrooms in Canada   133
  David Zandvliet

Chapter 8
Assessing and researching the online
learning environment   157
  John Clayton

Chapter 9
Computer laboratory environments: Providing
a sustainable practical learning experience   187
  Michael Newby

Chapter 10
Implementing the Internet learning environment
into the chemistry curriculum in high schools in Israel   209
  Miri Kesner, Marcel Frailich and Avi Hofstein

Chapter 11
Technology and maritime education and training:
A future perspective   235
  Peter Muirhead

Chapter 12
Designing a web-supported learning environment
on communication in multicultural classrooms   255
  *Jan van Tartwijk, Theo Wubbels, Perry den Brok,
  Yvonne de Jong and Ietje Veldman*

Chapter 13
Evaluating e-learning environments in Singapore
lower secondary science classrooms 285
   Quek Choon Lang and Angela F.L. Wong

Chapter 14
Students as change agents: The generation Y model 307
   Dennis Harper

Chapter 15
A system of reciprocity: Empowering stakeholders
to do more with less in educational technology 331
   Catherine P. Fulford and Ariana Eichelberger

Chapter 16
Web-based e-learning environments in Taiwan:
The impact of the online science flash program
on students' learning 343
   Hsiao-Ching She and Darrell Fisher

Chapter 17
Students' and teachers' perceptions of actual and
preferred classroom environments in Japanese
junior high school: The potential of psychological
measures in the classroom 369
   Sonomi Hirata and Darrell Fisher

Chapter 18
Design principles for web-based learning:
Balancing individual and social perspectives
in technology-rich learning environments 385
   David Hung and Tan Seng Chee

Selected Bibliography 407

Index 419

Chapter 1

THE VALIDATION AND APPLICATION OF A NEW LEARNING ENVIRONMENT INSTRUMENT FOR ONLINE LEARNING IN HIGHER EDUCATION

Vanessa Chang and Darrell Fisher
Curtin University of Technology
Australia

More and more academics are accepting the challenge of using web-based or online learning in higher education to deliver coursework. Many web-sites indicate that opportunities for students to receive coursework via the Web is routine at most universities. The Internet/Web has become an important change agent in higher education and universities are reviewing their strategic plans to incorporate online learning. As a result of the increase in online courses, it is timely for learning environment research to focus on the Web. However, to date, no comprehensive instruments have been developed to assess online learning environments for higher education. A new web-based learning environment instrument is described in this chapter. The Web-based Learning Environment Instrument (WEBLEI) contains four main scales. Three scales (Access, Interaction, and Response) are built upon the work of Tobin (1998). The other scale (Results) focuses on information structure and the design of online material. The rationale behind, and development of, the WEBLEI are described in the paper. Statistical analyses, Cronbach alpha reliability coefficient, factor analysis, and discriminant validity, indicated that the WEBLEI is a reliable and valid instrument. The chapter also reports on findings involving the perceptions of undergraduate and graduate students utilising this new instrument.

1. Introduction

The rise in computer literacy of users and the trend of Internet access have presented enormous challenges for universities world wide to improve outcomes and extend access to a broad range of students. Higher education now draws students from all backgrounds from all over the world and all age groups. The Web represents a paradigm shift in education and it signifies an evolving change in learning style where information is shared with a wider community (Brodsky, 1998). Many universities now are exploring technologies that may facilitate change in education and confront challenges that we will face as we move towards a new paradigm of continuous education in an online learning environment (Hicks, Reid, & George, 1999; Wilson, 1997).

Given the fact that the Web is being used in an increasing number of courses and in most universities, it is desirable to conduct research into the social and psychological aspects of online learning environment and to draw from it the students' perception of online learning environment. The study described here concentrates on online learning in higher education and its effectiveness as a learning environment. This is achieved by investigating students' perceptions of this learning environment.

2. Learning Environments

The concept of learning environment has existed since the 1930s (Fraser, 1994, 1998; Goh & Fraser, 1998). During the last 25 years, learning environment research has been firmly established in the traditional classroom environment particularly in the field of science education (McRobbie, Fisher, & Wong, 1998; Tobin & Fraser, 1998) and this research has recognised that students' perceptions are important social and psychological factors in classrooms (Fraser, 1994; Fraser, 1998). Very often these perceptions are assessed using questionnaires. Fraser (1998) has collated and explained a number of these learning environment questionnaires developed over the last three decades. These instruments have mainly been used in the assessment and investigation of classroom environments in primary and secondary schools (Fraser, 1998).

In recent times, there have been research studies into distance education environments for higher education levels. For example, Jegede, Fraser, and Fisher (1998) developed the *Distance and Open Learning Environment Scale* (DOLES) for university students studying in distance education. Lately, some research on learning environments has focused on the Web (Tobin, 1998). In particular, Tobin described a framework which can be used for the evaluation of learning environments in interactive environments. However, no comprehensive instruments have been developed to assess online learning environments for higher education. Thus, it was decided to develop a new web-based learning environment instrument building on the work of Tobin (1998). Furthermore, although interest in this environment has increased in recent time (Laurillard, 1993; Khan, 1997; Palloff & Pratt, 1998; Reeves & Reeves, 1997; Tobin, 1998), there is little research and almost none at the tertiary level in the psychosocial aspects of online learning environments.

3. Paradigm Shift in Learning Environment

Many students see web-based learning as an opportunity for them to gain higher education without having to physically attend classes and academics worldwide have realised the attraction and extent of this new learning mode. The change in the teaching and learning mode from the traditional environment to online environment presents a new way of teaching and learning for both teachers and students. The view of the online learning approach, which is discussed next, is one that carries all of the teaching and learning notions of a traditional environment with emphases on constructivist and cognitive perspectives.

The styles of teaching and learning in an online environment can be characterised in a quite different manner to the traditional teaching and learning environment. Online learning is defined as a system and process that connects learners with distributed and online learning materials. The learning in this environment is characterised by separation of place and time between the teacher and learner, between learners, and between learners and learning resources. In order for this online environment to be utilised effectively, the teaching and learning activities in this environment can be characterised as having a three way interaction: one-to-one; one-to-many; and many to many (McDonald & Postle, 1999).

A one-to-one communication can be characterised as activities that were carried out by answering students' queries via electronic mail. Also included in this would be students seeking advice regarding their course or other matters from their teacher. A one-to-many communication can be described as activities carried out when the facilitator is guiding and facilitating students' progress through study materials, readings, and other postings. The final interaction type of many-to-many can be deemed as activities where on-going discussions are established amongst learners and the facilitator. This is demonstrated where discussion of a particular topic takes place with the group sharing, collaborating, and cooperating with one another. This discussion is seen as promoting an effective and a rich learning environment.

Many authors such as Bannan and Milheim (1997), Dowling (1997), Jonassen (1994) and Laurillard (1993) have indicated that the online learning environment utilises the model of an integrated behaviourist or objectivist and constructivist model. It is claimed that this model offers a structured approach for basic skills or the content of the lesson (behavourist or objectivist approach) whilst the constructivist design of the course includes motivating and empowering the learners in their course of study. In order to benefit from this online learning environment, learners must collaborate and interact with other students and at the same time, be able to analyse, reflect, synthesise, organise, and restructure information as well as create and contribute their own ideas (Bannan & Milheim, 1997). In contrast to the behaviourist and objectivist views of traditional learning environment, the constructivist believes that the student ought to build an internal and personal interpretation and be able to construct new knowledge based on their prior knowledge and understanding of present knowledge (Bannan & Milheim, 1997).

Another consideration of this constructivist environment involves the control of learning activities. According to Hooper and Hannafin (1991), this control of learning activities is demonstrated by students selecting and sequencing their learning activities as well as creating their own learning opportunities and satisfying their own learning needs. This approach is view as students taking control of their own learning, students being more responsible for their own learning, and thus, creating a student-centred learning environment.

As online learning becomes more collaborative and interactive, it is important to consider the changing roles of the teacher. A study conducted by Hiltz (1994) confirmed that teachers should consider their new role in an online teaching environment and ought to foster a sense of community among learners. This may mean that teachers need to pursue the role of a facilitator or a guide, rather than being an instructor where stringent instructions were usually given to students in a face-to-face setting. Hiltz (1994) found that there are three basic principles that a teacher must consider in order to establish and maintain a learning community, the principles are to: be responsive; be competent; and be organised in their facilitation of student interaction. In addition, teachers were exhorted to provide frequent feedback, to encourage students to contribute, to acknowledge comments, and to periodically update and summarise reviews of discussion.

4. Roles of the Online Teacher and Learner

Clearly, the role of the teacher either in a classroom using face-to-face teaching or in an online setting is to ensure that some type of educational process occurs amongst the learners involved. In the traditional classroom setting, the teacher's role generally is to impart knowledge to learners (Relan & Gillani, 1997). Students in a face-to-face classroom setting see and work with one another and get to know each other well in the learning process. In the Web environment, the role of the teacher becomes that of an educational facilitator (Sherry & Wilson, 1997). As a facilitator, the teacher provides guidance and allows students to explore the course material as well as related materials without restriction.

Collins and Berge (1996) categorised the tasks and roles of the online teacher into four areas: pedagogical, social, managerial, and technical. They described pedagogical area as the functions and tasks that revolve around educational facilitation. Social function is described as the promotion of a friendly social environment which is needed in the process of online learning. The managerial aspect of online learning involves all organisational and administrative aspects of putting the learning materials online such as setting objectives, rules, and decision making norms. The technical aspect focuses on the teacher's proficiency with the use of the technology.

A successful learner should be active in the online learning environment. The roles of the online learners include knowledge generation, collaboration, and process management (Palloff & Pratt, 1998). In online learning environments, with guidance from the teacher, the learner is responsible for actively seeking solutions to problems confined within the knowledge area being studied. Students are expected to view problems and questions presented by the teacher and those of other students. Students are expected to participate actively, to learn collaboratively and cooperatively (Khan, 1997), and are expected to work together in order to generate deeper levels of understanding of the course material. Students are also expected to share the resources, and other materials that they find, with other learners. In the role of process management, students are expected to participate with minimal guidelines, interact with one another and be involved in the discussion. Furthermore, students must be willing to speak out when they have an opinion on something or when the discussion is moving into an uncomfortable zone or when they are offended (Palloff & Pratt, 1998).

5. Web-based Learning Application

The extent to which web-based learning is applied in a course is a decision that the individual instructor must make. The instructor is the person who knows the structure of his/her course, who is responsible for the instructional pedagogy that is involved in his/her course, who determines the assessments required, and who is familiar with the level of interactivity amongst students in the course. Having evaluated the nature of the course, the instructor may then apply any one or all of the web-based learning applications according to Finder and Raleigh's (1998) informational, supplemental, dependent, and fully developed use of the Web. These four web-based applications are described in the following sections.

5.1 Informational Use

The first Web-based learning application of informational use is described as presenting factual or static information. This informational use is also known as presenting declarative knowledge. According to Finder and Raleigh (1998), information about the course, assignment descriptions, the instructor, or the entire course plan for the duration of the semester are made available on the Web. Another example of this type of informational use is the posting of the course syllabus. This information is valuable to students who want to find out more about the course before enrolling in it. Normally, this form of web-based application of informational use is used in conjunction with traditional classroom teaching.

Instructors are able to update their web-site on a regular basis and are also able to post important information pertaining to their course, for example, notifying students of changes of assignments, class times, scheduled events and so on. In fact, students should be able to receive all notices about their course on this "informational" web-site.

The informational form of web-based application does not normally include key concepts of web-based learning such as interactivity, social, and collaborative learning. Another type of web application is that of supplemental use.

5.2 Supplemental Use

Supplemental use of the web is used in conjunction with informational use. According to Finder and Raleigh (1998), in supplemental use, students use the Web to complete part of the course. Students may also complete an assignment, or part of an assignment, using this form of web-based application. Instructors can give direction to students who are looking to further their understanding about certain lecture materials by incorporating links to related sources. By providing some guidance, students are able to explore and research similar web-sites that can explain a specific topic in greater detail (Pan, 1998).

5.3 Dependent Use

A third approach of the web-based application is dependent use, where students are encouraged to be active and collaborative learners. According to Finder and Raleigh (1998), most course materials exist on the Web as well as links to related sources, and students use the Web as a major course component when completing assignments. The mode of teaching used with this form of web-based application is normally mixed. Dependent use of the Web suggests that the material provided online includes some classroom teaching but the online component plays an integral part in the course and the access to the materials is normally planned for students to use in their course.

Instructors using the Web for dependent use must also take on a commitment in relation to the make up of the student's experience of the course. This involves the inclusion of a range of components such as course information, course content and materials, and additional learning resources in the overall online course material. Instructors must be able to provide guidance to students, especially when students use the Web to complete their assignments either individually or in a group. In order for this dependent use to be effective, instructors must be able to perform some of the roles of the online teacher.

5.4 Fully-Developed Use

The fourth approach of web-based application, namely, fully-developed use, covers all the earlier applications of informational, supplemental, and dependent uses of the Web. According to Finder and Raleigh (1998), in fully-developed use, the entire course is delivered via the Web, and students and teacher may never meet face to face. It is made clear that the primary source of learning is online. King (1993) describes the fully-developed use of the Web as the comprehensive replacement of earlier forms of delivery (i.e., traditional teaching) and the function of comprehensive replacement is to provide an extensive course in an electronic or online learning environment.

Instructors using the Web in fully-developed use must incorporate student-centred learning and a range of flexible teaching and learning strategies. The online course materials used in this approach must be comprehensively developed. Apart from including all components such as course information, course content and materials, which have already been described in the earlier approaches, administrative aspects such as maintenance of course assessment, and the entire management of the course must also be incorporated in this type of application.

Both instructors and students play an important role in this fully-developed use. As the course material is used totally online, where minimal or no face-to-face contact is present, instructors and students must adjust to the new way of teaching and learning.

Courses that are developed online and are within the approaches of dependent and fully developed use of the Web, are classified as courses conducted in an online learning environment. The rationale for this is that instructors must develop the online course materials focused on a student-centred approach and that they must use a range of online teaching and learning strategies to set up their learning tasks. Also, instructors and students must understand their online roles before they can contribute and participate successfully in an online environment.

6. Development of the Web-Based Learning Environment Instrument (WEBLEI)

As online learning is becoming more and more popular, it was decided to develop a learning environment questionnaire for use in university settings. This new instrument was named the *Web-Based Learning*

Environment Instrument (WEBLEI). This instrument was designed with four scales to capture students' perceptions of web-based learning environments. The first three scales of emancipatory activities, co-participatory activities, and qualia are adapted from Tobin's (1998) work on *Connecting Communities Learning* (CCL) and the final scale focuses on information structure and the design aspect of the web-based material. Each of these aspects is explained in the following sections.

6.1 WEBLEI Scale I: Emancipatory Activities

Tobin (1998) listed three main categories of convenience, efficiency and autonomy for emancipatory activities.

- Convenience is achieved when students can access the learning activities at convenient times.
- Efficiency is described as not having to attend on campus classes and therefore allowed for efficient use of time.
- Autonomy is described as allowing students to decide when and how to access the curriculum. (Tobin, 1998, p. 151)

6.2 WEBLEI Scale II: Co-Participatory Activities

According to Tobin (1998), "co-participation implies the presence of a shared language which can be accessed by all participants to engage the activities of the community, with a goal of facilitating learning." Included under the co-participatory activities are six categories of flexibility, reflection, quality, interaction, feedback and collaboration.

- Flexibility is described as allowing students to meet their goals.
- Reflection is noted as asynchronous interactions which encouraged reflective interactions.
- Quality is linked to the learning reflected in the level of activity undertaken by the students.
- Interaction is described as enabling students to interact with each other asynchronously.
- Feedback is described as the availability of feedback from students and the teacher.
- Collaboration enabled students to collaborate in a variety of activities. (Tobin, 1998 p. 152)

The focus of this aspect is on the learning activities in which the students participate. This includes structuring of activities in which students use their existing knowledge to apply to the present subject and build new understandings from the present subject. This co-participatory aspect is aligned with Laurillard's (1993) analysis of how learners 'come to know' through (1) active learning, (2) feedback, and (3) reflection.

6.3 WEBLEI Scale III: Qualia

Tobin (1998, p. 155) explained qualia as describing knowledge which is considered "as embodied in neural networks theory Churchlands (1989, 1996) which conceptualises knowing in terms of electronic loadings on a matrix of neurons that tightly couples qualia and cognitive ways of knowing."

Tobin (1998) described six categories of qualia. They are enjoyment, confidence, accomplishments, success, frustration and tedium.

- Enjoyment is associated with academic success and mastery of technology.
- Confidence is associated with successful learning and support for learning.
- Accomplishments are described as allowing student to display their course accomplishments regularly and publicly.
- Success has two dimensions - use of technology and conceptual aspects of the program.
- Frustration is associated with the use of technology and the conceptual aspects of the program.
- Tedium is associated with posting and responding to reviews on a regular basis. Tobin (1998, p. 155)

6.4 WEBLEI Scale IV: Information Structure and Design Activities

Information structure and design deals with how the web based learning materials are structured and organised, and whether the materials presented follow accepted instructional design standards, such as stating its purpose, describing its scope, incorporating interactivity, and providing a variety of formats to meet different learning styles. Included in this section are relevance and scope of content, validity of content, accuracy and balance of content, navigation, and aesthetic and affective aspects.

6.4 Rationale for WEBLEI

The rationale for selecting these four scales, together with their relationship with Tobin's work on *Connecting Communities Learning*, is represented in Figure 1.1. In order to study online, it is necessary to have accessed (Scale I) to some web-based learning material or a virtual subject. This scale, named Access, is necessary to ascertain the convenience of accessing the learning activities, the efficiency in terms of accessing the learning materials at a location suitable to the student and the autonomy of accessing the learning materials at a time convenient to the student.

Once access to the learning materials is established, it is vital that students interact with one another to achieve the learning outcomes set out in the learning materials. Scale II (Interaction), assesses the extent to which the students participate actively, and work in a collaborative and cooperative manner with other students in order to achieve the learning outcomes.

Once students have access (Scale I) to the learning materials and that they are actively participating (Scale II) in the learning activities, students should be able to indicate how they feel (Scale III: Response) in using this type of learning environment. Students are able to respond by indicating their perception of this learning environment and whether they have accomplished any learning objectives through this learning environment.

Having gone through all the learning activities, from access (Scale I) to interaction (Scale II) to response (Scale III), students should be able to determine what they have gained (Scale IV: Results) from learning in this environment. Therefore, the WEBLEI is composed of items arranged in four scales and is presented in Table 1.1. The instrument uses a 5-point Likert scale response options of Almost Never, Seldom, Sometimes, Often, and Almost Always.

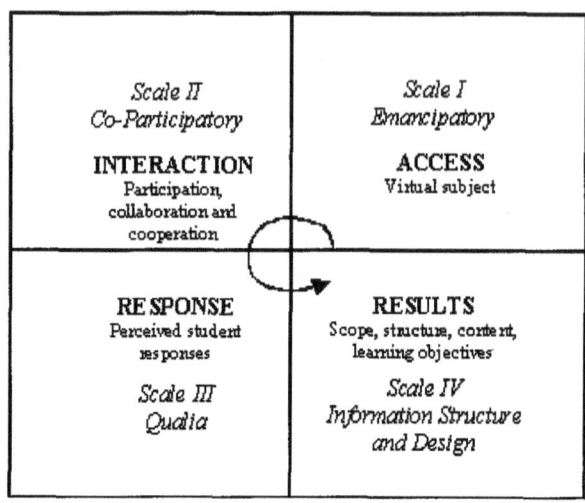

Figure 1.1. WEBLEI scales

Table 1.1. WEBLEI Scales and Items

Scale I: Access
1. I can access the learning activities at times convenient to me.
2. The online material is available at locations suitable for me.
3. I can use time saved in travelling and on campus class attendance for study and other commitments.
4. I am allowed to work at my own pace to achieve learning objectives.
5. I decide how much I want to learn in a given period.
6. I decide when I want to learn.
7. The flexibility allows me to meet my learning goals.
8. The flexibility allows me to explore my own areas of interest.

Scale II: Interaction
1. I communicate with other students in this subject electronically (email, bulletin boards, chat line).
2. In this learning environment, I have to be self-disciplined in order to learn.
3. I have the autonomy to ask my tutor what I do not understand.
4. I have the autonomy to ask other students what I do not understand.
5. Other students respond promptly to my queries.
6. I regularly participate in self-evaluations.
7. I regularly participate in peer-evaluations.
8. I was supported by positive attitude from my peers.

Table 1.1. Continued

Scale III: Response
1. This mode of learning enables me to interact with other students and the tutor asynchronously.
2. I felt a sense of satisfaction and achievement about this learning environment.
3. I enjoy learning in this environment.
4. I could learn more in this environment.
5. It is easy to organise a group for a project.
6. It is easy to work collaboratively with other students involved in a group project.
7. The web-based learning environment held my interest throughout my course of study.
8. I felt a sense of boredom towards the end of my course of study.

Scale IV: Results
1. The scope or learning objectives are clearly stated in each lesson.
2. The organisation of each lesson is easy to follow.
3. The structure keeps me focused on what is to be learned.
4. Expectations of assignments are clearly stated in my unit.
5. Activities are planned carefully.
6. The subject content is appropriate for delivery on the Web.
7. The presentation of the subject content is clear.
8. The quiz in the web-based materials enhances my learning process.

7 Reliability and Validity of the WEBLEI

7.1 Factor Analysis

The WEBLEI was administered to two groups of Electronic Commerce students from Curtin Business School at Curtin University, Perth, Western Australia.

A total of 344 responses were received. A factor analysis was conducted to examine the internal structure of the instrument. A principal factor analysis was carried out to extract four factors and this was followed by a varimax rotation. The results of the factor analysis confirmed that there were indeed four scales in the WEBLEI. Table 1.2 shows the items for each of the four factors.

Table 1.2. The WEBLEI Items on Four Factors

Item	Access	Interaction	Response	Results
1	0.428			
2	0.421			
3	0.505			
4	0.465			
5	0.607			
6	0.556			
7	0.609			
8	0.626			
9			0.435	
10		0.459		
11		0.348		
12		0.393		
13		0.601		
14		0.568		
15		0.648		
16		0.609		
17			0.677	
18			0.705	
19			0.595	
20		0.449		
21			0.502	
22			0.514	
23			0.439	
24			0.336	
25				0.642
26				0.637
27				0.668
28				0.631
29				0.662
30				0.582
31				0.678
32				0.394
% of Variance	25.2	5.3	4.9	4.1
Eigenvalue	11.9	2.5	2.3	1.9

Factor loading < 0.30 not included

7.2 Reliability and Discriminant Validity of the WEBLEI

Table 1.3 provides some information about the internal consistency, using Cronbach alpha reliability coefficient, and the discriminant validity, using the mean correlation of a scale with the other scales as a convenient index, of the WEBLEI. The Cronbach alpha reliability coefficients presented in the table show that the figures ranged from 0.68

to 0.87. According to Nunnally (1967), a reliability coefficient of 0.60 or greater is acceptable. Therefore, the figures indicate that they are satisfactory in terms of their internal consistency. The discriminant validity shows that the mean correlations ranged from 0.37 to 0.49 indicating that the scales of the WEBLEI measure distinct although somewhat overlapping aspects of the online learning environment.

Table 1.3. Cronbach Alpha Reliability and Discriminant Validity (Validation Statistics) and Descriptive Statistics of the WEBLEI Questionnaire

Aspects	Items	Valid Cases	Validation Statistics		Descriptive Statistics	
			Alpha Reliability	Discriminant Validity	Mean	sd
Scale I: Access	8	310	0.79	0.49	3.96	0.53
Scale II: Interaction	8	318	0.68	0.37	3.55	0.51
Scale III: Response	8	318	0.69	0.49	3.37	0.53
Scale IV: Results	8	312	0.87	0.49	3.72	0.57

8. An Application using the WEBLEI

8.1 Means and Standard Deviations

The mean scores (as shown in Table 1.3) of 3.96, 3.55, 3.37, and 3.72 for these four scales respectively, indicate that on average students gave a response of "Sometimes" to "Often" on the items in these scales. These are a relatively high means (3.65) for the scales.

The mean score of Scale 1 of Access of 3.96 shows that students generally agree that they can access the online learning materials in their learning environment in a convenient and efficient way. As such this learning environment apparently provides them the autonomy of when and how they intend to access the learning materials.

The mean score of Scale II of Interaction of 3.55, which ranges from "Sometimes" to "Often", indicates that the students believed they were able to participate and interact regularly with oine another and their lecturer enhancing their chance of being successful and effective learners in this environment.

Scale III of Response has a mean score of 3.37 and indicates that students feel a sense of achievement and satisfaction once they have completed the online learning unit. The course developer must also incorporate different learning activities in order to maintain students' interest in the course of study and to ensure that students do not feel bored towards the end of the course.

The last scale, Scale IV of Results has a mean score of 3.72 indicates that students agree that the learning objectives and organisation of the online materials were important in guiding them in their studies. It is imperative for course developers to know that having the unit activities planned carefully for students will assist the students in their course of study.

7.2.1 Demographic Profile

Demographic information also was gathered about the students who responded to the WEBLEI. These data helped explain the results obtained with the WEBLEI. Table 1.4 shows the number of students who were enrolled in an online unit for the first time. Interestingly the figures in Table 1.4 show that majority of students (95.3%) are new to the concept of studying a unit in an online mode.

Table 1.4. Number of Students Studying Online for the First Time

First Online Unit	Female	Male	Total
Yes	105	150	155
No	30	41	71
Did not indicate	4	3	7

Table 1.5 shows the use of different access methods in studying the unit. It is obvious that the use of electronic mail (mean score of 4.14, towards *Always*) was a popular method of interacting with other students and tutors.

Table 1.5. Mean and Standard Deviation of Student Access

	Cases		E-mail	Phone	Bulletin Board	Chat Line	Online Study Materials	Remote Library
Male	193	Mean	4.10	2.85	3.21	2.73	3.75	2.82
		SD	0.84	1.16	0.99	1.16	1.08	1.09
Female	139	Mean	4.19	2.75	3.18	2.62	3.60	2.90
		SD	0.86	1.20	1.00	1.21	1.10	1.27
Total	332	Mean	4.14	2.81	3.20	2.68	3.69	2.85
		SD	0.85	1.17	0.99	1.18	1.09	1.17

The use of the online study materials with a mean of 3.69 shows that the unit materials were accessed and used by most students. The use of bulletin board and remote library access was also an indication that assistance was sought online. Table 1.5 also shows that male and female students were similar in their patterns of access.

Table 1.6 shows that students spent most of their time studying at home (towards Often). This is consistent with the concept of online learning where students are encouraged to telecommute or to study in a virtual environment. Again male and female students were similar in their selections of a place for studying.

Table 1.6. Mean and Standard Deviation of Time Spent in Online Unit

	Cases		Home	Campus	Work	Library	Other
Male	193	Mean	4.07	3.09	1.53	2.88	2.17
		SD	0.86	0.93	0.92	0.88	0.992
Female	138	Mean	4.16	3.15	1.247	2.70	1.97
		SD	0.85	1.10	0.54	0.99	1.01
Total	331	Mean	4.11	3.11	1.41	2.80	2.09
		SD	0.86	1.00	0.79	0.93	1.00

9. Conclusion

This paper has described a new instrument, which assesses student perceptions of four core aspects of the Web-based learning environment, namely, Access, Interaction, Response, and Results. The development and validation of the WEBLEI is a significant outcome of this study. This instrument has been shown to have factorial validity and the WEBLEI scales of Access, Interaction, Response, and Results have acceptable reliability and discriminant validity from a statistical perspective. This instrument has been designed to be used by tertiary teachers who have their courses delivered as dependent and/or fully-developed Web-based learning applications. This instrument has also been carefully developed to incorporate the four scales of accessing the online materials (Scale I: Access), the interaction and participation of all parties involved in the online learning (Scale II: Interaction), the responses and perceptions of students learning in this environment (Scale III: Response), and finally, the students' learning outcome and achievement in this learning environment (Scale IV: Results). The survey of 334 students indicate that the concept of online learning is well received by these students. The availability of this instrument will allow researchers and developers to evaluate their own Web-based learning environments in accordance with the suggested scales.

References

Bannan, B., & Milheim, W. D. (1997). Existing Web-Based instruction courses and their design In B. H. Khan (Ed.), *Web-based instruction* (pp. 381-387). Englewood Cliffs, New Jersey: Educational Technology Publication, Inc.

Brodsky, N. H. (1998). Learning from learners Internet style. *Educom Review, 33* (2), March/April. Retrieved Oct 20, 2000, from http://www.educause.edu/pub/er/review/reviewArticles/33214.html.

Churchland, P. M. (1989). *A neurocomputational perspective: The nature of mind and the structure of science.* Bradford Book. Cambridge, MA: MIT Press.

Churchland, P. S. (1996). Toward a neurobiology of the mind In R. Lilnas & P. S. Churchland (Eds.), *The mind brain continuum* (pp. 281–303). Cambridge, MA: MIT Press

Collins, M. P. & Berge Z. L. (1996, June). Facilitating interaction in computer-mediated online classrooms. Paper presented at FSU/AECT Conference on Distance Learning, Tallahassee, Florida.

Dowling, D. (1997). Teaching literature on the World Wide Web In B. H. Khan (Ed.), *Web-based instruction* (pp. 411-416). Englewood Cliffs, New Jersey: Educational Technology Publication, Inc.

Finder, K., & Raleigh D. (1998). Web applications in the classroom, *Society for Information Technology in Education Conference*, Washington DC. Retrieved April 04, 2001, from http://www.uwec.edu/Info/IT/CITI/Examples/Pres/sld001.htm

Fraser, B. J. (1994). Research on classroom and school climate. In D. Gabel (Ed.), *Handbook of research on science teaching and learning* (pp. 493-541). New York: MacMillan.

Fraser, B. J. (1998). Science learning environments: Assessment, effect and determinants. In B. J. Fraser & K. G. Tobin (Eds.), *International handbook of science education* (pp. 527-564). Dordrecht: Kluwer Academic Publishers.

Goh, S. C., & Fraser, B. J. (1998). Teacher interpersonal behaviour, classroom environment and student outcomes in primary mathematics in Singapor. In B. J. Fraser and K. G. Tobin (Eds.), *International handbook of science education* (pp. 199-229). Dordrecht: Kluwer Academic Publishers.

Hicks, M., Reid, I. C., & George, R. (1999). Designing responsive Online learning environment: Approaches to supporting students. *The Australian Association for Research in Education Conference Proceedings*, Australia. Retrieved Mar 12, 2001, from http://www.aare.edu.au/99pap/hic99172.htm

Hiltz, S. R. (1994). The virtual classroom: *Learning without limits via computer networks.* Norwood, New Jersey: Ablex.

Hooper, S., & Hannafin, M. J. (1991). The effects of group composition on achievement, interaction, and learning efficiency during computer-based cooperative instruction. *Educational Technology Research and Development, 39*(3), 27-40.

Jegede, O., Fraser, B. J., & Fisher, D. (1998, April). *Development, Validation and Use of a Learning Environment Instrument for University Distance Education Settings.* Paper presented at the Annual Meeting of the American Educational Research Association, San Diego.

Jonassen, D. (1994) Thinking technology: Towards a constructivist design model. *Educational Technology, 4,* 34-37.

Khan, B. H. (1997). *Web-based instruction.* Englewood Cliffs, New Jersey: Educational Technology Publication, Inc.

King, B. (1993). Open learning in Australia: Government intervention and institutional response. *Open Learning, 8*(3).

Laurillard, D. (1993). *Rethinking university teaching: A framework for the effective use of educational technology.* London: Routledge.

McDonald, J., & Postle, G. (1999). Teaching online: Challenge to a reinterpretation of traditional instructional models. *Proceedings of the AusWeb99, The Fifth Australaian WWW Conference,* Ballina, NSW, April. Retrieved September 29, 1999, from http://ausweb.scu.edu.au/aw99_archive/aw99/papers/mcdonald/paper.htm

McRobbie, C. J., Fisher, D. L., & Wong, A. F. L. (1998). Personal and class forms of classroom environment instruments In B. J. Fraser & K. G. Tobin (Eds.), *International handbook of science education* (pp. 581-594.). Dordrecht: Kluwer Academic Publishers.

Nunnally, J. (1967). *Psychometric theory*. New York: McGraw-Hill.

Palloff, R. M., & Pratt, K. (1998). Effective teaching and learning in the virtual classroom. *World Computer Congress: Teleteaching 98*, Vienna/Austria and Budapest/Hungary, August.

Pan, A. C. (1998). Optimize the Web for better instruction. *Society for Information Technology and Teacher Education Conference*.

Reeves, T. C., & Reeves, P. M. (1997). Effective dimensions of interactive learning on the WWW In B. H. Khan (Ed.), *Web-Based Instruction* (pp. 59-66). Englewood Cliffs, New Jersey: Educational Technology Publication, Inc.

Relan, A., & Gillani, B. B. (1997). Web-Based instruction and the traditional classroom: Similarities and differences. In B. H. Khan (Ed.), *Web-Based Instruction* (pp. 41-46). Englewood Cliffs, New Jersey: Educational Technology Publication, Inc.

Sherry, L., & Wilson, B. (1997). Transformation communication as a stimulus to Web innovations In B. H. Khan (Ed.), *Web-Based Instruction* (pp. 67-73). Englewood Cliffs, New Jersey: Educational Technology Publication, Inc.

Tobin, K. (1998). Qualitative Perceptions of Learning Environments on the World Wide Web. In B. J. Fraser and K. G. Tobin (eds.). *International Handbook of Science Education* (pp. 139-162). Dordrecht: Kluwer Academic Publishers.

Tobin, K., & Fraser, B. J. (1998). Qualitative and quantitative landscapes of classroom learning environments In B. J. Fraser & K. G. Tobin (Eds.), *International Handbook of Science Education* (pp. 623-640). Dordrecht: Kluwer Academic Publishers.

Wilson, J. (1997). Distance learning for continuous education. *Educom Review, 32* (2 0, March/April. Retrieved Oct 23, 2000, from http://www.educause.edu/pub/er/review/review Articles/32212.html

Chapter 2

CREATING A TECHNOLOGY-RICH CONSTRUCTIVIST LEARNING ENVIRONMENT IN A CLASSROOM MANAGEMENT MODULE

Myint Swe Khine
Nanyang Technological University
Republic of Singapore

One of the major shifts in education today under the influence of information and communication technologies (ICT) is that classrooms at all levels are becoming technology-rich learning environment. ICT has provided new opportunities for delivering instruction in innovative ways. The chapter describes an attempt to develop a technology-rich learning environment that delivers course materials to students in a variety of formats. An indigenous CD-ROM was developed as a comprehensive resource to facilitate learning the concepts and skills associated with classroom management. The CD-ROM was designed in a web-enable format so that it could interface with video clips and multimedia materials that are relevant to classroom management issues. Communication with the students was maintained through Blackboard communication tools. The students also had opportunities to interaction on a face-to-face basis with their peers and the tutors during tutorials. The students also have an opportunity to explore the necessary information, make meanings and construct their own knowledge. This chapter describes the application of the new technologies in delivering a teacher education module on classroom management and the perception of students who participated in the experiment.

1. Introduction

One of the major shifts in education today under the influence of information and communication technologies (ICT) is that classrooms at all levels are becoming technology-rich learning environment. Jonassen (2000) said that technologies can support meaning making by students and knowledge construction. Technologies such as computers and network communication enhance access to information and support explorations and construction of knowledge. ICT has provided new opportunities for delivering instruction in innovative ways. The constructivism movement in instructional design emphasizes the importance of providing meaningful, authentic activities that can help the learner to construct understandings and develop skills relevant to solving problems and not by feeding them with more and more information (Wilson, 1996). The constructive perspective of learning states that "knowledge is built by the learner, not supplied by the teacher" (Papert, 1990, p. 3). According to Papert, instruction connotes more control and directiveness in teaching while constructivism connotes a flexible setting that fosters and supports learning. Creating such learning environments seems intrinsically problematic. Therefore, it is important that careful planning and design to the extent possible is employed, and that the environment also includes proper support and guidance and rich resources and tools. (Lourdusamy, Wong, & Khine, 2001).

An early approach to understanding learning was to look from the perception of communication processes, where the teacher was the sender of a message, and the student was the receiver of the message. But recent views on learning focus on a mental operation and knowledge is a constructed element resulting from the learning process (Lever-Duffy, McDonald, & Mizell, 2003). Educators argue that new learning and teaching strategies may have to be introduced to prepare students to become independent learners. ICT may provide an opportunity to introduce such strategies. Through the use of technology, teachers can provide opportunities for the students to learn, think critically and have discussions with their peers supported by ICT. Bitter and Pierson (2002) view that technology is an agent of change and appropriate use of technologies can make learning for students more interesting and enriching and prepare them for the demands of the workplace. Therefore, it is important that educators seriously consider matching the appropriate use of technology with content to maximize the student's potential in learning. Sharp (2002) envisaged that teachers will be "teaching" less and it is up to educators to inspire, motivate, and excite students about the use of technology for learning.

Wilson and Lowry (2000) believe that learners need to develop individual competence in effective participation in groups and communities. Among all the technology available, they, identified the Web as where constructivist learning can take place. In this connection, three core principles for effective use of the Web for learning are introduced: providing access to rich sources of information; encourage meaningful interactions with content; and bring people together to challenge, support, or respond to each other (p. 82). During these interactions scaffolding, encouragement and providing alternative perspectives are possible.

There are many ways technology can be used, but the best way and the most instructionally sound are those that provide students with real and authentic experiences (Solomon, 1999). This is especially so in the learning of process skills such as teaching and classroom management in teacher education. Authentic episodes in the classrooms can help would-be teachers to examine the events and reflect on the solutions. It could also lead to peer discussion of real-life encounters in the classroom.

Another aspect in learning that is considered important is collaboration. The focus of much learning has been on individual learning coming from the behaviorist perspective of learning. However, recent studies began to study learning as a collaborative process. Collaboration between students can take place by using software designed for interpersonal correspondence. Computer-mediated communication, such as on-line discussions, supports collaboration by overcoming the limitations of time and space (Barnes, 2003). Morrison and Guenther (2000) noted that providing a forum for students to discuss their dialogues and share results can be an effective way to integrate teaching and learning processes. However, they warned that online discussion requires careful planning and facilitation in order to be successful.

Newman, Griffin, and Cole (1989) feel that through the use of computers educators can help the students to communicate and collaborate on joint activities, by acting as support and providing assistance through which groups can collaborate with one another. Also a growing body of research provides evidence that organising learners into small communities has beneficial effects on students' achievements and psychological well-being (Oxley, 2001). Community imparts a common sense of purpose. Within a community, members grow by meaningful relationships. Learning communities are therefore defined as being characterized by associated groups of learners, sharing common values and a common understanding of purpose, acting within a context of curricular and co-curricular structures and functions that link traditional disciplines and co-curricular structures.

Technology has had a long presence in education and made great impact on information manipulation, distribution and communication in the teaching and learning process (Ross & Bailey, 1996). Emerging technologies such as the Internet and multimedia are even more empowering to learners if their uses are harnessed to meet learner characteristics and learning conditions.

2. The Context

Teaching and Classroom Management is one of the core modules in the Postgraduate Diploma in Education (PGDE) program at Nanyang technological University, Singapore and it aims to introduce beginning teachers to how they can facilitate learning and maintain orderliness in the classroom. The module emphasizes the fundamentals of instructional skills and teacher competencies in managing classroom teaching and pupil behavior which contribute to the making of an effective teacher. The design of the module is also based on the concept that an effective teacher should be adept at facilitating learning and maintaining orderliness in the classroom. To be able to do so, the teacher needs to acquire fundamental pedagogical knowledge and instructional skills. This module emphasizes teaching competencies in managing classroom teaching, especially in the management of student behavior.

The module aims are that student teachers will acquire an awareness of the dynamics of classroom teaching; realize the significance of interpersonal behavior on student's behavior and learning; develop and apply a repertoire of teaching strategies and skills for managing student learning and behavior.

The module is organized in to the following six inter-related themes.

- Classroom management and classroom environment
- Creating a positive learning environment
- Teachers' attributes and qualities
- Managing learning activities
- Managing pupil misbehaviour and
- School practices and support

The programme has a large intake of students and each year about 1200 trainee teachers take up the module.

3. Multimedia CD-ROM

For more than a century, text and verbal messages are predominant medium for human communication in imparting new knowledge and skills to the learners. Technological development in recent years allows the presentation of information in multimedia consisting of audio, video, animation, still pictures and text-based materials, into a hyper-linked structure to promote human learning. Previous research has indicated that with the use of multimedia, learners are able to retain information longer and they are able to apply learned information in a new situation (Mayer, 2001).

The curriculum team responsible for designing this module also believes that learning is an individual process and collaborative and cooperative learning environments are important means of constructing knowledge. It was decided that this module would be delivered using multimedia and ICT. The normal mass lecture sessions which use "direct instruction" were cancelled and the content of the lectures were made available on a specially designed interactive multimedia CD-ROM. This CD-ROM allows students to engage in an active learning process in which students work to construct their own meaning and understandings. The CD-ROM integrates observations, discussions and contextualised examples to help trainee teachers effectively apply the theories and principles of classroom management and understand the philosophies governing good classroom management.

The CD-ROM consists of multimedia-rich content and can be opened by any Web browser. This makes it easier for the user who is not required to install other application software. Knowledge bits are organised in different media format. These include still pictures, audio, video clips, and Word and PDF documents. Some quiz and practice questions on new concepts are also included.

Figure 2.1 shows the site map of the content in the CD-ROM. Selecting any one of the words or phrases will hyper-link to another page containing a knowledge bit related to that particular issue. Figure 2.2 depicts an example of one of the sections in the CD-ROM.

A resource section was provided to facilitate more reading and research into areas of interest. Some video episodes depict enactment of classroom management scenes. These include handling of disciplinary problems inside and outside the classroom. Some classroom teaching videos show how a teacher introduces a lesson, presents information and lesson closure. Other video episodes cover managing group instruction, monitoring group progress and ending group activities systematically. As teaching can be a mediated transaction between a student, the teacher and the learning objective, various classroom management strategies and teaching techniques are modeled in the video clip (see Figure 2.3). Figure 2.4 shows an example of a practice quiz section.

The students were briefed on how the CD-ROM was to be used in preparation for the tutorial activities that were designed in synchrony with the content of the CD. The students attended six face-to-face tutorials of two hours per session. At the end of the seventh week of the semester, students went out to school to do their Practicum for seven weeks. During this period, they were provided access to their tutors and peers through the Blackboard communication tools in order to develop a vibrant learning community.

Students are required to follow the instruction given in the weekly tutorial guide sheet before they come to the face-to-face tutorial class. Weekly tutorial sheet explains the details of the lesson, objectives, activity to engage and reading required, and the section to be explored in the CD-ROM. This prepared them to be ready for activity and related discussion during the tutorial. At the end of the semester, the students were invited for a feedback session.

The objectives of this study were to find out the views and perceptions of student teachers about the CD-ROM, tutorials and the Discussion Board interaction. An attempt was also made to find out views and perceptions of the module in general.

Technology-rich Constructivist Learning Environment 27

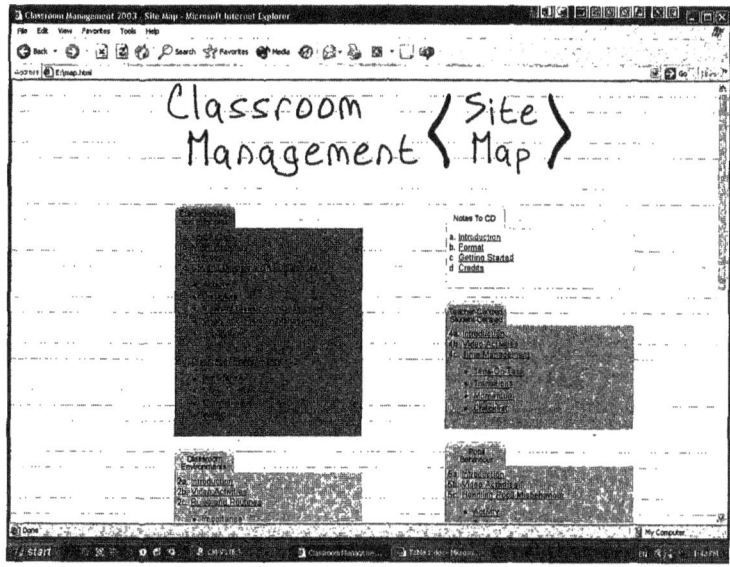

Figure 2.1. Site map of CD-ROM

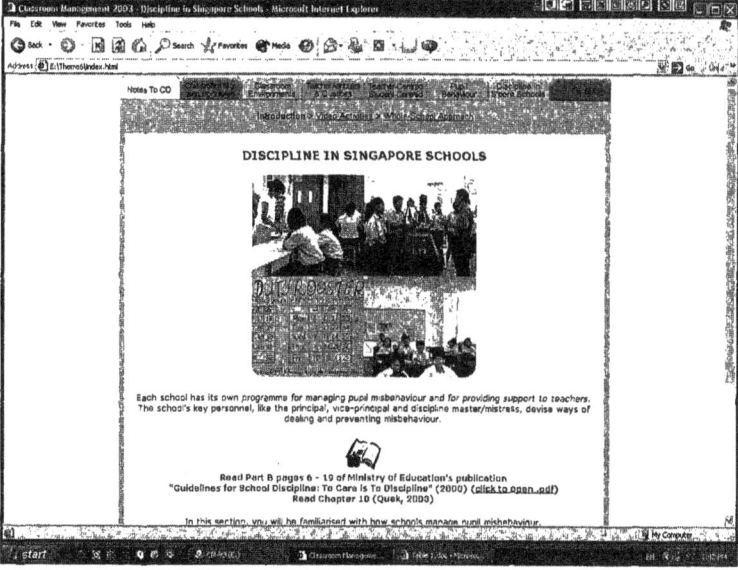

Figure 2.2. Section on discipline in Singapore schools

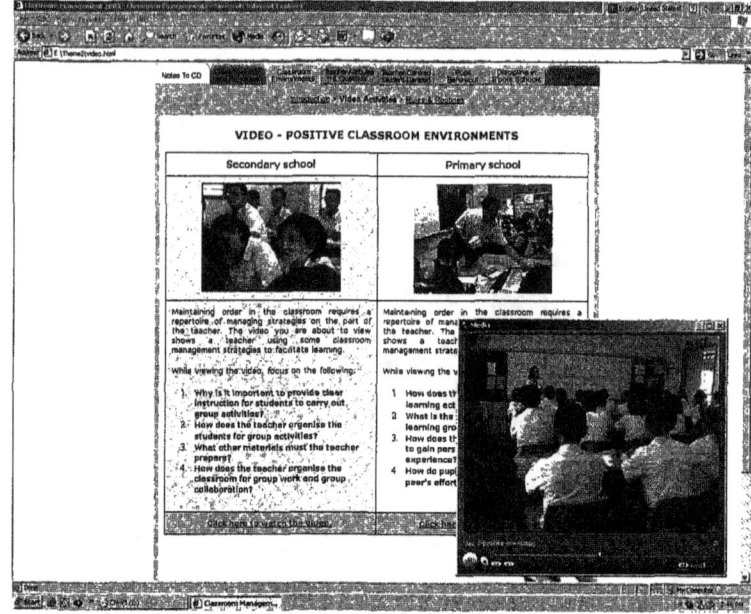

Figure 2.3. Examples of classroom video clips

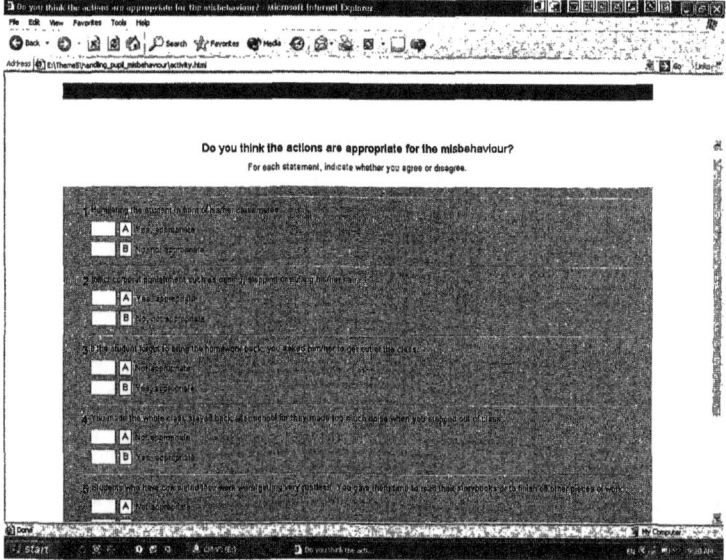

Figure 2.4. Examples of a practice quiz section

4. Data Collection and Analysis

The feedback data were collected from the January 2002 cohort which has an enrollment of 265 students. A total of 187 feedback questionnaires were received which was a response rate of 70%. The questionnaire consisted of items dealing with the use and evaluation of CD-ROM, Tutorial activities, Discussion Board and General Issues. In all, there were 32 items and the respondents were required to express their views on a 4-point scale, 1=strongly disagree, 2=disagree, 3=agree and 4=strongly agree to each of the items. The data were analysed using SPSS: PC software. Descriptive statistics were used to describe the perceptions of students about the technology-rich learning environment used in delivering the content of this module.

5. Results and Discussion

The results discussed in this section cover the four parts of the questionnaire. The first section deals with the students' perceptions of the content of CD-ROM and the second section covers the students' perceptions of Discussion Board. The third section covers the perceptions on the face-to-face tutorials. The perceptions of the module in general were given in the fourth section. The overall reliability of the questionnaire (Cronbach Alpha) was found to be 0.85.

5.1. Students' Perceptions of the Content of CD-ROM

The first ten items in the questionnaire obtained the views of the students on the usefulness, relevance and helpfulness of the content of the CD-ROM to give them a better understanding of teaching and classroom management. The responses of the students are listed in Table 2.1.

The mean scores of all 10 items are above 2.5 the mid-point on a four point scale except for the item on the usefulness of the activities in the CD (Item 8). This suggests that students on average perceive the content of CD-ROM to be of help for better understanding of the issues related to teaching and classroom management. Students seem to appreciate most the examples and video clips used to illustrate aspects of teaching and classroom management. The content of the CD-ROM has also helped them to think critically on issues related to teaching and classroom management. But between 10 to 25% of students are not convinced of the benefits of the content of the CD-ROM in helping them have a better understanding of the issues related to instruction and classroom management. Some of the students were not convinced by the fact that the module is enhanced with the use of materials found in the CD. But 70% of the students appreciated the use of the CD (Item 10). The students perceived that the contents in the CD-ROM are well integrated with the tutorial activities (76%) (Item 1) and interviews in the video clips are informative and relevant (78%) (Item 7).

Table 2.1. Students' Perceptions of CD-ROM Content

No	Statement	Frequency (Percentage)				Mean (SD)
		SD	D	A	SA	
1	The contents in the CD ROM integrate well with the tutorial activities.	3 1.6%	29 15.5%	129 69.0%	13 7.0%	2.67 (0.90)
2	I find it easy to navigate through the CD ROM.	5 2.7%	37 19.8%	117 62.6%	16 8.6%	2.64 (0.91)
3	I like the design and layout of the CD ROM.	4 2.1%	49 26.2%	104 55.6%	15 8.0%	2.72 (2.49)
4	I find the CD ROM text content useful for the tutorials.	2 1.1%	38 20.3%	121 64.7%	11 5.9%	2.59 (0.93)
5	I find the video clips appropriate as they illustrate various teaching points.	3 1.6%	22 11.8%	129 69.0%	21 11.2%	2.77 (0.91)
6	I find the newspaper clippings relevant to the module.	1 0.5%	16 8.6%	144 77.0%	5 2.7%	2.59 (0.99)
7	The interviews in the video clips are informative and relevant.	4 2.1%	23 12.3%	127 67.9%	20 10.7%	2.73 (0.94)
8	The activities in the CD ROM are useful to me.	5 2.7%	50 26.7%	108 57.8%	8 4.3%	2.47 (0.95)
9	The CD-ROM content provides good examples of classroom management principles.	6 3.2%	38 20.3%	112 59.9%	17 9.1%	2.60 (0.97)
10	I feel that the module is enhanced with the use of materials found in the CD ROM.	3 1.6%	40 21.4%	116 62.0%	15 8.0%	2.63 (0.92)

SD= strongly disagree; D= disagree; A= agree; SA= strongly agree
N = 187

5.2. Students' Perceptions of Discussion Board

The online communication with the students was maintained through Blackboard communication tools while they were in schools for Practicum. The students were provided with the opportunity to communicate and discuss with their tutors or peers problems which they encountered while they were teaching. This was a compulsory communication channel and they were given 10 marks to participate in the discussion. The students are required to submit at least one posting to share their school experience which includes teaching, students and discipline problems they encounter. They are also required to post at least one comment or response on their peer's experience.

The perceptions of those who used this collaborative communication tool were obtained by means of nine items in the questionnaire (Table 2.2). These items were computed to obtain the students' perceptions of Discussion Board. The mean scores of eight out of nine items are above 3.1. Item 1 of the questionnaire asks whether the reason for participation is due to 10 marks given. There is a disagreement among students on the reason for their participation. Some 42.2% felt that their participation was not due to the requirement and 57.8% think otherwise. This result is similar to the earlier findings by Lourdusamy and Wong (2002) where they found that 58.4% viewed that participation in Discussion Board is because of the marks allocated. However the students are convinced that one can learn a lot from peers through Discussion Board. An overwhelming majority (92%) agree to this fact (Item 5).

All the items have a mean score greater than 3.0 on a 4-point scale. This indicates that the students who have used the Discussion Board in generally appreciate the opportunity they had to communicate with their peer and tutors. The others may not have engaged in the electronic group discussion because of their heavy workload and not because this avenue of communication was not meaningful. However, a few students expressed the view that they feel more comfortable sharing their teaching difficulties with their peers face-to-face rather than through the electronic media. This suggests that some students prefer the person-to-person approach in the learning process.

Table 2.2. Students' Perceptions of Discussion Board

No	Statement	SD	D	A	SA	Mean (SD)
1	I participate in the discussion forum because of the 10 marks given.	12 6.4%	67 35.8%	85 46.0%	22 11.8%	2.61 (0.79)
2	I will participate even if no marks are given.	2 1.1%	23 12.3%	131 70.1%	30 16.0%	3.18 (2.33)
3	I feel encouraged by the numerous postings and discussions	2 1.1%	23 12.3%	115 61.5%	47 25.1%	3.11 (0.63)
4	I enjoy participating in the discussions.	0 0.0%	15 8.0%	139 74.3%	33 17.6%	3.10 (0.49)
5	I learn a lot from the postings of my classmates.	1 0.5%	14 7.5%	125 66.8%	47 25.1%	3.16 (0.59)
6	I find the postings relevant to me.	0 0.0%	11 5.9%	137 73.3%	39 20.9%	3.15 (0.49)
7	I appreciate the views expressed by my classmates to my postings.	0 0.0%	3 1.6%	139 74.3%	43 23.0%	3.18 (0.55)
8	I believe that one can learn a lot from peers through discussion boards.	0 0.0%	15 8.0%	103 55.1%	69 36.9%	3.45 (2.25)
9	The idea of using the discussion board to support us during practicum is appropriate.	2 1.1%	20 10.7%	104 55.6%	61 32.6%	3.20 (0.66)

SD= strongly disagree; D= disagree; A= agree; SA= strongly agree
N= 187

During the six-week Practicum, students are to post one original message to share their school experience and comment on another. This required them to post at least two messages. An average posting of 3.8 per student was recorded in the on-line discussion. Figure 2.5 shows the on-line group Discussion Board with discussion notes.

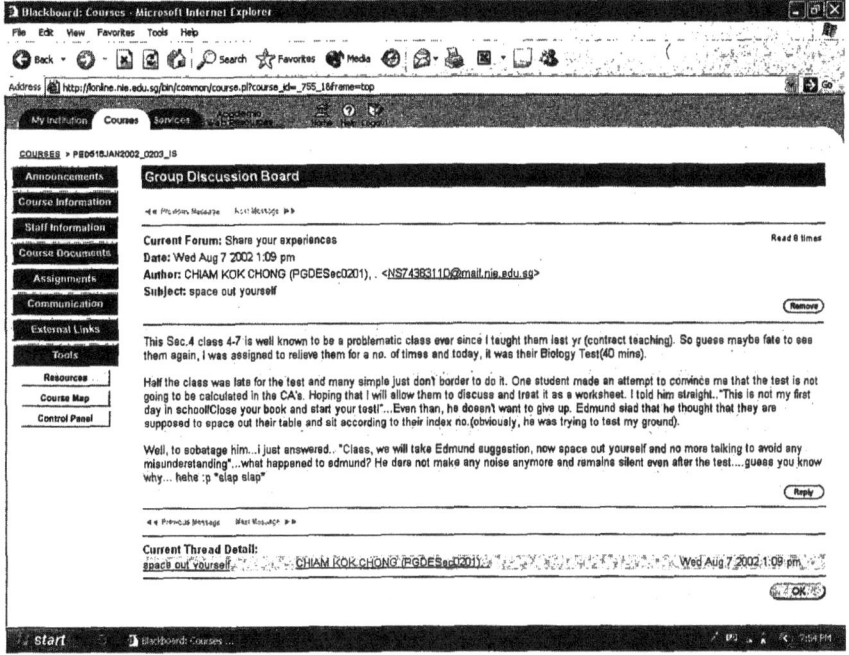

Figure 2.5. On-line group discussion board with discussion notes

The preliminary analysis shows that message ideas were practically all on their classroom encounters consisting of straightforward facts on current school practices, hear-say, 'how to' tips, woes and frustrations. The messages show the evidence of students linking theory and practice. The following Figures (2.6 and 2.7) are the excerpts from the Discussion Board.

5.3. Students' Perceptions on Tutorials

Weekly tutorial sessions are designed to be student-centred. The details of the tutorial activities are posted on the website in advance to enable the students to prepare themselves when they come to the tutorial class. This requires them to read relevant chapters in the books and to view the relevant section of the CD-ROM. During the tutorial, the tutors provide guidance and students perform the tasks required for the particular topic.

This includes presenting mock lessons, role play and brain storming (see Table 2.3).

Current Forum: Share your experiences Read 12 times
Date: Tue Jul 23 2002 10:59 pm
Author: Erwin
Subject: Sec 1students, the fish market and Kounin....

(Remove)

Teaching Sec 1 normal academic is horrendous... seems more like normal tech. You feel like you step into either a toddler's playground or a fish market.

Anyway, I am testing out my "layered disciplinary model" on them... it seems to have some practical use to it. What I do is that I use most of Kounin's principles as the "frontline" strategy and Canter as the "second line". Some may prefer a mixture but I find it too much of a hassle at the moment to remember which is which. Keep it simple coz I'm still new.

Personally, I find that these kids have very short attention span, they are not self motivated and need some kicking before they can get some work done... What Kounin says is true, get the kids attention, use interesting instructional activities (Hands on) and keep them occupied with something or other. Occasionally, talk about interesting things, build some rapport (creates noise too). Walk around the class and make sure you know what's going on everywhere and last but not least, teach theory for no more than 10 minutes. That's all they will last without giving you the glazed look.

Kounin's stuff solves about 80-90% of my classroom mgt problems...but it is very very taxing to come up with hands on learning activities e.g. worksheets, quizzes etc. The rest is encouraging (how did Dreikur get into this?) and positive pep talks.

For the remaining monkeys who can't behave themselves, I have to resort to assertive (more like aggressive) discipline. I rounded them up after school for counseling, scolding, explaining and "contract" building...

Didn't have too much problems after that.

(Reply)

Figure 2.6. Example of on-line group discussion posting

Current Forum: Share your experiences Read 11 times
Date: Wed Jul 24 2002 5:32 pm
Author: Yen
Subject: Re: Sec 1students, the fish market and Kounin....

(Remove)

Hmm...I am not teaching sec 1s this time round...but i agree with Erwin totally.. .

Sometimes, Kounin is quite effective in managing restless classes...but quite a lot of work is required in preparing the worksheets and activities...thankfully for me, I'm teaching mensuration for math so, there are a lot of 'hands-on' activities for the students to do...

anyway, i do not have any major discipline problems so i never had the opportunity to try the other theories....although i am trying to be an assertive teacher, but sometimes the little brats do not seem to appreciate my good intentions and I have to go down hard on them....sigh....

yen

(Reply)

Figure 2.7. Example of on-line group discussion response

Table 2.3. Students' Perceptions of Tutorials

No	Statement	Frequency (Percentage)				Mean
		SD	D	A	SA	(SD)
1	I find the tutorial activities interesting.	6 3.2%	43 23.0%	120 64.2%	17 9.1%	2.78 (0.672)
2	The viewing of the video clips during tutorial was helpful for initiating relevant discussion.	7 3.7%	34 18.2%	122 65.2%	23 12.3%	2.85 (0.695)
3	I find the discussions during the tutorial meaningful.	3 1.6%	24 12.6%	131 70.1%	29 15.5%	2.99 (0.591)
4	I benefited from the tutorial activities.	1 0.5%	29 15.5%	131 70.1%	26 13.9%	2.97 (0.563)
5	I did all the pre-tutorial activities before I went to the tutorials (viewing CD-ROM and reading the text, etc).	7 3.7%	58 31.0%	102 54.5%	19 10.2%	2.70 (0.723)

SD= strongly disagree; D= disagree; A= agree; SA= strongly agree
N = 187

As shown in Table 2.3, the mean scores of all 5 items are above 2.7 on the four point scale. This suggests that students perceived that the tutorial activities were relevant and useful for them. At least 85% of the respondents revealed that they benefited from the tutorials and activities are meaningful to them. However, in terms of preparation for the tutorials, only 65% of the students did the pre-tutorial activities in advance. This requires tutors to ensure that students come to class prepared. The preparedness of students can affect the quality and success of the tutorial sessions and maximize the time spent for the tutorials contact hours.

5.4. Students' Perceptions of the Module in General

Students' perceptions of the module in general were elicited using a set of eight statements. The students were asked to answer on a four point scale corresponding to the degree of agreement to the statement. As shown in Table 2.4 the students felt that they had benefited from the whole module. In all, 86% either agreed or strongly agreed to that fact

(Item 6). Overall, the students were happy with the way the module was run and 85.6% favored the module (Item 8).

Table 2.4. Students' Perceptions of the Module in General

No	Statement	Frequency (Percentage)				Mean (SD)
		SD	D	A	SA	
1	The case study task allowed me to apply what I have learned in the module.	2 1.1%	44 23.5%	126 67.4%	14 7.5%	2.80 (0.603)
2	The school-based assignment allowed me to link theory to practice.	4 2.1%	48 25.7%	117 62.6%	17 9.1%	2.78 (0.658)
3	The amount of work involved in the assignments is fair.	14 7.5%	45 24.1%	119 63.6%	8 4.3%	2.64 (0.708)
4	The textbook was useful and relevant to the module tasks.	5 2.7%	40 21.4%	128 68.4%	13 7.0%	2.79 (0.628)
5	The module has a balance between theory and practice in schools.	8 4.3%	46 24.6%	118 63.1%	15 8.0%	2.73 (0.684)
6	I feel that I have benefited from the whole module.	2 1.1%	24 12.8%	136 72.7%	25 13.4%	2.94 (0.624)
7	I am now able to apply what I have learned from the module in the classroom.	1 0.5%	47 25.1%	124 66.3%	14 7.5%	2.80 (0.597)
8	Overall, I am happy with the module.	00.00%	27 14.4%	144 77.0%	16 8.6%	2.92 (0.517)

SD= strongly disagree; D= disagree; A= agree; SA= strongly agree
N = 187

The students also felt that the case study task, which required them to analyse the classroom discipline problem, allowed them to apply the knowledge they learnt from the module. They also agreed that the school-based assignment allowed them to link theory to practice. The majority of the students (71.1%) (Item 5) felt that the module had a balance between theory and practice in school and 28.9% thinks otherwise. At the end of the module, students also felt that they were able to apply what they had learned from the module in the classroom. However, some anecdotal envidence suggests that students faced heavy workload during their practicum including observations of lessons by their cooperating teachers, preparation for their own teaching and completing assignments for other courses.

6. Conclusion

Mayer (2001) stated that when words and pictures are presented in multimedia format, students have an opportunity to construct mental models and built connections. The multimedia CD-ROM specially designed for the module provided a comprehensive resource to facilitate learning of the concepts and skills associated with classroom management. Throughout the module opportunities for students to have face-to-face interaction with their peers and their tutors were available. Communication with the students during the teaching practice period was kept open through Blackboard communication tools. In this technology-rich learning environment, students can explore new information, construct new knowledge and link theories into practice. As described by Breck (2002), the future offers virtually limitless opportunity for learning if the technology is appropriately used. However, it must be noted that students do not learn from the technology, but that technologies can support meaning making by students (Jonassen, 2000).

Constructivism does not mean that the instructor can leave the learners to explore all by themselves. A great deal of scaffolding, coaching and modeling are necessary to ensure that learning is on task. It is essential that the learners are actively engaged in deep learning which also involved articulating and reflecting (Weigel, 2002).

Many lessons can be learned from this experiment. Student teachers will gain knowledge and skills if the face-to-face tutorials are activity-based. This requires them to do preparation before they come to the tutorials. A meaningful experience can be gained if the materials given in the CD-ROM are authentic and contextually relevant. On-line discussion allows students to exchange their experiences and encourage thinking and reflection. As educators, we need to constantly expand our teaching repertoires and this technology-rich constructivist learning environment suggests that this mode of learning can be successfully used in teacher education.

References

Barnes, S. (2003). *Computer-mediated communication: Human-to-human communication across the internet.* Boston: Allyn & Bacon.

Bitter, G., & Pierson, M. (2002). *Using technology in the classroom.* Boston: Allyn & Bacon.

Breck, J. (2002). *How we will learn in the 21st Century.* Oxford: The Scarecrow Press.

Jonassen, D.H (2000). *Computers as mindtools for schools: Engaging critical thinking.* Columbus, Ohio: Merrill.

Lever-Duffy, J., McDonald, J., & Mizell. (2003). *Teaching and learning with technology.* Boston: Allyn & Bacon.

Lourdusamy, A., Wong, P., & Khine, M.S. (2001, December). *Creating a constructivist learning environment using ICT to teach concepts and skills in classroom management.* Paper presented at the International Educational Research Conference, University of Notre Dame, Australia.

Lourdusamy, A., & Wong, P. (2002, November). *Student teachers' view on their participation in the interactive electronic group discussion during Practicum.* Paper presented at Educational Research Association of Singapore Conference, Singapore.

Mayer, R. (2001). *Multimedia learning.* Cambridge: Cambridge University Press.

Morrison, G., and Guenther, P. (2000). Designing instruction for learning in electronic classrooms. In Weiss, R., Knowlton, D. and Speck, B. (Eds.). *Principles of effective teaching in the on-line classroom.* pp 15-21, San Francisco: Jossey-Bass.

Newman, D., Griffin, P., & Cole, M. (1989). *The construction zone: working for cognitive change in school.* New York: Cambridge Press.

Oxley, D. (2001). *Organising schools into small learning communities.* National Association of secondary school principles, NASSP Bulletin, 85(625), 5-16.

Papert, S. (1990). Introduction. In Idit Harel (Ed.) *Constructivist learning.* Boston: MIT.

Ross, T., & Bailey, G. (1996). *Technology-based learning: A handbook for teachers and technology leaders.* Illinois: Skylight.

Sharp, V. (2002). *Computer education for teachers: Integrating technology into classroom teaching.* New York: McGraw-Hill.

Solomon, G. (1999). Collaborative learning with technology. *Technology and Learning*, 19(5), 51-53.

Wilson, B. (1996). *Constructivist learning environments: Case studies in instructional design.* New Jersey: Educational Technology Publications.

Wilson, B., and Lowry, M. (2000). Constructivist learning on the Web. In E. Burge (Ed.) *The strategic use of learning technologies.* (pp 79-88). San Francisco: Jossey-Bass.

Weigel, V. (2002). *Deep learning for digital age: Technology's untapped potential to enrich higher education.* San Francisco: Jossey-Bass.

Chapter 3

EFFECTIVENESS OF A TECHNOLOGY-RICH AND OUTCOMES-FOCUSED LEARNING ENVIRONMENT

Jill M. Aldridge
Barry J. Fraser
Curtin University of Technology
Australia

This chapter reports a study that involved the validation of a widely-applicable and distinctive questionnaire for assessing students' perceptions of their actual and preferred classroom learning environments in technology-rich, outcomes-focused learning settings. Analysis of data from 1035 student responses from 80 classes provided evidence for the validity and reliability of the questionnaire for use at the senior high school level across a number of different subjects. Also, the data were used to investigate (a) associations between students' perceptions of the learning environment and their academic achievement, attitude towards the subject, attitudes toward computer use and academic efficacy and (b) the success of an innovative new school in promoting ICT-rich and outcomes-focused classroom learning environments.

1. Introduction

In numerous countries around the world, there currently is a major shift in school education from what teachers do to an 'outcomes-focus' on what students achieve and an emphasis on catering for student individual differences in backgrounds, interests and learning styles. Although an effective outcomes-focused system can be extremely difficult to achieve for practical reasons, integration of information communications technology (ICT) into the learning environment has considerable potential for providing teachers with the means to manage efficiently the diverse educational provisions needed to optimise each individual student's outcomes. In many schools, ICT is becoming more commonplace and, in some cases, the integration of ICT into the learning environment is becoming a major thrust. In the field of learning environments, therefore, there is a need for an instrument that can be used to monitor the development and effectiveness of the learning environments that teachers create which provide an outcomes-focus and which integrate the use of ICT into their teaching and learning.

This chapter reports the reliability and validity of a generally-applicable instrument, designed to monitor the evolution of technology-rich, outcomes-focused learning environments, as well as its use in two research applications: 1) how the learning environment created by teachers influences students' achievement, attitudes and self-efficacy and 2) whether an innovative new school is effective in terms of the classroom learning environments that it creates.

2. Aims of the Study

1. To validate a widely-applicable questionnaire for monitoring outcomes-focused and ICT-rich classroom learning environments and student attitudes.

2. To investigate whether outcomes-focused and ICT-rich learning environments promote student achievement, attitudes towards the subject, attitudes to use of ICT and academic efficacy.

3. To evaluate the success of educational programs at an innovative new school in terms of changes in learning environment and student attitudes

3. Background to the Study

3.1 Field of Learning Environments

The study draws on and contributes to the field of learning environments (Fraser, 1994, 1998a). Contemporary research on school environments partly owes inspiration to Lewin's (1936) seminal work in non-educational settings, which recognised that both the environment and its interaction with characteristics of the individual are potent determinants of human behaviour. Since then, the notion of person-environment fit has been elucidated in education by Stern (1970), whereas Walberg (1981) has proposed a model of educational productivity in which the educational environment is one of nine determinants of student outcomes. Research specifically on classroom learning environments took off about 30 years ago with the work of Walberg (1979) and Moos (1974) which spawned many, diverse research programs around the world (Fraser, 1994, 1998a) and the creation of *Learning Environments Research: An International Journal* (Fraser, 1998c). Although earlier work often used questionnaires to assess learning environments, the productive combination of qualitative and quantitative methods is a hallmark of the field today (Tobin & Fraser, 1998).

The dimensions measured by individual classroom environment instruments can be classified according to Moos' (1974) scheme for classifying human environments. Moos identified three basic dimensions including: the *Relationship Dimension*, which measures the nature and intensity of personal relationships; the *Personal Development Dimension*, which measures the directions in which personal growth and self-enhancement occur; and the *System Maintenance and System Change Dimension*, which measures the extent to which the environment maintains clear objectives and control and responds to change.

Past research on learning environments provides numerous research traditions, conceptual models and research methods that are relevant to the study presented in this chapter. This study draws on the rich resource of diverse, valid, economical and widely-applicable assessment instruments that are available in the field of learning environments (Fraser, 1998b) as a starting point for developing a new questionnaire ideally suited to technology-rich, outcomes-focused learning environments. Also, the study draws on past evaluations of educational innovations (Fraser & Maor, 2000; Maor & Fraser, 1996; Teh & Fraser, 1994) from the field of learning environments to investigate success in creating effective outcomes-focused and ICT-rich classroom learning environments.

3.2. Information and Communications Technology (ICT) and Education

Education and training are fundamental to achieving priorities for the economy in the twenty-first century. All citizens need to be "enterprising, innovative, adaptable and socially responsible participants in the information economy" (National Office of the Information Economy, 1999, p. 11). These national views also are reflected in state curriculum frameworks in Australia (e.g., Curriculum Council, 1997). Although education has a poor history of successfully meeting the challenges of major shifts in information technology (Trinidad, 1998), there has been far too little research into the implementation and educational benefits of technology-rich school learning environments. It is important to have a generally-applicable instrument that can help in monitoring the impact of the integration of ICT on the learning environment that teachers create.

4. Research Methods

4.1 Sample

The sample involved in data collection (learning environment and student attitudes, including academic efficacy) included Grade 11 and 12 students from across all learning areas at an innovative new school. The total sample available for the analyses reported in this chapter consisted of 1035 student responses from 80 classes. The students' scores, designated at the end of the academic year were used as a measure of achievement. These scores were obtained for 356 students.

The school in which our study was undertaken, is an innovative new school located in a lower socioeconomic suburb of Perth, Western Australia. The unique ICT infrastructure built into the new school is aimed at facilitating a truly outcomes-focused curriculum that allows the integration of ICT into the delivery of programs, and it provides online curriculum and electronic information management systems to teachers and students. Therefore, this innovative new school is an ideal setting for this study of the educational benefits of technology-rich, outcomes-focused learning environments.

4.2 Instrument Development and Validation

This chapter reports the reliability and validity of a widely-applicable questionnaire for assessing students' perceptions of their actual and preferred classroom learning environments in technology-rich, outcomes-focused learning settings (known as the *Technology-Rich Outcomes-Focused Learning Environment Inventory*, TROFLEI). The validation of the questionnaire involved conducting various statistical analyses with data from a sample of 1035 student responses (e.g., factor analysis and item analysis) to refine the scales and furnish validity and reliability information (see Fraser, 1998a).

To investigate students' attitudes, we developed a second instrument consisting of 18 items in three scales, namely, Attitude to Subject, Attitude to Computer Usage and Student Academic Efficacy. The first scale, Attitude to Subject, is based on a scale from the *Test of Science-Related Attitudes* (TOSRA; Fraser, 1981). The second scale is adapted from the Computer Attitude Scale (CAS) developed by Newhouse (2001). The third scale, Academic Efficacy, is based on a scale developed by Jinks and Morgan (1999).

5. Findings and Results

5.1 Description of the Technology-Rich Outcomes-Focused Learning Environment Inventory (TROFLEI)

The *What is Happening in this Class?* (WIHIC) questionnaire was drawn on especially during the development of the Technology-Rich Outcomes-Focused Learning Environment Inventory (TROFLEI). The WIHIC was originally developed by Fraser, McRobbie and Fisher (1996) and attempted to incorporate those scales that previous studies had shown to be predictors of student outcomes. The robust nature of the What is Happening in this Class? (WIHIC) questionnaire, in terms of reliability and validity, has been widely reported in studies that have used the instrument in different subject areas, at different age levels and in eight different countries. Since the initial development of the WIHIC, the questionnaire has been used successfully in studies to assess the learning environment in Singapore (Chionh & Fraser, 1998; Fraser & Chionh, 2000), Australia and Taiwan (Aldridge & Fraser, 2000; Aldridge, Fraser, & Huang, 1999), Brunei (Khine & Fisher, 2001; Riah & Fraser, 1998), Canada (Raaflaub & Fraser, 2002; Zandvliet & Fraser, 1998), Australia (Dorman, 2002), Indonesia (Margianti, Fraser, & Aldridge, 2001), the United States (Moss & Fraser, 2001) and Canada, Britain and the United States (Dorman, Adams & Ferguson, in press). Within these countries, the WIHIC has been used to assess a range of subjects including high school science (Aldridge & Fraser, 2000; Aldridge, Fraser & Huang, 1999; Moss & Fraser, 2001; Riah & Fraser, 1998), mathematics (Margianti, Fraser & Aldridge, 2001), mathematics and science (Raaflaub & Fraser, 2002) and mathematics and geography (Chionh &

Fraser, 1998; Fraser & Chionh, 2000). The robust nature of the WIHIC made it a sensible choice as a starting point for the present study that involved a sample of students undertaking a range of subjects.

The new instrument included all seven of the original WIHIC scales, namely, Student Cohesiveness, Teacher Support, Involvement, Investigation, Task Orientation, Cooperation and Equity. Three new scales were also developed for the purpose of this study, namely, Differentiation, Computer Usage and Young Adult Ethos scales. These scales were considered especially relevant to outcomes-focused and ICT-rich learning environments.

The initial version of the Technology-Rich Outcomes-Focused Learning Environment Inventory (TROFLEI) contained 80 items altogether with 8 items belonging to each of 10 scales. Extensive field-testing and instrument validation procedures led to a refined version of the TROFLEI consisting of 77 items in the same 10 scales. Items are responded to on a five-point scale with the alternatives of Almost Never, Seldom, Sometimes, Often and Almost Always.

All items were written to have a positive scoring direction in order to minimise confusion to students and they were grouped together in scales to provide contextual cues to readers. Historically, researchers have administered a separate actual and preferred version of questionnaires. To provide a more economical format, however, the TROFLEI pioneered the inclusion of two adjacent response scales on the one sheet (one to record what students perceived as actually happening in their class and the other to record what students would prefer to happen in their class).

5.2 Reliability and Validity of the Technology-Rich Outcomes-Focused Learning Environment Inventory (TROFLEI) and Attitude Scales

Data collected from the 1035 students in 80 classes were analysed in various ways to investigate the reliability and validity of both the actual and preferred versions of the TROFLEI. Principal components factor analysis followed by varimax rotation confirmed a refined structure of the actual and preferred forms of the instrument comprising 77 items in 10 scales. Nearly all of the remaining 77 items have a loading of at least 0.40 on their *a priori* scale and no other scale (see Table 3.1) for both the actual and preferred versions. With the exceptions being Item 6 from the Student Cohesiveness scale and Item 61 from the Differentiation scale that did not load 0.40 or above on its own or any other scale for either the actual or preferred versions. Also Item 43 in the preferred version of the Cooperation scale loaded at least 0.40 in its own scale as well as the Task Orientation scale. The percentage of the total variance extracted with each factor is also recorded at the bottom of Table 3.1. For the actual version, the percentage of variance varies from 4.17% to 7.32% for different scales, with the total variance accounted for being 55.60%. For the preferred version, the percentage of variance ranges from 4.21% to 7.93% for different scales, with a total variance accounted for being 61.00%.

For the revised 77-item version of the TROFLEI, three further indices of scale reliability and validity were generated separately for the actual and preferred versions. The Cronbach alpha reliability coefficient was used as an index of scale internal consistency. Analysis of variance (ANOVA) results were used as evidence of the ability of each scale in the actual form to differentiate between the perceptions of students in different classrooms. A convenient discriminant validity index (namely, the mean correlation of a scale with other scales) was used as evidence that each TROFLEI scale measures a separate dimension that is distinct from the other scales in this questionnaire.

The internal consistency reliability was determined for two units of analysis. Table 3.2 reports the Cronbach alpha coefficient for the actual and preferred versions for each of the 10 TROFLEI scales for two units of analysis (individual and class mean). Using the individual as the unit of analysis, scale reliability estimates for different scales range from 0.81 to 0.94 for the actual form and from 0.85 to 0.95 for the preferred form. Generally reliability figures are even higher with the class mean as the unit of analysis (from 0.87 to 0.97 for the actual form and from 0.89 to 0.97 for the preferred form). These internal consistency indices are comparable to those in past studies that have used the WIHIC (Aldridge & Fraser, 2000; Fraser & Chionh, 2000).

Using the individual as the unit of analysis, the discriminant validity results (mean correlation of a scale with other scales) for the 10 scales of the TROFLEI range from 0.18 to 0.40 for the actual form and between 0.21 and 0.49 for the preferred form (Table 3.2). With the class mean as the unit of analysis, discriminant validity ranges from 0.37 to 0.45 for the actual form and from 0.21 to 0.49 for the preferred form. The data suggest that raw scores on the TROFLEI assess distinct but somewhat overlapping aspects of learning environment. However, the factor analysis supports the independence of factor scores on the 10 scales.

Table 3.1. Factor Loadings for the Technology-Rich Outcomes-Focused Learning Environment Inventory (TROFLEI)

Item No.	Student Cohesiveness		Teacher Support		Involvement		Task Orientation		Investigation	
	Act	Pref	Act	Pref	Act	Pref	Act	Pref	Act	Pref
1	.64	.69								
2	.63	.68								
3	.62	.66								
4	.69	.72								
5	.57	.53								
6	–	–								
7	.49	.62								
9			.71	.66						
10			.81	.75						
11			.63	.70						
12			.57	.62						
13			.65	.73						
14			.64	.69						
15			.62	.69						
16			.61	.63						
17					.72	.67				
18					.65	.70				
19					.46	.69				
20					.60	.50				
22					.62	.51				
23					.47	.48				
24					.60	.50				
25							.55	.68		
26							.52	.64		
27							.64	.71		
28							.56	.68		
29							.71	.77		
30							.57	.70		
31							.50	.67		
32							.53	.69		
33									.68	.75
34									.46	.68
35									.77	.77
36									.59	.76
37									.79	.81
38									.78	.83
39									.79	.80
40									.78	.76
41										
42										
43									.44	
44										
45										
46										
47										
48										
49										
50										
51										
52										
53										
54										
55										
56										
59										
60										
61										
62										
63										
64										
65										
66										
67										
68										
69										
70										
71										
72										
73										
74										
75										
76										
77										
78										
79										
80										
% variance	4.23	5.09	6.20	7.00	6.56	4.34	5.11	7.93	5.13	7.87

<small>Note: The ".44" for item 43 appears in the Task Orientation area (between Pref columns of Task Orientation and Investigation).</small>

Table 3.1. Continued

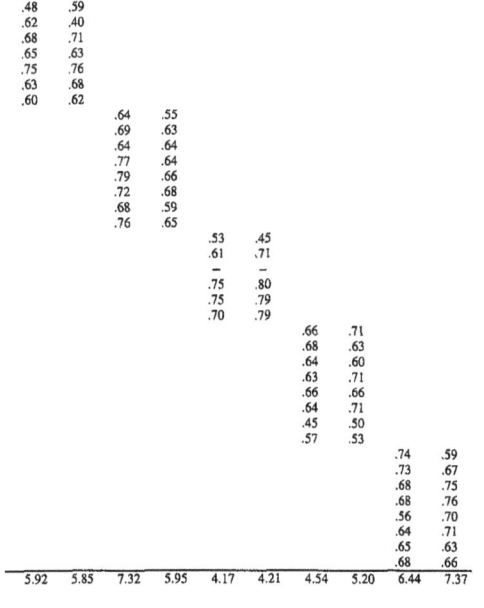

Factor loadings smaller than 0.40 have been omitted. The sample consisted of 1035 student responses in 80 classes.

An analysis of variance (ANOVA) was used to determine the ability of the actual version of each TROFLEI scale to differentiate between the perceptions of students in different classes. The one-way ANOVA for each scale involved class membership as the independent variable and the individual student as the unit of analysis. Table 3.2 reports the ANOVA results showing all 10 TROFLEI scales differentiate significantly between classes ($p<0.01$). Thus, students within the same class perceive the environment in a relatively similar manner, while the within-class mean perceptions of the students vary between classes. The eta^2 statistic (an estimate of the strength of association between class membership and the dependent variable) ranges from 0.07 to 0.18 for different TROFLEI scales.

The statistics obtained for the internal consistency (alpha reliability) and the ability of each scale to differentiate between the perceptions of the students in different classrooms (eta^2 statistic from ANOVA) can be considered acceptable. The data presented in Table 3.2, in conjunction with the factor analysis results in Table 3.1, support the contention that the TROFLEI is a valid and reliable classroom environment instrument for the assessment of students' perceptions of their psychosocial environments at the high school level.

To measure students' attitudes, the present study adapted selected scales from three instruments. The three scales are Attitude toward Subject, Attitudes toward Computer Use and Academic Efficacy. The original instrument consisted of 24 items, with 8 eight items in each of three scales.

The data collected from 1,035 student responses in 80 classes were used to perform a principal components factor analysis followed by varimax rotation. This resulted in the acceptance of a revised version of the instrument with the same three *a priori* factors, but with three items omitted, namely, Item 14 and 15 from the Computer Attitude scale and Item 22 from the Academic Efficacy scale. For the final version, all items loaded more than 0.40 on their own scale and no other scale (see the factor loadings reported in Table 3.3). The percentage of variance varies from 13.06 to 22.83 for different scales, with the total variance accounted for being 54.40%.

Table 3.2. Internal Consistency Reliability (Cronbach Alpha Coefficient), Discriminant Validity (Mean Correlation With Other Scales) and Ability to Differentiate Between Classrooms (ANOVA Results) for Two Units of Analysis for the Modified TROFLEI

Scale	Unit of Analysis	No of Items	Alpha Reliability		Mean correlation With other scales		ANOVA Eta^2
			Act	Pref	Act	Pref	Act
Student Cohesiveness	Individual	7	0.86	0.91	0.35	0.45	0.09**
	Class Mean		0.91	0.94	0.42	0.49	
Teacher Support	Individual	8	0.91	0.91	0.36	0.46	0.18**
	Class Mean		0.96	0.94	0.40	0.42	
Involvement	Individual	7	0.86	0.89	0.38	0.44	0.10**
	Class Mean		0.87	0.89	0.45	0.41	
Task Orientation	Individual	8	0.87	0.94	0.36	0.46	0.09**
	Class Mean		0.92	0.95	0.45	0.47	
Investigation	Individual	8	0.92	0.95	0.34	0.43	0.07**
	Class Mean		0.94	0.96	0.37	0.37	
Cooperation	Individual	8	0.90	0.92	0.40	0.49	0.08**
	Class Mean		0.90	0.93	0.42	0.48	
Equity	Individual	8	0.94	0.95	0.35	0.44	0.13**
	Class Mean		0.97	0.97	0.45	0.48	
Differentiation	Individual	6	0.81	0.85	0.18	0.21	0.10**
	Class Mean		0.89	0.91	0.21	0.24	
Computer Usage	Individual	8	0.86	0.88	0.20	0.30	0.17**
	Class Mean		0.92	0.91	0.20	0.21	
Young Adult Ethos	Individual	8	0.92	0.91	0.37	0.41	0.13**
	Class Mean		0.95	0.92	0.39	0.39	

* $p<0.05$ ** $p<0.01$
The sample consisted of 1,035 students in 80 classes.
The eta^2 statistic (which is the ratio of 'between' to 'total' sums of squares) represents the proportion of variance explained by class membership.

Table 3.3. Factor Loadings for the Student Attitude and Efficacy Scales

Item No	Factor Loading		
	Attitude to Subject	Attitude to Computer Usage	Academic Efficacy
1	0.75		
2	0.76		
3	0.74		
4	0.76		
5	0.64		
6	0.71		
7	0.64		
8	0.69		
9		0.83	
10		0.83	
11		0.44	
12		0.77	
13		0.63	
16		0.83	
17			0.74
18			0.74
19			0.71
20			0.73
21			0.76
23			0.51
24			0.63
% Variance	28.58	12.36	15.20
Eigenvalue	6.00	2.60	3.19

Factor loadings smaller than 0.40 have been omitted.
The sample consisted of 1,035 students in 80 classes.

Table 3. 4. Internal Consistency Reliability (Cronbach Alpha Coefficient) and Discriminant Validity (Mean Correlation With Other Scales) for Two Units of Analysis for the Student Attitude and Efficacy Scales

Scale	Unit of Analysis	No of Items	Alpha Reliability	Mean Correlation with other Scales
Attitude to Subject	Individual	8	0.87	0.24
	Class Mean		0.92	0.21
Attitude to Computer Usage	Individual	6	0.81	0.14
	Class Mean		0.83	0.15
Academic Efficacy	Individual	7	0.85	0.26
	Class Mean		0.88	0.23

** $p<0.01$
* $p<0.05$
The sample consisted of 1,035 students in 80 classes.

The internal consistency reliability (Cronbach alpha coefficient) of each of the three attitude and efficacy scales for two units of analysis (individual and class mean) is reported in Table 3.4. The scale reliability estimates range from 0.81 to 0.87 using the individual as the unit of analysis and from 0.83 to 0.92 using the class mean as the unit of analysis. As a convenient index of the discriminant validity of the attitude questionnaire, use was made of the mean correlation of scale with the other scale for the three scales of the attitude instrument. The mean correlation of a scale with the other scales ranged from 0.14 to 0.26 using the individual as the unit of analysis and from 0.15 to 0.23 using the class mean as the unit of analysis (see Table 3.4). The results in Tables 3.3 and 3.4 suggest strong factorial validity, internal consistency reliability and discriminant validity for the three attitude and efficacy scales.

5.3 Investigating Whether Outcomes-Focused and ICT-Rich Learning Environments are Associated with Student Outcomes

To investigate associations between four student outcomes and the 10 classroom environment scales, simple correlation and multiple regression analyses were conducted. The four student outcomes were student attitudes towards their subject, student attitudes towards using the computer, student self-efficacy and student achievement (the score designated to a student at the end of the year). A simple correlation analysis of relationships between each outcome and each of 10 learning environment scales was performed to provide information about the bivariate association between each learning environment scale and each student outcome. A multiple correlation analysis of relationships between each attitude scale and the set of 10 learning environment scales was conducted to provide a more complete picture of the joint influence of correlated environment dimensions on outcomes and to reduce the Type I error rate associated with the simple correlation analysis. To interpret which individual scales make the largest contribution to explaining variance in student attitudes, the regression weights were examined to see which ones were significantly greater than zero ($p<0.05$). The regression weight describes the influence of a particular environment variable on an outcome when all other environment variables in the regression analysis are mutually controlled. Table 3.5 shows the association between each of the student outcomes and each

TROFLEI scale using both the individual and the class mean as the units of analysis for all analyses except for the achievement outcome (for which the sample size was not large enough to permit analyses at the class level).

5.3.1 Student Attitudes towards their Subject

The results of simple correlation analysis (Table 3.5) indicate that all but two of the 10 TROFLEI scales, namely, Differentiation and Computer Usage, are statistically significantly and positively associated with student attitudes towards their class ($p<0.01$) at the individual level of analysis. Seven of the 10 scales are statistically significantly ($p<0.05$) related to the Attitude to Subject scale at the class mean level of analysis, namely, Student Cohesiveness, Teacher Support, Involvement, Task Orientation, Cooperation, Equity and Young Adult Ethos. The results of the simple correlation analysis suggest that improved student attitudes towards a subject are associated with more emphasis on these scales.

The multiple correlation (R) between students' perceptions of the set of 10 TROFLEI scales and the Attitude Toward Subject scale (reported in Table 3.5) is 0.52 at the student level of analysis and 0.76 at the class mean level of analysis, and is statistically significant ($p<0.01$) for both levels. Standardised regression weights were computed to provide information about the unique contribution of each learning environment scale to the Attitude Toward Subject scale when the other nine scales are mutually controlled. Table 3.5 indicates that three of the 10 TROFLEI scales uniquely account for a significant ($p<0.01$) amount of variance in student attitudes towards their subject (Teacher Support, Equity and Young Adult Ethos) at the student level of analysis. Teacher support is the only TROFLEI scale that is a significant independent predictor ($p<0.01$) of Attitude to Subject at the class level of analysis.

5.3.2 Student Attitude to Computer Use

With the individual as unit of analysis, the results of the simple correlation analysis (reported in Table 3.5) indicate that nine of the 10 TROFLEI scales (with the exception being Differentiation) are positively and statistically significantly ($p<0.05$) related to the Attitude to Computer Use scale. At the class mean level of analysis, seven of the 10 TROFLEI scales (namely, Involvement, Task Orientation, Investigation,

Cooperation, Equity, Computer Usage and Young Adult Ethos) are positively and statistically significantly ($p<0.01$) related to Attitudes to Computer Use.

Table 3.5. Simple Correlation and Multiple Regression Analyses for Associations Between Four Student Outcomes (Attitude to Subject, Attitude to Computer Use, Academic Efficacy and Achievement) and Dimensions of the TROFLEI for Two Units of Analysis

Scale	Unit of analysis	Outcome Environment Association							
		Attitude toward Subject		Attitude to Computer Use		Academic Efficacy		Achievement	
		r	β	r	β	r	β	r	β
Student Cohesiveness	Individual	0.19**	-0.06	0.14**	0.02	0.20**	0.05	0.04	-0.11
	Class	0.23*	-0.17	0.17	-0.22	0.34**	0.09		
Teacher Support	Individual	0.46**	0.24**	0.09**	0.05	0.25**	0.03	0.15**	-0.04
	Class	0.71**	0.49**	0.21	-0.12	0.33**	0.26		
Involvement	Individual	0.27**	0.05	0.18**	0.04	0.38**	0.26**	0.17**	0.13
	Class	0.34**	-0.04	0.39**	0.35*	0.41**	0.10		
Task Orientation	Individual	0.42**	0.18**	0.15**	0.05	0.33**	0.19**	0.19**	0.13
	Class	0.54**	0.22	0.26*	0.05	0.29**	0.23		
Investigation	Individual	0.20**	0.06	0.19**	0.08	0.35**	0.14**	0.19	-0.03
	Class	0.11	-0.14	0.31**	0.26	0.68**	0.43**		
Cooperation	Individual	0.22**	-0.09	0.19**	-0.01	0.21**	-0.05	0.13*	0.07
	Class	0.32**	0.13	0.27*	0.06	0.27*	-0.05		
Equity	Individual	0.42**	0.07	0.14**	0.07	0.22**	0.05	0.23**	0.17*
	Class	0.62**	0.06	0.30**	0.27	0.12	0.07		
Differentiation	Individual	0.02	-0.01	0.01	-0.15**	0.25**	0.09*	0.02	0.04
	Class	0.17	-0.23	-0.11	-0.52**	0.66**	0.46**		
Computer Usage	Individual	0.05	-0.01	0.33**	0.38**	0.17**	0.00	-0.07	-0.11
	Class	0.09	-0.04	0.23*	0.44**	0.41**	0.09		
Young Adult Ethos	Individual	0.39**	0.17**	0.14**	0.07	0.24**	0.10	0.11*	-0.03
	Class	0.55**	0.14	0.24*	0.00	0.10	0.18		
Multiple Correlation (R)	Individual	0.52**		0.40**		0.45**		0.29**	
	Class	0.76**		0.62**		0.81**			

*$p<0.05$ **$p<0.01$
N= 1,035 students for attitude scales and 356 students for achievement

The multiple correlation is 0.40 and 0.62, respectively, for the individual and class mean levels of analysis and is statistically significant ($p<0.01$) for both levels. The standardised regression weights reported in Table 3.5 indicate that two of the 10 TROFLEI scales (Differentiation and Computer Usage) are statistically significantly ($p<0.01$) and independently related to the Attitudes to Computer Use at both the student and class mean levels of analysis. Also Involvement is a significant ($p<0.01$) independent predictor of Attitudes to Computer Use at the class mean level. All relationships are positive except those for Differentiation, and this suggests the need for further research aimed at replicating and explaining this relationship.

5.3.3 Academic Efficacy

With the individual student as unit of analysis, the results of the simple correlation analysis reported in Table 3.5 indicate that all 10 scales of the TROFLEI are positively and significantly ($p<0.01$) related to the Academic Efficacy scale. At the class mean level of analysis, eight of the 10 TROFLEI scales are positively and statistically significantly ($p<0.05$) related to the Academic Efficacy scale (namely, Student Cohesiveness, Teacher Support, Involvement, Task Orientation, Investigation, Cooperation, Differentiation and Computer Usage). The multiple correlation (R) between students' perceptions of the learning environment and academic efficacy is positive and statistically significant ($p<0.01$) with both the individual (0.45) and class mean (0.81) as the unit of analysis. For the Academic Efficacy scale, scales that uniquely account for a significant proportion of variance are Involvement, Task Orientation, Investigation and Differentiation at the student level and Investigation and Differentiation at both the student and class levels. All relationships are positive for both the simple correlation and multiple regression analyses, thus suggesting a link between improved student Academic Efficacy and emphasis on the dimensions of the classroom environment that are assessed by the TROFLEI.

5.3.4 Student Achievement

The study also examined whether associations exist between student achievement and dimensions of the learning environment. The student's score, designated at the end of the academic year, was used as a measure of achievement. Given the limited sample sizes, analyses were conducted only at the student level. The results of the simple correlation analysis reported in Table 3.5 indicate that six of the 10 scales of the TROFLEI are positively and significantly ($p<0.05$) related to the student achievement score, namely, Teacher Support, Involvement, Task Orientation, Cooperation, Equity and Young Adult Ethos. The multiple correlation (R) between students' perceptions of the learning environment and achievement is statistically significant ($p<0.01$) at the individual level of analysis. According Table 3.5, only the Equity scale uniquely accounts for a significant proportion of variance in student achievement. All significant relationships between student achievement and learning environment scales are positive.

5.4 Evaluating the Success of Educational Programs at an Innovative New School in Terms of Changes in Learning Environment and Student Attitudes

To examine whether the TROFLEI and attitude scales could be used to monitor the evolution of technology-rich, outcomes-focused learning environments, the instrument was administered to students at the end of the school year in 2001 and then again at the end of 2002. The sample included 441 students attending the school in 2001 and 596 students in 2002. Profiles, based on student average item mean scores for the actual learning environment, at different grain sizes (whole school and by learning area), were generated and used as the basis for discussions between teachers about how the discrepancies between students' actual and preferred scores might be reduced.

To evaluate the programs in terms of changes between 2001 and 2002, one-way MANOVAs were conducted separately with the set of actual TROFLEI scales and the set of attitude scales as the dependent variables and the year as the independent variable. In each case, the multivariate test yielded significant results ($p<0.01$) in terms of Wilks' lambda criterion, indicating that there were subject differences in the set of criterion variables as a whole. Therefore, the univariate ANOVA was interpreted for each individual environment and attitude scale. Effect sizes were also calculated (as recommended by Thompson, 1998a, 1998b) to estimate the magnitudes of the differences. These results are reported in Table 3.6.

Table 3.6. Average Item Mean, Average Item Standard Deviation and Difference (Effect Size and MANOVA Results) between the Environments Perceived by Students in 2001 and 2002 Using the Individual Student as the Unit of Analysis

TROFLEI Scale	Average Item Mean		Average Item Std Deviation		Difference	
	2001	2002	2001	2002	Effect Size	F
Student Cohesiveness	3.90	4.02	0.72	0.67	0.17	1.70**
Teacher Support	3.62	3.58	0.86	0.85	0.05	0.77
Involvement	3.20	3.24	0.85	0.81	0.05	0.88
Task Orientation	3.82	3.94	0.76	0.69	0.17	1.64**
Investigation	2.88	3.01	0.93	0.85	0.15	1.54*
Cooperation	3.70	3.87	0.85	0.77	0.21	1.87**
Equity	4.02	4.08	0.93	0.89	0.07	1.05
Differentiation	2.92	2.76	0.97	0.96	0.17	1.65**
Computer Usage	3.40	3.37	0.94	0.89	0.03	0.81
Young Adult Ethos	3.97	4.14	0.85	0.69	0.22	1.86**
Attitude to Subject	3.42	3.55	0.88	0.93	0.14	1.48*
Attitude to Computer Use	3.77	3.91	0.85	0.80	0.17	1.63**
Academic Efficacy	3.17	3.14	0.84	0.81	0.04	0.70

*$p<0.05$ **$p<0.01$
N=441 students who participated in the research in 2001 and 596 students who participated in the research in 2002.

At the whole school level, the ANOVA results in Table 3.6 indicate that, in 2002, students generally perceived a more positive learning environment than in 2001. The results suggest that students perceived statistically significantly ($p<0.05$) more Student Cohesiveness, Task Orientation, Investigation, Cooperation and Young Adult Ethos, but significantly less Differentiation in 2002 than in 2001. These differences in perceptions are presented graphically in Figure 1. The effect sizes for the six scales for which differences are statistically significant range between approximately one sixth of a standard deviation (0.15) and one quarter of a standard deviation (0.22). The results indicate that the magnitudes of the differences on these TROFLEI scales is modest, with students who participated in the research in 2002 consistently perceiving their learning environment more favourably on all scales, except Differentiation, than those who participated in 2001 (see Figure 3.1).

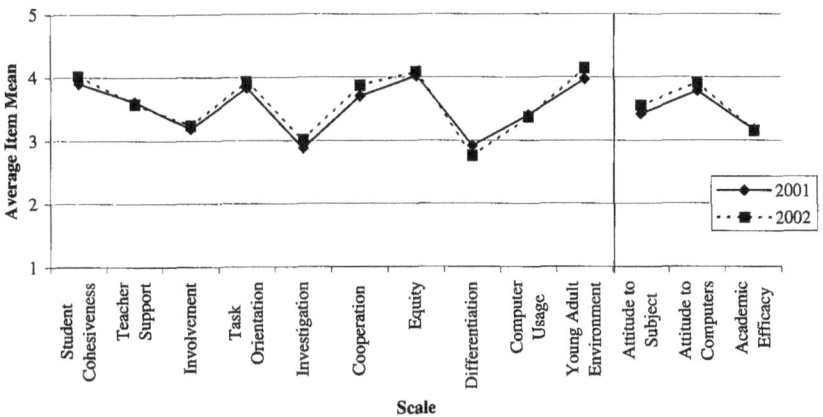

Figure 3.1. Average item mean for Actual and Preferred scores on the TROFLEI and Attitude scales for students enrolled in 2001 and 2002.

The ANOVA results for the attitude instrument (reported in Table 3.6) indicate that, in 2002, students had statistically significantly ($p<0.05$) more positive attitudes towards their subject and towards computer use than in 2001. The effect size for differences in Attitude to Subject is 0.14 and for Attitude to Computer Use is 0.17.

In addition to providing feedback at the whole school level, feedback regarding specific learning areas (such as English or science) was also provided. Table 3.7 provides the average item mean, average item standard deviations and effect sizes (for differences between 2001 and 2002) for two learning areas within the school. Figures 3.2 and 3.3 provide a graphical profile of student scores on the actual form of the TROFLEI and attitude instrument for 2001 and 2002 for each of the learning areas. The sample size for Learning Area 1 was 57 students enrolled in 2001 and 45 students enrolled in 2002. For Learning Area 2 the sample size was 82 students enrolled in 2001 and 54 students enrolled in 2002. It should be noted that the smallness of the sample sizes involved in these analyses make the findings tentative.

Table 3.7. Average Item Mean, Average Item Standard Deviation and Effect Size for Difference between 2001 and 2002 in Perceived Environment and Attitude Scores for Two Learning Areas Using the Individual Student as the Unit of Analysis

TROFLEI Scale	Learning Area	Item Mean		Std Deviation		Effect Size
		2001	2002	2001	2002	
Student Cohesiveness	Learning Area 1	3.97	4.05	0.59	0.68	0.13
	Learning Area 2	3.77	3.90	0.80	0.58	0.19
Teacher Support	Learning Area 1	3.37	1.07	0.79	0.82	0.87
	Learning Area 2	3.49	3.32	0.97	0.85	0.19
Involvement	Learning Area 1	3.19	3.47	0.75	1.04	0.31
	Learning Area 2	3.02	3.14	0.92	0.85	0.14
Task Orientation	Learning Area 1	3.69	4.08	0.67	0.63	0.60
	Learning Area 2	3.77	3.88	0.78	0.59	0.16
Investigation	Learning Area 1	2.89	3.07	0.82	0.92	0.21
	Learning Area 2	2.79	2.70	0.95	0.73	0.11
Cooperation	Learning Area 1	3.73	4.39	0.97	0.63	0.83
	Learning Area 2	3.56	3.63	0.82	0.85	0.08
Equity	Learning Area 1	3.96	4.39	0.97	0.66	0.53
	Learning Area 2	3.87	3.85	1.02	0.97	0.02
Differentiation	Learning Area 1	2.84	3.21	0.93	0.86	0.41
	Learning Area 2	2.99	2.37	1.06	0.77	0.68
Computer Usage	Learning Area 1	3.41	3.32	0.81	0.80	0.11
	Learning Area 2	3.57	3.28	0.75	0.79	0.38
Young Adult Ethos	Learning Area 1	3.93	4.29	0.78	0.64	0.51
	Learning Area 2	3.89	3.98	0.97	0.91	0.10
Attitude To Subject	Learning Area 1	3.22	3.89	0.85	0.99	0.73
	Learning Area 2	3.46	3.41	1.01	0.94	0.05
Attitude To Computer Use	Learning Area 1	3.88	3.59	0.85	0.86	0.34
	Learning Area 2	3.67	3.84	0.84	0.72	0.22
Academic Efficacy	Learning Area 1	3.08	3.43	0.84	0.79	0.43
	Learning Area 2	3.08	2.93	0.81	0.64	0.21

*$p<0.05$ **$p<0.01$
N= 57 students enrolled in 2001 and 45 students enrolled in 2002 for Learning Area 1, and 82 students enrolled in 2001 and 54 students enrolled in 2002 for Learning Area 2.

For Learning Area 1 (Figure 3.2), students perceived a learning environment that included more of nine of the 10 learning environment scales in 2002 than in 2001 (the exception being Computer Usage). The effect size (calculated to provide an approximation of the magnitude of the differences) for the scales of the TROFLEI range between approximately one tenth (0.11) and four-fifths of a standard deviation (0.87). For five TROFLEI scales, Teacher Support, Task Orientation, Cooperation, Equity, Differentiation and Young Adult Ethos, the effect sizes range from approximately half (0.51) to four-fifths of a standard deviation (0.87), suggesting a notable difference between the learning environment perceived in 2001 and 2002. Students' responses to the Attitudes to Subject and Academic Efficacy scales also improved markedly, whilst their Attitude to Computer Use deteriorated. The effect sizes for differences between 2001 and 2002 were 0.73 for Attitude to Subject, 0.34 for Attitude to Computer Use and 0.43 for Academic Efficacy.

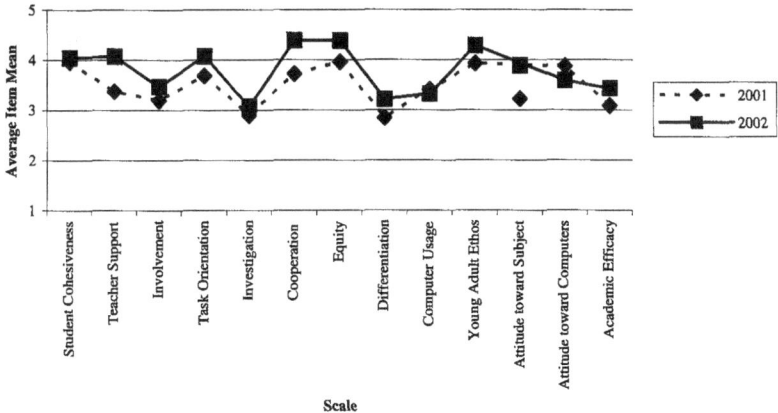

Figure 3.2. Average item mean for students enrolled in Learning Area 1 in 2001 and 2002 on Actual TROFLEI and Attitude scales.

For Learning Area 2 (Figure 3.3), students perceived very similar learning environments in 2001 and in 2002 on eight of the 10 learning environment scales (Student Cohesiveness, Teacher Support, Involvement, Task Orientation, Investigation, Cooperation, Equity and

Young Adult Ethos). The effect sizes (calculated to provide an approximation of the magnitude of the differences) for these scales are modest, ranging between 0.02 and approximately one fifth (0.19) of a standard deviation. Students perceived Learning Area 2 less favourably in 2002 than in 2001 on two TROFLEI scales, namely, Differentiation and Computer Usage. The effect sizes for differences between student scores in 2001 and 2002 for these two scales were 0.68 and 0.38, respectively, suggesting a notable difference in these two scales. In terms of student attitudes and academic efficacy, students held a slightly more favourable attitude to the subjects in this learning area in 2002 than in 2001 (effect size of 0.05 standard deviations). For Attitude to Computer Use and Academic Efficacy, students scored less favourably in 2002 than in 2002. The effect sizes for Computer Use and Academic Efficacy were 0.22 and 0.21, respectively.

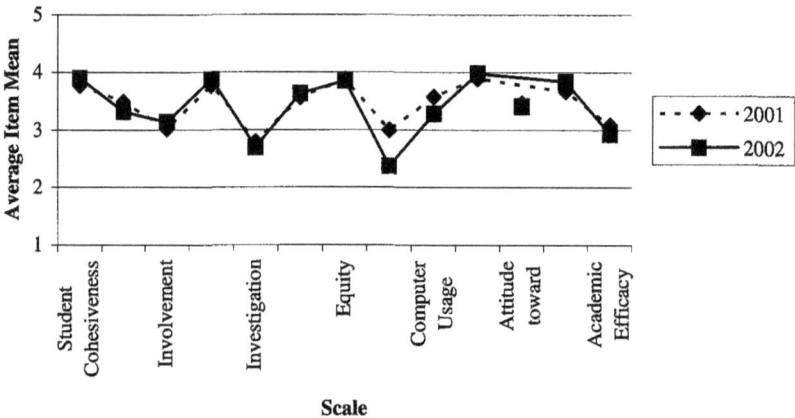

Figure 3.3. Average item mean for students enrolled in Learning Area 2 in 2001 and 2002 on Actual TROFLEI and Attitude scales.

6. Discussion and Conclusion

A major contribution of the present study is the development and validation of a widely-applicable and distinctive questionnaire for assessing students' perceptions of their actual and preferred classroom learning environments in technology-rich, outcomes-focused classroom learning settings. This research, by examining the learning environment in an innovative new school and its impact on student attitudes towards learning and computer use, academic efficacy and student achievement, has the potential to provide information to teachers on how ICT can be used in creating outcomes-focused education and promoting improved outcomes for all students.

A new questionnaire (Technology-Rich Outcomes-Focused Learning Environment Inventory, TROFLEI) measures 10 dimensions of the actual and preferred classroom environments at the high school level, namely, Student Cohesiveness, Teacher Support, Involvement, Investigation, Task Orientation, Cooperation, Equity, Differentiation, Computer Usage and Young Adult Ethos. The questionnaire has 77 items and includes a novel structure that incorporates the actual and preferred responses on the same form, thus providing an economical format that reduces the amount of administration time.

The total sample available for the analyses reported in this chapter consisted of 1,035 student responses from 80 classes. The sample included Grade 11 and 12 students from across all learning areas at an innovative new senior high school.

The TROFLEI was found to be valid and reliable at the senior high school level across a number of different subjects and learning areas. A series of item and factor analyses led to a refined version of the TROFLEI that displays satisfactory factorial validity for both the actual and preferred versions of the questionnaire. At both the individual and class mean levels of analysis, the internal consistency reliability and discriminant validity are satisfactory for both the actual and preferred form to the TROFLEI. Further analyses support the ability of the actual responses to differentiate between classrooms on all scales. These results support the reliability and validity of the TROFLEI and, therefore, teachers and researchers can use it with confidence in the future.

An attitude instrument was also developed for the present study. The three scales assess important affective outcomes of technology-rich, outcomes-focused learning environments, namely, Attitude to Subject, Attitude to Computer Use and Academic Efficacy. Satisfactory factorial validity, internal consistency reliability and discriminant validity were found for the new attitude instrument for both the individual and class mean as the units of analysis.

To explore the usefulness of the TROFLEI, data were analysed to examine two separate applications. The first involved an investigation of whether associations exist between the classroom learning environment and achievement and three affective outcomes (student attitude towards their subject, student attitude towards computer use and student academic efficacy). The results suggest that Teacher Support, Equity and Young Adult Ethos uniquely account for a significant amount of variance in students' attitudes towards their subject. For associations between student attitudes to computer use, the results indicate that Differentiation and Computer Usage are statistically significantly and independently related to the students' attitudes to computer use at the individual level of analysis. An examination of associations between academic efficacy and the learning environment suggest that, with the individual as the unit of analysis, Involvement, Task Orientation, Investigation and Differentiation independently account for a significant proportion of variance in Academic Efficacy. Finally, the study examined whether associations exist between students' achievement and dimensions of the learning environment. The results indicate that only the Equity scale uniquely accounts for a significant proportion of variance in student achievement.

The second application involved using the actual TROFLEI and attitude scales to evaluate the success of programs at the school in terms of changes in the learning environment and student attitudes. Data collected from students at the end of each academic year (2001 and 2002 were used to generate graphical profiles that could be used to examine whether changes to the learning environment had occurred. At the whole school level, the results indicate that students perceived statistically significantly more Student Cohesiveness, Task Orientation, Investigation, Cooperation and Young Adult Ethos, but significantly less Differentiation, in 2002 than in 2001. Also, in 2002, students' Attitude to Subject and Attitude to Computer Use scores were statistically significantly more positive than in 2001. Although differences on each of these scales were statistically significant, the effect sizes suggest that the differences were modest in size.

Graphical profiles, generated for the different learning areas within the school, reveal differences in the degree to which the learning environment and attitudes of students changed between 2001 and 2002. For Learning Area 1, students generally perceive the learning environment to be more favourable in 2002 than in 2001. Also, when compared to 2001, students appear to have more positive attitudes to their subject and more positive views of their academic efficacy in 2002.

The profile for Learning Area 2, however, appears to give quite a different picture of the development of the learning environment over the two years. The results suggest little change on eight of the 10 TROFLEI scales for Learning Area 2, with students perceiving less Differentiation and Computer Usage in 2002 than in 2001. Student responses to the attitude and academic efficacy scales were also similar for 2001 and 2002.

Since the school opened at the beginning of 2001, teachers have begun to introduce and integrate ICT into all facets of their work, thus generating a wealth of knowledge that is directly transferable to other schools. This study could have important implications for educational systems concerning how ICT can be used effectively to maximise educational outcomes for individual students. The study is innovative within the field of learning environments because of its focus on technology-rich settings and outcomes-based at an innovative new school.

Acknowledgements

The present study is funded by the Australian Research Council under its Strategic Partnerships with Industry: Research and Training Scheme (SPIRT). The contributions of a number of organisations have contributed to the study and we would like to acknowledge the assistance of the Australian Research Council, Education Department of Western Australia, AlphaWest6, CISCO Systems, ACER Computers and RM Australasia.

References

Aldridge, J. M., Fraser, B. J., & Huang, I. T.-C. (1999). Investigating classroom environments in Taiwan and Australia with multiple research methods. *Journal of Educational Research, 93*, 48-62.

Aldridge, J. M., Fraser, B. J., Taylor, P. C., & Chen, C.-C. (2000). Constructivist learning environments in a cross-national study in Taiwan and Australia. *International Journal of Science Education, 22*, 37-55.

Chionh, Y. H., & Fraser, B. J. (1998, April). *Validation and use of the 'What is Happening in this Class' (WIHIC) questionnaire in*

Singapore. Paper presented at the annual meeting of the American Educational Research Association, San Diego, CA.

Curriculum Council. (1997). *Curriculum framework*. Perth: Western Australian Curriculum Council.

Dorman, J. P. (2001). Associations between classroom environment and academic efficacy. *Learning Environment Research: An International Journal, 4,* 243-257.

Dorman, J. P., Adams, J. E., & Ferguson, J. M. (in press). Confirmatory factor analysis of the 'What is Happening in this Class' questionnaire and its structural invariance across groups. *Journal of Classroom Interaction.*

Fisher, D., Henderson, D., & Fraser, B. (1997). Laboratory environments and student outcomes in senior high school biology, *American Biology Teacher, 59*(2), 14-19.

Fraser, B. J. (1981). *Test of Science-Related Attitudes handbook* (TOSRA). Melbourne, Australia: Australian Council for Educational Research.

Fraser, B. J. (1994). Research on classroom and school climate. In D. Gabel (Ed.), *Handbook of research on science teaching and learning* (pp. 493-541). New York: Macmillan.

Fraser, B. (1998a). Science learning environments: Assessment, effects and determinants. In B. Fraser & K. Tobin (Eds.), *International handbook of science education* (pp. 527-564). Dordrecht, The Netherlands: Kluwer.

Fraser, B. J. (1998b). Classroom environment instruments: Development, validity and applications. *Learning Environment Research: An International Journal, 1,* 7-33.

Fraser, B. J. (1998c). The birth of a new journal: Editor's introduction. *Learning Environments Research, 1,* 1-5.

Fraser, B. J. (1999). "Grain sizes" in learning environment research: Combining qualitative and quantitative methods. In H. C. Waxman & H. J. Walberg (Eds.), *New directions for teaching practice and research* (pp. 285-296). Berkeley, CA: McCutchan.

Fraser, B. J., & Chionh, Y. H. (2000, April). *Classroom environment, self-esteem, achievement, and attitudes in geography and mathematics in Singapore*. Paper presented at the annual meeting of the American Educational Research Association, New Orleans, LA.

Fraser, B. J., Giddings, G. J., & McRobbie, C. J. (1995). Evolution and validation of a personal form of an instrument for assessing science laboratory classroom environments. *Journal of Research in Science Teaching, 32*, 399-422.

Fraser, B. J., & Maor, D. (2000, April). *A learning environment instrument for evaluating students' and teachers' perceptions of constructivist multimedia learning environments.* Paper presented at the annual meeting of the National Association for Research in Science Teaching, New Orleans, LA.

Fraser, B. J., & McRobbie, C. J. (1995). Science laboratory classrooms at schools and universities: A cross-national study. *Educational Research and Evaluation: An International Journal on Theory and Practice, 1*(4), 1-25.

Fraser, B. J., McRobbie, C. J., & Fisher, D. L. (1996, April). *Development, validation and use of personal and class forms of a new classroom environment instrument.* Paper presented at the annual meeting of the American Educational Research Association, New York.

Jinks, J. L., & Morgan, V. (1999). Children's perceived academic self-efficacy: An inventory scale. *Clearing House, 72*, 224-230.

Khine, M. S., & Fisher, D. L. (2001). *Classroom environment and teachers' cultural background in secondary science classes in an Asian context.* Paper presented at the annual conference of the Australian Association for Research in Education, Fremantle, Western Australia.

Lewin, K. (1936). *Principles of topological psychology.* New York: McGraw.

Maor, D., & Fraser, B. J. (1996). Use of classroom environment perceptions in evaluating inquiry-based computer assisted learning. *International Journal of Science Education, 18*, 401-421.

Margianti, E. S., Fraser, B. J., & Aldridge, J. M. (2001, April). *Classroom environment and students' outcomes among university computing students in Indonesia.* Paper presented at the annual meeting of the American Educational Research Association, Seattle, WA.

Moos, R. H. (1974). *The Social Climate Scales: An overview.* Palo Alto, CA: Consulting Psychologists Press.

Moss, C. H., & Fraser, B. J. (2001, April). *Using environment assessments in improving teaching and learning in high school biology classrooms.* Paper presented at the annual meeting of the American Educational Research Association, Seattle, WA.

National Office of the Information Economy. (1999). *The strategic framework for the information economy: Identifying priorities for action in Australia.* The Commonwealth of Australia. Department of Communications, Information Technology & the Arts Canberra. [Online] Available http://www.noie.gov.au/docs/strategicframework.html

Newhouse, C. P. (2001). Development and use of an instrument for computer-supported learning environments. *Learning Environment Research: An International Journal, 4,* 115-138.

Raaflaub, C. A., & Fraser, B. J. (2002, April). *Investigating the learning environment in Canadian mathematics and science classes in which computers are used.* Paper presented at the annual meeting of the American Educational Research Association, New Orleans, LA.

Riah, H., & Fraser, B. J. (1998, April). *The learning environment of high school chemistry classes.* Paper presented at the annual meeting of the National Association for Research in Science Teaching, San Diego, CA.

Stern, G. G. (1970). *People in context: Measuring person-environment congruence in education and industry.* New York: Wiley.

Teh, G. P. L., & Fraser, B. J. (1994). An evaluation of computer assisted learning in terms of achievement, attitudes and classroom environment. *Evaluation and Research in Education, 8,* 147-161.

Thompson, B. (1998a). Review of 'what if there were no significance tests?' *Educational and Psychological Measurement, 58,* 334-346.

Thompson, B. (1998b, April). *Five methodology errors in educational research: The pantheon of statistical significance and other faux pas.* Invited address presented at the annual meeting of the American Educational Research Association, San Diego, CA.

Tobin, K., & Fraser, B. (1998). Qualitative and quantitative landscapes of classroom learning environments. In B. J. Fraser & K. G. Tobin (Eds.), *The international handbook of science education* (pp. 623-640). Dordrecht, The Netherlands: Kluwer.

Trinidad, S. (1998). National overview: Table of state education department technology initiatives. *Australian Educational Computing, 13* (2), 4-5.

Walberg, H. J. (Ed.). (1979). *Educational environments and effects: Evaluation, policy and productivity.* Berkeley, CA: McCutchan.

Walberg, H. J. (1981). A psychological theory of educational productivity. In F. Farley & N. J. Gordon (Eds.), *Psychology and education: The state of the union* (pp. 81-108). Berkeley, CA: McCutchan.

Zandvliet, D., & Fraser, B. J. (1999, March). *A model of educational productivity for high school internet classrooms.* Paper presented at the annual meeting of the American Educational Research Association, Montreal, Canada.

Chapter 4

THE RELATIONSHIP BETWEEN ATTITUDES AND ACHIEVEMENT OF UNIVERSITY STUDENTS IN COMPUTER CLASSROOMS IN INDONESIA

Eko Sri Margianti
Gunadarma University
Indonesia

A study to investigate the relationship between attitudes and achievement of university students in computer classrooms was conducted with a sample of 2,498 third-semester computer students in 50 university classes in one of the private universities in Indonesia. To assess students' perceptions of the classroom environment a university-level version of the What Is Happening In This Class? (WIHIC) questionnaire (originally developed by Fraser, McRobbie, & Fisher (1996) was developed. This questionnaire provides a reliable and widely-applicable instrument that is suitable for use at the university level. Secondary aims of the present study were to examine the usefulness of the university-level learning environment to investigate whether differences exist between (a) students' perceptions of the actual and preferred classroom learning environment and (b) males' and females' perceptions of the actual classroom environment. The results of this study contribute towards explaining why students are achieving at less than desirable levels in their computing courses.

1. Introduction

University administrators consider learning environment at the tertiary level as important for many reasons, including the retention of students (Spreda & Donnay, 2000). A review of literature reveals that, throughout the world, relatively few studies have been conducted at the university level to investigate the impact of the learning environment on student outcome (Dorman, 1998). It is generally recognised that, contributing to this lack of research, is the shortage of reliable instruments available for use at this level. This study is distinctive in that it involved the modification and validation, for the university level, a learning environment instrument that has been used successfully in numerous countries around the world and across a range of subject areas at the school level. The addition of such a widely-applicable questionnaire to assess student's perceptions of their learning environment at the higher education level opens up a range of possibilities for researchers worldwide.

In addition to the modification and validation of this significant questionnaire, the study explored its usefulness in a range of applications, including the investigation of whether the learning environment created by university lecturers, influences students' outcomes (achievement and attitudes), and differences between perceptions on actual and preferred forms of the questionnaire and between males and females. This chapter describes this recent study conducted in a university in Indonesia involving 2,498 students in 50 computer classes.

2. Background

2.1 Studies of Learning Environments at the Higher Educational Level

Learning environment work has distinguished between classroom-level environment and school-level environment. At the university level, school-level research owes much in theory, instrumentation and methodology to earlier work on organization, such as the widely-used university-level instrument, the *College Characteristic Index* (CCI; Stern, 1970). In a more recent study, Dorman (1998) made an important contribution by developing the *University-Level Environment Questionnaire* (ULEQ) to assess lecturers' perceptions of the university environment and validating it with a sample of 489 academic staff from 52 department in 28 Australian universities.

Fraser and Treagust (1986) developed and used the *College and University Classroom Environment Inventory* (CUCEI) to assess students' perception of aspects of the learning environment. Using a sample of 127 university students, they reported that student satisfaction was greater in classes where students perceive higher levels of involvement, task orientation and innovation. In two more recent studies, the CUCEI has been used in examining changes in classroom environment across the transition from senior secondary school to the university level (Nair & Fisher, 2001) and in practical attempts to improve nursing education learning environments (Fisher & Parkinson, 1998).

Newby and Fisher (1997) adapted the *Science Laboratory Environment Inventory* (SLEI) to examine university students' perception of their computer laboratory classroom environments. Bain, McNaught, Mills and Lueckenhausen (1998) also described the computer-facilitated learning environment at the university level. This study was based entirely on archival material and was designed to provide the sampling plan for a second study.

In a study of mathematic courses at five universities in Australia, a learning environment instrument was developed based on factors implicated in decision making about pursuing mathematics at the university level. The questionnaire was validated using a sample of 1883 students attending university mathematic courses (Forgasz, 1998; Forgasz & Leder, 2000).

Spreda and Donnay (2000) validated a single learning environments scale, embedded in the *Strong Interest Inventory* developed for use in career counselling. The questionnaire was administered to 115 first-year students attending a Midwestern university in the USA enrolled in a career development course. The findings suggested that there were associations between the learning environment scale and students' career interests.

Khine and Goh (2001) reported the pioneering effort in a study of a university learning environment in Singapore which utilized the CUCEI in an attempt to examine associations between attitudes and environment. The findings provided the reliability of the instrument and a significant attitude-environment relationship, as well as gender-related differences among tertiary education students in Singapore.

Most recently, Lizzio, Wilson, and Simmons (2002) investigated relationships between students' perceptions of their academic environment, their approaches to study, and their academic outcomes at the university and faculty levels. A questionnaire was administered to a large, cross-disciplinary sample of undergraduate students. Data were analysed using higher-order path and regression analyses, and the results of the study indicated that students' perception of the learning environment influenced both academic achievement and student satisfaction.

2.2 Actual and Preferred Perceptions

Past research also has examined differences between students' and teachers' perceptions of their preferred and actual learning environment (Fraser, 1998). Such research has involved the use of a 'preferred' form of an instrument (which measures students' or teachers' perceptions of the learning environment that they would ideally like) and the 'actual' form of an instrument (which measure the students' and teachers' perception of the actual classroom environment). The wording of the items in these two instruments is similar. These studies also revealed that students and the teachers are likely to prefer a more positive environment than the one actually present in the classroom (Fisher & Fraser, 1983).

2.3 Gender Differences

In many countries, the proportion of males and females studying at the high school level is almost equal. However, a higher proportion of males than females pursue more demanding science and mathematic subjects (Forgasz, 1998). This gender gap is likely to widen as the social scale descends (Teese, Davies, Charlton & Polesel, 1995), and the learning environment could well be a crucial factor when university lecturers consider closing this gender gap.

Past studies that involved students in the higher education grade levels revealed that boys differ from girls in their perceptions of classroom environments. For example, in a study involving 1,733 grade 10 students and using the Individualised Classroom Environment Questionnaire (ICEQ: Fraser, 1990) to assess classroom environment in Singapore, Tock (1995) found that female students perceived higher levels of participation and independence, while male students perceived higher levels of differentiation in their actual classroom environment. Studies involving the use of the *Questionnaire on the Teacher Interaction* (QTI: Wubbels & Levy, 1993) showed that girls perceived their teachers' interpersonal behaviour more favourably than did boys (Rickards & Fisher, 1999). However, an exception to this pattern is Tamir and Caridin's (1993) finding of no gender difference in Israeli Arabic students' perception of the classroom environment when the *Learning Environment Inventory* (LEI Fraser, Anderson, & Walberg, 1982) was administered to students.

2.4 Studies of Learning Environments in Indonesia

The research literature indicates some initial efforts in learning environment research in Indonesia. Fraser, Pearse, and Azmi (1982) described a study in Indonesia involving an Indonesian translation of a modified version of the ICEQ and four scales from the *Classroom Environment Scale* (CES: Moos & Trickett, 1987). The sample consisted of grades 8 and 9 students in 18 co-educational social studies classes in Padang, West Sumatra. This study used student's satisfaction and anxiety as the learning outcomes. The findings indicated that student satisfaction was greater in classes perceived as having less independence and greater involvement, while anxiety was reduced in classes perceived as having greater differentiation, involvement and affiliation.

Paige (1978; 1979) translated and modified an instrument based on the CES and three LEI scales. The sample was a stratified random group of 1,621 sixth-grade students in 30 rural and 30 urban schools in East Java, using the revised and translated instrument. Paige examined relationships between perceptions of the classroom learning environment and the two outcomes of cognitive achievement and individual modernity. Specific findings included the trend that individual modernity was enhanced in classrooms perceived as having greater task orientation, competition and difficulty and less order and organisation, while achievement was enhanced in classes higher in speed and lower in order and organisation.

There was no further documented research in this area until 2000. This is fully understandable for during the period, Indonesia was in the middle of physical development, where almost all potential efforts and resources were directed to support national development programs (Margianti, 2002).

3. Aims of the Study

The study described in this chapter was carried out to provide evidence to support the validity and reliability of a university-level version of the *What Is Happening In this Class?* (WIHIC: Aldridge & Fraser, 2000; Fraser, McRobbie & Fraser, 1996) questionnaire and to investigate how students' outcomes (achievement and attitudes) are related to their perceptions of the learning environment. The study also aimed to determine whether differences exist between learning environment perception for actual and preferred form of questionnaires and male and female students.

4. Research Methods

For the present study, the WIHIC; was modified to make it suitable for use in classes at the university level in Indonesia. This parsimonious learning environment instrument, initially developed by Fraser, McRobbie and Fisher (1996), incorporates important scales from a wide range of existing learning environment instruments, together with scales assessing dimensions of current educational concern scale such as equity. A five-point frequency response format (Almost Never, Seldom, Sometimes, Often, and Almost Always) was used.

The original version of the WIHIC was developed in Australia and was found to have satisfactory factorial validity, internal consistency reliability and discriminant validity, and each scale was capable of differentiating between the perceptions of students in different classrooms (Fraser, McRobbie & Fisher, 1996). The WIHIC has subsequently been used and validated in a number of countries and in different subject areas, including Taiwan and Australia (Aldridge, Fraser & Huang, 1999), Singapore (Fraser & Chionh, 2000) and Brunei (Riah & Fraser, 1998). The WIHIC has also been shown to be reliable when used in a variety of subjects, including geography and mathematic (Fraser & Chionh, 2000), science (Aldridge & Fraser, 2000; Riah & Fraser, 1998) and computing (Khoo & Fraser, 1998).

The versatility and reliability of the WIHIC under a range of circumstances made it appealing to the researchers. An examination of scale and individual items revealed that, with modification, this instrument would be suitable for assessing the learning environment of university-level computing classes.

Close scrutiny of the seven scales of the WIHIC (Student Cohesiveness, Teacher Support, Involvement, Investigation, Task Orientation, Cooperation and Equity) showed that, with the exception of the Investigation scale, all other scales were suitable for use at the university level. The Investigation scale was replaced with a modified scale from the Classroom Environment Scale (Moos & Trickett, 1987). This scale, Order and Organisation, was considered to be appropriate for the learning environment created at the university level. Table 4.1 provides the name and a description of each scale of the WIHIC as used in the present study and a sample items for each scale.

Table 4.1. Scale Names, Descriptions and Sample Items in WIHIC

Scale Name	Scale Description	Sample Item
	The extent to which	
Student Cohesiveness	Students know, help and are friendly towards each other	I know other students in this class
Teacher Support	The teacher helps, befriends, trusts and is interested in students	The teacher helps help me when I have trouble with the work
Involvement	Students participate actively and attentively in class discussion and activities	I give my opinion during class discussion
Order and Organization	Teachers emphasise that students' behave in an orderly, quiet and polite manner, and on the overall organisation of classroom activities	The teacher decides which students should work together
Task Orientation	It is important to complete activities planned and to stay on the subject matter	I know the goals for this class
Cooperation	Students cooperate with other students, working together and sharing resources	I share my books and resources with other students when doing assignments
Equity	Students are treated in a fair and equitable manner by the teacher	The teacher gives as much attention to many questions as to other students' questions

Items within the questionnaire were examined to ensure their suitability for the university level. In some cases, individual words were changed (e.g., the word 'teacher' was replaced with the word 'lecturer') and less-frequently used phrases were replaced (e.g., "The tutor goes out of his/her way to help me" was replaced with "The lecturer respects me"). Once the actual form of the WIHIC had been modified for use at the university level, a parallel preferred form was created.

A pilot study, with 50 students from five classes and their five teachers, was conducted to ensure that the actual and preferred forms of the modified WIHIC were applicable to the university level. Analysis of the responses revealed that both teachers and students had very similar responses. Interviews with teachers and students were used to ensure that each item of the university-level version of the WIHIC was appropriate and suitable to the university context. On the basis of these interviews, a fine-tuning was made to individual items.

The study also involved assessment of students' attitudes and achievement. An attitude scale, based on the *Test of Science Related Attitudes* (TOSRA; Fraser, 1981), was developed to assess students' attitudes towards their classes. Also, students' achievement scores obtained from the university database, were used as a measure of achievement. The attitude questionnaire also was pilot tested using a sample 50 students and five lecturers.

Data were then collected using the actual and preferred forms of the WIHIC and the attitude scale with sample of 2,498 students in 50 university level mathematic classes in Indonesia. The students were all enrolled in the third semester of their computing course, and were selected from either their linear algebra or statistic classes.

To determine whether the university-level version of the WIHIC questionnaire was valid and reliable, students' responses were analysed to furnish evidence regarding the scales' factor structure, internal consistency reliability, and ability to differentiate between students in different classrooms.

To investigate associations between student outcomes and the nature of the learning environment, simple correlation and multiple regression analyses were conducted at both the student and class levels.

To examine differences in classroom environment perceptions between actual and preferred forms and between genders, data were analysed with a one-way MANOVA for repeated measure. Because the multivariate test produced statistically significant result, the univariate ANOVA for repeated measures was interpreted for each individual WIHIC scale to investigate whether differences in students' perceptions existed.

5. Analyses and Results

The analyses and findings are presented in four sections: validity and reliability of the questionnaires; associations between students' perceptions of the learning environment and students' outcomes; differences between students' and teachers' perceptions of the actual environment and their preferred environment; differences between males' and females' perceptions of their learning environment.

5.1 Validity and Reliability of the University-level WIHIC

The data collected from 2,498 students were analysed to provide statistical validation for the Indonesian version of the WIHIC questionnaire. Factor and item analyses were conducted to identify questionnaire items whose removal would improve the internal consistency reliability and factorial validity of each WIHIC scale. Item analysis of the 56 WIHIC items showed that all the items in the seven environment scales had sizeable item-remainder correlations (i.e. correlations between a certain item and the rest of the scale excluding that item).

Table 4.2. Factor Loadings for the Modified WIHIC

Item No.	Factor Loading						
	Student Cohesive-ness	Teacher Support	Involve-ment	Order and Organisation	Task Orientation	Co-operation	Equity
1	0.60						
2	0.45						
3	0.57						
4	0.46						
5	0.41						
6	–						
7	0.53						
8							
9		–					
10		0.54					
11		0.53					
12		0.47					
13		0.47	0.30				
14		0.63					
15		0.43					

Table 4.2. Continued

Item No.	Factor Loading						
	Student Cohesive-ness	Teacher Support	Involve-ment	Order and Organisation	Task Orientation	Co-operation	Equity
16		0.42					
17			0.55				
18			0.66				
19			0.44				
20			0.62				
21			0.46				
22			0.57				
23			0.47				
24			0.61				
25							
26				–			
27				0.45			
28				0.49			
29				0.61			
30				0.49			
31				0.40			
32				0.44			
33					0.39		
34					0.38		
35					0.55		
36					0.54		
37					0.73		
38					0.54		
39					0.50		
40					0.54		
41						0.50	
42						0.50	
43						0.46	
44						0.60	
45						0.63	
46						0.64	
47						0.69	
48						0.61	
49							0.37
50							0.66
51							0.77
52							0.67
53							0.71
54							0.74
55							0.58
56							0.75
% Variance	2.1	2.7	4.5	1.8	3.3	5.3	18.5
Eigen value	1.15	1.48	2.45	0.98	1.80	2.89	10.00

Loadings smaller than 0.3 omitted. N=2,498 students in 50 classes

A principal components factor analysis with varimax rotation was used to examine the internal structure of the 56 items of the WIHIC and to generate orthogonal factors for the data set. Based on the factor analysis, items 8 and 25 were removed in subsequent analysis, leaving a total of 54 of the 56 items. Only factor loadings of the conventionally-accepted value of 0.30 or greater are included in Table 4.2.

There are 392 possible loadings in Table 4.2 (56 items x 7 scales = 392). In only four of the possible 392 cases is the original seven-factor structure not replicated. Items 6, 9, and 26 each have a loading of less than 0.30 on their own scales. Item 13 loads on Involvement in addition to it's *a priori* scale, Teacher Support.

Therefore, the *a priori* seven-factor structure of the final version of the WIHIC questionnaire is replicated, with nearly all items having a factor loading of at least 0.30 on their *a priori* scale and no other scale. Previous studies conducted in Singapore, Australia, UK, Canada, Brunai and Taiwan have reported similar factor structures for the WIHIC questionnaire (Aldridge & Fraser, 2000; Fraser & Chionh, 2000; Khine & Fisher, 2001), thus further supporting this factor structure. The percentage of variance varies from 1.8% to 18.5% for different scales, with the total variance accounted for being 38.2%. Eigen values vary from 1.2 to 10.0 for the different scales.

The Cronbach alpha reliability coefficient was used as an index of scale internal consistency. Table 4.3 reports the Cronbach alpha coefficient of each of the seven scales of the actual form for the WIHIC for two units of analysis for the whole sample. The scale reliability estimates range from 0.65 to 0.87 for the individual as the unit of analysis and from 0.68 to 0.92 for the class mean as the unit of analysis. These internal consistency indices are comparable to those obtained when the WIHIC was used with an Australia sample (Fraser, McRobbie, & Fisher, 1996), which ranged from 0.67 to 0.88. The internal consistency reliability (Cronbach alpha coefficient) for the attitude scale is 0.77 with the individual and 0.87 for the class means.

As a further indication of the validity of the university-level version of the learning environment instrument, a one-way ANOVA was used to indicate whether each scale of the questionnaire was able to differentiate significantly between the perceptions of students in different classes. The results, reported in Table 4.3, suggest that only the Teacher Support and Task Orientation scales were able to do so. The eta^2 statistic (an estimate of the strength of association between class membership and the dependent variable) ranged from 0.02 to 0.05, and was statistically significant for two scale. On the whole, these figures are lower than those for the original WIHIC (Fraser, McRobbie & Fisher, 1996), which ranged from 0.18 to 0.35. This could be due to the nature of university classrooms, which could be more uniform that high school classrooms.

Table 4.3. Internal Consistency Reliability (Cronbach Alpha Coefficient) and Ability to Differentiate Between Classrooms (ANOVA Results) for Two Units of Analysis for the Modified WIHIC

WIHIC Scale	No of Items	Unit of Analysis	Alpha Reliability	ANOVA Eta^2
Student Cohesiveness	7	Individual	0.74	0.02
		Class Mean	0.68	
Teacher Support	8	Individual	0.77	0.05*
		Class Mean	0.92	
Involvement	8	Individual	0.83	0.03
		Class Mean	0.86	
Order and Organisation	7	Individual	0.65	0.02
		Class Mean	0.64	
Task Orientation	8	Individual	0.79	0.03**
		Class Mean	0.86	
Cooperation	8	Individual	0.85	0.03
		Class Mean	0.84	
Equity	8	Individual	0.87	0.05
		Class Mean	0.92	

** $p<0.05$
The sample consisted of 2,498 students in 50 classes.
The eta^2 statistic (which is the ratio of 'between' to 'total' sums of squares) represents the proportion of variance explained by class membership.

5.2 Associations Between Students' Perceptions of the Learning Environment and Student Outcomes

Each student's achievement score at the end of his or her mathematics course was obtained from the university's database, and used as a measure of achievement. Also, the attitude scale was used as a student outcome measure. Simple correlation and multiple regression analyses, for two units of analysis (the individual student and the class mean), were used to determine whether associations existed between students' perceptions of the learning environment and each student outcome measure.

The results of the simple correlation analysis (reported in Table 4.4) suggest a statistically significant ($p<0.01$) association between students' mathematics achievement and four of the seven learning environment scales with the individual as the unit of analysis, namely, Student Cohesiveness, Order and Organisation, Task Orientation and Equity. Five of the seven scales have a statistically significant ($p<0.01$) simple correlation with mathematics achievement with the class mean as the unit of analysis: Teacher Support, Involvement, Task Orientation, Cooperation and Equity.

The results of the simple correlation analysis in Table 4.4 also suggest a statistically significant ($p<0.01$) and positive association between students' attitudes and all seven scales of the learning environment instrument with the individual as the unit of analysis. With the class mean as the unit of analysis, there are statistically significant ($p<0.05$) simple correlations between student attitudes and all learning environment scales with the exception of Student Cohesiveness.

Multiple correlation analysis was undertaken using the set of seven scales of the WIHIC questionnaire as independent variables and either mathematics achievement or attitude as the dependent variable. This analysis provided more parsimonious information about relationships between correlated independent variables and reduced the risk of a Type I error often linked with simple correlation analysis. A multiple regression analysis was performed separately using the individual student and class mean as the unit of analysis.

Table 4.4 shows that the multiple correlation (R) between students' perceptions of the learning environment and students' mathematics achievement is 0.19 for the individual as the unit of analysis and 0.88 for the class mean as the unit of analysis, and is statistically significant in both cases ($p<0.01$). The regression coefficients (β), using the individual as the unit of analysis indicate that all of the WIHIC scales except Cooperation uniquely account for a significant ($p<0.05$) proportion of the variance in achievement. Using the class mean as the unit of analysis, two of the seven learning environment scales account for significant ($p<0.05$) proportion of variance in students' achievement beyond that attributable to other environment scales; these are Involvement and Order and Organisation. Overall, Involvement and Equity appear to be particularly strong and consistent predictors of student achievement.

Table 4.4. Simple Correlation and Multiple Regression Analysis for Associations Between Two Student Outcomes and Scores on the Modified WIHIC for Two Units of Analysis

Scale	Unit of Analysis	Mathematical Score		Student attitude	
		r	β	r	β
Student Cohesiveness	Individual	0.05**	0.07**	0.37**	0.06**
	Class Mean	0.12	-0.08	0.22	-0.30**
Teacher Support	Individual	-0.04	-0.10**	0.37**	0.09**
	Class Mean	0.59**	-0.15	0.65**	-0.06
Involvement	Individual	0.03	0.06*	0.41**	0.19**
	Class Mean	0.81**	1.04**	0.80**	0.46**
Order and Organisation	Individual	-0.05**	-0.04*	0.20**	-0.04*
	Class Mean	0.12	-0.33*	0.34*	0.01
Task Orientation	Individual	-0.07**	-0.12**	0.56**	0.43**
	Class Mean	0.47**	-0.07	0.64**	-0.28
Cooperation	Individual	0.03	0.02	0.29**	0.01
	Class Mean	0.55**	0.08	0.64**	0.01
Equity	Individual	0.11**	0.13**	0.31**	0.04*
	Class Mean	0.56**	0.12	0.82**	0.93**
Multiple Correlation (R)	Individual	0.19**		0.62**	
	Class Mean	0.88**		0.92**	

*$p<0.05$
**$p<0.01$
N=2,498 students in 50 classes

For the attitude outcome, the multiple correlation (R) between students' perceptions of the learning environment and students' attitudes is 0.62 for the individual as the unit of analysis and 0.92 for the class mean as the unit of analysis and is statistically significant for both

($p<0.01$). The multiple regression coefficients using the individual as the unit of analysis indicates that all learning environment scales except Cooperation uniquely account for a significant ($p<0.05$) proportion of variance in attitude beyond that attributable to other environment scales. Using the class mean as the unit of analysis, three of the seven learning environment scales account for a significant ($p<0.01$) proportion of attitude variation, namely, Student Cohesiveness, Involvement and Equity. It would appear from these results that students' attitudes are most strongly related to the extent to which classes emphasise Teacher Support, Involvement, Task Orientation and Equity.

These results replicate those of past studies in numerous countries (Fraser, 1998) and generally suggest that the learning environment perceived by students is related to their achievement and especially their attitudes. Although most associations between environment and outcomes are positive in Table 4.4, the presence of some negative relationships suggests the desirability of replicating the present study and employing qualitative methods to seek explanation for any replicated negative relationships in future studies.

5.3 Differences between Students' Perceptions of Actual Environment and Preferred Environment

During the collection of data, all students completed a questionnaire to determine their perceptions of their actual classroom environment. One week later, these same students also completed a questionnaire related to their preferred or ideal classroom environment.

To examine differences between students' perceptions of the actual and preferred classroom environment, data were analysed with a one-way MANOVA for repeated measures. The analysis was conducted separately for the individual student and the class mean as the unit of analysis. Because the multivariate test produced statistically significant results using Wilks' lambda criterion, the univariate ANOVA for repeated measures was interpreted for each individual WIHIC scale to investigate whether students had different perceptions of their actual and preferred classroom learning environments (see Table 4.5).

The results reported in Table 4.5 indicate a significant difference ($p<0.01$) between actual and preferred scores for all seven learning environment scales for both units of analysis. To estimate the magnitude of the differences between student's scores on the actual and preferred forms of the WIHIC, effect sizes were calculated. The effect size for each of the WIHIC scales, reported in Table 4.5, range between 0.17 and 0.97 for the individual as the unit of analysis and between 0.87 and 6.20 with the class mean as the unit of analysis. These results suggest that there are large differences between students' perception of the actual and preferred environment.

Table 4.5. Average Item Mean, Average Item Standard Deviation and Differences between Actual and Preferred Perceptions (Effect Size and ANOVA Results) on the Modified WIHIC for Two Units of Analysis

WIHIC Scale	Unit of Analysis	Average Item Mean		Average item SD		Difference between Actual & Preferred	
		Actual	Preferred	Actual	Preferred	Effect Size	F
Student Cohesiveness	Individual	3.70	4.10	0.58	0.61	0.67	5.44**
	Class Mean	3.70	4.11	0.08	0.14	3.73	4.74**
Teacher Support	Individual	2.32	2.99	0.57	0.81	0.97	6.32**
	Class Mean	2.33	3.00	0.12	0.22	3.94	5.34**
Involvement	Individual	2.46	2.96	0.64	0.72	0.74	5.76**
	Class Mean	2.47	2.97	0.10	0.18	3.57	5.43**
Order and Organisation	Individual	2.72	3.33	0.67	0.65	0.92	6.27**
	Class Mean	2.72	3.34	0.09	0.11	6.20	5.62**
Task Orientation	Individual	3.80	3.90	0.54	0.63	0.17	2.86**
	Class Mean	3.80	3.90	0.09	0.14	0.87	2.35**
Cooperation	Individual	3.40	3.83	0.71	0.72	0.60	5.06**
	Class Mean	3.41	3.83	0.11	0.17	3.00	4.42**
Equity	Individual	3.68	3.83	0.77	0.78	0.19	2.93**
	Class Mean	3.69	3.84	0.17	0.15	0.94	2.60**

**$p<0.01$
The sample consisted of 2,498 students in 50 classes

The average item mean (or the scale mean divided by the number of items in that scale) for students' scores on the actual and preferred forms are tabulated in Table 4.5 and graphed in Figure 4.1. The reason for using the average item mean is to provide meaningful comparisons between the means of scales containing differing numbers of item. Figure 4.1 shows that students would prefer a much more positive learning environment than the one they presently perceive on all WIHIC dimensions. This finding has important practical implications for university teachers and administrators in Indonesia.

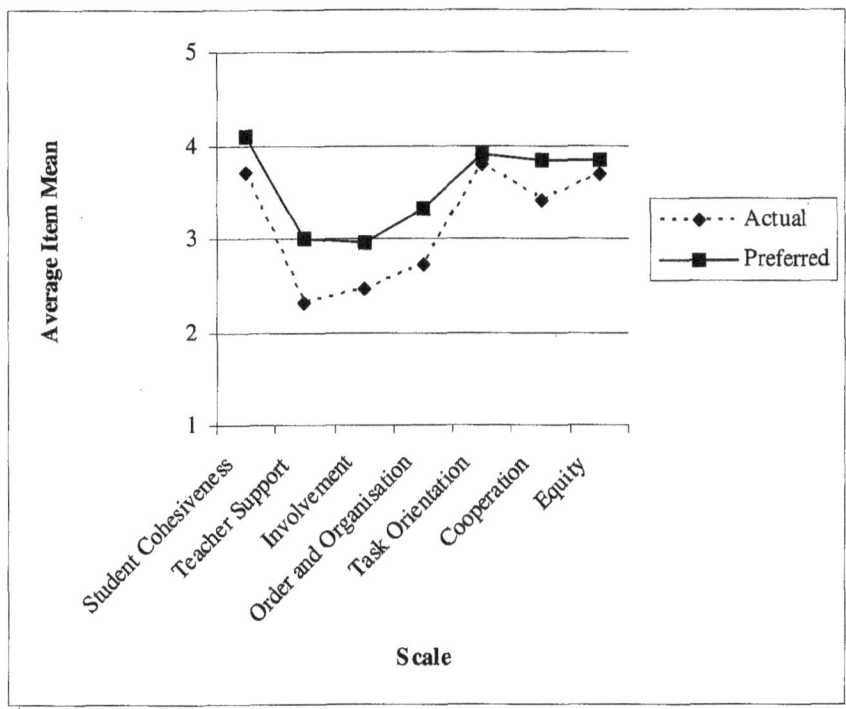

Figure 4.1. Differences in students' perceptions of Actual and Preferred learning environments for the WIHIC.

Students would prefer activities associated with WIHIC items to occur 'often' (average item mean of 4 in Figure 4.1) for the Student Cohesiveness, Task Orientation, Cooperation and Equity scales, and to occur approximately 'sometimes' (average item mean of 3) for Teacher

Support and Involvement, and to occur between 'sometimes' and 'often' for Order and Organisation. However, Figure 4.1 also shows that the level of each WIHIC dimension perceived to be actually present is lower for every scale. The lowest average item mean in Figure 4.1 occurs for Teacher Support, which is perceived to occur approximately 'seldom'.

The improvement of Teacher Support appears to be a high priority in these Indonesian university students' opinions. These results for Indonesian university students (with students preferring a more positive classroom environment than the one perceived to be actually present) replicates past research in secondary schools in several countries (Fraser & Fisher, 1983; Fraser & McRobbie, 1995; Hofstein & Lazarowitz , 1986).

5.4 Differences Between Males' and Females' Scores for Learning Environment and Attitude

To examine sex differences in classroom environment perceptions in the present study, data were analysed with a one-way MANOVA for repeated measures and using the within-class gender subgroup mean as the unit of analysis. Gender was the repeated measures factor, and the WIHIC scales formed the set of dependent variables. As males and females are not found in equal numbers in every class, the within-class gender mean was chosen as the unit of analysis to provide a matched pair of means – one within-class mean for males and one within-class mean for females. This reduces confounding in that, for each group of boys within a particular classroom, there is a corresponding group of girls in the same classroom.

Because the multivariate test produced statistically significant results using Wilks' lambda criterion, the univariate ANOVA for repeated measures was interpreted for each individual WIHIC scale to investigate whether males and females had different perceptions of their classrooms and different attitudes.

Table 4.6 reports the average item mean and average item standard deviation for male and female students for each actual WIHIC scale and each preferred WIHIC scale. Also, the results for the ANOVAs and effect sizes are reported in Table 4.6. The means generated using male and female scores on each actual WIHIC scale and the attitude scale were used to draw the graphical profile provided in Figure 4.2.

Table 4.6. Average Item Mean, Average Item Standard Deviation and Difference between Male and Female Scores (Effect Size and ANOVA Results) on WIHIC Actual, WIHIC Preferred and Attitude Scale Using the Within-Class Gender Mean as the Unit of Analysis

WIHIC Scale	Form of Questionnaire	Average item mean		Average item SD		Difference between Males and Females	
		Male	Female	Male	Female	Effect Size	F
Student Cohesiveness	Actual	3.69	3.71	0.09	0.12	0.19	0.90
	Preferred	4.07	4.15	0.13	0.17	0.53	2.20**
Teacher Support	Actual	2.33	2.32	0.12	0.15	0.07	0.14
	Preferred	2.97	3.03	0.15	0.25	0.30	1.74**
Involvement	Actual	2.47	2.46	0.11	0.13	0.08	1.03
	Preferred	2.96	2.98	0.16	0.25	0.36	0.88
Order and Organisation	Actual	2.67	2.76	0.11	0.14	0.72	1.85**
	Preferred	3.32	3.35	0.12	0.14	0.23	1.07
Task Orientation	Actual	3.72	3.88	0.07	0.15	1.45	2.61**
	Preferred	3.86	3,93	0.12	0.20	0.44	1.69**
Cooperation	Actual	3.50	3.32	0.11	0.14	1.44	3.18**
	Preferred	3.80	3.87	0.14	0.21	0.40	1.88**
Equity	Actual	3.73	3.65	0.24	0.16	0.40	1.46*
	Preferred	3.82	3.86	0.13	0.21	0.24	1.32
Attitude		3.42	3.40	0.18	0.10	0.14	-0.74

**$p<0.01$ *$p<0.05$
N= 50 within-class gender mean (2,498 students)

The results in Table 4.6 indicate that, while the magnitudes of the differences between male and female students' perceptions of the actual learning environment are small, female students perceived significantly ($p<0.01$) more actual Order and Organisation, Task Orientation and Cooperation than did male students. Male students, on the other hand, perceived significantly ($p<0.01$) more actual Equity than their female counterparts (see Figure 4.2). The effect size for each actual scale of the WIHIC (calculated to provide an approximation of the magnitude of the differences) ranged between 0.07 and 1.45 for different scales. Four of the actual learning environment scales, Order and Organization, Task Orientation, Cooperation and Equity, had an effect size of over one third of a standard deviation (0.40), suggesting that the magnitude of differences between male and female perceptions on these scales is educationally important.

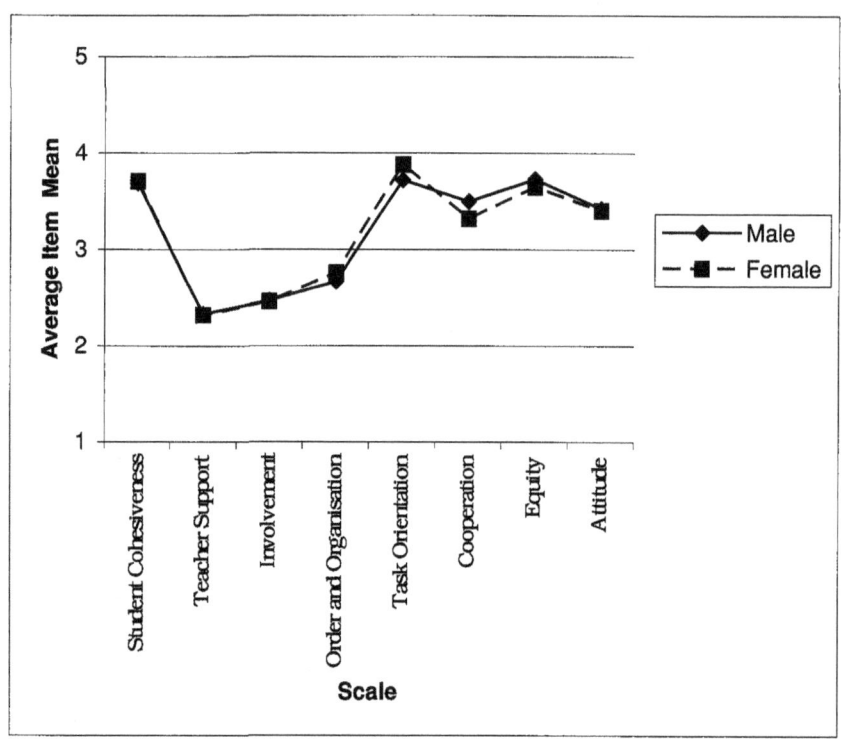

Figure 4.2. Differences between male and female students' scores on the Actual WIHIC and the Attitude scale.

Table 4.6 shows that females preferred a more favourable classroom environment than did males in term of more student Cohesiveness, Teacher Support, Task Orientation and Cooperation. Effect sizes for the preferred WIHIC scales range from 0.23 to 0.53. Overall, the finding that female Indonesian university students generally perceive and prefer a more favourable classroom environment replicates past research in Western primary and secondary schools (Fraser, 1998).

6. Discussion and Conclusion

This chapter reports the validity of a widely-applicable learning environment instrument modified for university-level classes in Indonesia. In addition, the study explored the usefulness of the questionnaire two applications. First, it examined whether the learning environment influence students' outcomes (achievement and attitudes) and, second, it investigated differences between students' perception for actual and preferred forms of the questionnaire and for males and females.

The *What is Happening in the Class?* (WIHIC) was modified for use at the university level, including the replacement of one scale and minor amendments to individual items. The university-level WIHIC and an attitude scale were administered to a sample 2,498 computing students in 26 linear algebra and 24 statistics classes in Indonesia. The data were analysed to determine the validity and reliability of the WIHIC questionnaire, in terms of its factor structure, internal consistency reliability and ability to differentiate between classroom. The *a priori* factor structure for the actual form of the WIHIC was replicated, with nearly all items having a factor loading of least 0.30 on their *a priori* scale and no other scale.

The internal consistency reliability estimate (Cronbach alpha coefficient) for each of the seven scale for both the actual and preferred form of the WIHIC, using both the individual and the class mean as the unit of analysis, was comparable with past studies. The result of one-way ANOVAs indicated that two of the seven scales were able to differentiate between the environments of different classes. Overall, the validation provides support for the confident future use of the Indonesian version of the WIHIC at the university level.

Simple correlation and multiple regression analyses were used to determine whether associations between students' perception of learning environment and students' attitude towards their university classes and their final achievement score. With the student as the unit of analysis, the results of the simple correlation analyses indicate that a statistically significant and the positive association exists between students' attitudes towards their mathematics classes and all seven learning environment scales. The multiple regression results indicate that all but one of the seven learning environment scale (Cooperation) uniquely account for a significant proportion of variance in students' attitude beyond that attributable to the learning environment scales. The multiple correlation between students' perceptions of the learning environment and students' attitude also was positive and statistically significant. These results suggest that the learning environment created by teachers at the university level could have an effect on their students' attitudes towards that subject. Therefore, teachers wishing to improve the learning environment at the university level should consider providing more Student Cohesiveness, Teacher Support, Involvement, Order and Organisation, Task Orientation and Equity.

With the class as the unit of analysis, the simple correlation results indicate a positive and statistically significant association between student achievement and two of the seven learning environment scales, namely, Task Orientation and Equity. The multiple regression results indicate that one of the seven learning environment scale, Equity, uniquely accounts for a significant amount of variance in student achievement beyond that attributable to other environment scales. The multiple correlation between students' perceptions of the learning environment and student achievement is positive and statistically significant. The results of the simple and multiple correlation analysis suggest that, to improve student achievement, teachers should be encouraged to increase the amount of Task Orientation and Equity in their classes.

MANOVA for repeated measure and effect sizes were used to investigate differences in scale scores between students' perception of the actual learning environment and their preferred learning environment. There was a significant difference for all seven learning environment scales, with students preferring a more positive learning environment than the one they presently perceive on all WIHIC dimensions. Overall, the finding that Indonesian university students generally perceive and prefer a more favourable classroom environment replicates past research in Western primary and secondary schools (Fraser, 1998).

To investigate differences between male and female students' perception of their learning environment, MANOVA for repeated measure and effect sizes, using the within-class gender mean as the unit of analysis, were used. Female students perceive significantly more Order and Organisation, Task Orientation and Cooperation and less

Equity than do males. These results for Equity make sense in the Indonesian context. Ninety percent of the population of Indonesia are Moslem, a religion in which males are given more freedom and independence in all aspects of their lives than females. This cultural background carries over from family life into the education of students, making such a difference in the degree of Equity perceived by male and female students very plausible.

A major contribution of the present study is the development of a widely-applicable, economical and valid learning environment instrument which is likely to prove to be a potentially powerful tool that lecturers can use monitor and guide the improvement of the learning environment in their classes. The present study is distinctive in that it is one of only a few studies in the field of learning environment to be carried out in Indonesia and one of the first studies worldwide in the field of learning environment to be carried out at the university level in Indonesia with base-line data, collected from a large sample of students, that can be used as the basis for assessing the success of curriculum reform, new teaching strategies and other attempts at improving teaching and learning.

References

Aldridge, J. M., & Fraser, B. J. (2000). A cross-cultural study of classroom learning environments in Australia and Taiwan. *Learning Environment Research: An International Journal, 3*, 101-134.

Aldridge, J. M., Fraser, B. J., & Huang, I. T.-C. (1999). Investigating classroom environments in Taiwan and Australia with multiple research methods. *Journal of Educational Research, 93*, 48-62.

Bain, D., McNaught, C., Mills, C., & Leuckenhausen, G. (1998). Describing computer facilitated learning environments in higher education, *Learning Environments Research, 1*, 163-180.

Dorman, J. P. (1998) The development and validation of an instrument to assess institutional-level environments in universities, *Learning Environments Research, 2*, 79-98.

Fisher, D. L. & Fraser, B. J. (1983). A comparison of actual and preferred classroom environment as perceived by science teachers and students, *Journal of Research in Science Teaching, 20*, 55-61.

Fisher, D. L. & Parkinson, C. (1998). Improving nursing education classroom environments, *Journal of Nursing Education, 36*, 87-108.

Forgasz, H. J. (1998). The typical Australian university mathematics students: challenging myths and stereotypes? *Higher Education, 36*, pp. 87-108.

Forgasz. H. J. & Leder, G. C. (2000). Perceptions of the tertiary learning environment: is mathematics worth the effort? *International Journal of Mathematics Education in Science and Technology, 31*, 37-42.

Fraser, B. J. (1981). *Test of Science Related Attitudes*. Melbourne: Australian Council for Educational Research.

Fraser, B. J. (1990). *Individualised Classroom Environment Questionnaire*. Melbourne: Australian Council for Educational Research.

Fraser, B. J. (1998). Science learning environments: Assessment, effects and determinants. In B. J. Fraser & K. G. Tobin (Eds.), *The international handbook of science education* (pp. 527-564). Dordrecht, The Netherlands: Kluwer Academic Publishers.

Fraser, B. J., Anderson, G. J., & Walberg, H. J. (1982). *Assessment of learning environments: Manual for Learning Environment Inventory(LEI) and My Class Inventory (MCI) (3rd vers.)*. Perth, Australia: Western Australian Institute of Technology.

Fraser, B. J., & Chionh, Y. H. (2000, April). *Classroom environment, self-esteem, achievement, and attitudes in geography and mathematics in Singapore*. Paper presented at the annual meeting of the American Educational Research Association, New Orleans.

Fraser, B. J., & McRobbie, C. J. (1995). Science laboratory classroom at schools and universities: a cross national study. *Education Research and Evaluation: An International Journal on Theory and Practice, 1*, 1-25

Fraser, B. J., McRobbie, C. J., & Fisher, D. L. (1996, April). *Development, validation and use of personal and class forms of a new classroom environment instrument*. Paper presented at the annual meeting of the American Educational Research Association, New York.

Fraser, B. J., Pearse, R., & Azmi (1982). A study of Indonesian students' perceptions of classroom psychosocial environment. *International Review of Education, 28*, 337-355.

Fraser, B. J., & Treagust, D. F. (1986). Validity and use of an instrument for assessing classroom psychosocial environment in higher education. *Higher Education, 15*, 37-57.

Hofstein, A. & Lazarowittz, R. (1986). A comparison of the actual and preferred classroom learning environment in biology and chemistry as perceived by high school students, *Journal of Research in Science Teaching, 23*, 189-199.

Khine, M. S. & Goh, S. C. (2001). Students' perceptions of the university learning environment in Singapore. *Journal of Applied Research in Education, 5*(1), 45-51.

Khine, M. S. & Fisher D.L. (2001, December). *Classroom environment and teachers' cultural background in secondary science classes in an Asian context,* Paper presented at the annual conference of the Australian Association for Research in Education, Fremantle, Western Australia.

Khoo, H. S., & Fraser, B. J. (1997, April). *Using classroom environment dimensions in the evaluation of adult computer courses.* Paper presented at the annual meeting of the National Association for Research in Science Teaching, San Diego.

Lizzio, A., Wilson, K., & Simons, R. (2002). University students' perceptions of the learning environment and academic outcomes: implication for theory and practice, *Studies in Higher Education, 27*, 27-52.

Margianti, E. S. (2002). Learning environment research in Indonesia. In S.C. Goh & M.S. Khine (Eds.). *Studies in educational learning environments: An international perspective* (pp 153-167). Singapore: World Scientific.

Moos, C. H. & Trickett, E. J. (1987). *Classroom Environment Scale manual* (2nd ed.) Palo Alto, CA, Consulting Psychologists Press.

Nair, C. S. & Fisher, D. L. (2001). Transition from senior secondary to higher education: a learning environment perspective, *Research in Science Education, 30*, 435-450.

Newby, M., & Fisher, D. (1997). An instrument for assessing the learning environment of a computer laboratory. *Journal of Educational Computing Research, 16*(2), 179-197.

Paige, R. M. (1978). *The impact of classroom learning environment on academic achievement and individual modernity in East Java, Indonesia.* Unpublished doctoral dissertation, Stanford University.

Paige, R. M. (1978). The learning of modern culture: Formal education and psychosocial modernity in East Java, Indonesia. *International Journal of Intercultural Relations, 3*, 333-364.

Riah, H., & Fraser, B. J. (1998, April). *The learning environment of high school chemistry classes.* Paper presented at the annual meeting of the American Educational Research Association, San Diego, CA.

Rickards, T., & Fisher, D. (1999). Teacher-student classroom interaction among science students in different sex and cultural background, *Research in Science Education, 29,* pp. 445-456.

Spreda, S.L. & Donnay, D.A.C. (2000, August). *Validating the Learning Environment Scale of the Student Interest Inventory for use with first year college students.* Paper presented at the annual meeting of the American Psychological association, Washington, DC.

Stern, G. G. (1970). *People in context: measuring person-environment congruence in education and industry.* New York: Wiley.

Tamir, P. & Caridin, H. (1993). Characteristics of learning environment in biology and chemistry classes as perceived by Jewish and Arab high school students in Israel. *Research in Science and Technological Education, 11,* 1-15.

Teese, R., Davies, M., Charlton, M. & Polesel, J. (1995). *Who wins at schools?* Melbourne Department of Education Policy and Management, University of Melbourne.

Tock, K. L. (1995). Perceptions of classroom environment, school, types, gender and learning styles of secondary school students. *International Journal of Experimental Educational Psychology, 15,* 161-169.

Wubbels, T., & Levy, J. (Eds.). (1993). *Do you know what you look like? Interpersonal relationships in education* (1st ed.). London, England: The Falmer Press.

Chapter 5

WORKING WITH TECHNOLOGY-RICH LEARNING ENVIRONMENTS: STRATEGIES FOR SUCCESS

Sue Trinidad
Hong Kong University
People's Republic of China

Technology is changing the way education is being delivered and educators across the world are faced with a number of challenges. Whilst many educational institutions move into the "technology-rich" arena, educators have found it difficult to follow and use such environments to their advantage. Technology-rich learning environments offer the potential to take teaching and learning beyond the four walls of the classroom where learning can be based on real-world problems and learners become active participants in constructing their own learning. This chapter looks at methods used with Hong Kong educators to develop e-learning projects that use interactive computer-based learning resources; linked with networked communities of peers and experts; and online collaborations in and beyond the classroom while accessing online information that goes beyond the textbook. It was found that once the process of learning was understood from its many perspectives, and the critical selection of strategies to ensure learning takes place, teachers could reflect on their own pedagogical practice in creating, maintaining and working in such technology-rich learning environments.

1. Introduction

Despite the introduction of technology to most learning environments there has been little change in the process of teaching and learning. Recently published findings of studies in the UK regarding teachers' use of technology in their teaching, reveal that little has changed in classrooms over the last fifteen years (ImpaCT2, 2002). Similar results were reported in a large-scale survey of more than 4,000 teachers in the USA on how they were using computers (Becker, 2001). The study revealed, "frequent use of computers by middle and high school teachers and their students in math, science, social studies, and English is still very much a rare phenomenon...outside of word processing, very few teachers have their students make frequent use of computers during class" (Becker, 2001, online). Interestingly, though this study found that the teacher's philosophies of learning and teaching made a difference to the way the computers were used with students. Of those teachers classified with the most constructivist teaching philosophies, they were reported to be the stronger users of computers, they used computers more frequently, they used them in more challenging ways, they used them more themselves, and they had greater technical expertise. It was also found that constructivist teachers were also much more likely to report having increased their use of computers over the past five years. As Law et al. (2000) reported in a study of 46 Hong Kong classrooms using technology, if the pedagogical beliefs of the teachers does not change, then the technology will just be used as a "substitution" to traditional methods, or to put it more succinctly, teaching is by old methods with new materials (technology).

With the advent of global communications networks learning environments can now utilise local and global communities, peer interaction and knowledgeable others and allow different, new and exciting approaches to teaching, learning and assessment. Educators can shift their pedagogical approach towards a balance between the appropriate uses of direct instruction with a collaborative, inquiry-driven, knowledge-construction approach allowing students to achieve far beyond expectations. The world of work demands the skills of negotiation, decision-making, and problem solving with understanding and application of knowledge, and such skills can be developed through authentic assessment tasks where the students continually receive feedback to enhance their understanding and build new knowledge and skills.

To enable students to acquire this knowledge and skills requires a shift from *teacher-centered instruction* to *learner-centered instruction* where the learner is able to make decisions about what they need to learn, how they need to learn and when it should be learned. Sandholtz, Ringstaff, and Dwyer (1997) reported a ten-year study of computer technology in five schools and identified the shift that needs to take place in changing from a focus on teaching to a focus on learning. This shift is illustrated in Table 5.1.

Table 5.1. Teacher-Centered and Learner-Centered Learning Environments

	Teacher-centred learning environments	Learner-centred learning environments
Classroom activity	Teacher-centered, Didactic	Learner-centered, Interactive
Teacher's role	Fact teller, primary source of information, content expert, and source of all answers.	Collaborator, mediator, mentor coach, sometimes co-learner and knowledge navigator. Gives students more options and responsibilities for their own learning.
Instructional emphasis	Facts Memorization Accumulation of facts	Relationships Inquiry and invention Transformation of facts
Students' role	Passive recipient of information, reproducing knowledge, learning as a solitary activity	Active participant in the learning process, producing and sharing knowledge, participating at times as expert, learning collaboratively with others
Concepts of knowledge	Quantity Comprehension	Quality of understanding Application, synthesis, evaluation
Demonstration of success	Norm referenced	Criterion referenced
Assessment	Multiple choice items Exams, Essays	Portfolios and performance or product based assessment
Technology use	Drill and practice, rote learning, presenting via Powerpoint™	Communication, access, collaboration, expression, sharing of data, e-learning

Adapted from: Sandholtz, Ringstaff, and Dwyer (1997) and UNESCO (n.d.)

The shift from a focus on teaching to a focus on learning is not easy. Support is needed to help educators teach in learner-centred and learner-directed environments with the educator being the key to creating, maintaining and working in such learning environments. In fact this entails a lengthy process of educators working together to develop new beliefs and attitudes towards how students can learn in technology-rich environments. As the ten year study of the Apple Classrooms of Tomorrow (ACOT) showed teachers who maintained traditional beliefs found the changes of working in technology-rich learning environments frustrating and reverted to lecture-style teaching (Dwyer et al., 1990a; 1990b; Sandholtz et al.,1997). So how do we help educators shift their pedagogical approach when using technology-rich environments from a teacher-directed approach to a learner-centred and learner-directed approach?

As long-term projects like ACOT show, educators must travel through a number of stages (entry, adoption, adaptation, appropriation, invention or innovation) to infuse technology successfully into their classrooms and their teaching programmes to change the learning environment. They must be exposed to models of good practice, and have the on-going support and scaffolding in the form of collaborative networks with peers. Due to lack of vision, models of good practice, and the structure of the learning environment, many educators stay embedded in their teacher-directed approach, but as Dwyer et al. (1990a; 1990b; 1991) found those who are able to change their pedagogy to be more learner-directed are more likely to be educators who work in collaborative environments that appear to have a more active orientation.

Using the process developed by Albon & Trinidad (2001; 2002) and Trinidad & Albon (2002; 2003) of the *Mediated Learning Approach* (MLA), 65 Hong Kong teachers participated in creating e-learning environments for their students. This took place over ten successive sessions during Term 1, September to November, 2002 and was aimed at helping these Hong Kong primary and secondary teachers experience, through collaboration, mentoring and modeling, an active, social-constructivist learning environment. Experiences in such a learning environment were to encourage them to construct learner-centred and learner-directed, real world products that could be used by their students, thus supporting the premise that using the technology will support a move to interactive learning that is learner-centred which Mandinach and Cline (1994, p.180) claim are "the two hallmarks of computer-based curriculum innovations".

2. Background

Hong Kong, like many countries, has spent millions of dollars on implementing technology into schools over the last five years. Every teacher has had to complete the compulsory computer training courses[1] and by December 2001 all teachers had attained a "basic" level of IT competence, that is, use a computer and the Internet. By the 2002-2003 school year 75% of teachers were to have reached the "intermediate" level of being able to use IT tools and make use of teaching resources available on the Internet and the Intranet in classroom teaching and lesson preparation; 25% were to have reached "upper-intermediate level" where a teacher handles computer networking, resolve simple hardware and software problems, makes more advanced use of Authorware™ for lesson preparation and understands the characteristics and use of different IT tools and resources; and 6% were to have reached "advanced level" where a teacher is able to understand the functions of computer managed instruction systems, evaluate the effectiveness of instructional computer programmes, design instructional materials with the use of IT and choose appropriate IT equipment to meet the school's needs (HKSAR, 2001). All Hong Kong schools provide labs of computers connected to the Internet for students to access during classes. Coupled with this technology implementation and training has been curriculum reform[2].

In Hong Kong, as with many other countries, there is the belief that educational reform will endorse lifelong learning with the help of technology. Many leaders and policy makers correlate the use of technology with pedagogical changes. The greater the skills of the teachers in using technology and the more computers available to students will relate to better learning. Unfortunately this is not always the case. For many Hong Kong classrooms the teachers remain teaching in a transmissive, exam driven culture (teaching for the test) and the technology is used for lower level activities such as teachers presenting lectures via Powerpoint™ and students word processing assignments and searching the Internet. As Fullan (1991) postulates there are three dimensions in the process of change, that of materials, methods and beliefs. Without pedagogical change, educators will teach with new materials (technology) using old methods, but when educators are able to

---

[1] The Hong Kong government pledged in its *IT in Education 5-year Strategy Plan (1998-1999 to 2002-2003)* to not only enhance IT infrastructure in all schools but to also raise the IT skills of both teachers and students by providing teacher training and reforming the curriculum.

[2] Reform Proposals for the Education System in Hong Kong: Learning for Life; Learning through life, September, Curriculum Development Council (2000).

reflect on their pedagogical approach then teaching in a technology-rich environment becomes a powerful change agent (Law et al., 2000).

3. The Teacher-directed Learning Environment

For the majority of educators, teaching, learning and assessment adheres to a mark driven agenda and is often supported by a transmissive (Barnes, 1987) and solitary approach to learning. In developing learning materials the focus is on teaching and not learning, the content or a syllabus are designed in response to what it is the students should be taught. The educator is seen as the expert with a specific knowledge base, and the student is seen as a passive receptor of that knowledge. The educator sets the objectives for what is to be taught. The educator, as knower of truth and information, espouses this to the students, thus using a transmissive mode of delivery that is teacher-directed providing one linear path through a narrowly bounded content area or sequence of standardized instructional units (UNESCO, u.d.). Students receive this information and through a product, produce the evidence of learning, usually in the form of something static such as a test or essay. Not only does this model promote a surface learning approach that is incompatible with today's need of producing lifelong learners who can think critically and strategically to solve problems in diverse situations of a rapidly changing world, but it is not based on a clearly articulated theory of learning (Albon & Trinidad, 2001; Nelson, 2001). If we add technology to this learning environment then often this is used to support a teacher-directed learning environment of materials, processes and beliefs illustrated in Figure 5.1.

Educators may be competent in analysing what teaching they will undertake and what learning they expect student to do, but unfortunately they are not always competent in knowing how a student actually learns. The emphasis made on constructing a learning environment that is learner-centred and based on learning with technology, as opposed to teaching with technology (Trinidad et al. 2001; Wood & Trinidad, 2001), is intentional here because once the process of learning with technology is understood from its many perspectives, the critical selection of strategies to ensure learning takes place should follow.

Teacher-Directed Learning Environment

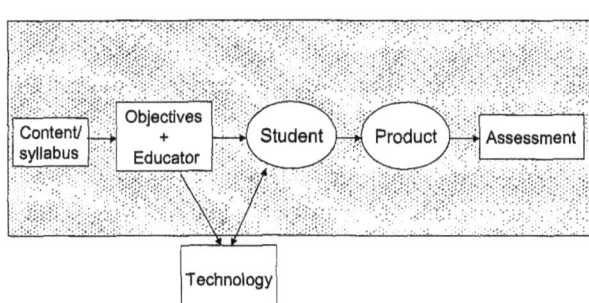

Figure 5.1. The teacher-directed learning environment with technology added.

4. The Learner-Centred Learning Environment

The educator can be involved in the restructuring of the curriculum and learning activities (Mandinach & Cline, 1994) to be more interactive and learner-directed which in turn can assist the transformation that is needed to take place, such as role changes, in a technology-rich environment. This process is illustrated in Figure 5.2 and was recorded as part of process of the Systems Thinking and Curriculum Innovation (STACI) project reported in the book *Classroom Dynamics: Implementing a Technology-Based Learning Environment*, where Mandinach & Cline (1994) offered insights and observations into the process of acceptance and utilization of technology in the technology-rich learning environment.

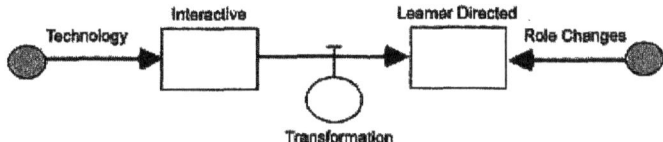

Source: Newhouse, Trinidad & Clarkson (2002, p. 22)

Figure 5.2. The interactive learning environment with technology added.

Integrating technology into the learning process requires educators to understand how technology can enhance the teaching and learning process. For learning to take place, the learners must be engaged in the learning process and one way to do that is to motivate learners through authentic learning experiences. Active learning provides learners with the opportunity to be involved and interested in their own learning and this gives them a sense of ownership of the learning that is taking place, that is, they are actively involved in their own learning process. Coupled with a "social-constructivist approach" (SCA) where the design of teaching and learning activities allow the learner to share and construct data with knowledgeable others, including their peers and the educator, a collaborative community of learners can be built. Here the educator mediates the learning by providing the appropriate scaffolding and support through the structure of the learning environment. The elements of this learner-centred learning environment are illustrated in Figure 5.3.

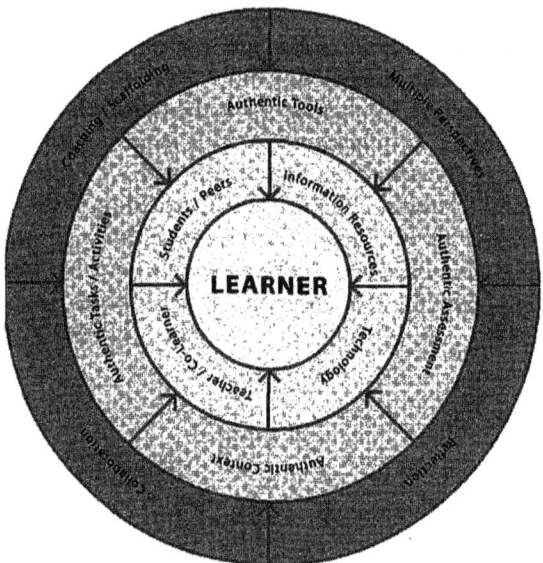

Source: UNESCO Report (n. d., p.10) ICT and Teacher Education: Global Context and Framework.

Figure 5.3. Learner-centred learning environment

If the learning environment is learner-centred and learner-directed, as illustrated in Figure 3, the educator focuses on the learner's learning in a community of learners. Here the learner is encouraged to be more responsible for their own learning, however that does not mean they work alone but they are encouraged to work with other knowledgeable students/peers along with the teacher/co-learner on authentic content, tasks, activities and assessment using authentic tools. Such a learning environment enables the learner to construct their own learning as learning is not seen as a solitary approach, but is seen part of the collaboration, coaching, scaffolding, reflection and multiple perspectives encouraged within the social-constructivist learning environment. The technology and information resources support this learning environment. A sense of empowerment and engagement for the learner emanates from a multitude of learning situations, where they are no longer dependent on the specific and often limited knowledge of their educator, but work within the community of learners mediated by the educator. This approach has been called the Mediated Learning Approach or MLA (Albon & Trinidad, 2002).

5. The Mediated Learning Environment

The *Mediated Learning Approach (MLA)* includes the nature of teaching, the learner's approaches to learning, the use of technology and access to information and resources. In MLA (Figure 5.4), the educator brings their expertise to the learning environment, has a syllabus or content, and has objectives but the major change is the recognition of learning through technology and mediation. The learning is learner-focused which recognises that this learner brings prior knowledge, attitudes, skills and a variety of approaches to their own learning. Outcomes/attributes provide the vision of what the learner should achieve, that of thinking critically, analysing information and problem solving. The learner is seen as one who is actively and meaningfully engaged in their own learning, which is embedded in a social interactive environment.

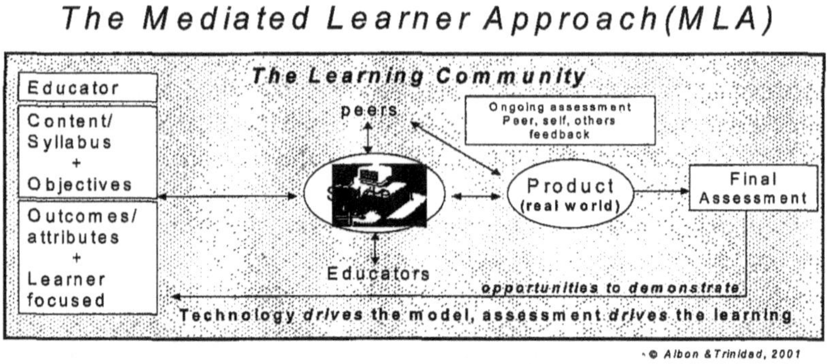

The Mediated Learner Approach (MLA)

Educator	The Learning Community	
Content/ Syllabus + Objectives Outcomes/ attributes + Learner focused	peers — Ongoing assessment Peer, self, others feedback — Product (real world) — Educators — opportunities to demonstrate	Final Assessment

Technology *drives* the model, assessment *drives* the learning

- © Albon & Trinidad, 2001

Figure 5.4. The Mediated Learner Approach (MLA).

MLA revolves around the learner and the technology, which *drives* the model. In the model technology is the vehicle for communication, collaboration and the framework for mediated learning that takes place between educators, peers and the wider community to produce authentic tasks, projects or investigations. Interactive technologies provide an opportunity for new and self-sustaining communities of learners, large and small, formal and informal, to exist alongside established, traditional approaches. Bransford, Brown & Cocking (1999) state, "the new technologies provide opportunities for creating learning environments that extend the possibilities of "old –but still useful —technologies— books, blackboards, and linear, one-way communications media, such as radio and television shows—as well as offering new possibilities" (online). So multiple information resources are used from books through to the Internet. Interactive technologies allow the educator to build a learning community that transcends the four walls of classrooms but is not restricted by traditional class timeframes. Social constructivist theory is applied to MLA allowing learners to increase the opportunities to learn from each other. Further, in producing learners who are competent communicators, educators have little recourse but to provide learning experiences in all forms of communication, both online and face-to-face. In this way technology drives a model of learning that reflects the criteria identified by Burns (1995) and Knowles (1998) for adult learners.

However, in MLA the effectiveness of learning is driven by the nature of the assessment and not technology alone. As in the teacher-directed learning approach, assessment is an integral component, but the purpose has now changed. Assessment is part of the learning process in which challenge, decisions, reflections are experienced through the development of a real world product or authentic tasks, activities or assessment (Trinidad & Albon, 2002). Learning is more than knowing content. It is about developing competency in applying knowledge. In this way assessment drives the learning. This means assessment is no longer a vehicle for the learner proving what they know, but instead is open-ended, negotiable, educative, explicit and informative. In this performance-based assessment learners are involved in weaving the content of the learning to produce the product using group work over a period of time. Processes include peer-reviewed forms of presentations, reflections, interviewing, interpreting and applying research findings. Such performance-based assessment is generative in that it allows learners to construct their knowledge, to produce real world products and services, perform in some way, organise peer conferences, create artistic works and so on (Trinidad & Albon, 2002). Assessment is seamless and ongoing in a community of learners, as is the feedback to the learners. These critical elements in MLA, are linked, as shown in Figure 4, and were used to build the ten-week module for Hong Kong teachers.

6. Building a Technology-Rich Learning Environment using MLA

The ten-week module was constructed using the principles of MLA with the outcome of involving teachers actively in their learning so they could reflect on their own pedagogical practices while developing an e-learning module suitable for a group of students in their school. The 65 primary and secondary teachers met once a week for three hours over a ten-week period. During this time they were invited to form groups of four (teams) and participate in a number of authentic based activities and tasks, including evaluating other e-learning examples, analysing, synthesising and evaluating what constitutes good e-learning and using that information to design a suitable e-learning module.

Woven into this authentic content were the theories of learning and what constitutes good learning. Therefore the module modeled effective learning, especially as it might be used in e-learning[3] and was built around cognitive processes reflecting the higher order thinking skills of evaluation, synthesis and analysis (Bloom, 1974). The strategies used to develop processes included peer-review critiques, reflections, interpretation and application of research findings. For example designing a table in teams based on core information that was posted to the Forum in the Interactive Learning Network (ILN[4]) and completed by others was one task and another was the development of one set of criteria by many small groups over a period of a week to be used by each group to evaluate posted websites. These tasks are complex, involve all learners within their groups and result in deep learning. The learner cannot just "cut-and-paste" answers from the Internet as for an essay, but must be involved in the analysis, synthesis and evaluation of data. The application of technology and a community can extend these processes and the invisible boundaries of a social-cultural view of learning to access and build a wider community. Strategies such as share posting and shared data building are powerful learning experiences and were the basis of the module. Therefore throughout the module the teachers were encouraged to reflect on their own learning, share data, present to peers and participate in self and peer assessment.

Following the premise of MLA that "the technology *drives* the model, the assessment *drives* the learning" the teachers were invited to submit a journal of their learning during the ten weeks and a working e-learning module developed by the group at the end of the ten weeks. All groups successfully achieved their target of developing a working e-learning module with 13 out of the 17 mounted on the web to be used by a group of students in their school. By participating in building their own e-learning modules they were writing for a purpose and an audience, which makes their work more meaningful and related to the real world. These teachers developed e-learning modules in the areas of mathematics,

---

[3] Electronic learning or e-learning as defined by Jackson (2002) *Defining eLearning - Different Shades of "Online"* can be technology-enhanced learning and/or technology-delivered learning. Both dimensions describe the e-learning that was used in this module.

[4] Interactive Learning Network (ILN) is a community-building environment designed to support virtual education communities of practice where teachers/students work as teams and engage in reflective, collegial patterns of work. It facilitates both cognitive scaffolding as well as social scaffolding, which enables teachers/students to become progressively more involved in the community and to sustain their commitment and interests. This environment is designed to support academic programs that rely heavily on pedagogies that emphasize the emergence and growth of autonomous collaborative learning, rather than teacher-directed delivery of learning materials. See http://iln.cite.hku.hk/

science, the environment, information technology and general education based on the vision and good practice principles modeled during the ten week module.

A mixed mode delivery of face-to-face and online was used during the ten weeks. This mixed mode of delivery was dependent on the Learner Management System ILN, which enabled the educator to interact, manage and track learner's learning experiences, especially with large numbers (65) of learners. Through the ILN Forum, email and chat the teachers were also able to further their experiences, methods and beliefs in a technology-rich environment. This ILN learning environment included accessing multiple information resources, where learners had to develop a repertoire of information processing skills, such as setting goals, organising facts, classifying and identifying key words and concepts, controlling and synthesising data, and comparing and evaluating ideas.

When asked what were the most helpful aspects of the module, comments from the teachers included being able to put the theory of curriculum reform into practice using technology, applying the principles of collaboration with the social-constructivist approach (SCA), and learning about the theories of good learning then applying these to real world situations. Many of them commented on being able to apply these strategies straight into their own classrooms during the course of the module, using these strategies and activities immediately with their own students.

7. Conclusion

It can be said that "Hong Kong students [and teachers] are often perceived as particularly exam-oriented in their study [and teaching] and that they prefer spoon-feeding to pass exam rather than learning for learning's sake" (TEHE, 2002) but with the experience of creating, maintaining, and working in technology-rich learning environments that are based on learning not teaching, a group of 65 Hong Kong teachers were able to experience how to create new, rich and engaging e-learning environments for their students based on sound principles of learning. The ten-week module was carefully constructed using these sound principles of learning applied to e-learning and MLA, which involved a mixed mode delivery that was dependent on the Learner Management System ILN. This enabled the educator and learners to interact and manage the learning experiences and work with peers to support each other through a social-constructivist approach. This was achieved by building a supportive, collaborative, e-learning environment that focused on working within a community of learners where they had to actively participate in the social, interactive learning environment that modeled best practice. Such a learning environment enabled them to reflect on their own pedagogical practice and helped them develop real-world products that they could use in their own technology-rich school environments. The ability to publish work electronically as e-learning modules allowed this group of teachers to present their work to the wider community. A wider community of e-learners, that is, those who respond to the needs of others, has the potential to mutually support each other and extend each other's learning and in so doing, empower the individual in their own learning. In addition, the use of a community of e-learners provided these teachers with models of good practice which encouraged them to reflect, create, maintain and work in their own school learning environments where lifelong learning skills and strategies can be modeled with their students.

This project has shown that technology-rich learning environments using e-learning can engage the learner giving them a sense of empowerment, where they are no longer dependent on the specific and often limited knowledge of their educator, but work within a community of learners who can participate in the process of pedagogical change that involves practical application of new materials, new methods and new beliefs. Given the opportunity to apply new methods (learner-centred and learner-directed learning principles) to new materials (e-learning) these primary and secondary teachers were able to make the shift from the focus on teaching to the focus on learning.

References

ACOT. (1995). *Changing the conversations about teaching, learning and technology: A report on 10 years of ACOT research.* Apple Classrooms of Tomorrow. Apple computer Australia Pty. Ltd: Frenchs Forest, NSW.

Albon, R., & Trinidad, S. (2001). Tapping out new rhythms in the journey of learning. In A. Herrmann and M.M. Kulski (Eds), *Expanding Horizons in Teaching and Learning.* Proceedings of the 10th Annual Teaching Learning Forum, 7-9 February 2001. Perth:

Curtin University of Technology. [verified 10 Jan 2003].
http://cleo.murdoch.edu.au/confs/tlf/tlf2001/trinidad.html
Albon, R. & Trinidad, S. (2002). Building learning communities through technology. In K. Appleton, C. Macpherson, & D. Orr (Eds.), *International Lifelong Learning Conference: Refereed papers from the 2nd International Lifelong Learning Conference*, (pp. 50-56) Yeppoon, Central Queensland, Australia.
Barnes, D. (1987). *From communication to curriculum.* United Kingdon: Hazel Watson & Viney.
Becker, H. (2001). How are teachers using computers in instruction? Paper presented at the *2001 Meetings of the American Educational Research Association.* [verified 10 Jan 2003] http://www.crito.uci.edu/tlc/FINDINGS/special3/
Bloom, B. (1974). *Taxonomy of education objectives. Book 1 cognitive domain.* London: Longman.
Bransford, J., Brown, A., & Cocking, R. (1999). *Technology to support learning. How people learn: Brain, mind, experience and school.* National Research Council. [verified 10 Jan 2003] http://books.nap.edu/html/howpeople1/ch9.html [10/02/02]
Burns, R. (1995). *The adult learner at work.* Sydney: Business and Professional Publishing.
Curriculum Development Council. (2001). *The Learning to Learn: The Way Forward in Curriculum Development ~ Web Edition.* Hong Kong. [verified 10 Jan 2002] http://cd.ed.gov.hk/report/sept/eindex.htm
Dwyer, D., Ringstaff, C. & Sandholtz, J. (1990a). *Teacher beliefs and practices part i: patterns of change the evolution of teachers' instructional beliefs and practices in high-access-to-technology classrooms: First–fourth year findings.* Cupertino, Apple Computer Inc.
Dwyer, D., Ringstaff, C. & Sandholtz, J. (1990b). *Teacher beliefs and practices part ii: support for change the evolution of teachers' instructional beliefs and practices in high-access-to-technology classrooms: First–fourth year findings.* Cupertino, Apple Computer Inc.
Dwyer, D., Ringstaff, C., & Sandholtz, J. (1991). Changes in teachers' beliefs and practices in technology-rich classrooms. *Educational Leadership, 48*(8), 45–52.
ImpaCT2. (2001). *ImpaCT2:Pupils and teachers perceptions of ICT in the home, school and community.* Department for Education and Skills (DfES) and BectaICT Research. [verified 10 Jan 2003] http://www.becta.org.uk/research/reports/docs/ImpaCT2_strand_2_r eport.pdf

Jackson, R. (2002). *Weblearning resources*. [verified 10 Jan 2003] http://www.knowledgeability.biz/weblearning/#Different%20Shades%20of%20Online

Fulan, M. (1991). *The new meaning of education change*. London: Cassell.

HKSAR, Hong Kong Special Administrative Region. (2001). *Digital 21 Hong Kong: Building a digitally inclusive society*. Hong Kong Government Report, September.

Law, N., Yuen, H.K., Ki, W.W., Li, S.C., Lee, Y. & Chow, Y. (2000). (Eds.) *Changing Classrooms & Changing Schools: A Study of Good Practices in Using ICT in Hong Kong Schools*. Hong Kong: Centre for IT in School and Teacher Education, The University of Hong Kong.

Knowles, M. (1998). *The adult learner. The Definitive Classic in Adult Education and Human Resource Development*. Houston, TX: Gulf Publishing.

Mandinach, E. & Cline, H. (1994). *Classroom dynamics: Implementing a Technology-Based Learning Environment*. Lawrence Erlbaum and Associates Inc.: New Jersey.

NCREL North Central Regional Educational Laboratory, (2001). *New times demand new ways of learning*. [verified 10 Jan 2003] http://www.ncrel.org/sdrs/edtalk/newtimes.htm

Nelson, K. (2001). *Teaching in the Cyberage: linking the Internet to brain theory*. Skylight Training and Publishing. Arlington Heights: Illinois.

Newhouse, P., Trinidad, S., & Clarkson, B. (2002). *Quality teaching and learning practice with Information and Communications Technology (ICT): A review of literature*. Specialist Educational Services: Perth.

Teaching Effectively in Higher Education in Hong Kong (TEHE) web site (2002). *Functions & Effect of Assessment on Student Learning*. [verified 10 Jan 2003] http://teaching.polyu.edu.hk/

Sandholtz J., Ringstaff C., & Dwyer, D. (1997). *Teaching with technology: creating student-centered classrooms*. New York: Teachers College Press.

Trinidad, S., Macnish, J., Aldridge, J., Fraser, B., & Wood, D. (2001). Integrating ICT into the learning environment at Sevenoaks Senior College: How teachers and students use educational technology in teaching and learning. Paper presented at *Australian Association for Research in Education AARE2001 Conference*, December 2nd-5th Fremantle: Notre Dame University.

Trinidad, S. & Albon, R. (2002). Using the potential of technology to reconceptualise assessment. Paper presented at the *Ninth International Literacy and Education Research Network Conference on Learning*, July 16th – 20th. Beijing: Peoples Republic of China.

Trinidad, S. & Albon, R. (2003). Building a community of elearners. Paper presented at *South Africa 2003 - 3rd International Conference on Science, Maths and Technology Education*, January 15th-18th, East London: Rhodes University.

Wood, D., & Trinidad, S. (2001, June). Sevenoaks Senior College: Transforming learning for the 21st century in Western Australia. In G.D. Chen & J.C. Yang (Eds.), *Proceedings of the 10th International conference on Computer-Assisted Instruction/5th Global Chinese Conference on Computers in Education: Creation of Chinese Cyberspace* (Vol. 2, pp. 611-614). Chung-Li, Taiwan: National Central University.

UNESCO Report (n. d.*) ICT and Teacher Education: Global Context and Framework.* [verified 10 Jan 2003] http://www.gcu-uec.org/UNESCOreport-chap1.rtf

Chapter 6

TECHNOLOGY-RICH LEARNING ENVIRONMENTS AND THE ROLE OF EFFECTIVE TEACHING

Tony Rickards
Curtin University of Technology
Australia

This chapter examines how the technology-rich classroom learning environments of today can better prepare students to make an effective contribution to their technology-based futures. It supports the role of the teacher as the primary driving force behind effective utilisation of technology in the classroom and the mechanisms that can enhance effective teaching and learning in the classroom. The classroom teacher after all determines the level of access and utilisation of computers and other technologies in schools by making curriculum choices that may control to a large degree how students are exposed to technology. These are typically based on the individual teacher's level of competence with the technologies at hand or their ability to manage classes in these technology-rich environments.

1. Introduction

Becoming a technology-rich society and a global leader in technology integration in education are perceived by many as globally desirable outcomes. This desire to get involved in the challenges and opportunities that a technology-rich environment can bring are not limited to advanced western societies. Countries such as Vietnam, not typically perceived as a technological leader in the East Asian region, have begun to address the issue of national development of an Information technology Infrastructure plan. This is evidenced by recent government programs such as the *IT Master Plan* in Vietnam (see http://www.idgnet.com/english/crd_it_13708.html), that seeks to support the rapidly developing information technology market in Vietnam which is expanding at between 40 to 50 percent per annum.

The development of an effective Information and Communications Technology (ICT) infrastructure, and the commensurate level of local skills to fully utilise the investment in these ICT's, is seen as pivotal in the development of a more modern and internationally competitive country.

The Vietnam example is a particularly salient one as it shows a country that has typically relied on low technologies to support its economy making the transition toward a more high technology future. This transition to a knowledge-based high technology environment will be a major change for Vietnam, however, a necessary one when other countries in the region are examined more closely. For example, Singapore, Taiwan, Korea, Hong Kong and mainland China have all made giant leaps forward in technology investment and the provision of an effective technology based infrastructure. Each of these countries has made plans for the future of ICT in education as evidenced by their education department web sites, and each deems effective use of technology-rich learning environments as pivotal in the development of their country.

One needs only to travel to these countries to see how readily available are Internet Café access and public shopping mall access points to the World Wide Web and email. Even airport departure lounges, such as at Hong Kong Airport, have public and free access to email and the World Wide Web. Access to the World Wide Web is important as it provides valuable resources as well as a means to communicate and collaborate with others, globally.

It is interesting to note some of the social aspects of this Internet access. People have to be able to adapt to gaining access in a public place rather than at home. In many countries, this is for economic reasons. Mostly, this means that people are not able to afford to personally purchase computer hardware and gain access to the Internet at home, but see the access as vital to their personal development. This leads them to seek access in lower cost and more public ways, particularly in Internet Café and University or library-type settings.

The problem now for many societies, including Australia, is not so closely linked to gaining access to technology and information on the Internet, it is more about having the skills to effectively utilise it in a meaningful way. It is in this area that teachers can make a particularly strong contribution to their students. For example, having free access to the Internet at an airport is a possibility now, but what use it is to an individual without the skills to make use of it. If a person does not know how to utilise email or the web, providing free access to the web is an expensive and wasted resource. In addition, those people that do know how to utilise the provision of these free resources need to be aware of some of the dangers that they present, such as virus access and security of personal data. Again, teachers with the appropriate skills and knowledge can make a strong contribution here by educating students about Internet crime, ethics and security of personal data for example.

People using public access points have less physical privacy. For example, when entering data such as usernames and passwords they are in a public place, so keeping information private as you type it in takes on a greater importance. Typically users tend to use the public access points for web based information browsing and personal email, based on observations by the author recently in Hong Kong and the United States. This is public access is particularly valuable for school age children, the topic of this chapter, due to the low cost to the individual. It enables a wider cross section of student socio-economic levels to have access out of school hours.

The rapid and continual development of knowledge-based economies requires a greater proportion of the population in any country to be "IT savvy". That is, being able to interact with the technology in a meaningful way and communicate and share information with others. It includes being able to be selective in searching for information and knowing what to do with information once you have found it. These are basic skills that are required with non-technology based access to information, and teachers have been teaching how to develop effective information handling skills since before computers came along. Teachers who can utilise technology-rich environments to assist in the development of these skills in their students will be at a distinct advantage over those that cannot, as they are multi-skilled and can offer their students additional experiences in their quest for knowledge.

Without local skills and expertise in effective utilisation and application of information technologies, education (like business) has to "buy in" this expertise. This is expensive and is a very short-term solution to gaining the knowledge to effectively manage technology-rich environments and couple this with effective education and teaching. The better path for any country to take is that of a move toward the national development of local expertise, support and infrastructure within that country. Without development of an effective technology plan, governments risk widening the gap between globally competitive and non-competitive knowledge-based societies. This same pattern applies in the school level environment, the subject of this chapter.

The desire to improve technology-rich educational learning environments is becoming a priority at the government level for many countries. This is usually evidenced by national and/or state guidelines for the development of infrastructure and pedagogy that supports this priority.

One particularly successful example of an ICT development plan is the IT Master Plan that has been implemented in Singapore. It sought to integrate the development of a society wide telecommunications infrastructure, with systemic change in the way that education, hardware infrastructure and the culture of technology use in Singapore was implemented. Today in Singapore, all schools have access to high-speed interconnected networks of computers, computer support and software of a high standard. This is continually updated and managed and is funded well. In addition to this, teachers have training and support to develop their teaching to include a minimum of 30 percent of technology based content in their lessons, for every lesson. This is audited and recorded within each school by each teacher as an imperative. As a result, Heads of Department can monitor their staff and audit computer and other educational technology use, in their technology-rich environments.

The idea that classroom teaching interactions, that were initially just between people face to face, can continue uninterrupted, is a mistake. There are many occasions where classes are interrupted to allow for the needs of the educational technologies. Negative pressures that impact on the effective teaching of students using computers either as the medium of instruction or as an assisting technology include the extra demands on teaching time that the start-up and shutdown times required by all personal computers exert. If students have to "log in", or "boot up" their computers, this takes time away from teaching time. Now assuming that the technology in a learning environment has all of the hardware and software necessary for one to operate it effectively, and that they are in fact working and the server that they are connected to has not crashed, this will take several minutes. It will take longer if all the students try to do it at once, and will be time added onto the normal settling in time for any class. This sounds cynical, but observations from some learning environments show that teachers take for granted that there will be some machines that do not work, and that there will be inevitable "system crashes" to deal with.

Having a technology-rich environment does not ensure that high quality effective teaching and learning takes place. Teachers have shown that they can achieve high quality outcomes and be effective teachers whether they use educational technologies or not (Fisher & Stolarchuk, 1998). In terms of student outcomes the study by Fisher and Stolarchuk (1998) observed that in classrooms where technology was used, there were no significant improvements in student outcomes, when compared to classes that did not utilise laptop technology. Others argue that presentation and writing skills as well as personal communication skills improve when access to notebook computers are used in a classroom Fouts and Stuen (1997).

In a typical ICT lesson, in say a middle school setting, time is taken away from effective teaching by the technology. In addition to the time needed to start up the machines, log in and open applications, find and open documents or create new ones, there are breakdowns and system "freezes" that can reduce the machines available to students in a class. Computers remain a highly unreliable device despite their popularity and their value in education as a research and communications tool. This may be in a large part due to their need to interact with many more complex online systems than they once had to and their increasingly complex programming code.

It could be argued that in some environments, teachers do not have enough time to cover all the things that they need to cover in a year. The introduction of new technologies, computers in particular, reduces time taken out of teaching and is a net loss to the education for children at all levels of education. This is not to say that we should get rid of computers, far from it. But what impact does the mere introduction of technology have on effective teaching?

Having the skills to fully utilise whatever technologies, or lack of technologies, are present in your learning environment is a more desirable outcome. It transforms the technology into a valuable asset. With appropriate teaching and technology skills, a teacher can adapt an environment where the technology may not be fully operational and take a more flexible delivery approach. This flexible delivery mode may lead to more effective and responsive pedagogy. It also models to students that people need to be responsive in the workplace and adapt to new environments quickly.

A successful future in education and the later life of our teachers and students is not about having the latest, fastest or most impressive technology; it is about making the most effective use of what you have and what is readily available to you. This is independent of technology as it is a personal attribute in students and teachers and so can operate in technology-rich environments just as well as it can in no technology environments. It is about the difference between being you as a teacher or student being personally IT savvy rather than being a Luddite (see http://carbon.cudenver.edu/~mryder/itc_data/luddite.html). It is about taking charge of your own path toward personal empowerment with technology and selecting what is most appropriate for you and the tasks that you have to achieve today either as an individual or as part of a collaborative team.

You cannot rely on others to do all the learning for you when it comes to technology, as there will not always be someone else around to help you out. You have to learn by doing, as you tend to do what you have learned with technology. This can be a limiting factor as you are only able to do what you know. A discovery-based social constructivist epistemology as well as some directed learning in functionality available in technology-rich learning environments is advocated here as an appropriate way to take charge of a successful personal technology future and becoming a more effective teacher.

Using a constructivist view of the world is particularly complementary in this case as it allows you, the individual, to build on what you already know about any particular technology. There is no end to the learning and there is no one right answer. In fact, the hard part is not about wondering where to find an answer, it is about making sure that you narrow the focus of your questions carefully and stay on task. The learning can be so interesting at times, and there is so much information available, say on the Internet, that it is easy to become distracted.

This chapter supports the view that the future of education is inextricably linked to the effective delivery of knowledge and information. In a constructivist world, where the learner may work with others to support one another as they access a variety of information sources and tools to guide their individual problem-based learning and

The Role of Effective Teaching

personal goals, technology-rich learning environments are a key factor in access and delivery of timely information (Wilson, 1996).

2. Technology-based futures

Computer technology has been used in education for many years now. Computers in particular have pervaded nearly every kind of learning environment, at great cost to education in terms of money, time and space. In terms of a progression of key events, the introduction of the very first personal computers into school classrooms took place in the early 1980s; the advent of more user friendly machines in the mid to late 1980s and access to the Internet and the world wide web for many in the late 1990s. These dates may seem a little incongruous to those who have followed the release of these technologies. It must be remembered that the focus here is on examining the future of information and communication technologies in the field of education. Education tends to have a delay between the release of new technology and the implementation of that technology into the learning environment.

The nature of technology-rich learning environments is in a constant state of change. This is unique in many respects as few other learning environments are so closely tied to the hardware and software that is available. Hardware and software to a large extent acts as a driving force for the defining of technology-based futures. They do this by altering and constantly developing new ways to deliver "what is possible". An example of this would be the need for faster central processors in computers when the software for video conferencing and web-delivered video materials became available. The first images from video were slow and jerky, but as the hardware improved and faster processors and modem speeds became available, the ability to videoconference and view video images became more of a reality for many. This development opened the possibility of supporting remote students, or students working at home, with a low cost synchronous videoconference system that was once the domain of expensive consoles with dedicated ISDN lines.

Technology-based futures in education have several issues of certainty. They will always be linked to the technology that is currently available, which in turn will be partly driven by what people want to use technology for. For example, currently MP3 music players are popular at the moment, so hardware suppliers are providing devices that include

MP3 players. These include mobile phones, personal organisers and even external hard disk devices like the Apple iPod ©.

Whether these technological solutions are a product or a process they will always be dynamic, flexible and have multiple pathways to correct solutions in any problem based learning environment. Most importantly, they will require effective, multi-skilled and enthusiastic teachers to manage the learning environment.

3. Availability of Technology in Schools

Since the early 1980s there have been many types of personal computers and other technologies available to schools. These have been developed to be significantly faster, cheaper and smaller than they once were. Graphic calculators are one such technology that have become powerful, small and very capable at achieving the tasks that they were designed to perform.

Computers, like some biological organisms, have evolved into different forms that allow them to adapt to a wider variety of environments. For example, the telephone and the computer were once two separate entities. These two technologies have now both evolved to be inextricably linked in many cases. The phone became mobile, the computer linked to the telephone network and we now have mobile network access devices that can utilise the benefits of Internet communications along with standard telephony services. These are always changing and already there are hybrid systems such as SMS (Short Message Services) that can be sent from a computer to a phone. This has opened yet another avenue for tele-marketing and direct marketing, but can also be utilised in education. Cost at present is a little high, but this too in time will decrease and empower teachers with another effective tool to communicate with their students.

In another Darwinian similarity with biological counterparts, the development of computers has exercised the precept of the survival of the fittest in terms of market acceptance. In Australia, this has typically resulted in a great proportion of technology-rich learning environments utilising one of two key computer based platforms. They are either the Apple Macintosh or IBM PC based platform. The decision to utilise a commercially available and well-supported platform such as one of these in the early days of involvement with computers in schools has had an impact on the software that has been available to technology-rich learning environments. More importantly, teacher skills and expertise in those schools has evolved to suit the chosen platform. Once a decision had been made to outlay many dollars to purchase technology of a particular platform, and then the appropriate software, the path was set for a long-term acceptance of that particular platform and its particular methods of interacting with the user interface.

In the early days of computer education in the mid 1980's in Australia, access to software that was available to any particular selected computer platform was limited. Software producers were not able to economically produce a version for all platforms available. What was available on one platform was not necessarily available on another. This created a limiting factor that has largely disappeared as software has become more compatible and available for multiple platforms and operating systems.

Access to technology in schools is almost always limited by budget constraints. In addition schools have to plan carefully to avoid buying today's latest "out-of-date-before-you-buy" technology. Access to effective support and self-education help to keep teachers up to date with the latest knowledge about what is available, but do they have to keep up with the latest? Perhaps making smart choices based on upgradeable and multifunctional devices will reduce the need to upgrade so often as will better utilisation of software that is in place already.

If users, both teachers and students, have better skills training in the use of software that they use when it is introduced, they would be able to make more advanced use of the software and hardware that they already have access to. Access to even moderately technology-enhanced environments coupled with effective and well informed and technically supported teaching would enable schools to get more out of what they already have and reduce some costs of upgrading. For example, many computer users may not be fully utilising the features that their current software offers as they are not aware that these features are available due to lack of training.

There are many other technologies that are available today, but not yet being utilized by students and teachers in schools effectively. For example, the wider availability in many countries of cheap wireless networked web enabled Personal Digital Assistants (PDA's) that combine powerful computing and telephony in a palm-sized unit. These allow users to access services in the form of SMS (Short Message Service) messaging. As educators we can capitalise on these technologies as students in many cases already have personal access to the technology in the form of a mobile phone.

Systems integrated with the Internet such as SMS that students already use on a daily basis with peers are not utilised widely in education. Based on informal observations, SMS is utilised widely in student peer groups in Japan, the United States and to a lesser extent in Australia,.

Governments at the national and state levels in all states in Australia have provided many millions of dollars to assist in the establishment of computer infrastructure and support since the early 1980s (Computer Education Group of Victoria, 1984). Parents too have invested many millions of dollars of their own money to provide technology-rich learning environments in homes across Australia. Access to technology is no longer an overly limiting factor in itself. In fact it may be time to reconcile the access to technology that teachers and students have against the skill development and basic competencies found in those that have had access to the technology. In addition, an examination of whether there have been improved outcomes as a result of the introduction of these technology-rich environments may be quite sobering also. Have the skills of teachers for example developed to the point where they are technologically literate in all of the areas necessary to interact with the technology effectively? What are these areas of competence? How can they be improved? These will be discussed later in this chapter.

4. Budget Considerations

As mentioned previously, huge sums of money have been spent on technology infrastructure globally since the more widespread availability. One only needs to walk into many schools in Australia, South East Asia, Europe or the USA to see evidence of this expenditure. It is what some may call the "Shop Front" approach to technology use, where the school site looks very new and advanced, but where the utilisation of those resources may not be commensurate with the perceptions that outside observers may have, namely prospective parents of the school. In other cases, these resources are utilised fully and students have access to well trained and supported staff in the school, but how does the school ascertain if they are in this, or the former category? Also, how can the school get the most out of its investment before it has to renew it all?

The problem of the service life of this equipment is a very real one for schools. An effective service life for computer equipment in schools is typically about 24 months in user terms before they are deemed to be "slow" machines and about four years in terms of economic service life based on the author's experience. What this means for schools is that they either need to invest in a completely new set of computers every four years, or they need to have a large initial layout of funds followed by a retirement regime for the hardware and software that has been purchased. The assumption being that the technology is no longer usable after four years.

There are some parallels with business here. Schools could look at the strategic directions of competitors, look at available technologies and budget constraints and make a plan that includes complementary technologies that are upgradeable to keep up with technology more cost effectively. Things like memory upgrades are usually cheap, so buying the fastest processor, with a little less memory to start with may allow a slightly longer service life for computers. Also, hard disks can be upgraded relatively cheaply, so again, more speed, less space to start with may be a good idea. Having responsive hardware can enhance effective teaching in a single lesson, so a fast processor to start with is a good idea. As student skills improve, they may save work to their own disks, reducing the school's need to provide more hard disk space. This is a simple example, but over many schools, and many classes it can save a lot of money and resources.

5. Effective Pedagogy and the Role of the Classroom Teacher

Information and communication technologies can enrich the learning environment and enhance the learning experience for students, but only if an effective teacher facilitates the experiences and responds to student needs individually. They do this by allowing access to information and communications between people globally, from the classroom as well as by providing some learning experiences that may not be possible in traditional classrooms. Things such as simulations and access to expert knowledge, directly via email or indirectly via web sites. Technology cannot replace the role of the effective teacher or facilitator completely. It can enhance what an effective teacher can provide in a classroom, even with reliability issues discussed earlier present.

Teacher technology skill development out of necessity tends to be self-directed and self-motivated. Computer training for example is typically expensive in terms of time and money. In many cases the new skills learnt are developed "just in time" by teachers for the next assessment or reporting process, or in response to a new pedagogical need. This process was particularly evident in conference presentations and in schools in the mid to late 1990s when the education sector became more interested and then ensconced in the use of the Hyper Text Markup Language (HTML). Some teachers started to learn about HTML because they were intrigued as to what the Internet and web delivery could do for them and their teaching. The best way to learn HTML was to learn by doing. The effect on pedagogy was that teachers were able to customise content for individual classes, and indeed individual students. This is now much simpler to do with present day technology as many software packages are web enabled and have a simple "save as HTML" option to make web deliverable resources.

This chapter proposes a new paradigm for effective pedagogy. That of moving the user from knowledge about the software that they operate from the inch deep and inch wide box, to the inch wide and mile deep box. What this means is that users should be encouraged to learn more about what their current software is capable of and utilise more of the features that are resident in the software before having to upgrade. Teachers are good at teaching, they need to get better at teaching with ICT in varying technology environments.

As mentioned earlier, most users of word processing software in education utilise a small fraction of the total capabilities of the software to manage documents. There are many automated functions in the software that go unnoticed and unused. When these features are advertised as "new" features in the next edition of the software, some users become aware of them and may be tempted to consider that they need these "new" features and upgrade, rather than look for ways to achieve the same outcome with current software. This may sound a little simplistic, but it can be observed in many learning environments.

By learning more about what existing software is capable of, users empower themselves to be less reliant on outside support and more able to deal with complex tasks using older technology. There will of course come a time when a particular technology will be just too slow and too old to deal with user demands for a rapid response. Learning more about what you can do with what you already have will save some time and money and enable a longer service life from existing technology in schools. Given that schools typically do not have large amounts of money available to constantly invest in new computers, an extra year every four years can help out. If new technology does not have to be bought so often, it will enable better systems to be purchased when the upgrade interval does eventuate.

6. Defining Minimum Standards of Competency and Systemic Change in Teacher Skills

There are examples in Australia of emerging requirements for teachers to display their individual level of competence with technology. This has presented in the form of state-driven initiatives as well as nationally-funded and distributed initiatives. The current models of teacher professional development for the integration of information and communication technology (ICT) into classroom practice are summarised in a Department of Science and Technology document *Making Better Connections* (Commonwealth Department of Education, Science and Training, 2001). This is the report of a study into ways in which classroom teachers, pre-service teacher educators and educational leaders are being supported to acquire the skills and knowledge they need to ensure the effective use of ICT in the classroom setting. The report examines existing models of pre-service teacher education and in-service professional development, both in Australia and overseas. The report identifies barriers and critical success factors, and provides advice and recommendations that will help inform decisions by school systems, teacher professional associations and university teacher education faculties (Commonwealth Department of Education, Science and Training, 2001).

One excellent example of an Australian state initiative is the *Schooling 2001* project that operated in Queensland. It was implemented in 1997 at about the time that some Australian near neighbours, such as Singapore, were developing IT plans for their regions. Since the conclusion of the *Schooling 2001* project, all schools in Queensland have had an Internet connection (Beattie, 2001). This suggested that there was a realisation that IT skills in teachers were somehow lacking and that there was international concern in the Asia Pacific region about this.

The Queensland example was proactive and included materials for pre-service teacher education as well as for practicing teachers. The state government initiated a program of improvement and education to develop and improve teacher and student competencies in the effective integration and use of Information and Communication Technologies. The effective and timely development of teacher professional development practices was a key component of the program. It had, as part of its blueprint, the stipulation that all teachers in Queensland must have attained the 'Minimum Standards' in technological competence and applied them in their teaching by the end of the year 2001.

In reality, before the program was completed in 2001, there was a realisation that teachers in the state were not going to meet the deadline in terms of attaining the required competencies (Murphy & Poyatos-Matas, 2001). The Education Department had made a major investment in the development of teacher skills and competencies. A major achievement of this program was the greater awareness of support for teachers on the web and a valuable set of guidelines that allow teachers to guide their utilisation of ICT in the classroom.

The contribution of locally-based professional associations should not be underestimated as a contributing factor to the development of more effective use of ICT in education.

Professional associations, such as QSITE (Queensland Secondary Information Technology Educators), also benefited by gaining increased interest and membership from teachers that may have not otherwise developed an interest in improving ICT integration without outside support to do so.

It is clear that the move toward state and nationally recognised minimum standards of technology competence is of great importance for teachers in Australia. It signals that government at the national and state levels realise that generally, teacher competencies in the effective utilisation and integration of ICT in the classroom is poor. This is of concern as investment into the provision of high technology into schools by parents, schools and the government has been high. This investment has also come at the expense of support for other areas of the curriculum in terms of time, to clear access in the timetable for students to have "lab time" and in terms of money and resources including staff.

Another factor to consider, as a driving force for the effective introduction and implementation of a set of minimum standards, in the need to gain some commonality of student experience across school systems inter-state and intra-state.

Currently, the development of technology-rich environments is divergent in nature because of the way computers came into schools, i.e. in an ad-hoc way based usually on a set of individual state supported recommendations for computer systems, but then individual school decisions on what to purchase. This is not bad, but students need at least some commonality of experience driven by the factors that are the minimum that students need to know to make an effective contribution to their technology-rich knowledge-based societies. The development of "computer departments" was disjointed and many staff has interesting and very divergent career paths. This is reflected in the offerings in many schools that closely align school offerings with curriculum imperatives and staff expertise.

Informal observations by the author in a small number of Californian schools show that typically the computer teacher is also the technical support. They teach and fix computers that fail. Though they can support other teachers, they do not have time to do it in a way that empowers teachers to do more for themselves. In Australia the situation was much the same, though this has evolved over that last 15 years to the point where on an individual schools basis there are many different models of success based in differentiation of technical and teaching roles.

What is missing is a core set of agreed and minimum standards for every teacher. As part of the craft of teaching, teachers should be able to all utilise technology effectively as a tool in their teaching. Many teachers can now do this, but many can not and students in these classes are missing out on developing their skills because their teacher does not have the confidence to make more use of the technology-rich learning environments that many schools provide.

Often students at all levels of education have better access to educational technologies at home than they do at school. This may be due to a number of factors, but one clear one is that parents want the best for their children. This is not to say that all can afford to provide excellent computer facilities for their children at home, but they tend to make every effort to do so.

The high value given to the education of children is a key factor in many societies. It is particularly evident in cultures that have undergone major societal turmoil. Afghanistan and East Timor serve as valuable examples of this. Immediately following the cessation of civil unrest and war, one of the first public functions to be restored is education. The next may be public health. This tends to return a sense of normalcy to an otherwise devastated society for the inhabitants.

The provision of superior computers in the home compared to those provided in the wider context of a school has been a difficulty for schools since the early 1980's in Australia. If schools are examined more closely, several different solutions seem to have been evident. One was to mandate that all students had Laptops of the same specification to reduce competition and the issues of compatibility. Another was to provide labs of computers so that all students regardless of access at home could gain access sufficient to complete all school based tasks in those labs. These both provide access for students, but could not hope to keep up with the latest. This serves as another example of why students and teachers should learn to make more use of what they already have, as they can not necessarily afford to constantly upgrade computers each year.

The craft of teaching, positive teacher-student interaction and productive problem based learning environments that foster creative skill development and lateral thinking may be decisive factors for successful student futures. To this end, some pre-service teacher education courses in Australia are being adapted to better reflect changes in the learning environments that are dominated by technology. These changes may come from the state imperatives such as described earlier in Queensland. They seek to better prepare teachers before they enter the profession. In this way that can acts as a catalyst for already practicing teachers in the schools that they are sent to in their first year out. The changes should emphasise remaining sensitive to the needs of students in learning environments where technology is effectively integrated as a tool to support the learning process at all levels of education.

7. Conclusions

The introduction of educational technologies, particularly graphing calculators and personal computers, was hailed by many as a panacea for the drudgery in some areas of the curriculum. The thought was that computers in themselves brought great promise. With this came an initial fear that computers could replace teachers, particularly when computer assisted learning programs became more readily available. The introduction of computers into schools also saw students being free to communicate globally and able to access information from the Internet.

A major driving and indeed controlling force in the school environment is the leader of the school, the principal. These people need to be enthusiastic and informed about the use of technology in their learning environments and be able to look to the future to ensure that tomorrows needs are being addressed by today's thinking. They need to support the development staff skills and model these themselves.

Associated with this is the need to exercise an economically-rational model of expenditure so that the school does not end up being able to only buy a small number of computers, or a proportion of what they have planned for. This is enhanced in the decision makes are effective teachers and are technologically literate.

The role of effective teaching has never been so important as it is now. It is the one major factor in the development of young people that can make a strong contribution to a technology-based society. Effective teaching and effective teacher utilisation of technology-rich learning environments serves as a role model for the young, as well as a breeding ground for the development of creative, capable and empowered problem solvers for the future.

References

Beatie, P. (2001). *The Premier's media statement.* [Online] Available: http://statements.cabinet.qld.gov.au/portfolio-display/tmp/1044341891.html

Computer Education Group of Victoria, (1984). *Computing and education: 1984 and beyond.* Balaclava: Acacia Press.

Commonwealth Department of Education, Science and Training, (2001). *Making better connections: Models of teacher professional development for the integration of information and communication technology into classroom practice.* [Online] Available: http://www.dest.gov.au/schools/publications/2002/professional.htm

Fisher, D., & Stolarchuk, E. (1998). *The effect of using laptop computers on achievement, attitude to science and classroom environment in science.* In Proceedings of Western Australian Institute for Educational Research Forum 1998. [Online] Available: http://cleo.murdoch.edu.au/waier/forums/1998/fisher.html

Fouts, J., & Stuen, C. (1997). *Copernicus project: Learning with laptops: Year 1 evaluation report.* ERIC Document Reproduction Service (ED 416 847).

Marshall, P. (2000). *A review of educational technology competency standards.* [Online] Available: http://www.cegv.vic.edu.au/acec2000/paper_ref/p-marshall/paper11/paper11.PDF.

Murphy, M., & Poyatos-Matas, C. (2001). A pilot study to test the effectiveness of Education Queensland's 'Schooling 2001' Project from the LOTE teachers' point of view. *The Australian Journal Of Teacher Education, 26*(2). [Online] Available: http://www.ecu.edu.au/ses/educ/AJTE/vol26no2.html

Wilson, B.G. (Ed.). (1996). *Constructivist learning environments: Case studies in instructional design.* Englewood Cliffs, NJ: Educational Technology.

Chapter 7

LEARNING ENVIRONMENTS IN NEW CONTEXTS: WEB-CAPABLE CLASSROOMS IN CANADA

David Zandvliet
Simon Fraser University
Canada

This chapter reports on a study of classroom environments in emerging Internet (web capable) classrooms in British Columbia, Canada. The study involved an evaluation of the physical and psychosocial learning environments in these settings through a combination of case studies and questionnaires. This study focuses on the results obtained from the administration of a student questionnaire designed to measure aspects of the psychosocial learning environment in these settings and to relate these factors to students[1] satisfaction with learning and to other physical aspects of the learning environment. A version of the What is Happening in this Classroom (WIHIC) instrument and Computerized Classroom Environment Checklist (CCEC) were administered to 358 high school students in 22 classrooms from 6 schools around the province. Analysis of classroom environment data revealed that student autonomy/independence and task orientation were associated with satisfaction with learning. Relating data to physical measures such as the workspace and visual environments demonstrated significant associations between the physical and psychosocial learning environment in technology-rich classrooms. Further qualitative data suggest that factors related to teaching styles, classroom design and the learning environment, interact to influence students[1] satisfaction with learning.

1. Introduction

This chapter describes a study of the overall physical and psychosocial learning environment associated with classrooms using Internet (web based) technologies. Importantly, it also attempts to explore the degree to which physical and psychosocial factors interact to either facilitate or constrain students' satisfaction with their learning in these settings. These factors should be considered in the context of whether or not they enable current ideas about teaching and learning. Factors that work to constrain these methodologies should be seen as unproductive, whereas factors which facilitate or enable them should be viewed as desirable and productive. Most importantly, the chapter gives a broad, descriptive look into one province's (British Columbia) emerging Internet classrooms and gives recommendations as to what may or may not be working for classroom teachers.

There are many different rationales for the use of Internet technologies, however, these can be roughly categorized into two basic types: (1) the premise that the increasing use of technology in society alone justifies the greater implementation of information technology in our schools, and (2) the premise that the unique attributes of new information and communications technologies (ICTs) in themselves offer great potential to increase the effectiveness of teaching and learning, and may enable current efforts for educational reform and curriculum revision. In this chapter, the focus is on the latter argument that makes a case for using ICTs specifically as learning and teaching tools.

2. Learning and Teaching with ICT

As in the past, successful use of ICTs for teaching means involving students and educators in the learning process in new ways; however, the use of ICT's and the vitality of their use depends fundamentally on good teaching practices. Such factors as the relationship between technology and instruction, teachers' familiarity with Internet resources, teachers' competence in using technology, familiarity with constructivist and other developing pedagogical frameworks, and teacher access to professional development, are all key indicators of instructional success using ICTs.

Considering the relationship between technology and instruction is an important way to begin talking about classroom teaching. Collaborative technologies have often been explored as catalysts for changing teacher practices and introducing a variety of network-based tools can be an effective means for helping teachers develop a more student-directed, constructivist-learning environment. Further, student mentors can form an effective technical support group for teachers involved with implementing new technologies (Resta, 1998). Success with collaborative technologies requires extensive training and professional development, on-site support, easy access to technology and strong school administrative support. In the USA, the delivery of the Internet to schools has become a national priority. The US Department of Education aims to meet the technology literacy challenge; computers have been described as 'the new basic' of education, and the Internet as 'the blackboard of the future' (US Congress, 1996, p. 3).

Technology currently used in school classrooms includes word processing, spreadsheets, and the use of the Internet for research, practising drills, solving problems and analyzing data. Teachers also use computers to create instructional materials, research for planning lessons and for communicating with colleagues (National Center For Education Statistics, 2000). Teachers are also more likely to use computers and the Internet when these technologies are available in their classrooms as opposed to computer designated rooms or labs. In the hands of students, technology can assist in the process of learning through assisting in the gathering and evaluation of information, defining and solving problems and drawing conclusions. Technologies that may aid in the learning process include simulation and strategy software, CD/ROMs, videodiscs, and multimedia/hypermedia. However, technology by itself is not the answer; methods of teaching need to change to complement the new technologies that are available (Rice & Wilson, 1999).

As more technology finds its way into classrooms, there is a continued and growing interest in how technology is being used there and what is its relationship to pedagogy. Currently there is a lack of empirical research on the effectiveness of various emerging instructional approaches and applications of technology, compared to research on more traditional tutorial based applications. This may in part be due to a lack of well-defined models for assessment of educational outcomes within so called 'constructivist' learning practices. Conventional (standardized) multiple-choice tests offer the advantage of widespread availability and straightforward scoring. In addition, there is both familiarity and credibility with the general public for these tests. However, standardized tests place an emphasis on the understanding of isolated facts and basic skills and less on the acquisition of higher order thinking and problem based skills that are those emphasized in the more recent 'constructivist' models of teaching and learning.

3. Learning Environments and ICTs

While the implementation of information and communication technology (ICT) into schools in the form of infrastructure, professional development and new curricula are important components for educational reform. It is also important to continue research in this area in order to determine what are the tangible results of this investment in a recent (and relatively unproved) educational resource. One promising methodology, which can be used to investigate both the effects and affects of the integration of ICT's into school classrooms, is found in an area of the literature described as the study of 'learning environments'.

Studies describing psychosocial learning environments have demonstrated much about the factors that may influence or determine learning in classrooms (Fraser, 1994) and educators are adding their findings to the body of research within the fields of psychology, sociology, physiology, architecture and engineering. In part, the interdisciplinary nature of learning environment research points to the diversity of factors involved. These include many psychosocial factors including student perceptions of independence, cohesion, motivation, etc. but can be expanded to include a variety of physical or material factors such as classroom dimensions, classroom densities and lighting.

3.1 Psychosocial Learning Environments

Fraser's (1998a) summary of two decades of learning environment research revealed that the methods used in the study of learning environments tend to be descriptive, multivariate and correlation in nature. A short list of the instruments used in educational settings includes the *Individualized Classroom Environment Questionnaire* (ICEQ), *Learning Environment Inventory* (LEI) and the *Classroom Environment Scale* (CES). These include scales proven to be effective predictors of student achievement, behaviours and attitudes. An instrument known as the *What is Happening in This Class?* (WIHIC) questionnaire was the one selected for use in this study. This instrument was created by combining the most salient scales from many earlier instruments (Fraser, 1998a) and has been shown to be a valid and reliable instrument in many different international contexts (Chionh & Fraser, 1998; Khoo & Fraser, 1997; Margianti, 2000; Riah & Fraser, 1998; Zandvliet & Fraser, 1998). The WIHIC scales used in this study included those of: student cohesiveness, autonomy/independence, involvement, task orientation and cooperation.

Classroom environment instruments have also been effectively used in the evaluation of educational innovation. For example, the use of a classroom environment inventory to assess the use of a computerized database indicated that the students became more inquiry orientated through its use (Maor & Fraser, 1996). In Singapore, classroom environment measures were used in evaluations of computer-assisted learning (Teh & Fraser, 1994, 1995b) and computer application courses for adults (Khoo & Fraser, 1997). Dryden and Fraser (1996) used a learning environment inventory known as the *Constructivist Learning Environment Survey* (CLES) to illustrate a lack of success in achieving constructivist-orientated reform of science education, as part of an urban systemic initiative in Texas. Another common line of research involves associations between students' perceptions of their learning environments and their cognitive and affective learning outcomes (Fraser, 1998b; Fraser & Fisher, 1983a, 1983b). Fraser (1994) collected 40 past studies that presented data concerning student outcomes and their classroom environments. These studies replicated outcome-environment associations in a wide variety of countries and student grade levels. For example, Teh and Fraser (1995a; 1995b) found associations between classroom environment, student achievement and student attitudes in computer-assisted learning classrooms.

The inclusion of learning environment instruments and measures provide one effective methodology for investigating the impact of an educational innovation, such as the widespread introduction of networked resources into classroom settings investigated in this study. While they provide important information about student perceptions of the teaching/learning environment they have also been linked with other cognitive and affective student learning outcomes (e.g. satisfaction with learning, or performance on standardized tests). When taken together with the other methodologies used in this study, information about the learning environment in classrooms helps to provide a more holistic picture of the 'ecology' of these new environments created by the introduction of ICTs. Importantly, psychosocial factors such as these have also been linked with the physical environment of a classroom, which itself can be dramatically impacted by the significant introduction of ICT into classroom spaces and into the curriculum.

3.2 Studying Physical Learning Environments

Considering ergonomic issues in the investigation of classroom learning environments involves looking at a wide range of physical and psychosocial factors and determining together, how they are influenced by the use of technology. Two recent reports have broke some new ground in this area (Harris, Straker, & Zandvliet, 2000; Straker & Zandvliet, 2001) by demonstrating that the physical environment in school classrooms can be positively or negatively impacted by the introduction of ICT's depending on the principles used during their implementation. An important consideration then, is the relationship between technology and classroom design. For example, plentiful lighting ensures that students can read notes and stay alert. Also, different lighting levels are required for certain technologies (Kirby, 1999). Teachers need simple pre-set controls to switch between different lighting needs. Lack of ventilation is another common complaint from students and administrators; most classrooms do not meet minimum ventilation guidelines (Kirby, 1999).

Technology needs to become a shaper of school design. When wiring a school for technology we need to consider safety, security and ease of connectivity. Schools require modular furniture that can fit together in different configurations to accommodate general-purpose classrooms (Swanquist 1998). Ergonomically correct furniture promotes comfort and research confirms that students who are comfortable have better attention, and thus retention, of information. All students need to be considered, and so a range of sizes and adjustable height chairs and desks are essential to good design. Computers in classrooms also need to be placed so that students can easily move to see the instructor and their monitors. Movable chairs and wide walkways should be provided in order to encourage students to work and interact with each other. Classroom spaces should be designed so that as different learning approaches develop, the framework of the classroom and the school should support changes with minimal expenditure. Designs should combine computers and teaching spaces; these activities need to be related we should consider fittings that allow desks to be easily reconfigured (Ehrenkrantz, 1999).

This study considered specific aspects of the physical learning environment in classrooms through the development and use of an ergonomic checklist that allowed researchers to objectively compare the suitability of the selected physical aspects of a classroom through comparison with published ergonomic standards. In addition, students were administered a questionnaire developed specifically for use in school classrooms. The *Computerized Classroom Environment Checklist* (CCEC) asked students to rate their perceptions of specific aspects of the physical learning environment as they experienced it in the studied classrooms. The adoption and interpretation of ergonomic standards, developed for business and industry provided a good starting point for the categorization of the physical learning environment within schools (i.e. Knirk, 1992).

Some more recent studies have begun to draw on analogies between ergonomics in business and industry environments and investigations of the learning environment in schools (i.e. Zandvliet & Fraser, 1998; Zandvliet & Straker, 2001) and compares matches these data with traditional educational research methods (such as qualitative interview and case study). This synergy promises to inspire a broader view for research on learning environments. Ultimately, the educational productivity model that Walberg (1991) espoused was useful for the consideration of a wide range of factors operating within school classrooms in this study. This model maintains that a variety of factors when taken together could influence outcomes such as student attitudes, satisfaction and achievement. Walberg's model of psychosocial factors was broadened in this study to include other physical dimensions in what we describe as a holistic or ecological study of technological learning environments. Importantly, this study builds on previous studies that demonstrate links between the physical and psychosocial learning environments and other important cognitive and attitudinal outcomes.

4. Conceptual Framework

The conceptual framework used for this study considered a concurrent examination of: methodologies used by teachers when working with ICTs, A consideration of relevant psychosocial factors operating within these classrooms and in addition, a consideration of physical factors which also influence students learning environments. These components are detailed in the model presented as Figure 7.1.

Primarily, this study hoped to determine to what extent does the introduction of Internet resources in classrooms enable progressive approaches to teaching and learning? The study also investigated how the psychosocial environment in Internet classrooms would be described by students and whether certain factors were closely associated with students' satisfaction with learning? We further endeavoured to describe how computers have been physically implemented in classrooms to determine whether these situations meet basic guidelines for safe and productive use. Additionally we hoped to determine which physical factors influence the learning environment and student satisfaction

Importantly, we also hoped to determine through this investigation what types of interactions occur between physical and psychosocial factors in promoting student satisfaction in networked learning environments? Which are significant? How do these interactions impact on teaching and learning?

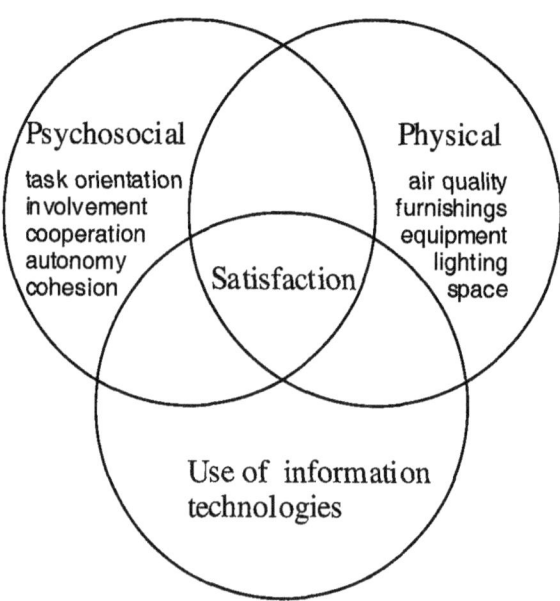

Figure 7.1. Model of potential factors influencing student satisfaction (adapted from Gardiner, 1989)

5. Research Methodology

The type of classroom identified for the purposes of this study can be described as the 'technologically-rich' classroom. This type of classroom was identified as having a number of networked computers installed, with the general availability of Internet resources for students and their substantial use in the delivery of curriculum. For each classroom, a general profile of the learning environment was constructed by evaluating a number of selected psychosocial and physical factors, then validating the results by intensely investigating a subset of the original sample. A number of different methodologies were used to accomplish this: first, the use of questionnaires and ergonomic inventories/checklists to be completed for a wide number of technological classrooms; and, second, the use of semi-structured interviews conducted with selected teachers working in these settings. Student satisfaction is seen as the major dependent variable for the study as it has been shown to be a good predictor of learning in school settings and in addition has been shown to be an important predictor of productivity in commercial settings.

5.1 Questionnaires

The psychosocial measures in the study were obtained by administering five scales selected and adapted from a the What is Happening in this Classroom (WIHIC) learning environment instrument (Fraser, Fisher, & McRobbie, 1996) which has been shown to have high reliability and validity in educational settings. Specifically, the scales measuring cohesiveness, involvement, autonomy, task orientation and cooperation were selected for this study as they are viewed as consistent with the goals of current reform efforts aimed at individualizing curriculum and instruction and increasing student interactions. These constructs are also consistent with variables considered important by ergonomists. The 'actual' form of the questionnaire was administered in each setting to students and they were asked to reflect on their perceptions of the classroom environment as they experienced it. The unit of analysis for the questionnaire measure was the individual classroom. As an additional (though conceptually different) measure, the questionnaire also included the items by which students provide their rating of satisfaction with learning in that particular environment – this scale was adapted from the

'Satisfaction with learning' scale adapted from the *Test of Science Related Attitudes* (Fraser, 1981).

5.2 Ergonomic checklists

The study also investigated a selection of physical environmental factors through the use of a general ergonomic evaluation and a related questionnaire developed specifically for this purpose. The inventory employs a hierarchical rating scale (scored out of five) which could allowed the researcher to objectively determine a classroom's degree of "fit" within currently published ergonomic standards. It includes a variety of general physical variables discretely measured or noted by the researcher, then grouped into the overall physical domains of workspace, computer, visual and spatial environments, and a rating of overall air quality. In order to ensure consistency, the inventory was completed by the same observer in each classroom setting. In addition to this, a related Computerised Learning Environment Checklist (CCEC) was administered to students in order to investigate the student perceptions of these same physical factors operating in the classrooms studied. Together, the evaluations and questionnaires give a rich description of the physical characteristics of the various learning spaces and configurations observed.

5.3 Semi-structured Teacher Interviews

Following the initial quantitative portion of the study, a number of teachers were invited to participate in a series of semi-structured interviews as part of the case study method for each school location. These interviews were conducted immediately following the lab evaluations described in the previous section. Teachers were invited to respond individually or in small focus groups to a series of open-ended interview questions that corresponded roughly to the learning environment factors (both physical and psychosocial) that were investigated by the initial questionnaire. The time allotted for each interview session was approximately one hour in length. The interviews were tape recorded and then later transcribed for analysis. The primary purpose of these open-ended questions was first to obtain data about classroom practices and clarification as to the nature of students technology-based assignments in each classroom. Secondly, it was intended that interview data would be used to triangulate results from the initial survey portion of the study with these qualitative data providing a richer more humanistic description of the classroom routine and learning environment. The teacher interview also provided a great deal of anecdotal information which helped describe each classroom setting for the purposes of the case study descriptions.

5.4 Sample

The target population for this study was adult continuing education and high school classrooms in the Canadian province of British Columbia. The study involved investigations conducted in technological (web capable) classroom settings as identified by the teachers. In total, 22 classes in six schools located around the province participated in the study, with a total of 358 students completing the questionnaire portion. Lastly, a total of 22 teachers were interviewed during the second phase which involved semi-structured interviews. Detailed case studies were completed in six locations: two from the Lower Mainland, two locations on Vancouver Island and two from the province's interior.

6. Results and Discussion

This section summarizes and discusses the results of the three different methodologies used in this study: the perceptions of students regarding the learning environment in the networked classrooms as measured by the WIHIC questionnaire; evaluations of the physical learning environment in these setting as measured by researchers and perceived by students; and finally, qualitative questionnaire data from semi-structured teacher interviews. To sum up how these data interact, a synthesis of the case study data is presented and followed by a summary analysis of this study's major findings.

6.1 Questionnaire Responses

The What is Happening in This Classroom (WIHIC) questionnaire was selected for use in this study as it had already proved a reliable and valid instrument in an earlier study conducted in Australian and Canadian classrooms (Zandvliet & Fraser, 1998). Statistical analyses for the WIHIC learning environment scales and the TOSRA Satisfaction scale provided amply support the validity and reliability of these instruments for obtaining information about relevant aspects of the psychosocial environment and students' level of satisfaction in the current studied settings.

Questionnaires were distributed in class sets to teachers who were working in computerized settings. Mean scores for each class were then calculated using individual scale scores and aggregating the data by class. This analysis yielded a number of descriptive statistics for the studied classrooms. These data are presented in Table 7.1.

Table 7.1. Descriptive Statistics for Learning Environment Scales (WIHIC) and Student Satisfaction (TOSRA) for Student Responses

Questionnaire and Scale	Mean Score	Standard Deviation	Min. Score	Max. Score
WIHIC				
Student Cohesiveness	3.47	0.63	1.4	5.0
Involvement	3.20	0.67	1.1	5.0
Autonomy / Independence	2.63	0.72	1.0	4.7
Cooperation	3.68	0.65	1.6	5.0
Task Orientation	3.37	0.72	1.2	5.0
TOSRA				
Satisfaction	3.24	0.77	1.3	4.5

N=22 classes
The following response key was used:
1=Almost never, 2=Seldom, 3=Sometimes, 4=Often, 5=Almost always.

Interpretation of the student questionnaire data presented in Table 7.1 yields one perspective on the learning environment in Internet classrooms. Mean scores of greater than 3 are considered positive and indicate that the majority of respondents perceived practices related to this psychosocial variable to be occurring more than *sometimes* and in the direction of *often* or *almost always*. Conversely, scores of less than three are considered negative as these practices were viewed by students as happening less frequently than *sometimes* and in the direction of *seldom* or *almost never*. Although there was considerable variability in the scores, overall, students perceived most aspects their learning environments to be positive and characterized them as higher in Student Cohesiveness and Task Orientation than other scales. The scale measuring Autonomy/Independence scored lowest (less than three) of the five learning environment scales. Finally, students rated their level of Satisfaction with learning in these environments as generally positive.

6.2 Associations Between Psychosocial Factors and Satisfaction

The key dependent variable in this study is the measure Satisfaction, and associations were explored between this attitudinal variable and various pyschosocial and physical factors. Both the psychosocial measures and the measure of student Satisfaction were obtained using student questionnaires and descriptive statistics regarding these measures were presented in the previous section. This section describes associations between the psychosocial environment and students' satisfaction with learning.

Questionnaire data were analysed for associations between the outcome variable student Satisfaction and the five psychosocial scales in the WIHIC questionnaire. To accomplish this, simple correlations and multiple linear regressions were performed using the SPSS (version 10) statistical package. In this analysis, Satisfaction was identified as the dependent variable and the other five psychosocial scales were identified as independent variables. These regression statistics are presented as Table 7.2.

The results show that the simple correlations with Satisfaction was statistically significant for all five WIHIC scales. When all five environment scales are considered together, the multiple correlation of Satisfaction with the set of five psychosocial scales was high (0.528), indicating that approximetely 28% of the variation in the Satisfaction scores was explained by psychosocial environmental variables. In addition, the ß weights shown in Table 7.2 suggest independent, strong associations between Satisfaction and each of the psychosocial scales of Autonomy/Independence and Task Orientation when the influence of other factors are controlled. Of these associations, Task Orientation had the strongest individual association with student Satisfaction (.396).

Table 7.2. Associations between WIHIC Scales and Student Satisfaction in Terms of Simple Correlations (r) and Standardised Regression Coefficients (ß)

WIHIC Scale	r	ß
Student Cohesion	0.314*	0.115
Involvement	0.271*	0.003
Autonomy / Independence	0.341*	0.255*
Task Orientation	0.455*	0.396*
Cooperation	0.276*	0.089
Multiple correlation (R)		0.528*

N=358
*$p < 0.01$

6.3 Ergonomic inventories and checklists

Evaluations of physical factors in the learning environment in the study settings were derived from two sources. The first was a perceptual measure called the Computerised Classroom Environment Checklist (CCEC) developed specifically for this study. The second was through ergonomic evaluations conducted by the research team as part of the overall case study methodology. These evaluations consisted of actual measurements and ratings taken on location using the Computerised Classroom Ergonomic Inventory (CCEI). Both types of evaluations consisted of an examination of the workspace, computer, visual and spatial environments as well as an estimate of air quality at each location.

The Computerised Classroom Environment Checklist (CCEC) was administered to students at the same time as the other learning environment questionnaire (WIHIC) described in the previous section. Summary data for the administration of this questionnaire is presented in Table 7.3. While there was considerable variability in the ratings, these data show that students generally rated the computing environment as very positive (mean score of 4.32 on a scale of 5), while other factors in the learning environment such as the visual environment (quality of lighting) and air quality were rated poorly (mean scores of 2.91 and 2.53 respectively). The spatial environment (quality of the space) was also rated marginally (3.08 on a scale of 5).

Table 7.3. Descriptive Statistics for Physical Factors (CCEC) According to Student Responses on Questionnaire

Questionnaire & Scale	Mean Score	Standard Deviation	Maximum Score	Minimum Score
Workspace Environment	3.78	1.18	5.0	0.0
Computer Environment	4.32	0.88	5.0	0.0
Visual Environment	2.91	1.06	5.0	0.0
Spatial Environment	3.08	0.93	5.0	0.0
Air Quality Rating	2.53	0.94	5.0	0.0

N=22 classes

In addition to the questionnaire data, ergonomic evaluations were conducted by the researchers in 13 different settings as part of the overall case study methodology. These evaluations consisted of actual measurements and ratings taken on location using the Computerised Classroom Ergonomic Inventory (CCEI) and associated worksheets. These consisted of an examination of the workspace, computer, visual and spatial environments as well as an estimate of air quality at each location. Similar, to the questionnaires, these data show considerable variability in the physical learning environment from location to location. In particular, the workspace environment (quality and adjustability of furnishings) for this portion of the study was the most problematic. These data are presented as Table 7.4.

The two types of evaluations showed a slightly different picture of the physical learning environment in the classroom settings studied. In particular, student perceptions were less than positive on most of the environmental measures rated by the questionnaire (with the exception of the computer environment). Actual measures taken by the researchers were quite variable but more positive than the student perceptions. The exception was the workspace environment which students had rated favourably but was quite poorly rated in the researcher evaluated settings.

Overall, the evaluations of the ergonomics or physical environmental factors in the classrooms studied showed a number of problematic issues for students. While they generally rated the quality of the computer resources as positive, students perceived deficiencies in the visual environment of their classrooms which indicated that their might be issues with inadequate lighting or perhaps reflective glare when they are working with the computers. In addition, they perceived problems with the air quality in these classrooms suggesting perhaps problems with inadequate ventilation.

These findings would indicate similar issues which have arisen in earlier studies which have demonstrated that few resources are directed towards creating a positive and safe learning environment in computerized classrooms as the bulk of resources are allocated for the purchase of computer hardware and software. While no statistical links were found between students' satisfaction and the measured perceptions of students on the physical factors described in the questionnaire a link was identified between the psychosocial measure of task orientation and the physical factor of spatial environment. An earlier study (Zandvliet & Fraser, 1998). linked positive psychosocial learning environments with the provision of positive physical spaces. In this, the provision of a positive physical environment becomes an educational issue. Students preoccupied with negative aspects of their surroundings can become distracted from their main task – learning.

Table 7.4. Ergonomic Evaluations of Selected Computer Settings According to Researcher Measurements and Ratings

Setting / Scores	Workspace Environment	Computer Environment	Visual Environment	Spatial Environment	Air Quality
Lower Mainland 1	0	4	2	3	4
Lower Mainland 2a	2	5	5	3	5
Lower Mainland 2b	3	5	5	4	5
Lower Mainland 2c	3	5	5	5	5
Vancouver Island 1	3	4	5	5	4
Vancouver Island 2a	3	5	4	5	4
Vancouver Island 2b	2	5	4	4	4
Vancouver Island 2c	0	4	3	5	4
Interior 1a	3	5	5	3	4
Interior 1b	1	5	3	4	1
Interior 2a	0	4	2	5	5
Interior 2b	1	5	2	5	4
Interior 2c	1	4	2	4	4

6.4 Case Study Results

Case studies were conducted in a number of different geographic regions of the province including: southern Vancouver Island, the Fraser Valley and urban areas in the Lower mainland. Together, the three cases represent different perspectives for the learning environment in BC's emerging networked classrooms. For each of these selected case studies, an analysis of the individualized results for that location were given followed by the results by class on both the physical and psychosocial questionnaire results for the location.

As part of the case studies, school visitations were arranged to most study locations. During these visits, the researchers conducted semi-structured interviews either individually or with small focus groups of teachers. For each aspect of the study, participants were asked open-ended questions about their teaching practices in their internet (web) capable classrooms. Following this, teachers were asked to elaborate on their perceptions of the physical and psychosocial aspects of the learning environment – using the questionnaire scales from the WIHIC and CCEI as a rough guideline for the questioning. In total, 22 teachers were involved with this portion of the study and their anecdotal comments are summarized in this analysis.

6.5 The Physical Setting (Ergonomics)

With reference to the physical environment in networked classrooms, teachers had a number of issues that they believed need addressing by school administrations and government. Firstly, space is an issue with many teachers stating a need for a better design for both computers and an improved workspace which would allow students to use other resources (eg. books, worksheets, etc.) at the same time as they are using the computers. Also, there are issues around the need for adjustable chairs, as students vary significantly in size and stature and this can create unhealthy postures when students work at incorrectly adjusted work stations. Lighting and air quality were also noted as being problematic in many settings supporting the findings of the student questionnaire which rated student perceptions of this variable as consistently low. Agreement on this point probably indicates that this is a serious issue requiring immediate attention. Below are a few teacher comments made by about the physical environment which were typical:

> *Standard chairs don't work, they should be adjustable, so the students can be at the appropriate height for their individual needs ...*
>
> *The height of the desks and tables is inconsistent ...*
>
> *The I-macs are quieter, while the windows machines are nosier. When you design a computer room, you have to think about that ...*
>
> *The I-macs are small and they save a lot of space. Whereas windows machines are not as good in terms of space saving ...*
>
> *In terms of design, I don't like ... having the computers facing the front of the class ...*
>
> *(There is) inconsistent Internet access, with numerous log-offs and crashes ...*
>
> *Students complain about the warm air in the computer room ...*

6.6 Teaching and Learning Practices: Use of the Internet

Teachers stated often that they themselves are using the Internet for research, information, materials and lesson plans. They also commented that their students in a variety of subject disciplines are researching information from Internet sites. Students are using the Internet for research on careers, university and government web sites and library database searches and students taking multimedia and design classes can also use the Internet extensively for a source of graphics and other resources for use in their own web sites and multimedia presentations. Some teachers reported that their students were using the web to understand copyright issues and e-mail. Below are a few typical comments made by teachers about their teaching and learning practices:

Using library sources on the Internet, the students can gather information from many sites ...

(students) use the web for project based research ... (there is a) lack of time to plan more use of the Internet ...

In class, students focus on what's happening and that takes them to the Internet...

Students use the computers to create presentations and they enjoy their assignments a lot better...

Students' work is a lot more representative, more colourful and interesting using (the web) ...

6.7 Psychosocial Learning Environment

Teachers also frequently reported that students collaborate well with each other when using the Internet and that the classroom seems to be more cooperative. Many stated that when there is a disruption, it is when students are off task and are into chat rooms and e-mails. Also, students with good ICT skills are readily involved with group and project work, even if they are not as informed about the subject matter said many teachers. However, research skills for many students were reported as short of adequate and the notion of using the internet for research is a skill to be taught. The following comments were typical:

Students work on projects in combinations: working individually, in pairs or in a small group ...

It's more challenging for regular classrooms ... whereas, in a computer class, there's always something that the students can work on with the computers ...

When the assignment involves a task which involves computer skills, the students who are good on computers, even though they are not necessarily good in the subject area, will be snapped up into a group more easily than they would in a regular classroom ...

It is important for teachers to know that they have a limited amount of time to spend with the class before the students go off into interaction ...

The case study data presented here described a great deal about the context of the emerging web capable classrooms. First, it describes a range of ways in which these settings were being used by teachers across a range of subject disciplines. Second, it highlighted variations and potential deficiencies found in these environments (in both the physical and psychosocial sense). Interviews with teachers indicated that the Internet medium is used largely to assist with projects, research and individualised assignments. Also, students and teachers largely feel positively about their learning environments, but expressed a number of concerns about physical factors such as room layout, workstation height and the temperature and air quality in these settings.

7. Significance and Limitations

This study has presented a unique theoretical framework in a study of a new learning environment -- the networked, computerized classroom. Holistically, the study has interpreted information from three realms of influence relating to Gardiner's (1989) model of conceptual change in technological environments (namely, the technosphere, the sociosphere and the ecosphere). This model was presented at the beginning of this chapter and was embodied in this study by considering jointly the educational context of technology use in schools, relevant ergonomic information about the implementation of computer technology, and the psychosocial learning environment of these new educational 'habitats' for students. All of these factors were considered in relationship to how they influenced a key outcome variable -- students' satisfaction with learning in these environments.

This study is significant because it also jointly considers the physical and psychosocial learning environments in a single study. The study is also significant for its holistic approach to the study of an important new learning environment: the technological classroom. Its approach mirrors methods that have proven effective in a wide variety of research in other settings, including ergonomic studies of technological settings in business and industry.

The major limitations in this study are that results are only descriptive of the learning environment in technological classrooms. Without an experimental design, definitive causal relationships could not be inferred from the data, and so caution would be needed in using the research results to inform educational policy. However, it is hoped that some important trends have emerged from the data that may serve to focus further, more specific research within this area. In particular, the inclusion of the qualitative component to the study is likely to help in clarifying causes and framing future research questions. Another limitation is in the inclusion of only high schools in the study, as results may not be applicable to younger age groups. Further, there may be fundamental, significant differences in learning environments operating within the different districts and regions where this study was conducted. This further complicates an already complex research methodology.

8. Conclusions

Educational institutions are continuing to implement a wide range of instructional technologies in the classroom. With the advent of Internet technologies, the pace of this technological change has become quickened and its implementation becomes more costly. Meanwhile, societal pressures to implement these technologies have continued to increase. In considering the new technological (web capable) classroom, this study makes a case for the closer integration of information technology, curriculum and instruction, and the design of suitable physical learning spaces. In future, all educators will need to be more involved in both the design and implementation of new technologies, the devising of new curricula and teaching methods and, finally, the physical design of schools and of classrooms themselves.

This study describes the learning environment in computerized classrooms as being a complex system in which many competing and interrelated physical, psychosocial and contextual factors are at work which need to be fully considered in shaping good instruction. While many aspects of the computerised/networked classrooms were evaluated as being positive, many other factors such as workspace environments, lighting levels, and air quality showed marked deficiencies, while students also perceived their degree of autonomy and independence as being less than ideal. All of this points to the fact that educational implementations of IT can and should be improved. This may involve diverting some of the resources currently allocated for equipment purchase towards other neglected areas.

Finally, if the considerable potential of the new information technologies (such as web and e-mail resources) is finally to be realised, coherent guidelines must be developed to ensure the technology's effectiveness as a learning tool. Minimally, such guidelines should include consideration of physical and psychosocial factors (with their potential ability to influence outcomes) and give concrete suggestions for the suitable installation and configuration of this equipment in classroom environments. Optimally, such guidelines would also include a detailed consideration of the professional development needs of teachers, in response to the new duties and responsibilities expected of them as they continue to shape physical and psychosocial environments in their new web capable classrooms.

References

Chionh, Y.H., & Fraser, B.J. (1998, April). *Validation of the "What is Happening In This Class" questionnaire.* Paper presented at the annual meeting of the National Association for Research in Science Teaching, San Diego, CA.

Dryden, M., & Fraser, B.J. (1996, April*). Evaluating urban systemic reform using classroom learning environment instruments.* Paper presented at the annual meeting of American Educational Research Association, New York.

Ehrenkrantz, E. (1999). *Planning for Flexibility, Not Obsolescence.* Available:http://www.designshare.com/Research/EEK/Ehrenkrantz1.htm.

Fraser, B.J. (1981). *Test of Science Related Attitudes.* Melbourne: Australian Council for Educational Research.

Fraser, B.J. (1994). Research on classroom and school climate. In D. Gabel (Ed.), *Handbook of research on science teaching and learning* (pp. 527-564). New York: Macmillan.

Fraser, B.J. (1998a). Science learning environments: Assessments, effects, and determinants. In B.J. Fraser & K.G. Tobin (Eds.), *International handbook of science education* (pp. 1-61). London: Kluwer.

Fraser, B.J. (1998b). Classroom environment instruments: Developments, validity and applications. *Learning Environment Research: An International Journal, 1*, 7-33.

Fraser, B.J., & Fisher, D.L. (1983a). Student achievement as a function of person-environment fit: A regression surface analysis. *British Journal of Educational Psychology, 53*, 89-99.

Fraser, B.J., & Fisher, D.L. (1983b). Use of actual and preferred classroom environment scales in person-environment fit research. *Journal of Educational Psychology, 75*, 303-313.

Fraser, B. J., Fisher, D. L., & McRobbie, C. J. (1996, April). *Development, validation and use of personal and class forms of a new classroom environment instrument.* Paper presented at the Annual Meeting of the American Educational Research Association, New York, USA.

Fraser, B.J., Giddings, G.J., & McRobbie, C.J. (1995). Evolution and validation of a personal form of an instrument for assessing science laboratory classroom environments. *Journal of Research in Science Teaching, 32*, 399-422.

Gardiner, W.L. (1989). Forecasting, planning, and the future of the information society. In P. Goumain (Ed.), *High technology workplaces: Integrating technology, management, and design for productive work environments* (pp. 27-39). New York: Van Nostrand Reinhold.

Grandjean, E. (1988). *Ergonomics in computerized offices.* London: Taylor and Francis.

Khoo, H.S., & Fraser, B.J. (1997, April). *The learning environments associated with computer application courses for adults in Singapore.* Paper presented at the annual meeting of the American Educational Research Association, Chicago, IL.

Kirby, C. (1999). Making demands. *American School and University, 72* (4), 34a-34b.

Knirk, F. (1992). Facility requirements for integrated learning systems. *Educational Technology, 32*(9) 26-32.

National Center for Education Statistics (2000, Sept.). *Teacher's tools for the 21st century: A report on teachers, use of technology.* Washington: U.S. Department of Education.

Resta, P. (1998). *Collaborative technologies as a catalyst for changing teacher practices.* Washington: US Department of Education.

Rice, M, & Wilson, E. (1999). How technology aids constructivism in the social studies classroom. *Social Studies, 90*, 28-34.

Straker, L., Harris C., & Zandvliet, D. (2000, Aug.). *Scarring a generation of school children through poor introduction of IT in schools.* Paper presented at the triennial meeting of the International Ergonomics Association.

Swanquist, B. (1998). Wire wise. *American School and University, 71* (4), 32-34.

Teh, G., & Fraser, B.J. (1995a). Associations between student outcomes and geography classroom environment. *International Journal of Research in Geographical and Environmental Education, 4*(1), 3-18.

Teh, G., & Fraser, B.J. (1995b). Development and validation of an instrument for assessing the psychosocial environment of computer-assisted learning classrooms. *Journal of Educational Computing Research, 12*, 177-193.

U.S. Congress, Office of Technology Assessment. (1995). *Teachers & technology: Making the connection.* Washington, DC: U.S. Government Printing Office. ED386155

Walberg, H.J. (1991). Educational productivity and talent development. In B.J. Fraser & H.J. Walberg (Eds.), *Educational environments: Evaluation, antecedents and consequences* (pp. 93-109). London: Pergamon.

Zandvliet, D., & Fraser, B.J. (1998, April). *The physical and psychosocial environment associated with classrooms using new information technologies.* Paper presented at the annual meeting of the American Educational Research Association, San Diego, CA.

Zandvliet D.B. and Straker L. (2001, July). Physical and psychosocial ergonomic aspects of the learning environment in information technology rich classrooms. *Ergonomics, 449*, 838-857.

Chapter 8

ASSESSING AND RESEARCHING THE ONLINE LEARNING ENVIRONMENT

John Clayton
Waikato Institute of Technology
New Zealand

Educational activity is no longer constricted to or confined by text, print based materials, time or space. Online educators are challenged to develop appropriate strategies to deal with new information and communication technology-rich ways of teaching and learning. It appears that the same features that are important to explore in classroom environments, the perceptions of students and teachers of the psychosocial environment, are equally important in the digital world. Student and tutor reactions to and perceptions of this environment will have a significant impact on their performance. Therefore, the use and development of a perceptual measure that explores the online learning environments would be a valued tool. This chapter explores the concepts and procedures used in the development of an online learning environment perceptual measure. Initially the five broad categories of activity that can be identified in the connected computer or online environment are outlined. This overview is followed by a description of the scales and items, the web based delivery and storage procedures used in the creation of the *Online Learning Environment Survey* (OLLES).

1. Introduction

The advent of the microcomputer in the 1980s, the creation of the Internet and the development of the World Wide Web (WWW) have influenced all aspects of modern society including learning (Clayton, 2001; Sangster, 1995; Reid, 1994). Increasingly the perceived benefits of information stored in a digital format are being exploited. The sophistication and ease of supporting web browsers, the creation of Internet search engines, the advancing computer skills of students, mean educational institutions at all levels are using the WWW and Internet to supplement classroom instruction, to give learners the ability to connect to information (instructional and other resources) and to deliver learning experiences (Bonk, Cummings, Hara, Fischler, & Lee, 1999; Zhu & McKnight, 2001). In short the Internet and the WWW have altered approaches to education, have changed, and are continuing to change, the way teachers communicate with learners and the ways learners communicate with each other (McGovern & Norton, 2001; Newhouse, 2001a). Educators are challenged to develop appropriate strategies to deal with new information and communication technology-rich ways of teaching and learning (Bates, 2000).

Over the last three decades, learning environment researchers have recognised student and tutor reactions to, and perceptions of, the learning environment they participate within have a significant impact on their performance (Fraser, 2001; Fraser & Fisher, 1994). This chapter will focus on the concepts and procedures used in the development of an online learning environment perceptual measure. Initially, the five broad categories of activity that can be identified in the connected computer or online environment will be outlined. This will be followed by an overview of learning environment research and the social climate dimensions used in the construction of scales and items. This overview will be followed by a description of the scales and items, the web-based delivery and storage procedures used in the creation of the *Online Learning Environment Survey* (OLLES), a perceptual measure currently being developed and piloted by the author.

1.1 What is 'Online' Learning?

By reviewing the term 'online learning' we could provide a simple definition, 'the use by learners and tutors of connected (online) computers to participate in educational activities (learning)'. While this definition is technically correct it fails to explain the full range and use of connected computers in the classroom. To Radford (1997) the term 'online learning' is used to denote material that is accessible via a computer using networks or telecommunications rather than material accessed on paper or other non-networked medium. Chang & Fisher (1999) would describe a web-based learning environment as consisting of digitally formatted content resources and communication devices to allow interaction. Zhu and McKnight (2001) describe online instruction as any formal educational process in which the instruction occurs when the learner and the instructor are not in the same place and technology is used to provide a communication link between the instructor and students.

The range of definitions of online learning is a reflection of the variety of ways educators, at all levels, use connected computers in learning. For example, in one situation, **scenario one,** a group of 14-year-old students, following a pre-prepared unit in a supervised computer laboratory, may use the information storage capacity of the WWW to gather additional resources to prepare a presentation on Antarctica. A second group, **scenario two**, of 16-year-olds, studying the same topic in a classroom with a dedicated computer work station situated by the teachers' desk, could use the communicative functions of the Internet to establish mail lists with Antarctic staff to follow studies being undertaken on weather patterns. A third group, **scenario three,** of 12-year-olds, consisting of small pockets of learners in isolated locations using home-based connected workstations, may use an educational courseware package, incorporating information storage and communicative functions, to participate in a complete distance unit studying animal life in the Antarctic. Each of the groups described have used connected computers in different ways to achieve different objectives. The technical competencies required, the learning support needed and the physical location of the students in each case appears to be distinct.

Scenario one illustrated how the information storage and retrieval functions of the WWW could be used to expand available student resources. In this scenario, students could be directly supervised and assisted in their tasks by a teacher, physically present, responsible for a dedicated computer suite established at the school.

Scenario two demonstrated how the communication features of connected computers could be used to provide authentic examples to enrich student understanding. In this scenario students could work independently of the teacher, who was however present to offer guidance and support.

Scenario three described how web-based educational management platforms could be used to provide educational opportunities for isolated pockets of students. In this scenario, students are completely independent and they rely on the information and communication technologies provided by their tutor for guidance and support. Initially, it appears to be impossible to investigate each scenario using a common instrument, there does not appear to be any 'commonality'. However, on closer examination we find this is not the case. Relationships identified within the online learning environment that can be described and investigated are explained in more detail in the following section.

1.2 Identification of Broad Features of Online Learning Activity

In each of the scenarios described in the previous section, there is an assumption that students have a functional knowledge of computer operations and are able to:

- know if the computer is turned on or turned off,
- use a keyboard and computer mouse,
- view information presented on a visual display unit,
- select and/or use appropriate software applications.

A student-computer relationship, common to all scenarios, can be identified and therefore investigated. This can be further expanded by focusing on our understanding of the process of learning and the relationships created in this process. In each of the scenarios, the learners engage in purposeful learning activities designed and facilitated by a tutor. A tutor-student relationship, common to all scenarios, can once again, be identified and therefore investigated. Morihara (2001) broadens these two relationships to include student-student interaction, student-media interaction (content knowledge in a variety of formats) and the outcomes of learning in the environment created. Haynes (2002) outlines four features of online activity. These are:

- student – interface relationship,
- student – tutor relationships,
- student – student relationships,
- student – content relationships,

Although these four broad categories appear to identify all aspects of online learning they do not investigate how the learner, as an individual, reacts to and reflects on his/her experiences in this environment.

The importance of creating time for and encouraging self-reflection of the learning process is well documented by constructivists (Gilbert, 1993; Gunstone, 1994; Hewson, 1996; Posner, Strike, Hewson, & Gertzog, 1982). It would appear to be crucial to investigate if, when and how, reflective activity takes place. Therefore, there appears to be 5 broad categories of online learning activity that can be identified, described and therefore investigated in the online environment. These are:

1. **Student - Interface Interaction** (What are the features of the interface created that enhance / inhibit student learning and navigation?)
2. **Student - Student Relationships** (How, why and when students communicate with each other and what is the nature of this communication?)
3. **Student - Tutor Relationships** (How, why and when students communicate with their tutor and what is the nature of this communication?)
4. **Student - Media Interaction** (How is the student is engaged with digitally stored information and how do they relate to the information presented?)
5. **Student Reflection Activities.** (How are students encouraged to reflect on their learning, are they satisfied with the environment and how do they relate to the environment created?)

How these relationships can be investigated is explained in the next section.

2. Researching Online Learning

Investigations of computer-networked learning: the use of the World Wide Web (WWW) and students' and teachers' perceptions of the learning environments created, is still in it's infancy. A number of studies have focused on tutor and/or student acceptance of electronic delivery of course materials (Benson & Vincent, 1997; Clayton, 2000), the most appropriate computer technologies to use in teaching in these new environments (Cottman, 1997; Ortiz, 1993), the costs of developing and delivering technology rich courses (Bartolic-Zlomislic & Bates, 1999; Harapnuik, Montgomerie, & Torgerson, 1998; Morgan, 2000). While these studies are informative and serve to highlight the potential of using connected computers and the WWW in teaching and learning, they fail to critically examine the actual learning environment created or the interactions that take place within it.

2.1 Learning Environment Research

For over 30 years researchers have found the perceptions of participants undertaking educational activities, provide a comprehensive insight into the environment they work within (Fraser, 2001). Indeed research has noted that student achievement was enhanced in those environments which students felt comfortable in and positive about (Dorman, Fraser, & McRobbie, 1994; Newby & Fisher, 1997; Yarrow, Millwater, & Fraser, 1997). The investigation of learning environments using widely applicable questionnaires is a rich and growing research area (Fraser, 1998a). Therefore, the development and use of a perceptual measure to investigate the learning environment created in online learning activities would be a valued tool.

Through ongoing research, instruments developed have been proved to be flexible (Ommundsen, 2001), reliable and cost effective (Fraser & Wubbels, 1995). The influence of constructivism and growing use of computers in education is reflected in the number of surveys and inventories that have been developed and tested exploring the influence they are having on learning environments (Maor, 2000; Taylor & Maor, 2000). The strong background of learning environment research demonstrates the feasibility of developing perceptual measures capable of successfully analysing the learning environments created when using computer-connected and web-based teaching and learning.

2.2 Social Climate Dimensions and the Influence of Rudolf Moos

Moos (1976) has convincingly argued that there are three dimensions underpinning all socially created environments. Vastly different social environments, including educational, can be investigated using these social climate dimensions.

Relationship Dimensions – assess "the extent to which people are involved in the setting, the extent to which they support and help each other, and the extent to which they express themselves freely and openly" (Moos, 1979, p. 14).

Personal Development Dimensions – assess "the basic directions along which personal growth and self-enhancement tend to occur in the particular environment" (Moos, 1976, p. 331).

System Maintenance & System Change Dimensions – measure the "extent to which the environment is orderly and clear in it's expectations, maintains control and is responds to change" (Moos, 1979, p. 16)

These three broad categories of dimensions are based upon individual dimensions or scales. For example the relationship dimensions could include dimensions of involvement, cohesiveness, and support. The personal development dimensions could include dimensions of independence, competition and autonomy. The system maintenance and system change dimensions could include dimensions of order and organization, clarity, control and innovation (Moos, 1976, pp. 330-331). These dimensions are not isolated, independent elements they are interactive. The broad dimensions and interactions are illustrated in Figure 8.1.

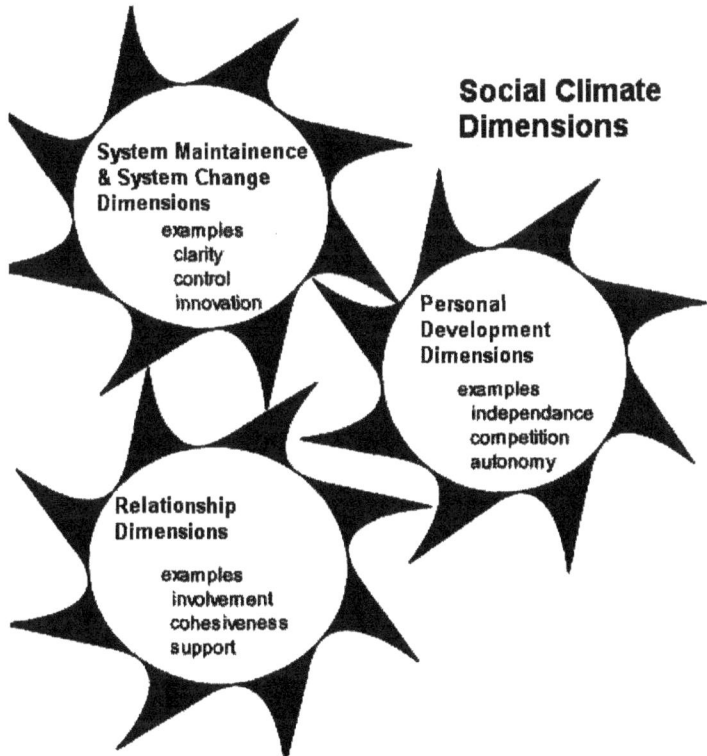

Figure 8.1. Moos' social climate dimensions

The three dimensions crafted by Moos have been used extensively in the construction and development of a number of learning environment inventories and surveys (Fraser, 1998a, 1998b; Walker, 2002a; Yarrow et al., 1997) and should be used in the development of any instrument investigating the online learning environment which is the focus of the next section.

3. Online Learning Environment Survey (OLLES)

Any instrument developed to explore the online learning environment should firstly, be based solidly on past research in learning environment research, secondly, incorporate and where necessary expand upon previous studies undertaken in this area and finally, be aware of and incorporate constructivist views of learning on the need to create environments that promote conceptual change. The development of a perceptual measure incorporating these criteria, the identification of potential scales and items is the focus of this section.

3.1 Student Interface Interaction

3.1.1 Overview
When the learner 'logs on' to the computer, (i.e. establishes a connection), immediately an interactive relationship is created. The learner through input devices (key board mouse, microphone, scanner) interacts with the computer. The computer through a range of output devices (printer, visual display unit, sound card, video card) interacts with the learner. The relationship created, while apparently 'two way', is input dependant. For example, to print a page the learner, must instruct the computer to print. When the computer receives the instruction, it processes the command and carries out the task. Without input the computer does not function. Online activities are also input dependant. The learner must select an appropriate 'tool' to participate fully in the course. It would appear important to investigate how this interface is structured, laid out and organized.

Schroeder (1997) found, when studying activities in virtual worlds, two levels shaped how virtual worlds were organized. Students continual use of, or the lack of use of, particular tools influenced the shaping of the system. Tools consistently used are expanded and developed. Tools rarely used are modified or eliminated. Morine-

Dershimer and Kent (1999) investigated organizational or structural issues; they argued students must understand the specific rules and expectations of communication within the environment. Student participation and achievement will be governed by how well they understand the rules. However, too detailed explanations of how to use the site and the tools provided can be detrimental. The support tools used, and the explanation of their use should be minimal (Swaak & De Jong, 2001). In short the interface should be carefully designed, structured and explained to orient the user and provide a sense of direction (Zhu & McKnight, 2001). It is assumed that an easily navigable interface, with clear instructions, will reduce anxiety and correspondingly increase student confidence and achievement.

There are three broad factors to be considered when designing or investigating the interface for online courses. Firstly, there is what could be regarded as technological issues. What is the level of technology required to make the system operate smoothly? This would include software applications, browser capabilities and plug-ins. Secondly, what is the required level of student technological capability to successfully learn within the environment? This would include the types of software applications students are required to use and the types of activities students will be engaged in. Thirdly, how is the environment organized and ordered? This would include the ease of navigation, the visual layout of tools on the screen and the explanations provided.

3.1.2 Potential Scales and Items
Previous research has, to some extent, investigated the broad factors outlined above. Newby and Fisher (1997) in the instrument *Attitudes toward Computers and Computer Courses* developed items using the scales, 'Lack of Anxiety' and 'Enjoyment'. These scales explored the extent to which the student felt comfortable using a computer and the extent to which students enjoyed using a computer. It was found these two scales were reliable, and although needing further testing, could be used with some confidence. For this instrument it is proposed a scale 'Computer Competence' will be developed. The scale, the Moos dimension it fits within, and an example of an item associated with the scale are presented in Table 8.1.

Fraser et al., (1992) in the *Science Laboratory Environment Inventory* (SLEI) developed items using the scale 'Rule Clarity'. This scale investigated the extent to which behaviour in the laboratory is guided by formal rules. Teh and Fraser (1994) in exploring the effects of computer-assisted learning in the development of the *Geography Classroom Environment Inventory* (GCEI) developed items using the scale "Resource Adequacy". This scale investigated the extent to which the computer hardware and software used by students was adequate to run the software application. Maor and Fraser (1993) in the instrument *Computer Classroom Environment Inventory* developed items using the scale 'Material Environment'. This investigated the extent to which the computer hardware and software was adequate and user friendly. All three scales have been found to be reliable. For this instrument it is proposed a scale 'Material Environment' will be developed (see Table 8.1).

3.2 Student - Student Relationships

3.2.1 Overview
Applications have been developed in web-based environments for groups of people to share ideas and resources. In web enclosed environments, (those environments accessed with individual entry codes), these applications have been expanded and specific tools, for example Activity Room (Maor, 1998), have been developed to provide the ability to share ideas, concerns, thoughts and resources. The user, by using the appropriate tool, is able to establish relationships with others connected to their network. Three relationships can be created in a computer connected or web based environment. Firstly, private communication between individuals can occur (i.e., one-to-one). Secondly, individuals can communicate with small, or large groups (i.e., one-to-many). Thirdly, communication can occur that involves all participants (i.e., many-to-many) (Miller & Miller, 1999). The individual's participation, the perceived success or failure of these communication groups established, is dependant upon individuals being able to use the tool to pose queries or respond to others' queries. When investigating student-student relationships a focus should be placed on how the learner generates and responds to the queries generated by individuals and groups on a personal level.

3.2.2 Potential Scales and Items
Previous research has, to some extent, investigated the factors outlined above. Newby and Fisher (1997) in the perceptual measure *Computer*

Laboratory Environment Inventory (CLEI) developed items using the scale 'Student Cohesiveness'. This scale explored the extent to which students know, help, and are supportive of each other. Newhouse (2001b) in the *New Classroom Environment Instrument* (NCEI) developed items using the scale 'Affiliation'. This scale explores the level of friendship that students feel for each other, that is, the extent to which they help each other with homework, get to know each other easily, and enjoy working together. In the development of this instrument it was proposed a scale 'Student Collaboration' be developed (see Table 8.1).

3.3 Student - Tutor Relationships

3.3.1 Overview
While student - student relationships, allowing students to contribute to each other's growth and development and providing students with a sense of autonomy, is important, student - student interaction in isolation is insufficient. There is a need for guidance from the tutor on aspects of content the students may find difficulty comprehending or concepts they do not fully understand (Roth, Tobin, & Ritchie, 2001). The moderating of, and the tutor's ability to guide and monitor students' discussion is regarded as the key to successful e-education (Bunker & Ellis, 2001; Salmon, 2000). There is a notion of circularity in this communication process. Input from one part of the communication structure established leads to changes in the other parts of the system. For example, student communication on a particular concept will affect how the tutor responds. The tone and detail of the tutor's response will affect students' future postings. It could be argued students' perceptions of the tutor's interpersonal behaviour are an important aspect of the learning environment and will influence their achievement and performance (Levy, Rodriguez, & Wubbels, 1993). Although, in a connected computer environment, the tutor is only one node on the network there are a number of relationships the tutor can create and maintain. Firstly, private communication between the tutor and individual students can occur (i.e., one-to-one). Secondly, the tutor can communicate with small, or large groups, established within the course (i.e., one-to-many) (Miller & Miller, 1999).

In many connected computer or web-based courses there is a second, invisible, level of tutor-student communication, this is in the form of preset computer marked activities. The communication channel can be regarded as invisible in that there appears to be no direct relationship between student activity, marks, and feedback received, and students. The computer - student relationship appears to be the dominant and sole relationship. However, this does not take into account the tutors' creation of the activities and their pre-recorded responses to student actions. The tutor instructs the computer to respond in particular ways to student input. Since the tutor is responsible for the task design, type of input and nature of response, the relationship established is a student - tutor relationship, mediated by the computer (Clayton, 2002). Since the types of questions posed will influence student achievement (Morine-Dershimer, & Kent, 1999), tutors must be able to ask suitable questions and sequence those questions in an order that will generate understanding (Gilbert, Boulter, & Rutherford, 2000). The pre-recorded feedback preset by the tutor to activate on student input, will influence student motivation, interaction and progress (Ho & Tabata, 2001). It has been argued there is a positive relationship between academic efficacy, students' perceptions of their competence to do specific activities, and academic motivation, effort and performance (Dorman, 2001).

When investigating tutor-student relationships there are two considerations that must be taken into account. Firstly, how the tutor responds to the queries generated by individuals and groups on a personal level, secondly, how they create and maintain computer mediated interactive activities.

3.3.2 Potential Scales and Items

Previous research has, to some extent, investigated the broad factors outlined above. Newhouse (2001b) in the NCEI developed items using the scale 'Teacher Support". This scale explored the amount of help, concern, and friendship, which the teacher directs towards students and the extent to which the teacher talks openly with students, trusts them, and is interested in their ideas. Taylor and Maor (2000) in the *Constructivist On-Line Learning Environment Survey* (COLLES) developed items using the scale 'Affective Support'. This scale investigated the extent to which sensitive and encouraging support is provided by tutors. Walker (2001) in the *Distance Education Learning Environment Survey* (DELES) developed items using the scale 'Instructor Support'. This scale investigated the extent to which the teacher is approachable and responds quickly with feedback. For this instrument it is proposed a scale 'Tutor Support' will be developed (Table 8.1).

Maor and Fraser (1993) in the CCEI developed items using the scale 'Open-Endedness'. This scale investigated the extent to which computer activities emphasized an open-ended approach to inquiry. Teh and Fraser (1994) in the GCEI developed items using the scale 'Innovation'. This scale investigated the extent to which the teacher planned new and varying activities and techniques, and encouraged students to think creatively. Walker (2001) in the DELES developed items using the scale 'Active Learning'. This scale investigated the extent to which students had the opportunity to take an active role in their learning. For this instrument it is proposed a scale 'Active Learning' will be developed (Table 8.1).

3.4 Student - Media Interaction

There are a number of aspects that need to be taken into account when reviewing content provided to students in a connected computer environment. Firstly, there are physical considerations. When using print based materials, the student generally reads the material at 'arms length' moving from page to page by hand. The physical position of the arms in relation to the eyes means the print material is held below head level and the reader looks down on the information presented. Computer-presented information is viewed on a visual display unit (VDU) that is in a fixed position, generally positioned at eye-level. The presence of input devices in front of the VDU, keyboard and mouse, ensures the material is presented at a distance further than arms length. To view the information, the reader uses the keyboard or mouse to move from section to section. Secondly, there are differences in presentation. Information in print can be regarded as static, the text, graphics and photos used to explain concepts or illustrate processes remaining constantly unchanging. While it is possible to enhance material by supplementing the text with audio or videotapes, these are separate and distinct items utilizing specialist devices. Information presented via the computer is dynamic, the text, graphics and photos can be animated to illustrate complex relationships. Audio and video components can be embedded in the material and be reviewed on the same device.

There are many critical components to online education, none of which have anything to do with the presentation or the technology used in the production or delivery. Learning materials must be complete and well organized (Kearsley, 1998), students need to know what is going to happen, what is to be learned, why it is to be learned, the purpose of it, and how they will be assessed. Therefore a guide, which outlines learning objectives, provides self-evaluation exercises, glossary of key terms and summaries of the material presented, should be an integral part of the learning package (Gilbert, et al., 2000; Kearsley, 1998). Swaak & De Jong (2001) argue that if information is clearly organized and assignments are well defined, students should have no problem in following the sequence and making sense of content provided. As well as providing the student with an overview of how the course is structured and organized, tutors must take care to sequence and chunk material to meet the needs of the students participating in the course. Firstly, tutors must be able to anticipate students' level of reasoning skills and be aware of problems they may encounter when dealing with particular concepts or reviewing content presented (Zembal-Saul, Starr, & Krajcik, 1999). The importance of the teacher knowing the subject and being able to intervene at the appropriate moment is critical (Roth et al., 2001). While students should have sufficient information, either provided within the course or hyper-linked to, to complete tasks set (Frazer, 1986), material to be learned needs to broken down into comprehensible chunks to facilitate understanding and retention (Kearsley, 1998). The most general ideas of a subject should be presented first and then progressively differentiated in terms of detail and specificity (Chang & Fisher, 2001). In chunking information, it is argued students are more likely to form an opinion if they are forced to think about it. The tutor must be able to provide objective information so the students can reflect and form their own opinion (Frazer, 1986). Owen (2000) has argued students engage in activities, which generate ideas and knowledge (they are producers not consumers) in order to 'trigger' prior knowledge we should make at least a minimum amount of knowledge available, particularly explanations. Chang and Fisher (2001) argue that instruction should be designed to facilitate extrapolation and or fill in the gaps (going beyond the information given) and to facilitate perception; realistic environmental settings should be used in the presentation of materials.

When investigating student – media interactions there are two considerations that must be taken into account, firstly, how the information is sequenced and chunked and does the sequencing and chunking assist the online learner, secondly, how is information visually displayed and does this presentation appeal to participants?

3.4.1 Potential Scales and Items

Previous research has, to some extent, investigated the broad factors outlined above. Teh and Fraser (1994) in the GCEI developed items using the scale 'Innovation". This scale investigated the extent to which the teacher plans new and varying activities and techniques, and encourages students to think creatively. Maor and Fraser (1993) in the CCEI developed items using the scale 'Organization'. This scale investigated the extent to which classroom activities were planned and well organized. Newhouse (2001b) in the NCEI developed items using the scale 'Involvement' This scale investigated the extent to which students had attentive interest in class activities and participated in discussions and the extent to which students did additional work on their own and enjoyed the class. Chang and Fisher (2001) in the *Web-Based Learning Environment Inventory* (WEBLEI) developed items using the scale 'Information Structure and Design Activities'. A section of this scale explored if the course was well structured and organized. For this instrument it is proposed a scale 'Order and Organization' will be developed (Table 8.1).

Maor and Fraser (1993) in the CCEI developed items using the scale 'Organization'. This scale investigated the extent to which classroom activities were planned and well organized. Chang and Fisher (2001) in the WEBLEI developed items using the scale 'Information Structure and Design Activities'. A section of this scale explored whether the materials presented followed accepted instructional design standards. Instructional design standards include the visual display of material reviewed. For this instrument it is proposed a scale 'Information Design and Appeal' will be developed (Table 8.1).

3.5 Student Reflection Activities

In web-based and computer-connected learning environments, the computer mediates all the relationships created within that environment. Electronic mediation eliminates traditional physical cues that are present in face-to-face relationships. The tutor cannot smile, glare or raise an eyebrow if things are going right or wrong. Students cannot nudge or wink at each other or look bored, excited or vacant when the tutor is explaining concepts. These physical cues within the face-to-face classroom environment prompt students and teachers to stop, modify or continue with the behaviour being exhibited. In the web-based and computer-connected environments these physical cues are not present. To attract attention, from the tutor or other participants in this virtual environment, they have to use the input devices and tools provided to communicate with others, to respond, to ask for clarification or provide support. Students then have to be conscious of their own learning and be able to recognize when they must actively seek answers or provide support. After the course has been completed, students must also reflect on the environment they have been participating within and ask themselves if they were satisfied with learning in the environment created. For example, did they enjoy learning in this environment, were they motivated by the environment, did the course meet their learning needs? In short, students must reflect on the way they learn both during the activities within the virtual learning environment and after the course has been completed.

Zariski and Styles (2000) have argued that very little is known about how students acquire, modify or adapt appropriate learning strategies to suit the new environment of online learning. Zariski and Styles have speculated it is likely that students need be highly self regulated and be responsible for organizing and reflecting on their learning. They must become self-directed learners. Radloff and De La Harpe (2001) argue that self-directed learners will not only have knowledge and understanding of content, they will also have a positive attitude to learning and to themselves as learners. They will have the ability to reflect on their learning and a willingness to continue learning throughout life. To achieve this, students must have opportunities for reflection and introspection in order to make sense of experience gained (Armarego & Roy, 2000). There are a number of strategies that can be employed to achieve this result. Zariski & Styles (2000) argue students will have a more self-regulatory and more sympathetic approach if they have the opportunity to frankly discuss the benefits and drawbacks of online learning. Maor (1999) provided students with the opportunity to have shared control over 20% of their assessment. She believed this self-assessment would increase self-reflection amongst the participants. Fairholme, Dougiamas, and Dreher (2000) outline the strategy of students compiling weekly online journals based around probing questions that would encourage students to reflect on their activities.

When investigating student–reflective activities there are two considerations that must be taken into account. Firstly, in what ways are students encouraged to reflect on their learning? Secondly, are learners satisfied with their online learning experience?

3.5.1 Potential Scales and Items
Previous research has, to some extent, investigated the broad factors outlined above. Taylor and Maor (2000) in the COLLES developed items using the scale 'Reflective Thinking'. This scale investigated the extent to which critical reflective thinking is occurring in association with online peer discussion. Fraser (1990) in the *Individualized Classroom Environment Questionnaire* (ICEQ) developed items using the scale 'Investigation'. This scale explores the emphasis on the skills and processes of inquiry and their use in problem solving and investigation. Maor and Fraser (1993) in the CCEI developed items using the scales, 'Investigation' and 'Satisfaction'. These scales investigated the extent to which the student was encouraged to engage in inquiry learning and the extent to which the student was interested in using the computer and in conducting investigations. Walker (2002b) in the DELES developed items using the scale of 'Enjoyment. This scale investigated the extent to which students enjoyed learning in a distance environment. It must be noted Walker regards this scale as a 'measure' and as such cannot be regarded as a social climate dimension. Chang and Fisher (2001) in the (WEBLEI) developed items using the scale 'Qualia'. This scale explored six categories, enjoyment, confidence, accomplishments, success, frustration and tedium. For this instrument it is proposed a scale 'Reflective Thinking' will be developed (Table 8.1).

4. Electronic Delivery and Collection of Data

The sophistication of electronic databases and the interconnectivity of dynamic WebPages with these databases would appear to make the electronic collection storage and manipulation of data generated by perceptual measures an attractive and cost effective option. Therefore, it is envisaged that *Online Learning Environment Survey* developed in this study will use these features. The procedures used are explained in this section.

Table 8.1. Description of Scales and Sample Items for each Scale of the OLLES

Scale Name	Moos' Dimension	Description of Scale Extent to which...	Sample Item
Computer Competence	Personal Development	The student feels comfortable and enjoys using computers in the online environment.	I have no problems using a range of computer technologies.
Material Environment	System Maintenance & System Change	The computer hardware and software are adequate and user friendly.	The instructions provided to use the tools within the site are clear and precise.
Student Collaboration	Relationship	Students work together, know, help, support and are friendly to each other.	I communicate regularly with other students in this course.
Tutor Support	Relationship	The tutor guides students in their learning and provides sensitive, ongoing and encouraging support.	The feedback I receive from my tutor helps me identify the things I do not understand.
Active Learning	Personal Development	The computer activities support students in they're learning and provide ongoing and relevant feedback.	The feedback I receive from activities / quizzes are meaningful.
Order and Organization	System Maintenance & System Change	Class activities are well organized and assist student comprehension.	The learning objectives are clearly stated for each topic.
Information Design and Appeal	System Maintenance & System Change	Class materials are clear, stimulating and visually pleasing to the student.	The material presented is visually appealing.
Reflective Thinking	Personal Development	Reflective activities are encouraged and how students enjoyed learning and participating in this environment.	I feel a sense of satisfaction and achievement about this learning environment.

4.1 Delivery of Instrument and Collection of Data

The growth of connected computing technologies has meant web-based surveying is becoming more widely used in educational research (Shannon, Johnson, Searcy, & Lott, 2002). It has been argued the Web offers significant advantages over more traditional survey techniques (Solomon, 2001). For example, the use of connected computing technologies offers researchers a simpler, more streamlined method for the collection of data. With effective software, the tedious data entry stage is eliminated and there is a greater assurance that data are acquired free from common entry errors (Schmidt, 1997). Since there is no separate data entry phase, tabled results can be available for analysis soon after the data collection phase (De Leeuw & Nicholls II, 1996). The costs in terms of both time and money for publishing a survey on the web are low, compared with costs associated with conventional surveying methods. For example, costs of data entry, paper, ink and printing are eliminated, and as a result, research can be much less expensive (Baron & Siepmann, 2000). It also appears that web-based surveys are reliable. Carini, Hayek, Kuh, and Ouimet (2001) in analyzing data collected from first year and Senior College students in both web-based and conventional methods, found that when discrepancies exist they tend to be very small. Indeed it appeared that items related to computing and information technology exhibited moderately more favourable responses when answered via the Web. They concluded, that given the very small effects observed for most items, their study should help allay concerns that data gathered via the Web may be very different than those collected from paper. These findings are supported by Baron and Siepmann (2000). Their research also found there were no significant differences between web and interview subjects in any variables.

In the field of learning environment research it has been common to use 'pencil and paper' forms (Fisher & Fraser, 1990; Fraser et al., 1992; Fraser & Walberg, 1995). However, as in general educational research, web-based surveys are growing in popularity and use. For example, Maor (2000) has developed the *Constructivist Virtual Learning Environment Survey*, which uses a digitally submitted questionnaire as the method of gaining data. Joiner, Malone and Haimes (2002) in the collection of data during an investigation of the effects of calculus reform, used electronically connected database. Walker (2002a) during the development of the DELES found a web-based version of the actual form, while taking longer to develop initially, is much faster to reduce and analyse. It could be argued the use of web-based surveys in learning environment research will continue to grow as the software programmes and electronic databases used for conducting surveys and collecting data grow in sophistication and ease of use.

4.2 Database Procedures

When using dynamic web pages to generate data to be stored on a digital database, a clear set of procedures must be established to ensure data are gathered, stored, retrieved and manipulated in a consistently reliable manner. Before outlining the procedures to be followed it would be profitable, at this early stage, to distinguish between the terms data and information. Data can be seen to be a collection of raw facts stored in isolation. In this raw state, data have generally little meaning. On the other hand, information can be seen to be raw pieces of data that have been selected and manipulated to convey meaning; in short, it is useful (Whitten, Bently, & Barlow, 1994). If we accept these definitions are useful it becomes important when creating a database, to ensure that the data generated, by the participants' completion of an online form, in this case the OLLES, is lodged in a specific place established within the database and that this data is able to be easily manipulated to produce information in the form of reports that is useful to the researcher. It would appear that a relationship database would meet the requirements outlined above. A relational database stores all its data inside tables. All operations (searching, manipulating, analyzing) on data are done on the tables themselves. The results of these operations are the creation of other tables, which can then be utilized to report on the data collected (Lozano, 1999). Since a relationship database is to be created, we need to identify the types of tables we are going to create and how these tables are internally structured. To best illustrate the procedures to be used a brief scenario is outlined below.

Participant Action	Database Procedure
Individual participant accesses the OLLES form.	A numerical identifier, a key, is randomly produced for each participant.
Participant views a scale based upon the three social climate dimensions identified by Moos.	A separate table is created for each scale. This table is uniquely identified using alphabetic characters.
Participant completes individual items within the scale.	Each item in the scale is uniquely identified using the alphabetic characters used in the table produced for each scale and a numeric character to identify each item.

From this brief scenario, we can now create the tables and identify the relationships used in the collection of electronic data. The database will have the generic heading of 'Online Learning Environment Survey'. This database will be divided into three overarching categories based upon the social climate dimensions identified by Moos. These three

Assessing and Researching the Online Learning Environment 177

categories will be further divided into tables to represent individual scales. These tables will be structured upon individual items. A table of the database structure and the created relationships is illustrated in Figure 8.2.

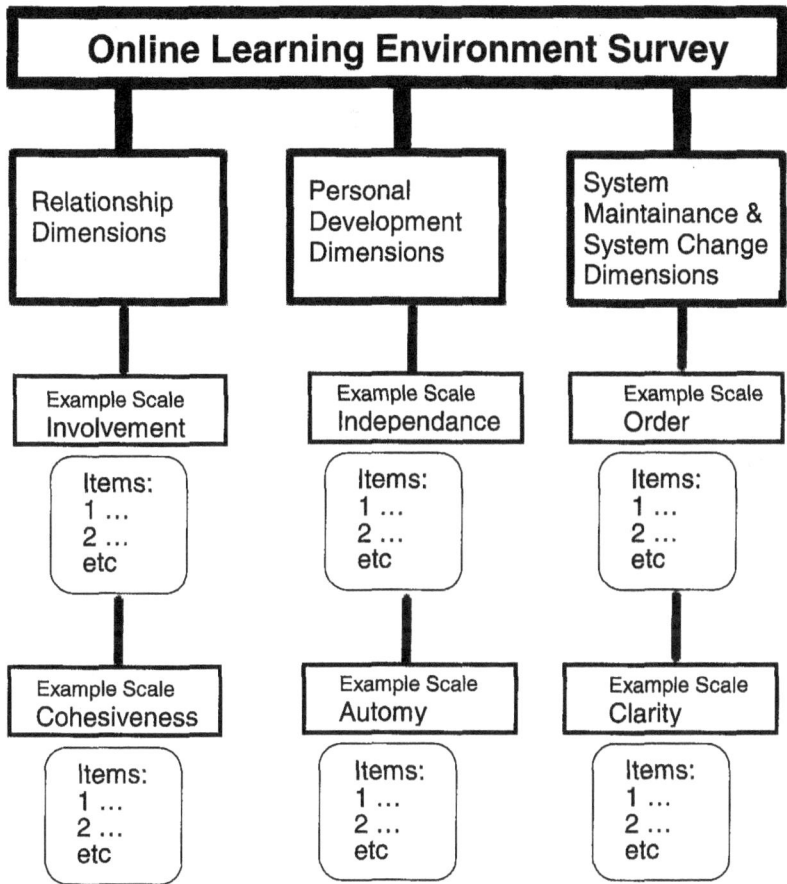

Figure 8. 2. Database structure and relationships

To effectively investigate or query different tables within the database each table and item must be clearly identified and labelled. For example, a table based on the scale of Involvement is within the relationship dimensions outlined by Moos. The items that make up this scale can be identified numerically (1, 2, 3, ... etc). The social climate dimension and scale can be identified alphabetically, I = Involvement,

RD = Relationship Dimension. By using these alphabetical and numerical identifiers we can label each item within the table. For example, the third item within a table created to store data generated by the scale involvement would be labelled RDI 3. The label is made up of a base identifier (RDI) and a numerical identifier for the particular item. An example, using the relationship dimension and codes is illustrated below.

Dimension	Relationship (Code **RD**)	
Scale	Involvement (Code **I**)	
Base Identifier	**RDI**	
Item 3		Code
I communicate regularly with other students in this course.		*RDI 3*

5. Summary

In the not too distant future educational activity will no longer be constricted to or confined by text, print based materials, time or space. Educationalists will be challenged to develop appropriate strategies to deal with new information and communication technology-rich ways of teaching and learning. It appears evident those features explored in learning environment research, the perceptions of students and teachers of the environment, the social and psychological factors, will be as equally important to research in digital environments. The development of a perceptual measure investigating the online learning environment is timely and can make a significant contribution to teaching, learning and research.

- Firstly, online educators in the move to develop courses for online delivery should be careful to ensure participants, both learners and tutors, are comfortable in and benefit from the learning environment created. The availability of this instrument, and the data generated by it's application, will serve to illuminate practices assisting learners and tutors adjust to the online environment and identify practices creating barriers to learning.
- Secondly the availability of this instrument, illustrates how online learning environments, and the changes that might occur within these environments, can be monitored for effectiveness.
- Thirdly, while the instrument should not, at this stage, be regarded as consistent, reliable or valid, it could be viewed as contributing

significantly to the larger research field of learning environment studies.
- The demand for more flexibility in education, the improvement in information and communication technological capabilities, and the reducing costs of such technologies are making electronically mediated education increasingly more viable, attractive, cost effective and valued. This growth of online educational opportunities needs to be matched by a similar growth in educational research focused upon the learning environments created in the digital world. The development and refinement of learning environment instruments such as OLLES are recommended as one way to conduct such research.

References

Armarego, J., & Roy, G. G. (2000, February). Management of a student centred online environment. In A. Herrmann & M. Kulski (Eds.), *Flexible Futures in Tertiary Teaching* Proceedings of the 9th Annual Teaching Learning Forum. Perth: Curtin University of Technology. http://cea.curtin.edu.au/tlf/tlf2000/armarego.html.

Baron, J., & Siepmann, M. (2000). Using web questionnaires for judgment and decision making research. In M. Birnbaum (Ed.), *Psychological experiments on the Internet* (pp. 235-267). New York: Academic Press.

Bartolic-Zlomislic, S., & Bates, T. (1999). Investing in online learning: potential benefits and limitations. *Canadian Journal of Communication, 24*, 349 - 366.

Bates, T. (2000). *Distance education in dual mode higher education institutions: Challenges and changes.* Retrieved March 15, 2003, from University of British Columbia, Continuing Studies: Distance Education & Technology Web site: http://bates.cstudies.ubc.ca/

Benson, R., & Vincent, M. (1997, September, October). *Electronic delivery of study materials: the students' response.* Paper presented at the Open, Flexible and distance learning: Education and training in the 21st century conference, Launceston: University of Tasmania.

Bonk, C., Cummings, J., Hara, N., Fischler, R., & Lee, S. (1999). A ten level Web integration continuum for higher education: New Resources, Partners, Courses, and Markets. Retrieved March 15, 2003, from Personal Home Page of Curtis Bonk, Presentations, Website: http://php.indiana.edu/~cjbonk/paper/edmdia99.html

Bunker, A., & Ellis, R. (2001, February). Using bulletin boards for learning: What do staff and students need to know in order to use boards effectively? In A. Herrmann & M. Kulski (Eds.), *Expanding Horizons in Teaching and Learning*. Proceedings of the 10th Annual Teaching Learning Forum. Perth: Curtin University of Technology. http://cea.curtin.edu.au/tlf/tlf2001/bunker.html

Carini, R., Hayek, J., Kuh, G., & Ouimet, J. (2001, June). *College student responses to web and paper surveys: Does mode matter?* Paper presented at the meeting of the Association for Institutional Research, Long Beach, CA.

Chang, V., & Fisher, D. (2001, December). *The validation and application of a new learning environment instrument to evaluate online learning in higher education.* Paper presented at the Australian Association for Research in Education, Fremantle.

Clayton, J. (2000, December). *Does online teaching add value to the teaching of science?* Paper presented at the Science in Nursing Education Conference, Hamilton.

Clayton, J. (2001, July). *Visual clues and the online environment: Issues and implications.* Paper presented at the Tertiary Teaching and Learning: Dealing with Diversity Conference, Northern Territory University, Darwin.

Clayton, J. (2002, April). *Using web-based assessment to engage learners.* Paper presented at the DEANZ: Evolving e-Learning Conference, Wellington.

Cottman, C. (1997, September, October). *It is the pedagogy, not the technology that counts'.* Paper presented at the Open, Flexible and distance learning: Education and training in the 21st century conference, Launceston: University of Tasmania.

De Leeuw, E., & Nicholls II, W. (1996). Technological innovations in data collection: Acceptance, data quality and costs. *Sociological Research Online. 1*(4) Retrieved March 15, 2003, from http://www.socresonline.org.uk/socresonline/1/4/leeuw.html

Dorman, J. (2001). Associations between classroom environment and academic efficacy. *Learning Environments Research: An International Journal, 4*(3), 243-257.

Dorman, J., Fraser, B., & McRobbie, C. J. (1994). Rhetoric and Reality: A study of classroom environments in catholic and government secondary schools. In D. Fisher (Ed.), *The Study of Learning Environments* (Vol. 8, pp. 124-141). Perth: Curtin University of Technology.

Fairholme, E., Dougiamas, M., & Dreher, H. (2000, February). Using online journals to stimulate reflective thinking. In A. Herrmann & M.

Kulski (Eds.), *Flexible futures in tertiary teaching.* Proceedings of the 9th Annual Teaching Learning Forum. Perth: Curtin University of Technology. http://cea.curtin.edu.au/tlf/tlf2000/fairholme.html.
Fisher, D., & Fraser, B. (1990). School climate (SET: *Research information for teachers No. 2*). Melbourne: Australian Council for Educational Research.
Fraser, B. J. (1990). *Individualised classroom environment questionnaire: Handbook and test master set.* Hawthorn: The Australian Council for Educational Research.
Fraser, B. (1998a). Classroom environment instruments: Development, validity and applications. *Learning Environments Research: An International Journal, 1*(1), 68-93.
Fraser, B. (1998b). Science learning environments: Assessment, effects and determinats. In B. Fraser & K. Tobin (Eds.), *International handbook of science education* (pp. 527-564). Dordrecht: Kluwer Academic Publishers.
Fraser, B. (2001). Twenty thousand hours: Editors introduction. *Learning Environments Research: An International Journal, 4*(1), 1-5.
Fraser, B., & Fisher, D. (1994). Assessing and researching the classroom environment. In D. Fisher (Ed.), *The Study of Learning Environments* (Vol. 8, pp. 23-39). Perth: Curtin University of Technology.
Fraser, B., Giddings, G. J., & McRobbie, C. J. (1992). Assessing the climate of science laboratory classes (What Research Says, No. 8). Perth: Curtin University of Technology.
Fraser, B., & Walberg, H. (Eds.). (1995). *Improving science education.* Chicago: The University of Chicago Press.
Fraser, B., & Wubbels, T. (1995). Classroom learning environments. In B. Fraser & H. Walberg (Eds.), *Improving science education* (pp. 117-143). Chicago: The University of Chicago Press.
Frazer, M. (1986). Teaching styles. In M. Frazer & A. Kornhauser (Eds.), *Ethics and social responsibility in science education* (pp. 141-145). Oxford: Pergamon Press.
Gilbert, J. (1993). Teacher development: a literature review. In B. Bell (Ed.), *I know about LISP but how do I put it into practice?* (pp. 15 - 39). Hamilton: CSMER University of Waikato.
Gilbert, J., Boulter, C., & Rutherford, M. (2000). Explanations with models in science education. In J. Gilbert & C. Boulter (Eds.), *Developing models in science education* (pp. 193-209). Dordrecht: Kluwer Academic Publishers.

Gunstone, R. (1994). The importance of specific science content in the enhancement of metacognition. In P. Fensham, R. Gunstone & R. White (Eds.), *The content of science: A constructivist approach to its teaching and learning* (pp. 131-147). London: The Falmer Press.

Harapnuik, D., Montgomerie, T., & Torgerson, C. (1998, November). *Costs of developing and delivering a web-based instruction course.* Paper presented at the WebNet 98 - World Conference of the WWW, Internet, and Intranet, Orlando.

Haynes, D. (2002, April). *The social dimensions of online learning: Perceptions, theories and practical responses.* Paper presented at the DEANZ: Evolving e-Learning Conference, Wellington.

Hewson, P. (1996). Teaching for conceptual change. In D. Treagust, D. Duit & B. Fraser (Eds.), *Improving teaching and learning in science and mathematics* (pp. 131-141). New York: Teachers College Press.

Ho, C. P., & Tabata, L. N. (2001, May). *Strategies for designing online courses to engage student learning.* Paper presented at the TCC 2001: The Internet and Learning virtual conference. Retrieved March 15, 2003, from http://leahi.kcc.hawaii.edu/org/tcon01/index.html

Joiner, K., Malone, J., & Haimes, D. (2002). Assessment of classroom environments in reformed calculus education. *Learning Environments Research: An International Journal, 5*(1), 51-76.

Kearsley, G. (1998). *Educational technology: A critique of pure reason.* Retrieved March 15, 2003, from http://home.sprynet.com/~gkearsley/critique.htm

Levy, J., Rodriguez, R., & Wubbels, T. (1993). Teacher communication style and instruction. In D. Fisher (Ed.), *The Study of Learning Environments* (Vol. 7, pp. 11-19). Perth: Curtin University of Technology.

Lozano, F. (1999). Introduction to Relational Database Design. *EDM/2: The electronic developer magazine*(msql17). Retrieved March 15, 2003, from http://www.edm2.com/0612/msql7.html

Maor, D. (1998). How does one evaluate students' participation and interaction in an Internet-based unit? In B. Black & N. Stanley (Eds.), *Teaching and learning in changing Times, 176-182.* Proceedings of the 7th Annual Teaching Learning Forum, The University of Western Australia, February 1998. Perth: UWA. http://cea.curtin.edu.au/tlf/tlf1998/maor.html

Maor, D. (1999). Teacher and student reflections on interactions in an Internet based unit. In K. Martin, N. Stanley & N. Davison (Eds.), *Teaching in the disciplines/ Learning in context,* (pp. 257-261). Proceedings of the 8th Annual Teaching Learning Forum, The

University of Western Australia, February 1999. Perth: UWA. http://cea.curtin.edu.au/tlf/tlf1999/maor.html

Maor, D. (2000). *Constructivist Virtual Learning Environment Survey.* Retrieved March 15, 2003, from http://www.curtin.edu.au/learn/unit/05474/forms/CVLES_form.html

Maor, D., & Fraser, B. (1993). Use of classroom environment perceptions in evaluating inquiry-based computer learning. In D. Fisher (Ed.), *The Study of Learning Environments* (Vol. 7, pp. 42-57). Perth: Curtin University of Technology.

McGovern, G., & Norton, R. (2001). *Content critical: Gaining competitive advantage through high-quality web content.* London: Financial Times Prentice Hall.

Miller, S. M., & Miller, K. L. (1999). Using instructional theory to facilitate communications in web-based courses. *Educational Technology and Society, 2*(3). Retrieved March 15, 2003, from http://ifets.ieee.org/periodical/vol_3_99/miller.html

Moos, R. H. (1976). *The human context: Environmental determinants of behaviour.* New York: Wiley-Interscience.

Moos, R. H. (1979). *Evaluating Educational Environments.* San Francisco: Jossey-Bass.

Morgan, B. (2000). *Is distance learning worth it? Helping to determine the costs of online courses.* Retrieved March 15, 2003, from http://www.marshall.edu/distance/distancelearning.pdf

Morihara, B. (2001, May 1-3). *Practice and pedagogy in university web teaching.* Paper presented at the TCC 2001: The Internet and learning virtual conference. Retrieved March 15, 2003, from http://leahi.kcc.hawaii.edu/org/tcon01/index.html

Morine-Dershimer, G., & Kent, T. (1999). The complex nature and sources of teachers' pedagogical knowledge. In J. Gess-Newsome & N. Lederman, (Eds.), *Examining pedagogical content knowledge* (pp. 21-51). Dordrecht: Kluwer Academic Publishers.

Newby, M., & Fisher, D. (1997). An instrument for assessing the learning environment of a computer laboratory. *Journal of Educational Computing Research, 16,* 179-190.

Newhouse, P. (2001a). Wireless portable technology unlocks the potential for computers to support learning in primary schools. *Australian Educational Computing, 16*(2). Retrieved March 15, 2003, from http://www.acce.edu.au/journal/

Newhouse, P. (2001b). Development and use of an instrument for computer-supported learning environments. *Learning Environments Research: An International Journal, 2*(2), 115-138.

Ommundsen, Y. (2001). Students' implicit theories of ability in physical education classes: The influence of motivational aspects of the learning environment. *Learning Environments Research: An International Journal, 4*(2), 139-158.

Ortiz, E. (1993). Perceived robustness in a computer-managed learning environment. In D. Fisher (Ed.), *The Study of Learning Environments* (Vol. 7, pp. 121-128). Perth: Curtin University of Technology.

Owen, M. (2000). Structure and discourse in a telematic learning environment. *Educational Technology & Society, 3*(3). Retrieved March 15, 2003, from http://ifets.ieee.org/periodical/

Posner, G., Strike, K., Hewson, P., & Gertzog, W. (1982). Accommodation of scientific conception: Toward a theory of conceptual change. *Science Education, 66*(2), 211-227.

Radford, A. J. (1997). The future of multimedia in education. *First Monday, 2*(11). Retrieved March 15, 2003, from http://www.firstmonday.dk/issues/index.html

Radloff, A., & de la Harpe, B. (2001). Expanding what and how we assess: Going beyond the content. In A. Herrmann & M. Kulski (Eds.), *Expanding Horizons in Teaching and Learning*. Proceedings of the 10th Annual Teaching Learning Forum, 7-9 February 2001. Perth: Curtin University of Technology. http://cea.curtin.edu.au/tlf/tlf2001/radloff.html

Reid, T. A. (1994). Perspectives on computers in education: the promise, the pain, the prospect. *Active Learning*(1). Retrieved March 15, 2003, from
http://www.ilt.ac.uk/public/cti/ActiveLearning/index.html

Roth, W., Tobin, K., & Ritchie, S. (2001). *Re/constructing elementary science*. New York: Peter Lang.

Salmon, G. (2000). *E-Moderating: The key to teaching and learning Online*. London: Kogan Page

Sangster, A. (1995). World Wide Web - What can it do for education? *Active Learning*(2). Retrieved March 15, 2003, from http://www.ilt.ac.uk/public/cti/ActiveLearning/index.html

Schmidt, W. C. (1997). World-Wide Web survey research: Benefits, potential problems, and solutions. *Behaviour Research Methods, Instruments, & Computers, 29*(2), 274-279.

Schroeder, R. (1997). Networked Worlds: Social Aspects of Multi-User Virtual Reality Technology. *Sociological Research Online, 2*(4). Retrieved March 15, 2003, from http://www.socresonline.org.uk/socresonline/2/4/5.html

Shannon, D., Johnson, T., Searcy, S., & Lott, A. (2002). Using electronic surveys: advice from survey professionals. *Practical Assessment, Research & Evaluation, 8*(1). Retrieved March 15, 2003, from http://ericae.net/pare/getvn.asp?v=8&n=1.

Swaak, J., & De Jong, T. (2001). Learner Vs system control in using online support for simulation-based discovery learning. *Learning Environments Research: An International Journal, 4*(3), 217-241.

Taylor, P., & Maor, D. (2000). Assessing the efficacy of online teaching with the Constructivist On-Line Learning Environment Survey. In A. Herrmann & M. Kulski (Eds.), *Flexible Futures in Tertiary Teaching.* Proceedings of the 9th Annual Teaching Learning Forum, 2-4 February 2000. Perth: Curtin University of Technology. http://cea.curtin.edu.au/tlf/tlf2000/taylor.html.

Teh, G., & Fraser, B. (1994). An evaluation of computer assisted learning in geography in Singapore. *Australian Journal of Educational Technology, 10*(1), 55 - 68.

Walker, S. (2001, November). Distance Education Learning Environments Survey. Retrieved April 4, 2002, from Scott's Doctoral Pages, Publications Web site: http://www.itouch.net/~swalker/smec/index.html

Walker, S. (2002a,). *Measuring the distance education psychosocial environment.* Paper presented at the TCC 2002: Hybrid Dreams: The Next Leap for Internet-Mediated Learning virtual conference. Retrieved March 15, 2003, from http://www.itouch.net/~swalker/publications/TCC_2002/index.html

Walker, S. (2002b, January). *Evaluation, description and effects of distance education learning environments in higher education.* Paper presented at the Ninth Annual Distance Education Conference., Austin, Texas.

Whitten, J., Bently, L., & Barlow, V. (Eds.). (1994). *Systems analysis and design methods* (3rd ed.). Boston: Irwin.

Yarrow, A., Millwater, J., & Fraser, B. (1997). Improving university and primary school classroom environments through pre-service teachers' action research. *International Journal of Practical Experiences in Professional Education, 1* (1), 68-93.

Zariski, A., & Styles, I. (2000). Enhancing student strategies for online learning. In A. Herrmann & M. Kulski (Eds.), *Flexible futures in tertiary teaching.* Proceedings of the 9th Annual Teaching Learning Forum, 2-4 February 2000. Perth: Curtin University of Technology. http://cea.curtin.edu.au/tlf/tlf2000/zariski.html

Zembal-Saul, C., Starr, M., & Krajcik, J. (1999). Constructing a framework for elementary science teaching using pedagogical content knowledge. In J. Gess-Newsome & N. Lederman (Eds.), *Examining pedagogical content knowledge* (pp. 237-257). Dordrecht: Kluwer Academic Publishers.

Zhu, E., & McKnight, R. (2001). *Principles of online design.* Retrieved March 15, 2003, from Florida Gulf Coast University, Office of Instructional Technology Web site: http://www.fgcu.edu/onlinedesign/

Chapter 9

COMPUTER LABORATORY ENVIRONMENTS: PROVIDING A SUITABLE PRACTICAL LEARNING EXPERIENCE

Michael Newby
California State University, Fullerton
USA

The use of information and communications technologies in education has increased dramatically over the past decade. At the university level, computers are now used in most disciplines, either as an adjunct to the traditional lecture or to deliver the material on-line. Consequently, students are now required to master computer skills before they can master the subject being taught. To accommodate this need, tertiary institutions have provided access to computer laboratories. A computer laboratory is an expensive resource in terms of equipment and people, and should be used as effectively as possible. Computer laboratory classes may be organized as closed laboratories which are scheduled and staffed in the same way as other classes, or as open laboratories where students come and go as they please. This chapter reports the results of a study that investigated differences between students' perceptions of aspects of the learning environment of open and closed computer laboratories, and also the differences in student outcomes from courses that adopt these approaches. There was no significant difference in achievement between the two groups but there was a difference in their attitudes towards computers with those students gaining their practical experience from closed laboratories having a more positive attitude.

1. Introduction

The use of information and communications technologies in education has increased dramatically over the past decade. At the university level, computers are now used in most disciplines, either as an adjunct to the traditional lecture or to deliver the material on-line. Consequently, students are now required to master computer skills before they can master the subject being taught. To accommodate this need, tertiary institutions have provided access to computer laboratories. A computer laboratory is an expensive resource in terms of equipment and people, and should be used as effectively as possible. Computer laboratory classes may be organized as closed laboratories which are scheduled and staffed in the same way as other classes, or as open laboratories where students come and go as they please. This chapter reports the results of a study that investigated differences between students' perceptions of aspects of the learning environment of open and closed computer laboratories, and also the differences in student outcomes from courses that adopt these approaches. There was no significant difference in achievement between the two groups but there was a difference in their attitudes towards computers with those students gaining their practical experience from closed laboratories having a more positive attitude.

The first electronic computer was developed in the 1940s, and up to the mid-1950s, the use of computers was restricted to scientific and engineering applications. Commercial applications of computers started in a small way in the late 1950s and expanded rapidly over the following 20 years. However, up to 1980, computer usage was not very widespread. At that time, organizations used a central computer and had a specialist Data Processing or Information Systems Department. These departments were usually the only part of the organization with access to computers. This situation changed with the advent of the microcomputer in the 1980s, and later the local area network. Following their introduction, the use of computers spread to all levels of organizations and today it would be unusual to find a desk in any organization without a workstation on it.

This evolution in the use of computers is mirrored in the provision of computer education and training. Initially, computer manufacturers ran specialist intensive courses in programming and operating systems over three to five days; this practice continues and indeed has been extended to cover many aspects of the computing and communications industries. The first university computing courses started in the 1960s. They had titles such as Computer Science, Computer Studies or Electronic Data Processing and were intended for the computing specialist, who would start their careers as programmers or systems analysts. Computer Science has established itself firmly as a discipline in most universities. The other terms mentioned have, in general, been replaced by Information Systems, which has emerged as a discipline in its own right with its focus on the application of computers to business problems. All academic programs within these disciplines involve the study of programming as the means by which computer-based systems are developed.

The introduction of the microcomputer in the early 1980s led to the wider use of computers throughout post-secondary education in programs such as business, education and engineering. Here the computer is often used as a tool to assist in learning, as a means of delivering educational material and for on-line assessment. More recently, the availability of multimedia has extended the use of computers to graphic design and architecture, and the Internet has made the workstation an invaluable educational and research tool. This has led to the inclusion of some form of computer education in virtually every discipline at the university level. In any course that uses computers either as an integral part of the course or as a medium of instruction or as a tool to assist in understanding the subject matter, it is necessary to provide a practical experience for the students. Computer laboratories can provide such experience. However, computer laboratories are expensive in terms of space, equipment and technical support. Furthermore, if they are integrated into teaching, there is an overhead with respect to faculty commitment and faculty time required to learn new software environments. Given the expense associated with computer laboratories, it is important that computer laboratory classes are organized in a way that will optimize student outcomes.

2. Computing Laboratories

The use of a laboratory as part of a computing course began with the advent of interactive computing in the 1970s. It is understandable that laboratories play such a prominent role in such courses given that using a computer, particularly for programming, is perceived as a skill which cannot be learned by simply reading a book and needs practice in order for it to be acquired (Azemi, 1995). This skill must be mastered before any progress can be made, and laboratory classes provide an opportunity for students to gain proficiency. However, proficiency is not the only aim of a computer laboratory class. Other aims would include:

- familiarizing students with the computing environment;
- reinforcing material taught in the lecture;
- teaching students the principles of using computers;
- providing closer contact between staff and students;
- stimulating and maintaining interest in the subject;
- teaching theoretical material not included in lectures;
- fostering critical awareness e.g. avoiding systematic errors;
- developing skills in problem solving;
- simulating conditions in an information systems development environment;
- stimulating independent thinking;
- developing skills in communicating technical concepts and solutions;
- providing motivation to acquire specific knowledge;
- bridging the gap between theory and practice.

(adapted from Boud, Dunn, & Hegarty-Hazel (1986))

The joint Association of Computing Machinery – Institute of Electrical and Electronic Engineers (ACM-IEEE) Curriculum Task Force recommended that introductory computer science courses should be supported by extensive laboratory work (Denning et al, 1989; ACM/IEEE-CS, 1991). The ACM SIGCSE (Special Interest Group on Computer Science Education) Working Group on Computing Laboratories published guidelines for the use of laboratories in computer science education (Knox et al, 1996). Their report was predicated on a number of assumptions, one of which was that laboratory experiences are relevant almost all computer science courses across all levels from literacy and language courses for non-specialists to graduate level theory courses. In a collaborative effort, the Association of Computing Machinery (ACM), the Association for Information Systems (AIS), the Association of Information Technology Professionals (AITP), and the International Conference on Information Systems (ICIS) developed guidelines for an undergraduate Information Systems Curriculum (Davis, Gorgone, Cougar, Feinstein, & Longenecker, 1997). In their report, they identified three types of laboratories, the structured laboratory, the open laboratory and the specialized laboratory.

The structured laboratory is a closed or formal laboratory (Prey, 1996; Lin, Wu, & Chiou, 1996). It is scheduled in the same way as lectures and tutorials with specific exercises being set for students. Such laboratories are generally staffed by the instructor who is available to help guide the students. On the other hand, open or public laboratories are provided so that students may complete exercises and assignments outside scheduled laboratory classes. Students are allowed to come and go as they please with technical assistance, if any, being provided by laboratory assistants who are often senior students. For open laboratories an instructor assigns a problem and students work on it in their own time usually individually but sometimes in groups. Finally, there is the specialized laboratory, which is provided to support up-to-date programs with state of the art technology. Examples of specialized laboratories are systems development laboratories, providing access to CASE (Computer Assisted Software Engineering) tools, data communication laboratories with hands-on access to network management tools, and decision conferencing laboratories with access to group support systems software (Cougar, et al., 1995).

There are a number of ways in which a computer laboratory may be staffed, and these can affect the way in which the instructor interacts with the students. For closed laboratories, it is usual for these to be staffed by the instructor themselves, with an alternative being a graduate teaching assistant. In either case, the instructor would be able to give a high level of interaction, answering questions on advanced concepts, as well as on technical details. One advantage of closed laboratories is that they tend to encourage both active learning (Huss, 1995; McConnell, 1996) and cooperative learning (Prey, 1996).

The level of assistance provided in open laboratories varies from none to the provision of technical help supplied by non-academic staff. Many universities use undergraduate student assistants in this role to help students with basic questions. Often, because of staffing problems, this is the only help that students get, particularly in open laboratories. This can lead to senior students passing on bad practice to their junior colleagues and generating a philosophy of 'getting it to work at all costs' (Newby, 1994). One reason for providing technical help in laboratories is the need for rapid feedback (Pitt, 1993). A student can spend hours looking at a program which will not compile and which produces an unhelpful error message, when all that is needed is for a semi-colon to be removed.

Institutional support is necessary for the success of computer laboratory classes. The provision of computer laboratory facilities does not just involve a room full of workstations. There must be an infrastructure of technical support for both hardware and software, together with a help desk available to both staff and students. A number of issues arise from using computer laboratories as an integral part of teaching and learning, and these include technology, both hardware and software, physical environment, organization, assignment difficulty, technical support, and staff training. Problems can arise when any of these aspects are not addressed (Pitt, 1993). The hardware must be capable to running the software satisfactorily and in the case of shared resources such as multi-user systems or networks, able to handle the required number of users. The software must be suitable for the curriculum, and enable some of the requirements of laboratory classes given above to be satisfied, as deemed necessary by the instructor. At the very least such classes should teach practical skills and reinforce the theoretical aspects covered in lectures and tutorials. Also, the fundamentals of such software must be able to be mastered in a relatively short period of time, for example, half a semester. It has been recognized that some software is extremely complex (Knox et al, 1996). This applies particularly to commercial software, and it often means that the learning curve for its use is too extensive for such software to be included in a single course (Granger & Little, 1996). This difficulty makes the provision of realistic laboratory assignments problematic. In some cases, this situation is exacerbated by an unrealistic use of software. For example, in a laboratory class where students access a multi-user system, there may be as many as 30 students performing similar tasks using the same software whereas in a practical (commercial) environment there would be only two or three at any one time. In the student environment, this may lead to poor performance with slow response time, giving the impression that the software is inadequate, an attitude that may remain with students after they graduate.

As many university computing courses are preparing students for a career in a commercial or public sector environment, both the hardware and software must have commercial credibility. Of course, this requirement sometimes conflicts with the need for the software to be easy to learn. Organizations would obviously prefer graduates who have been exposed to the systems that they use rather than having to go to the expense of training. However, this is a somewhat contentious point and many surveys indicate that employers are at least interested in general skills as in specific ones (Trauth, Farwell, & Lee, 1993; Richards & Pelley, 1994). As stated earlier, to develop practical computing skills, students will have to complete various computer-based tasks such as laboratory exercises or assignments. Such tasks must be within the average student's capability. If they are too simple, they give the wrong impression regarding the subject. If they are too difficult or time consuming, this can lead to frustration and a negative attitude towards the course, the software or computing in general. In recent years, there have been changes in the style of development software from text-based systems to graphical user interfaces (GUI) and multimedia. Systems developed using GUIs are usually easier for the user, but the development tool itself is more complex and more difficult to learn (Mutchler & Laxer, 1996; Wolz, Weisgarber, Domen, & McAuliffe, 1996).

Clearly, open and closed laboratories provide different levels of support and different learning experiences. In Australian and British universities most computing classes provide formal scheduled laboratory classes, with different levels of prescription with respect to the work to be done. However, in the United States, it seems that the open laboratory is the norm (Prey, 1996). One study showed that only about a third of the university courses surveyed used formal laboratory classes (Denk, Martin, & Sarangarm, 1994). One factor that undoubtedly affects the provision of closed laboratories in the USA is the way that workloads are measured. It is done on the basis of course credits and in most US universities, a laboratory class counts as only half a credit. In Australia and the UK, laboratory classes carry the same weight as lectures or tutorials.

3. Studies Involving Computer Laboratory Environments

There have been a number of studies of the learning environments of classroom involving either computer-based learning or computer laboratories, and these have shown that the introduction of computers into the classroom changes the learning environment (Maor & Fraser, 1993; Levine & Donitsa-Schmidt, 1995). It was found that using computers effectively creates a classroom that is more student-centered and cooperative. This is consistent with the observation made earlier that the use of closed laboratories in computing courses is seen as an opportunity to introduce cooperative learning strategies (Prey, 1996). Other studies have focused on the psychosocial environment in computer-assisted learning classrooms (Teh & Fraser, 1995), professional computer courses (Khoo & Fraser, 1997), university computer courses (Newby & Fisher, 1998) and secondary school computer classrooms (Zandvliet & Fraser, 1998). All of these showed that the environment variables were strongly related to student attitudes, satisfaction and achievement. Further statistical analysis also indicated that between 16% and 36% of the variance in attitude could be explained simply by the environment.

In a study to investigate the effect of scheduled laboratory classes on students' ability to complete assignment projects and tutorial exercises, Duplass (1995) compared two classes of the same course for one semester. The course was introductory and included use of an application package. Both classes had the same number of hours of instruction, but one of them had 25% of the time in a scheduled laboratory, where the instructor gave "over the shoulder" advice, whereas in the other class, this time was spent in demonstration of the process. Open laboratories were available to both groups of students. The study showed that those who had the benefit of the scheduled laboratory completed their projects in significantly less time (about 14%) than those who did not, but there was no significant difference in times taken to complete the tutorial exercises. This indicates that computer laboratory classes may have greater influence on students' ability to tackle larger problems.

The association between learning environment and student outcomes is well established (Fraser, 1991), and the studies mentioned above support this association. The purpose of the current study is to compare the learning environments of open and closed laboratories to see if there are any differences between how students perceive the psycho-social environment of different types of computer laboratory classroom and whether these perceptions have any effect on students' attitudes or achievement.

4. Methodology

This study involved the use of two previously developed instruments, one called the *Computer Laboratory Environment Inventory* (CLEI) for measuring aspects of a computer laboratory environment and the other, the *Attitude to Computers and Computing Courses Questionnaire* (ACCC) used to measure students' attitudes (Newby & Fisher, 1997). The research focused on whether there were differences in a student's perception of aspects of their computer laboratory environment or in their course outcomes if they received their computer laboratory experience via open or closed laboratories.

4.1 The Computer Laboratory Environment Inventory

The instrument for assessing aspects of a computer laboratory environment has five scales, Student Cohesiveness, Open-Endedness, Integration, Technology Adequacy, and Laboratory Availability. Each scale consists of seven items, with each item being measured on a Likert scale of 1 to 5 with some questions being reversed. Table 9.1 gives a description of each scale with a sample item.

Table 9.1. Description of CLEI Scales

Scale	Description	Sample Item
Student Cohesiveness	Extent to which students know, help and are supportive of each other	I get on well with students in this laboratory class (+)
Open-endedness	Extent to which the laboratory activities encourage an open-ended, divergent approach to use of computers	There is opportunity for me to pursue my own computing interests in this laboratory class (+)
Integration	Extent to which the laboratory activities are integrated with non-laboratory and theory classes	The laboratory work is unrelated to the topics that I am studying in my lecture (-)
Technology Adequacy	Extent to which the hardware and software are adequate for the tasks required	The computers are suitable for running the software I am required to use (+)
Laboratory Availability	Extent to which the laboratory is available for use	I find that the laboratory is crowded when I am using the computer (-)

Items designated (+) are scored 1,2,3,4 and 5, respectively for responses Almost Never, Seldom, Sometimes, Often, Almost Always

Items designated (-) are scored 5,4,3,2 and 1, respectively for responses Almost Never, Seldom, Sometimes, Often, Almost Always

The first three scales are based on similar scales of a well-validated instrument called the Science Laboratory Environment Inventory (Fraser, Giddings, & McRobbie, 1993), and the scales Technology Adequacy and

Laboratory Availability were designed specifically for this instrument. The use of the first four scales is justified by the guidelines for the use of computer laboratories (Knox et al., 1996). In the report the authors discuss the relationship between the lecture and laboratory in terms of how the laboratory component is organized within the curriculum, the content level, the type of activity, the type of interaction, and the objectives of the laboratory.

The laboratory component may be independent of the lecture, a situation which is desirable in some literacy courses where students are required to gain knowledge about computers and also skills in using them. The lecture and laboratory may be connected across semesters, with the theory course first followed by the practical laboratory course, or both may be integrated so a course consists of both theory and practical components in the same semester. The scale Integration measures students' perceptions of this aspect of the laboratory experience.

The content level of a laboratory may vary from purely mechanical knowledge of a computer system, such as which key to strike to perform a certain task, to developing a computer based solution to a problem. Laboratories may also be used for exploration and the illumination of difficult concepts. The activity type describes what the student is doing in the laboratory. This could be using a computer-based learning (CBL) system for a tutorial and/or on-line assessment, developing a software system from scratch, modifying existing software, analyzing data, exploring a system to find out how it works, or using the Internet as a research tool. Each activity type will have different laboratory needs. Open-Endedness will measure students' perceptions of these aspects.

The interaction type is indicative of how the class members work together: students could work on their own, or in groups, and in addition, the staff member may be involved with students either individually or in groups. Closed laboratories allow for greater interaction between staff and students and amongst the students themselves. Student Cohesiveness will measure this aspect.

The uses of technology in computer laboratory classes may be classified by the activities they support and the concepts they reinforce. They include learning to use the technology, using the technology as a tool, using the technology to develop new systems, and using technology to support group work. In each of these cases, different demands will be put on the laboratory class, and the hardware and software must be able to cope with those demands. The Technology Adequacy scale measures students' perceptions of how well the technology performs.

The scale Laboratory Availability recognizes that access to computers outside scheduled classes is needed for students to complete their work. Although most university students have access to computers off-campus, the required software may not be available and so they will have to use the university computers in the laboratory.

4.2 Attitude towards Computers and Computer Courses Questionnaire

The instrument for assessing students' attitudes towards computers and computer courses (ACCC) has been described in earlier studies (Newby & Fisher, 1997). For assessing attitude towards computers, the scales Anxiety, Enjoyment, and Perceived Usefulness of Computers were based upon an instrument devised by Loyd and Loyd (1985). A fourth scale was included to measure the student's perception of the usefulness of the course. As with the CLEI, all the scales have seven items and a description of the scales used in the instrument is given in Table 9.2 together with a sample item from each scale.

Table 9.2. Description of ACCC Scales

Scale	Description	Sample Item
Anxiety	Extent to which the student feels comfortable using a computer	Working with a computer makes me very nervous (+)
Enjoyment	Extent to which the student enjoys using a computer	I enjoy learning on a computer (+)
Usefulness of Computers	Extent to which the student believes computers are useful	My future career will require a knowledge of computers (+)
Usefulness of Course	Extent to which the student found the course useful	I do not think I will use what I learned in this class (-)

Items designated (+) are scored 1,2,3,4 and 5, respectively for responses Strongly Disagree, Disagree, Not Sure, Agree, Strongly Agree

Items designated (-) are scored 5,4,3,2 and 1, respectively for responses Strongly Disagree, Disagree, Not Sure, Agree, Strongly Agree

4.3 Samples

The instrument was administered to 104 students undertaking courses within the Business School of Curtin University of Technology in Western Australia, and to 109 students within the College of Business and Economics at California State University, Fullerton. All courses involved the use of a computer to solve problems. The Curtin courses provided the laboratory experience by means of formal closed laboratory classes. At Fullerton, laboratory classes were not scheduled and the laboratory experience was provided by open laboratories. In both surveys, the classes included those in which the development of software was the focus of study, such as Information Systems, and others in which the computer was used as a tool. The surveys were carried out in the last third of the semester in which the course was given so that students would have had a sufficient exposure to the laboratories. However it should be pointed out that although the surveys were conducted at different times of the calendar year, they were conducted at equivalent times of the academic year.

The program at Curtin is accredited by the Australian Computer Society and follows their curriculum guidelines (Australian Computer Society, 2002). At Fullerton, the program is accredited by AACSB and the Information Systems courses are based on those in the IS '97 curriculum (Davis, et al., 1997). The Information Systems courses in both programs are similar as the Australian Computer Society core requirements draw heavily upon the IS '97 curriculum. The major difference in the programs is the length. As is the norm in Australia, the program at Curtin is 3 years, whereas the one at Fullerton is 4 years, but it should be noted that the Curtin program contains no General Education courses.

The students at Curtin take their first computing course in Semester 1 and those surveyed were in their 4th semester. At Fullerton, the students take their first computing course in Semester 3 and those surveyed were in their 6th semester. This means that both sets of students were at the same stage of their program and were similar in both academic level and computer experience. The samples were also similar in terms of gender, age, and mode of study (part-time or full-time) as is indicated in Table 9.3 which gives the frequencies of these variables for both samples.

Table 9.3. Frequencies of Demographic Variables in Australian and US Samples

Variable		Australian Frequency	Australian Percentage	United States Frequency	United States Percentage
Age	< 20	21	20.2	12	11.0
	20-25	54	51.9	63	57.8
	26-30	16	15.4	24	22.0
	30-35	3	2.9	7	6.4
	> 35	2	1.9	1	0.9
	Missing	8	7.7	2	1.8
Gender	Female	34	32.7	50	45.9
	Male	63	60.6	57	52.3
	Missing	7	6.7	2	1.8
Mode of Study	Full-time	89	85.6	97	89.0
	Part-time	9	8.7	10	9.2
	Missing	6	5.8	2	1.8
Sample Size		104		109	

4.4 Achievement

Achievement was measured as the grade obtained in the course, as a mark out of 100. This grade was contributed to by three components, a final examination, assignments and laboratory exercises. Both the examination and the assignments tested knowledge and skills that should have been gained mainly in the laboratory classes, whose major purpose was to give practical experience of material covered in the lectures. Using means and standard deviations obtained for each course, each grade was converted into a z-score. Of the 104 students from Curtin, 77 provided their student number and of the 109 students from Fullerton, 74 did so. This allowed the grades of these students to be determined.

4.5 Research Questions

Closed computer laboratory classes require more resources and greater commitment than open laboratories and this provides the rationale for Research Question #1:

Do students who receive their laboratory experience via open computer laboratories perceive their learning environment differently from those who receive their laboratory experience via closed computer laboratories?

Previous research shows an association between classroom environment and student outcomes (Fraser, 1991) and this formed the focus of Research Question #2:

Are the course outcomes in terms of attitude and achievement different for students who receive their laboratory experience via open computer laboratories from those who receive it via closed computer laboratories?

5. Results

Table 9.4 shows the alpha reliabilities and mean correlations with other scales for the scales of the CLEI for both samples. The reliabilities for the Australian sample vary from 0.56 to 0.89, and for the US sample from 0.61 to 0.80. These are consistent with previous studies and indicate that the reliabilities of the scales are satisfactory.

Table 9.4. Internal Reliability and Mean Correlations for the Scales of the CLEI

Scale	Australia		United States	
	Alpha	Mean Correlation	Alpha	Mean Correlation
Student Cohesiveness	0.64	0.13	0.72	0.10
Open-Endedness	0.56	0.14	0.61	0.07
Integration	0.89	0.08	0.80	0.13
Technology Adequacy	0.84	0.23	0.78	0.24
Laboratory Availability	0.81	0.22	0.71	0.23
Sample Size	104		109	

The mean correlation with other scales varies from 0.08 to 0.23 for the Australian sample and 0.06 to 0.24 for the US sample. These demonstrate that there is little overlap in what the scales are measuring and the results are consistent with previous studies in which factor analysis was used to confirm that there are five distinct scales (Newby, 1998).

Table 9.5. Internal Reliability and Mean Correlations for the Scales of the ACCC

	Australia		United States	
Scale	Alpha	Mean Correlation	Alpha	Mean Correlation
Anxiety	0.89	0.36	0.88	0.47
Enjoyment	0.90	0.41	0.89	0.47
Usefulness of Computers	0.82	0.36	0.81	0.49
Usefulness of Course	0.64	0.28	0.72	0.36
Sample Size	104		109	

Table 9.5 shows the alpha reliabilities and mean correlations with other scales for the scales of the ACCC. The alpha reliabilities vary from 0.64 to 0.90 for the Australian sample and from 0.72 to 0.89, indicating that the scales have a satisfactory internal consistency for these samples. The mean correlations show that the scales measure distinct but overlapping aspects of students' attitudes towards computers and the course. Factor analysis has been used in a previous study to confirm a structure of four factors (Newby, 1998).

An independent samples t-test was carried out on the environment variables, the attitudinal variables and on achievement measured by the z-score, using country of study as the grouping variable. The results for the environment variables are given in Table 9.6, and for the attitudinal variables and achievement in Table 9.7.

Of the environment variables, the difference in the mean for Open-Endedness was significant ($p<0.01$), with courses having closed laboratories being higher. Both Technology Adequacy ($p<0.01$) and Laboratory Availability ($p<0.001$) were significantly higher for courses which provided the laboratory experience via open laboratories.

Of the attitudinal variables, only Anxiety showed a significant difference ($p < .01$) in the means with courses using open laboratories being higher. There was no significant different between the means of achievement for the two groups.

Table 9.6. Comparison of the Means for Environment Variables

Scale	Australia		United States			
	Mean	Std	Mean	Std	t	p
Student Cohesiveness	23.1	3.65	22.2	4.31	0.83	0.411
Open-Endedness	23.5	3.22	22.4	2.65	2.88	0.004
Integration	24.6	5.52	25.8	4.05	-1.83	0.068
Technology Adequacy	22.7	4.65	24.4	4.38	-2.74	0.007
Laboratory Availability	19.7	5.58	22.3	4.96	-3.57	0.000

Table 9.7. Comparison of the Means for Attitudinal Variables and Achievement

Scale	Australia		United States			
	Mean	Std	Mean	Std	t	p
Anxiety	13.7	4.61	15.4	5.39	-2.40	0.007
Enjoyment	29.0	4.96	28.3	4.83	0.97	0.334
Usefulness of Computers	30.8	4.11	30.2	4.14	1.07	0.286
Usefulness of Course	25.2	3.45	25.4	4.06	-0.39	0.695
Achievement	0.35	1.01	0.22	0.89	0.83	0.411

6. Discussion

The first research question that was posed for this study was:

Do students who receive their laboratory experience via open computer laboratories perceive their learning environment differently from those who receive their laboratory experience via closed computer laboratories?

The results demonstrate that there are some important differences in students' perceptions of their computer laboratory environment depending whether they received their laboratory experience via closed laboratories or open laboratories. The only scale in which the mean was higher for courses employing closed laboratories was Open-Endedness. At first sight, this seems somewhat surprising as closed laboratories are designed to be much more structured than open laboratories. However, a possible explanation is that in a closed laboratory setting, students are more confident about experimenting with different ways of solving problems. In an open laboratory, students are more reliant upon laboratory assistants and each other and are likely to be satisfied when they get a solution that works. Of the remaining environment variables, both Technology Adequacy and Laboratory Availability have a significantly greater mean for courses using open laboratories. In many ways, the higher mean for Laboratory Availability is to be expected. With an open laboratory setting, the laboratories are available for use by students all day since there are no classes scheduled in them. The only competition comes from other students. Where closed laboratories are in use, much of the available time is taken by scheduled classes, and students are competing for the time that is unscheduled.

The higher mean for Technology Adequacy for courses with open laboratories could have a number of explanations, most of which are not directly related to open and closed laboratories. One such explanation is that the technology at Fullerton is more suitable than that at Curtin for the courses being taught. Certainly, the fact that about half of the students in the Curtin sample used a centralized computer and the rest used a network of PCs, whereas all Fullerton students used a network of PCs could be a contributing factor. Another possibility is that the instructor using closed laboratories set exercises that would more consciously extend the student's knowledge of how to solve problems in such an environment. Being on hand to answer questions immediately as would be the case with closed laboratories makes this more feasible. With open laboratories, the instructor must be more aware that they are setting exercises where the students will, in general, be obtaining limited help. It is interesting to observe that although not significant ($p = 0.068$), the mean for Integration is higher for open laboratories than for closed ones. This could be also be explained by the awareness of the instructor of the limited assistance available to students, and so they make the laboratory work closely related to the material of the lecture.

The second research question was:

Are the course outcomes in terms of attitude and achievement different for students who receive their laboratory experience via open computer laboratories from those who receive it via closed computer laboratories?

Of the student outcome variables, the only one that shows a significant difference in the means is Anxiety, where the mean is significantly greater ($p < .01$) for courses with open laboratories than for those with closed ones. This suggests that the presence of a faculty member when students are using unfamiliar software or hardware may reduce their anxiety about using computers. The lack of significant difference in the means for the other outcomes including achievement would indicate that there are factors other than laboratory environment that influence these outcomes.

7. Conclusion

This study compared the provision of computer laboratory experience by the use of closed laboratories and the use of open laboratories. It has demonstrated that there are some significant differences in both environment and attitudinal variables for the two groups of students. A previous study (Newby & Fisher, 2000) indicated that computer laboratory environment affects attitude which in turn affects achievement. An even earlier study (Marcoulides, 1988) demonstrated that there is a significant association between computer anxiety and achievement as measured by performance on computing assignments. Although the present study did not show a significant difference in the means for achievement, it did show a lower mean for anxiety those courses with closed computer laboratories. This would imply that the use of closed laboratories within courses could improve achievement by changing student attitudes towards computers. On the other hand, using closed laboratories would appear to reduce laboratory availability so students have less opportunity to work in a laboratory on campus outside formal classes. To some extent encouraging students to purchase laptop computers, which some universities already do, could overcome this.

However, software must be available to students at a reasonable cost. Overall, the results would also indicate that the students' perceptions of their laboratory environment could be optimized by the adoption of a judicious mix of both open and closed laboratories so as to obtain the best of both worlds. Such a strategy would require more resources, particularly in the provision of closed computer laboratory classes, which requires a commitment on the part of faculty and college administrators, but this study indicates that such an investment would be worthwhile.

References

ACM/IEEE-CS. (1991). Computing curricula 1991 report of the ACM/IEEE-CS Joint Curriculum Task Force. Palo Alto, CA: IEEE Computer Society Press.
Australian Computer Society (2002). *Guidelines for the accreditation of IT courses at the professional level.* Retrieved October 8, 2002 from the Australian Computer Society Web site: http://www.acs.org.au
Azemi, A. (1995). Teaching computer programming courses in a computer laboratory environment. *Proceedings - Frontiers in Education Conference,* 2a5.18-2a5.20.
Boud, D., Dunn, J., & Hegarty-Hazel, E. (1986). *Teaching in laboratories.* Guildford, Surrey, UK: SRHE & NFER-Nelson.
Davis, G. B., Gorgone, J. T., Cougar, J. D., Feinstein, D. L., & Longenecker, H.E. (1997). *IS '97 model curriculum and guidelines for undergraduate degree programs in Information Systems.* Association of Information Technology Professionals.
Denk, J., Martin, J., & Sarangarm, S. (1994). Not yet comfortable in the classroom: A study of academic computing at three land-grant universities. *Journal of Educational Technology Systems, 22*(1), 39-55.
Denning, P.J., Comer, D.E., Gries, D., Mulder, M.C., Tucker, A., Turner, A.J., & Young, P.R. (1989). Computing as a discipline, *Communications of the ACM, 32*(1), 9-23.
Duplass, J.A. (1995). Teaching software: Is the supervised laboratory effective? *Computers and Edication, 24*(4), 287-291.
Fraser, B. J. (1991). Two decades of classroom environments research, in B. J. Fraser and H. J. Walberg (eds.), *Educational environments: Antecedents, consequences and evaluation,* Pergamon Press, London.
Fraser, B. J., Giddings, G. J., & McRobbie, C. J. (1993). Development and cross-national validation of a laboratory classroom environment instrument for senior high school science. *Science Education, 77,* 1-24.

Granger, M.J., & Little, J.C. (1996). Integrating CASE tools into the CS/CIS curriculum. *SIGCSE Bulletin, Special Edition - Integrating Technology into Computer Science Education,* 130-132.

Huss, J.E. (1995). Laboratory projects for promoting hands-on learning in a computer security course. *SIGSCE Bulletin,* 27(2), 2-6.

Khoo, H.S., & Fraser, B.J. (1997, April). *The learning environment associated with computer application courses for adults in Singapore.* Paper presented at the annual meeting of the American Educational Research Association, Chicago, IL.

Knox D., Wolz U., Joyce D., Koffman E., Krone J., Laribi A., Myers J. P., Proulx V. K., & Reek, K. A. (1996). Use of laboratories in Computer Science Education: Guidelines for good practice, *SIGCSE Bulletin, Special Edition - Integrating Technology into Computer Science Education,* 167-181.

Levine, T., & Donitsa-Schmidt, S. (1995). Computer experience, gender, and classroom environment in computer-supported writing classes, *Journal of Educational Computing Research,* 13(4), 337-357.

Lin, J.M-C., Wu, C-C., & Chiou, G-F. (1996). Critical concepts in the development of courseware for CS closed laboratories, *SIGCSE Bulletin, Special Edition - Integrating Technology into Computer Science Education,* 14-19.

Loyd, B.H., & Loyd, D.E. (1985). The reliability and validity of an instrument for the assessment of computer attitudes. *Educational and Psychological Measurement,* 45, 903-908.

Maor, D. & Fraser, B. J. (1993). Use of classroom environment perceptions in evaluating inquiry-based computer learning. In D.L Fisher (Ed.), *A Study of Learning Environments, Volume 7* (pp. 57-71). Perth, Western Australia: Curtin University of Technology.

Marcoulides, G.A. (1988). The relationship between computer anxiety and computer achievement. *Journal of Educational Computing Research,* 4 (2), 151-158.

McConnell, J.J. (1996). Active learning and its use in computer science. SIGCSE Bulletin, Special Edition - Integrating Technology into Computer Science Education, 52-54.

Mutchler, D., & Laxer, C. (1996). Using multimedia and GUI programming in CS 1. SIGCSE Bulletin, Special Edition - Integrating Technology into Computer Science Education, 63-65.

Newby, M. (1994). Legacy systems, software maintenance, and computing curricula. In M. Purvis (Ed.), *Proceedings, Software Education Conference (SRIG-ET'94)* (pp. 96-102). Los Alamitos, CA: IEEE Computer Society Press.

Newby, M. (1998). *A study of the effectiveness of computer laboratory classes as learning environments.* Ph.D. thesis, Curtin University of Technology, Perth, Western Australia.

Newby M., & Fisher D. L. (1997). An instrument for assessing the learning environment of a computer laboratory, *Journal of Educational Computing Research 16* (2), 179-197.

Newby M., & Fisher D. L. (1998, April). *Associations between university computer laboratory environments and student outcomes.* Paper presented at the American Educational Research Association Annual Meeting, San Diego, CA.

Newby, M., & Fisher, D. L. (2000). A model of the relationship between computer laboratory environment and student outcomes in university courses. *Learning Environments Research, 3*(1), 51-66.

Pitt, M. J. (1993). What is missing from the computer laboratory?. *British Journal of Educational Technology, 24* (3), 165-170.

Prey, J. C. (1996). Cooperative learning and closed laboratories in an undergraduate Computer Science curriculum [Special issue: Integrating Technology into Computer Science Education]. *SIGCSE Bulletin, 28*, 23–24.

Teh, G.P.L., & Fraser, B. J. (1995). Development and validation of an instrument for assessing the psychosocial environment of computer-assisted learning classrooms. *Journal of Educational Computing Research, 12* (2), 177-193.

Trauth, E.M., Farwell, D.W., & Lee, D. (1993). The IS expectation gap: Industry expectations versus academic preparation. *MIS Quarterly,17*(3), 293-307.

Wolz, U., Weisgarber, S., Domen, D., & McAuliffe, M. (1996). Teaching introductory programming in the multi-media world. *SIGCSE Bulletin, Special Edition - Integrating Technology into Computer Science Education,* 57-59.

Zandvliet, D.B., & Fraser, B.J. (1998, April). *The physical and psychosocial environments associated with classrooms using new information technologies.* Paper presented at the annual meeting of the American Educational Research Association, San Diego, CA.

Chapter 10

IMPLEMENTING THE INTERNET LEARNING ENVIRONMENT INTO THE CHEMISTRY CURRICULUM IN HIGH SCHOOLS IN ISRAEL

Miri Kesner
Marcel Frailich
Avi Hofstein
The Weizmann Institute of Science
Israel

In the Internet era, the teacher and the school do not comprise the only source of information. Surfing the Internet and information and communication facilities are now an integral part of our daily life. The Internet can serve as a source /database for a variety of educational activities and learning tasks used for enrichment, investigative learning, exercises, and cooperative learning projects. The Internet site *General Chemistry and Industrial Chemistry for the Use of Mankind* (http://stwww.weizmann.ac.il/g-chem/learnchem) was developed to serve as a useful resource to complement the teaching materials for high school chemistry students and teachers in Israel. It has been developed according to a curriculum based rational, flexible enough to adapt to future changes in the syllabus. This site can be used to enrich and vary chemistry studies, mainly with relevant everyday life contexts and industrial applications. The project is accompanied by intensive implementation procedures, including teachers' workshop and continuous support. In the academic year 2002-2003 the Internet site is implemented in the educational system. In the chapter we tell the story of two teachers in order to illustrate different uses of the site.

1. Introduction

In 2003, as this chapter is being written, we are entering a new era of reform in science education. Both the content and pedagogy of science learning and teaching are being scrutinized, and new standards intended to shape meaningful science education are emerging. The release of the *National Science Education Standards* (NRC, 1996) in the USA was an important first step in identifying goals to achieve scientific literacy for all students. The standards detail the content, teaching strategies and assessment, professional development, and support necessary to enable high quality science education for all students in K to 12th grades.

Achieving scientific literacy for all students has become a national goal for education in Israel and in many other countries. In 1992, the *Tomorrow 98* report on reform in science, technology, and mathematics education was released. This report includes 43 recommendations for special projects, changes, and improvements, both educational and structural, in the area of curriculum development and implementation, pedagogy of science and mathematics, as well as the directions and actions to be taken in the professional development of science and mathematics teachers. This chapter describes the development of an Internet site in an attempt to make a significant contribution to both teaching and learning chemistry in high schools in Israel.

2. Teaching and Learning Science

The literature contains numerous suggestions about how one can enhance students' motivation to learn science within the context of school activities (Hofstein & Kempa, 1985; Hofstein & Walberg, 1995; Kempa, 1983). These suggestions can be divided into two categories:

- suggestions relating to the nature, content, structure, and presentation of the subject matter; and
- suggestions concerning the nature of pedagogical and instructional procedures to be adopted and implemented by the science teachers in their classrooms.

2.1 The Content and Structure of the Subject Matter

In recent years, science educators and curriculum developers have realized that science should be taught not only to prepare students for university studies and academic careers in the sciences, but also to become citizens in a society that is highly dependent upon scientific and technological advances. Therefore, it is suggested that more emphasis should be placed on the relevance of science to everyday life and to the integral role that it plays in industry, technology, and society. Also in the last 20 years, the chemistry curriculum has changed dramatically, from focusing on the structure of the disciplinary approach to a multidimensional approach. Even as early as 1983, Kempa claimed that the future development of teaching and learning materials in chemistry should include the following six dimensions: the conceptual structure of chemistry, the processes of chemistry, the technological manifestations of chemistry, chemistry as a 'personally relevant' subject, the cultural aspect of chemistry, and finally, the societal implications of chemistry. In order to make chemistry more relevant to students' lives and to the society in which they live, it should be taught as an applied science of major economic and technological importance. This approach emerged in an effort to produce an informed citizenry capable of making crucial decisions about current problems and issues, who will take personal actions as a result of those decisions. In addition, Johnstone, Percival, and Reid (1981) showed that students who were exposed to learning modules in chemistry that combine scientific, technological, and societal aspects, found their chemistry studies more relevant, more appealing, and motivating.

In the last decade, the science education community has expanded its knowledge of students' understanding of concepts and the nature of science. In addition, based on developments in cognitive psychology, there has been a substantial paradigm shift in thinking about the ways in which learners construct their scientific knowledge and understanding. Based on a comprehensive study, Krajcik (2000) suggested that when students acquire new information in a meaningful context and relate it to what is already known, they link new information to a better and larger, more linked, conceptual network of understanding. Moreover, there is a growing sense that learning is contextualized and that learners construct knowledge by solving genuine and meaningful problems (Brown, Collins, & Duguit, 1989; Williams & Hmelo, 1998).

2.2 The Pedagogy of Teaching Science

A widely accepted notion is that instructional techniques should be matched to the learners' characteristics and needs if the effectiveness of the teaching/learning process is to be maximized. Learners' characteristics that have received attention include cognitive characteristics such as achievement, cognitive level, conceptual level, and certain affective traits such as attitudes, interests, and motivation.

Hofstein & Kempa (1985) suggested that students have preferences for particular types of learning activities and that these reflect their motivation. Adar (1969) identified four motivational "needs": the need to achieve; the need to satisfy curiosity; the need to discharge a duty; the need to affiliate with other people. After studying the relationship between students' motivational needs and their preference for a particular instructional strategy, she concluded that:

> The application of different teaching techniques will affect
> A student motivation only if the method interacts with the
> students' motivational pattern.

Hofstein and Kempa (1985) elaborated this theory for science education. They postulated that a number of relationships exist between students' motivational needs and their preferences for particular modes of instruction in science education. This was verified in a study conducted in Spain by Kempa and Diaz (1990). These findings should be taken into consideration in the design of learning experiences and teaching interventions, both by teachers, curriculum developers, as well as those who are responsible for the organization of science education in schools. Clearly, it is difficult in practice to respond to each student's needs but much could be achieved if teachers would use a wide repertoire of instructional strategies in an attempt to vary the science classroom-learning environment. Hofstein & Kempa (1985) wrote that:

> Most of our science teaching has to take place in
> heterogeneous classes and thus we face the task of having to
> cater for a variety of students of different needs and
> motivations towards the learning of science. This calls for
> use of a variety of instructional procedures and techniques
> on the part of the teachers so that the needs and motivational
> aspirations of many different types of students can be
> satisfied (p. 228).

3. Using the WWW as a Teaching and Learning Resource in Science

Abad (1999) suggested that integrating an Internet-based learning environment into the teaching and learning of science in general and of chemistry in particular has great educational potential. In recent years the Internet has found its place in the educational system mainly as a source and database for varied educational activities and learning tasks used for enrichment, investigative learning, exercises, cooperative learning, and projects (Yaron, Freeland, & Milton, 2000).

However, in regard to research on the Internet's educational effectiveness, the literature revealed mixed findings. For example, Carpi (2001), in the context of chemistry education, suggested that the web holds several advantages over traditional teaching resources for enhancing the teaching and learning of chemistry. First, he mentioned the ability of the web to provide interactive multimedia content that overcomes the static resources such as textbooks in conveying broad-range, complex, and dynamic subject matter (the dynamic nature of the content). Second, he mentioned the capacity of the web to allow the users to control the pace and order of content presented, which creates a learning environment tailored to the needs of the individual teacher and individual students (flexible implementation). In addition, the web expands the boundaries of the classroom and allows students to interact with the learning materials, with their teachers, and with their peers in an informal setting (learning environment). Finally, in order to learn chemistry, its technological application, and its societal ramifications, the learners need primary data sources that can be easily provided by the web site. Access to resources is central to the learning of chemistry based on the six dimensions of chemistry education suggested by Kempa (1983), discussed previously. However, although educators speak positively of the use of the web in teaching and learning science, no clear evidence was found in the educational literature regarding the educational effectiveness of learning through web sites in comparison with other instructional techniques often used in science education (Krajcik, 2000; Lookatch, 1995). Moreover, in a series of studies conducted at the University of Michigan (e.g., Krajcik et al, 2000), it was concluded that students have difficulty locating and using resources in online environments and that very often teachers lack pedagogical skills regarding the teaching of science in an enriched technological environment.

4. Using the WWW as a Teaching and Learning Resource in Chemistry Education

Little information exists regarding the use of the Internet in the context of teaching and learning high-school chemistry. Usually, it is used for searching information when conducting projects (Gagan, 2001). Java applets have been used in molecular modeling (Barnea, & Dori, 1999) or simulations (Yaron, Freeland, & Milton, 2000), along with web-based materials and computer-based experiments (Aksela, & Meisalo, 2001) but they are not commonly used. Usually these interventions are integrated into university and college chemistry courses and less in high-school chemistry classes.

One of the main goals of teaching high-school chemistry is to open a window to the outside world. One way to attain this goal is to introduce industrial chemistry topics, issues, and ideas into the curriculum. It is suggested that industrial chemistry topics can provide an interesting and useful opportunity for introducing relevant issues to high-school students (Kesner, Hofstein, & Ben-Zvi, 1997a & b). In regard to the industrial issues, the web provides an excellent source for data about industrial plants, their products, raw materials, as well as technological, economical, and environmental issues regarding certain plant and industrial sites. There are a variety of sites available. Some were developed for educational purposes and some were not initially planned to serve for learning and teaching but can indeed be used indirectly for these goals. Note that the dynamic properties of the Internet, including the possibility of easily performing changes, can serve as an excellent tool for refreshing and updating the curriculum with new subject content and initiatives (Alister, 1999).

5. Integrating Web-based Learning into the Chemistry Curriculum

5.1 Rationale and Principles of the Internet Site

Our goal was to create a computer/Internet-learning environment for the use of chemistry teachers and their students. The rationale behind the project of building a chemistry-oriented Internet site was to use the Internet and computer tools for the enrichment of chemistry studies, both in content and in teaching and learning methods. The wide range of options and the unlimited possibilities enable establishing a variety of learning environments and activities, planned to be adaptable to the varied populations of students and teachers. Thus, the site must offer different learning units adapted for heterogeneous classes and for different types of students with diverse backgrounds. The site mainly focuses on curriculum-based activities in order to make it attractive and useful for everyday classroom practice.

The site was developed with the following goals in mind:

1. To enrich the whole syllabus by complementing it with varied and applied industrial aspects, emphasizing the relevance of chemistry to daily life in order to increase interest and motivation to study.
2. To enhance the students' investigative and thought process skills.
3. To introduce the Internet learning environment to the chemistry classroom.
4. To raise students' interest in chemistry studies.
5. To develop enrichment resources for the motivated students.

Our goal was to plan and construct a site that will be dynamic, appealing and captivating, up-to-date, user-friendly, applicable to diverse-types of students (both cognitively and affectively), interactive by involving the students in the learning process, and based on information technology principles. In addition, we wanted the contents to be practical in terms of learning objectives, classroom resources, and applied to chemistry topics in the curriculum relevant to daily life aspects of chemistry; to present industrial applications based on chemistry principles and concepts; to contribute to teachers' and students' advancement, offer varied teaching methods, consist of varied activities, and to be flexible regarding various learning styles.

5.2 Programming Outlines

Each item on the site is selected from one central database and thus the site is actually an information system. In this way, the entire site is dynamic and can be maintained very easily by a web application back office restricted to authorized managers. Moreover, it is very user-friendly and convenient, and it does not require a knowledge of programming.

The Internet site is written using mostly ASP technology and contains Java and VB components. With this structure, it is very easy to incorporate future developments, thus it decreases the maintenance costs.

The input procedure possesses much freedom and has a high level of flexibility, which is essential to an Internet site in general and to an educational site in particular. This technology requires very little dependence on the system supplier and the content management is separate from the programming demands.

5.3 Involving Teachers in the Process of Development and Implementation

In order to design a site that will serve the teachers' needs in their daily classroom work and that will contain teaching and learning materials that will align with the curriculum and the teachers' and students' needs, we decided to involve teachers in the actual process of constructing the site. A small group (n=7) of leading-teachers was selected for a year-long (112 hours) workshop. The main goal of the workshop was to involve those teachers who are enthusiastic about using technological devices in their classroom, in the design, selection of appropriate activities, and development of the various components of the site. It was assumed that involving teachers in the developmental process will ensure a richness of ideas and alignment of activities to the teachers' teaching style and the chemistry classroom learning environment. During the meetings, the teachers discussed the nature and characteristics of the Internet site needed to encourage the teachers to surf regularly. They discussed the design of the home page and its graphics. The teachers were presented with relevant Internet facilities such as java applets and simulations, a virtual lab, molecular modeling tools, and databases. Most of the applications were new to them, but after trying them by themselves, they were ready to use them for developing their own learning materials. The teachers designed learning activities related to subjects in the syllabus that focused on the relevance to daily life applications and the industrial implications. In addition, a discussion was held regarding different pedagogical approaches and various models for classroom practice. This was done in an attempt to try to create a variety of teaching and learning materials that would eventually serve as examples for further development. As mentioned in the introductory part of this chapter, the use of the Internet in the classroom causes changes in the role of the teacher, who now becomes more of a guide and consultant in this rather student-centered learning situation. This issue was discussed with the teachers and was used as the rationale for the development of the various Internet-type activities.

5.4 The structure of the Internet site: "General Chemistry and Industrial Chemistry for the Use of Mankind"

The Internet site "General Chemistry and Industrial Chemistry for the Use of Mankind" (http://stwww.weizmann.ac.il/g-chem/learnchem) was developed (rationale, structure, selection of contents and teaching strategies) to serve as a useful resource to complement the teaching materials for high-school chemistry students and teachers. It was developed according to a curriculum-based rationale, flexible enough to adapt to future changes in the syllabus. This site also has the potential to enrich and vary chemistry studies, mainly with relevant everyday life issues and industrial applications (see Figure 10.1).

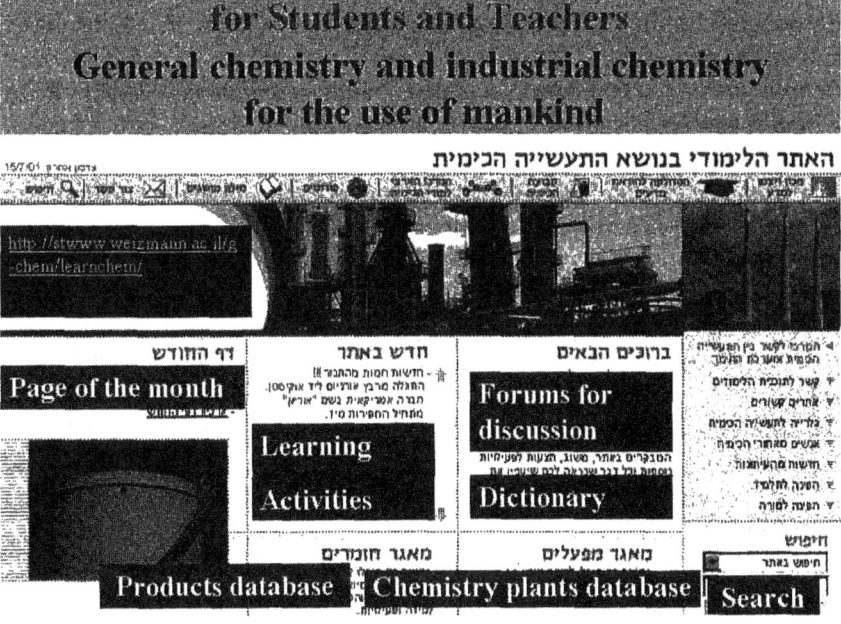

Figure 10.1. An Educational Internet Site for Students and Teachers

The main components of the Internet site are as follows:

About the Israeli Chemical Industry-Education Link Center: information, publications, activities, and courses.
Link to the syllabus (learning materials and activities related to each of the following topics in the syllabus): Atomic structure, structure and bonding, oxidation-reduction, stoichiometry, acids and bases, carbon compounds, energy, equilibrium, thermodynamics, industrial chemistry, electrochemistry, polymers, the interaction between radiation and matter, sugars, and proteins.
Relevant links: organizations, museums, chemical industries abroad, governmental links, and Internet resources
Galleries: pictures, articles/newspaper clippings, presentations, videos, and production process flow charts
The chemical industry in Israel: the products database (information on 100 products of the Israeli chemical industry relevant to the syllabus, see an example in Appendix 1), the chemistry plants database (information on 30 main chemistry plants in Israel, see an example in Appendix 2), introduction to the products database, introduction to the plants database, and maps
People behind chemistry: scientists and researchers, Nobel Prize winners, employees from industry, and prominent figures in the history of chemistry.
The students' corner: games, experiments at home, questions of interest, an open line to experts, why chemistry?
The teachers' corner: an open line to experts, a collection of exams, subjects for discussion, and interesting articles
From the news: "hot" newspaper clippings
Page of the month: chemistry related to the car, chemistry on the beach, etc.
Industrial initiatives (a new program): guides, programs, and activities
Selected subjects in daily life chemistry: medicines and health, foods and drinks, clothing, plastics, forensic chemistry, and environmental chemistry
Forums (students, teachers): questions and dilemmas discussed by classes, support forums for in-service training courses and experimental groups of teachers
Contact us: messages, questions, and problems
Guides: student guides, teacher guides
Search: the whole site, the databases

In Table 10.1, we present the characteristics of the site according to its rationale and the principles described before, and the methods that were used to attain these characteristics.

Table 10.1 Characteristics of the Internet Site and Methods that were Used to Attain these Characteristics

Characteristics	Methods
Dynamically up-dated	Most of the items are in the form of Microsoft Word documents and Power Point presentations that can be very easily downloaded by the teachers or students, and changed or adapted according to their needs Special notes about new items in the site. Items can be very easily up-dated by authorized managers. Informing about the date of updating. Includes a counter.
Appealing and captivating	Galleries with lots of colorful pictures. Short video films. Games. Lots of links to important institutions (universities, government, libraries, plants...)
User-friendly	A very simple portal structure. Includes a teacher's guide. Includes a student's guide. Most of the activities have notes for the teacher. Includes search possibilities.
Applicable to diverse students	Different sizes, levels, styles of learning activities. Activities oriented to all grades.
Interactive by involving and motivating the students in the learning process	Forums for discussion. Questions for experts. Make direct e-mailing.
Based on information technology principles	Includes content organized databases. The databases are A-Z organized. Includes a dictionary. Internal searching.
Practical in terms of learning objectives and applied to chemistry topics in the curriculum	Links to the syllabus-learning activities are organized in the portal according to the subjects in the syllabus. The portal has special programs and their outlines. Examples of teachers' practices. Includes practical suggestions for alternative assessment tools.

Table 10.1. Continued.

Characteristics	Methods
Relevant to daily life aspects of chemistry	A special place in the portal is devoted to chemistry in daily life. Most activities are planned to include daily life aspects of chemistry. Includes a gallery of articles and newspaper clippings from daily journals.
Presents industrial applications based on chemistry principles and concepts	A resource about the main chemistry plants in Israel. A resource about the main chemistry products of Israeli Industry. Most activities are planned to include industrial aspects of chemistry.
Contributes to teachers' and students' advancement	Contains enrichment materials beyond the syllabus.
Offers varied teaching methods and activities, flexible regarding various learning styles	The activities are designed to be varied regarding length (time needed to perform), level of difficulty, learning styles (individual /cooperative), contents, etc. The activities are classified into categories (following a table that shows the main categories and specific examples).

6. Implementation of the Site in the Context of High-School Chemistry

Implementation is an important part of the process of curriculum development. This includes the four stages of initiation, planning, development of materials, and implementation. One of the lessons that was learned from the reforms in science education in the '60s was that even the best programs or learning materials will not be educationally effective without appropriate implementation procedures that include the continuous professional development of teachers. Technologically-rich environments are new for many teachers and most of the chemistry teachers in Israel had only limited experiences with such technological devices in general and in monitoring the chemistry classroom in which instruction is regulated by the Internet in particular.

Next, we describe the procedures that were used with the goal in mind of helping teachers to adopt the newly developed site into their regular chemistry classroom instruction. The implementation included continuous support provided to the teachers and also qualitative and quantitative assessment procedures aimed mainly for formative purposes of the web site.

6.1 Stages in the Implementation

Stage 1: Assessing the implementation and selecting teachers to participate in a workshop

The first stage in the implementation procedure was aimed at obtaining an objective picture regarding the availability of the relevant technology in schools (access to Internet and e-mail), the degree of involvement of the teachers and students in learning through technologically-rich environments, and finally the use of computer-assisted instruction in chemistry education. The survey showed that in only 50% of the schools teachers had access to computers in the context of chemistry education, and that only a few used the Internet in the context of chemistry education. Based on this survey, the teachers who had the initial potential to implement the web site in their chemistry classes were invited to participate in a three-day-long intensive workshop.

Stage 2: The workshop

The main goal of the summer workshop was to familiarize teachers with the pedagogy of teaching chemistry in a technologically-rich environment, to familiarize them to the rationale, structure, and philosophy of the web site, the various components of the website, and to discuss issues and problems that can arise in teaching the concepts and models that are presented to the student. During the workshop, the chemistry teachers, who worked collaboratively in small groups, were provided with opportunities to familiarize themselves with the various components of the site in the same way as their students. It was assumed that in order to teach chemistry using the web site, teachers need to undergo intensive professional development in order to equip them with the necessary knowledge and abilities. Moreover, studies have shown that in order to ensure effective implementation, teachers need to undergo Internet-type experiences similarly to their own students (Kennedy, 1998; Kracjik, Mamlok, & Hug, 2001).

Stage 3: Implementing the site in schools

Ten teachers opted to try the new site in their schools (10 classes, n=210 students). Each teacher was asked to adopt at least one activity from each of the categories described in Table 10.2.

In Appendix 3 we provide an example of an activity involving stoichiometry that is in the category of using Internet resources for visualization and realization. This was developed based on the use of a free applet from the web in order to help students in understanding calculations of chemical processes, but according to the aim of the Internet site, various tasks and aspects of industrial and daily life applications of the substances are included.

Table 10.2. Categories and Examples of Activities in the Internet Site

Category	Types of activities	Examples
Short focused activity	Treasure hunt (a focused inquiry on a specific topic based on a written text conducted by a few leading questions). An activity based on a newspaper clipping /article from the web/galleries. A game. An activity based on one of the resources (products of industry, chemistry plants).	Metals and alloys, why did the World Trade Center collapse? Acid rain: the scientific background. Substances around us. Looking for ionic/molecular compounds and their properties. Exploring the Israeli chemical industry.
Large scale inquiry-type activity	Web quest Multi-dimensional inquiry (a challenging and relevant question coming from a newspaper clipping /article, advertisements, T.V. program, etc. leads to research conducted in various learning environments including the WWW).	Fertilizers, yes or no? Distillation of water, yes or no? Nuclear energy and us, yes or no? Fluorine in water, yes or no? Recycling of plastics, yes or no? The world of ions. Carbohydrates for our use. Batteries around us.
Use of Internet resources for visualization and realization	Virtual lab. Use of an applet. Virtual visit. Short video.	Applets (stoichiometry, organic compounds families, bond energies, etc.) Actual visits to chemistry plants Internet sites Short videos on industrial chemistry topics.

Table 10.2. Continued

Category	Types of activities	Examples
Group discussion	Forums for discussion of topics related to the chemistry curriculum.	Is chemistry related to everyday life? (10th grade) Methyl bromide use for agriculture-yes or no? (12th grade) Ireen Brokovitz –does the film relate to chemistry (10th grade)
An "open" web-based project	Based on a general topic for exploration	A project on an everyday life products

6.2 The Story of Two Teachers

The site was constructed so that the chemistry teachers will have maximum flexibility to choose activities that will be aligned with their teaching style and in addition will be suitable to the cognitive ability, learning style, and motivational pattern of their students. In order to illustrate the idea of "flexible implementation", we chose to describe two case studies of two teachers in their grade 10 classroom.

6.2.1 The Story of "M"

"M" came to the course with little experience regarding teaching chemistry in a technologically-rich learning environment. However, she was highly motivated and enthusiastic about the idea of trying the new instructional technique in her chemistry classroom. Her headmaster provided her with technical support and encouraged her efforts to use the site. We observed her behaviour in the classroom and it is clear that she makes a big effort to create an effective learning environment. More specifically, she has clear goals that she wants to attain, she provides constant guidance to her students in this student-centered learning, and she prepares clear and valid work sheets for her students. Moreover, it is clear that she is following the guidelines that she obtained from the site developers, and she is implementing the activities and experiences in which she was involved in the summer workshop.

We observed that "M" underwent a pronounced professional change regarding her attitude toward and interest in technologically rich teaching and learning tools. Her confidence in using the computer as a communication device, as a source for enhancing her content knowledge and her pedagogical content knowledge, and as a tool to vary the classroom learning environment was increased significantly.

6.2.2 The Story of "S"

"S" came to the summer workshop with a lot of uncertainty regarding the use of an Internet site in the chemistry classroom. She had many reservations and questions regarding the effectiveness of this instructional technique. However, after the summer workshop her confidence increased and she thought that the Internet could help her in increasing the students' motivation to learn chemistry in general and to enroll in more advanced courses in chemistry in particular. Our observation of "S" showed that she was using the site as a basis and a starting point for her teaching, in contrast to "M", who was using the site as instructed by the developers; "S" elaborates, and develops more activities for her science-oriented class. All the teaching of grade 10 chemistry is conducted in the computer laboratory, since she has a highly motivated class with a majority of computer-literate students. Moreover, her students report their homework on the computer (using e-mail) and she provides them with feedback electronically. In addition, she encourages her students to use the Internet also at home in order to extend their chemistry knowledge regarding issues that were discussed in class. She used the site with a lot of flexibility, including inserting more activities and ideas. She reported that the teaching style that she had adopted enhanced and improved her communication and interaction with her students. Thus, we believe it had a positive impact on her classroom learning environment. Recently she decided to involve her students' parents in the activities with the goal in mind of improving the home learning environment and gaining the parents' support for her students.

We described two teachers "M" who adopted the site as it was, without making changes or inserting additional items, and "S", who used the site as a vehicle for reforming the way she taught chemistry in general and for the purpose of improving her communication skills in the chemistry classroom. Each of them adopted the site to her own teaching style and to her students' interest and abilities.

7. Summary

The Internet site: *General Chemistry and Industrial Chemistry for the Use of Mankind,* which was developed for teaching chemistry in Israel, is a useful resource to complement the formal teaching of high- school chemistry in Israel. Preliminary research results show that both students and teachers are very satisfied with the site and its contents. The contribution of its use is in raising the motivation of teachers for implementation of the Internet in the chemistry classroom and for students to deal with chemistry issues relevant to industry and daily life applications.

Obviously, in addition to the advantages, there are in some respects also disadvantages, for example, the need for an additional budget, a lot of development work, a change in the duty of the teacher, who is now more a consultant and facilitator than an instructor, the need for intensive training courses for teachers, constant computer maintenance, and a need for training in integrating alternative ways of evaluation (different ways of learning and different ways of assessment).

We operate in an era of new *standards* in science education. These standards are characterized by the need to ensure that all students will be scientifically literate. There is no doubt that in order to attain such an ambitious goal, the teachers themselves must be equipped with tools that will help in decision-making regarding the pedagogy of teaching and learning science in general and chemistry in particular. Teachers must have flexibility regarding the use of learning materials and must be able to tailor these to their classroom. It is clear that using the Internet as a teaching device has great potential in varying the classroom environment. However, it is suggested, in regard to its educational effectiveness, that we are still in an "embryonic" stage. Moreover, we need to explore and develop research methodologies and assessment measures that will help the research community in exploring important issues and research regarding learning in and from such sites, the effectiveness of such learning in comparison with other pedagogical interventions used in the science classroom, students' and teachers' behavior in this unique learning environment, and finally, questions regarding effective implementation procedures, i.e. support that should be given to teachers in implementing technologically rich instructional techniques.

References

Abad, V.J. (1999). Hebdo-Chim, a Web application to support learning in a chemistry methods pre-service course. *Journal of Science Education and Technology, 8*, 283 - 290.

Adar, L. (1969). *A theoretical framework for the study of motivation in education.* Jerusalem: The Hebrew University. (In Hebrew).

Alister, B. F. (1999). Colleges should tap the pedagogical potential of the World Wide Web. *Chronicle of Higher Education. 48*, 8.

Aksela, M., & Meisalo, V. (2001). School chemistry in inspiring ways: a web-based investigative environment for interactive chemistry education. In A, F. Cachapuz (Ed.), *Proceedings of the 2nd European Conference on Chemical Education.* Aveiro, Portugal, University of Aveiro.

Barnea, N., & Dori, Y. J. (1999). High-school chemistry students' performance and gender differences in a computerized molecular modeling learning environment. *Journal of Science Education and Technology, 8*, 4, 257-271.

Brown, J. S., Collins, A., & Duguid, P. (1989). Situated cognition and the culture of learning. *Educational Researcher, 18*, 32-41.

Carpi, A. (2001). Improvements in undergraduate science education using web-based instructional modules. *Journal of Chemical Education, 78*, 1709-1712.

Gagen, M. (2001). The molecular world: a new, integrated, multimedia-rich course from the UK Open University. In A, F. Cachapuz (Ed.), *Proceedings of the 2nd European Conference on Chemical Education.* Aveiro, Portugal, University of Aveiro.

Hofstein, A., & Kempa, R. F. (1985). Motivating aspects in science education: An attempt at an analysis. *European Journal of Science Education, 7*, 221-229.

Hofstein, A., & Walberg H, J. (1995). Instructional strategies. In B. J. Fraser & H. J. Walberg (Eds.), *Improving Science Education. The NSSE Yearbook.* Chicago, IL: The International Academy of Education.

Johnstone, A. H., Percival, F., & Reid, N. (1981). Is knowledge enough? *Studies in Higher Education, 6*, 77-84.

Kempa, R. F. (1983). Developing new perspectives in chemical education. *Proceedings of the 7th International Conference in Chemistry, Education, and Society* (pp. 34-42). Montpellier, France.

Kempa, R.F., & Diaz, M. (1990). Motivational traits and preferences for different instructional modes in science. *International Journal of Science Education, 12*, 195-203.
Kennedy, M. M. (1998, April). *The relevance of content in in-service teacher education*. A paper presented at the annual meeting of the American Educational Research Association, San Diego, CA.
Kesner, M., Hofstein, A., & Ben-Zvi, R. (1997a). The development and implementation of two industrial chemistry case studies for the Israeli high school chemistry curriculum. *International Journal of Science Education, 19* (5), 565-576.
Kesner, M., Hofstein, A., & Ben-Zvi, R. (1997b). Student and teacher perceptions of industrial chemistry case studies. *International Journal of Science Education, 19* (6), 725-738.
Krajcik, J. Mamlok, R., & Hug, B. (2001) Learning science through inquiry. In L. Corno (Ed.), *Education Across a Century: The Centennial Volume*. The NSSE Yearbook, Chicago: Chicago University Press.
Krajcik, J. S. (2000). *Advantages and challenges of using the world-wide-web to foster sustained science inquiry in middle and high school classrooms*. Keynote speech, Taipei: Taiwan.
Krajcik, J., Blumenfeld, B. Marx, R., & Soloway, E. (2000). Instructional, curricular, and technological supports for inquiry in science classrooms. In Minstrell, J. & Van Zee, E. (Eds.). *Inquiring into inquiry: Science learning and teaching* (pp. 283 – 315), Washington, D.C: American Association for the Advancement of Science Press.
Lookatch, R.P. (1995). The strange but true story of multimedia and the type 1 error. *Technos, 4*, 10-13.
National Research Council (1996). *The National Science Education Standards*. Washington DC: National Academy Press.
"Tomorrow 98" (1992). *Report of the superior committee on science and technology education*. Jerusalem: The Ministry of Education and Culture (English version).
Williams, S. M., & Hmelo, C. E. (1998). Guest editors' introduction. *The Journal of the Learning Sciences, 7*, 265-270.
Yaron, D., Freeland, R., Lang D., & Milton J. (2000). *Using simulations to transform the nature of chemistry homework*. A progress report, Department of Chemistry, Carnegie Mellon University, Pittsburgh, PA.

Appendix 1

Products database
Each product has a data sheet containing the following information:

- Name in Hebrew
- Name in English
- Chemical formula
- Molar mass
- Structure
- The molecular or ionic model/picture
- Properties: Boiling temperature, melting temperature, density, solubility...
- Typical reactions
- Toxicity
- Flammability
- Production processes
- Uses
- Where to implement in the curriculum
- Internet links

Appendix 2

Chemistry plants database
Each plant has a data sheet containing the following information:

Name of the plant
General information
Location
Address
Internet site
Products and processes
Environmental care
Timetable/history of the plant
Visits
Implementation in the curriculum
Teaching materials
Related links

Appendix 3

Stochiometry (An example of a large scale inquiry-type activity)
Marcel Frailich, Dr. Tirza De-Vris (developed in the workshop conducted by Dr. Miri Kesner, 2002)

Target population: Tenth grade students
Objectives of the activity:
a. Acquaintance with the applet and its use.
b. Use of stoichiometry in industrial contexts.
c. Varying the subject of stoichiometry in teaching.

Part 1 - Being acquainted with the production process of Urea
This exercise deals with the production process of Urea.
At the beginning you will become acquainted with Urea and then be asked to make various calculations. At the following Internet address, you can find information about Urea (Materials database):

1. Look in the Urea data page and record its production process.
2. Write down the structural formula of Urea.
3. Describe the geometry around the carbon atom.
4. Write down the properties of Urea.
5. How is Urea used?
6. Examine the production process of Urea (question number 1) and answer the following questions:
    a. 2 moles of Ammonia were added to the reaction vessel. How many grams of Urea were formed? Show your method of calculation.
    b. In another experiment, 50 grams of ammonia were added to the reaction vessel. Calculate:
        - How many moles of ammonia were used for the experiment?
        - How many moles of carbon dioxide were used in the experiment?
        - How many moles of Urea were produced in the process? (Assume the process goes to completion).

7. In the "Fertilizers and Chemicals" plant Urea is produced. 1 ton of Urea was by ordered by a certain client. Calculate:
   - How many moles of Urea the plant has to produce?
   - How many moles of ammonia are needed?
   - How many grams of Ammonia are needed for the process?
   - How many grams of carbon dioxide are needed for the process?
8. Give your answers to the teacher.

Part 2 - Being acquainted with the applet and working with it.

At the following Internet address there is an applet dealing with the production process of Urea.
http://ir.chem.cmu.edu/irproject/applets/stoich/Applet.asp

1. Look at the applet and define its different components:
   b. Find the area where the reactants and products are presented.
   c. Find the area where the masses of the reaction components are presented.
   d. Find the area where the number of moles is presented.
   e. Use the button at the bottom of the applet and define its task. How do you know when the reaction is finished?
2. Find a way to input in data for the reaction in the applet. For example, input data for the following reactants: 2 moles of ammonia and 1 mole of carbon dioxide (use the button at the bottom of the applet). Describe what happens as a result of inputting the number of moles. (Note: Start the reaction after inputting the data about all the reactants.)
3. Use the applet in order to check your answers in part 1.
   Get from the teacher your corrected worksheet from part 1.
   Note: you have to input in the number of moles of all the reactants in order to get correct answers for all the components involved.
4. Choose one of the reactions given in the applet (by pressing the button representing the reactants or the products). Use the applet to create 3 exercises for calculating moles and quantities in grams, similar to the exercises that you already had.
5. Show the teacher your exercises.

Part 3 - Urea in industry and in daily life
Urea is produced in a "Fertilizers and chemicals" plant. The Internet address of the Internet site of the plant is
http://www.deshanim.co.il/deshanim/daf2.html

Press the button representing the product catalogue and answer the following questions:
1. In what states of matter is Urea marketed?
2. Why is Urea so popular as a fertilizer?
3. In the catalogue it is written that spreading Urea on the ground without covering it with earth can cause a loss of nitrogen because of the evaporation of ammonia. Explain this effect. Examining the production process of Urea can help you.
4. The written data on Urea indicates it is rich in Nitrogen. The percentage of Nitrogen is 46%. Calculate the percentage on your own, show your way of calculation, and check the data.
5. Ammonia is produced when proteins decompose in our body. It is a very dangerous substance. Thus, Urea is produced in order to decrease the concentration of ammonia in our bodies (especially in the liver). In following Internet address you can find a description of the metabolic path in the liver where Urea is produced:
http://www.nature.com/nrm/journal/v1/n3/slideshow/nrm1200_225a_F2.html

Look at the left diagram (a) and answer the following questions:

A. Try to explain the diagram in your own words.
B. The diagram describes the mechanism of Urea production in the liver. Write down the names of the reactants and the products.
C. Note the number of moles (of reactants and products); write the chemical equation for the production process of Urea in the liver. Compare the biological process to the industrial one.
D. Explain how Urea in our body can be produced at a temperature of 37^0C where as the industrial production process needs a temperature of 167^0C and a pressure of 140 atmospheres.

Part 4 - Uses of Urea in our daily life

It is possible to integrate these questions into the chapter on chemical equilibrium or at the end of the chapter on acids and bases.
Note that the production process of Ammonia is also an equilibrium process.
In part 1 you wrote down the chemical equation describing the production process of Urea. (Also in part 2 it is written in the applet.)
Read the technical information about Urea at the Internet site of "Fertilizers and chemicals" and answer the following questions:
http://www.deshanim.co.il/deshanim/asg/Category_0.html

1. The element nitrogen is absorbed by plants in its ionic state as $NH_4^+{}_{(aq)}$ and $NO_3^-(aq)$. Prilled urea is spread on the ground or hidden inside it a short time before it rains or there is irrigation.
   A. What is the process that makes Urea available for the plants?
   B. Write the chemical equations describing the change from Urea to both ions.
   C. Prilled Urea is packed in polypropylene bags with an inner coating of polyethylene (sealed). Why?
2. A. Write down the chemical reaction that takes place when ammonia is added to water.
   B. When Urea is added to the irrigation water (system), one must take care to do it in small quantities in order to avoid the precipitation of scale ($CaCO_{3(s)}$) that blocks the dropper holes in the drip irrigation system. Explain why. (Hint: Remember how scale in the kettle is being removed).
3. When spreading a solution there is a loss of Urea, thus splitting the amount of fertilizer into little quantities is recommended. Explain why.
4. A. Check the concentrations that are used for spreading Urea on leaves.
   B. Compare the concentrations of putting fertilizer beneath the ground to those used to spray it on leaves.
   C. In what stage of growth is it possible to use the spaying of leaves for fertilization?
   D. Why when spraying the part of the plants that are above the ground one uses much lower concentrations than used when fertilizer is put beneath the ground.

5. In 1981 it was found that the bacteria *Helicobacter pylori* is responsible for the stomach ulcer. Until then scientists thought that because of the high acidity in the stomach (pH~1-2 (there are no bacteria that can grow in it. Read the article "The bacteria, ulcer and the solution" (the second article at the Internet site).
http://www1.snunit.k12.il/heb_journals/galileo/008008.html

Answer the following questions:

A. What mechanism enables the bacteria to live in such an environment?
B. Write down the chemical equation described in this process.
C. What causes injury of the stomach walls?
D. What was the recommended treatment for stomach ulcer before the discovery of the bacteria? What is the recommended treatment today? Explain.

Enjoy your work!

Chapter 11

TECHNOLOGY AND MARITIME EDUCATION AND TRAINING: A FUTURE PERSPECTIVE

Peter Muirhead
World Maritime University
Sweden

The chapter considers the influence that computers and information technology links are having on traditional ways of delivering maritime education and training, and examines how these features can be used to open up future avenues of learning. In this regard the potential of marine simulation, satellite communications and distance learning methods to deliver training and education to the seafarer on the ship, using the global links of the Internet and Worldwide web is considered.

1. Global MET and the Impact of New Technology

The world of maritime education and training (MET) is being subjected to many changes resulting from new international agreements on global standards of education and training. Most conventions and codes affecting global competency standards of seafarers today are of relatively recent origin, having been enacted over the past 25 years. Education and training in the maritime sphere is conducted within vastly different infrastructures, varied institutional frameworks and course programs using a wide variety of standards in equipment and staff capability. Institutions may be established as vocational training centres, technical or secondary colleges, or tertiary polytechnics or universities producing a plethora of diverse systems. The operation of ships themselves has changed and continues to change in a marine environment where not only is legislation affecting the master and his officers in their daily lives, but the introduction of new ship design and technology and data communications systems are rapidly altering the work environment. Today ships are being delivered with built in Local Area Networks (LANs) to allow links via hubs directly to and from the shipowner's office ashore. The office at sea concept is based on the growing use of the IT highway (via satellite communications systems) and means that the shipmaster is no longer isolated from the office ashore when the ship sails over the horizon. The international shipping industry itself is faced with the challenge in the 21st century of manning its fleets of modern technology ships with highly skilled crews. Yet many in the maritime education and training community still follow traditional teaching and training approaches, lack modern equipment and facilities, and lack an understanding of how to apply new technology and educational methodologies.

New technology is going to have a considerable impact on how ships are operated and managed in the next few decades. While satellite position fixing and communications systems, computers and automation have penetrated the market extensively, the potential use of the Internet, the World Wide Web, e-mail, multimedia, simulation and distance education services for training has not yet been fully realised. Another influence at work is the revised Standards of Training, Watchkeeping and Certification (STCW 95) Convention that encourages a greater use of marine simulation to measure the competence of seafarers to perform functions and tasks.

A recent survey by the author (2002) of 90 global MET institutions showed that many of them are thinking about the future use of new technology. The penetration of modern instructional media is relatively good and many institutions appear to have plans for the progressive upgrading of classrooms and laboratories with PC projectors and video tablets. Accessibility to newer technology in the form of video and digital cameras is modest but growing. Marine simulation facilities have quite a wide variety of penetration. The use of these and other multimedia tools will play a greater role when institutions pursue the development of online learning materials and distance learning delivery systems. Where to with distance learning? The survey clearly indicates that it is still in its infancy in the maritime education sector. Very few institutions offer full maritime educational courses by distance learning. Developmentally, it is a costly and time consuming step and needs to be considered carefully. The growing accessibility to the Internet and e-mail services ashore and at sea, however, will assist in making such decisions easier in the future.

So what of the future? The perception is of one focused on the use of computer technology, access to the Internet and World Wide Web and utilising these facilities and multimedia tools for enhanced learning and for extending educational opportunities beyond the walls of the institution. Judging from the responses, most MET institutions are very aware of the changes taking place in technology and the challenge it poses to their future survival. The two most supported intentions are the creation of CBT laboratories and the provision of IT/CBT training to teachers.

2. Onboard Training – Current Trends and Future Perspectives

The world is changing rapidly due to technical innovation. The maritime industry cannot isolate itself from such influences and yet there is still a reluctance by some to go forward and embrace new methods and new techniques that will meet the challenge of change. Many shipowners, of course, recognise the need to change and embrace new methods. New technology offers the ship operator an opportunity to improve vessel operation efficiency and maintenance. Norwegian ship management companies have designed vessel specific training systems, using CBT modules onboard and at specific locations ashore. Experience has shown that officers and crew embrace onboard PC based training with a high degree of enthusiasm. A follow-up Norwegian project, completed at the end of 2001, called 'Flexible Learning System for the Shipping Industry' involved the cooperative effort of government, shipowners', research council and industry. A number of maritime institutions plan to offer programs to the seafarer via the Internet in future. E-mail and the Web will become standard everyday tools onboard ship opening up new opportunities in education and training, remote polling and monitoring of ship operations, improved maintenance management and stock control, and cost effective operations.

Current technology developments have opened up the possibility of transferring much training to the onboard environment. While this is the ideal place to gain practical experience, many people are concerned at the level of expectation industry has towards training outcomes. A new ship may very well be supplied with CD-ROM programs, developed by the manufacturer of equipment, to assist in familiarisation and operational efficiency, but trade routes and manning levels may inhibit effective use in many cases. The mandatory requirements of STCW 95 for approved training record books for trainees at sea may reap some benefit from technology, but much of the program to be covered relies on experiential outcomes. In this area of training there is great potential for using the electronic medium. Training record book activity could be returned electronically to the company training manager, an institutional assessor or to the master of the trainee's next ship. The provision by Maersk Line of simulation training facilities onboard a number of its ships marks a watershed in the transfer of training to the shipboard environment. Interactive multimedia programs are increasingly being delivered to the ship by the suppliers of bridge, engine room and cargo handling equipment. Total software solutions for meeting obligations under the International Safety Management (ISM) Code are available for the shipowner and shipmaster The training demands of the future relate very much to the degree of familiarisation of officers and masters with computers and computer systems and software.

In addition, computer based training lends itself to crew safety and familiarisation training required under STCW 95. With the quick turn-round time of many ships today (cruise ships, ferries and container ships) crew changes present owners with a particularly difficult problem in meeting the foregoing obligations. Many are turning to self-learning computer based technology and multimedia tools.

If MET institutions are to meet such demands, their computer based resources and instructors' skills must be upgraded, if they to are to continue to turn out trainees acceptable to industry. The maritime industry itself can expect growing pressure from technological developments to continue to change the manner in which they operate and manage vessels in the future. Strategic planning for new training requirements is clearly a major key to the future success of the shipping industry and the enhancing of global standards.

Consider the problem of attracting young people to sea today. If owners of highly sophisticated modern ships are to take advantage of IT and satellite communications technology, the source of recruitment needs to be carefully thought out. To what extent will the company need to provide training in the use of its onboard systems, for example? Can this be done onboard or in conjunction with a local educational institution? The Cyberspace University concept is starting to revolutionize education and training thinking ashore, with many institutions now offering online courses via the Internet. Hall (2001) noted, for example, that in 1988 there were 400 corporate universities in the USA, today there are over 1600 and, if the trend continues, by 2010 they will exceed the number of traditional universities. Such developments are starting to encroach upon the shipboard environment. Indeed, if shipowners and operators are to attract well-educated personnel to operate their fleets in the 21st century, the provision of Internet and e-mail facilities as a matter of course will both be expected and required. Shipowners need to review future training requirements and plan ahead as to how they will make optimal use of the new tools and IT methods available to them.

But can training keep pace with advances in technology today? The will to change and adapt is there but a lack of training equipment and resources may inhibit rapid progress. As well, the shipping industry needs to be clear on where it is heading and what level of skills it requires from its seafarers tomorrow. MET institutions are ready and willing to meet the new IT challenge, but funding support by governments and the maritime industry must enable institutions to have appropriate resources. But must new training requirements be carried out in shore based training institutions? Today technology provides the innovative owner and operator with a window of opportunity to transfer some of the training for required operational skills to the onboard environment. Indeed, new technological developments also provide increasing potential for the assessment.

An example of the new approach to training, is the work of the Norwegian company Seagull AS. Their ambitious plan to cover the seven functional training areas of the STCW 95 Convention through a CBT database is well advanced. More than 60 CD-ROM based training modules, covering STCW 95 functions, were available at the end of 2002. A further nine modules provide computing and language training. These can be placed onboard a ship or downloaded to the ship's server and managed via the Seagull Navigator system (see Figure 11.1). The Seagull Administrator is a database that takes care of recording and storing assessment reports created by each individual trainee. The latter information can be transferred to the company office ashore via built-in export and e-mail functions.

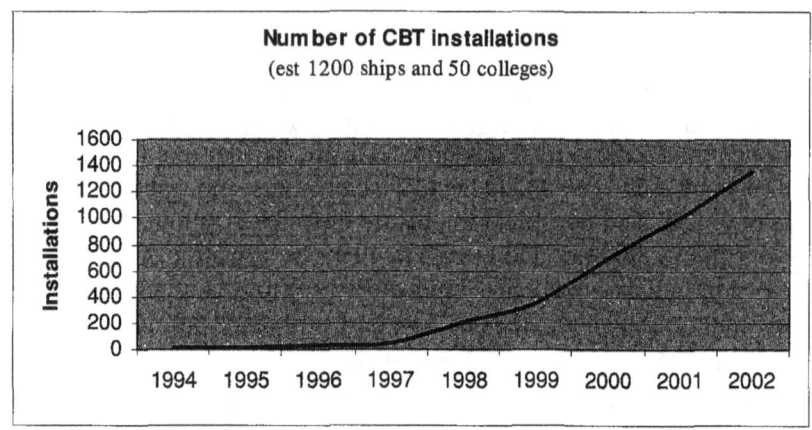

Source: Ringstad, 2002

Figure 11.1. Seagull AS: CBT deliveries to ships and colleges 1995-2002.

A competency evaluation system, CES 4.1, a CBT based assessment program from Seagull, aims to assist shipowners to meet their obligations STCW regarding the competence of seafarers they employ.

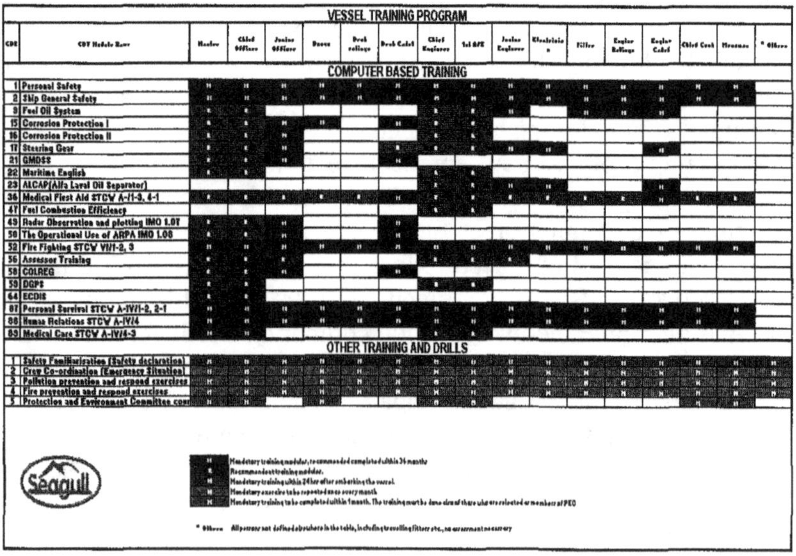

Figure 11.2. Example of a vessel's CBT training program

In the latest release the system uses a large databank of over 5,000 questions to generate an objective test based on rank, vessel type and functional areas (see Figure 11.2). Thus it can also be used to screen new applicants, verify the competence of existing crew, assess personnel for periodic compliance with standards, and assist in pinpointing training needs.

Similarly, Videotel, a company set up 25 years ago to provide training onboard ships via 35mm films, later using video, also provides an extensive suite of programs on CD-ROM.

3. Computer Technology and the Ship

The shipboard network is here. As long ago as 1995, Bergesen Line made the decision to fit each of its 44 ships with a Novell local area network (LAN) and in the late 1990s Stolt Tankers installed fibre-optic LANs throughout its new ships (Muirhead, 1998). Many companies today have computerized their ships and supplied their whole fleet with ship-shore communication software systems from companies such as Rydex (Rydex Express, RMX2), EasyLink (Ocean Connect range), Globe Wireless, Stratos, Bass, and Xantic (AMOS Express, etc). A growing area is in electronic procurement systems for maintenance, spare parts, stores, etc. with systems such as Unitor and Shipserv being just a few of the many companies established in this field. For example, Unitor draws upon a database of over 10,000 products, and in 2001 supplied more than 15,000 ships in 1063 ports and 145 shipyards (Unitor. 2002). Some companies such as Wallem Ship Management have set up their own hub to optimise flexibility for owners of their managed ships. Today in 2003, a ship can access online programs covering bunkering, shipbroking, chartering and ship sales.

How will the shipowner and shipboard personnel use such facilities? Who will be allowed to use the network and what will the shipowner allow the system to be used for? A survey by Davies and Parfett (1997) looked into the possible role of the Internet in improving the welfare and education of seafarers. The report found that unfortunately many companies were opposed to its use by seafarers, often due to a lack of knowledge of how the Internet works and how it affects their systems and costs. However, the new 21st century is seeing a growing realization by many companies of the need to open up communication links to crew members also. The growing availability of hand held satellite telephones on ships in the coming years, promises to create an alternative personal crew calling service, as costs come down. What are the objectives for such technology? Major focus of the shipowner is on improved profitability, efficiency, productivity, safety and operating standards. For the crew improved social services and access to self education and leisure interests.

Some concerns need to be addressed, however. If the Master, officers and crew are to be expected to increasingly use IT for the safe and effective management of the ship, then it is necessary to know the extent to which basic communication and computing facilities and services will be employed. Cost considerations may colour a company's use of the medium. Will satellite video services be used for maintenance purposes? How are High Speed Data links to be used? What range of software will the company employ to conduct business between ship and shore?

Training implications flow in both directions. Communication is a two way process. The potential for improved flows between the ship and the office and vice versa implies the need for a better understanding of each other's role in this increasingly interactive environment. Is this reflected in the company training policy for both seagoing and shore based staff?

4. Information Technology and the Ship

In considering some of the aspects raised earlier, what can the future shipmaster and officer expect to find influencing operational behaviour onboard? The Internet today has become the significant harbinger of the Information Society, using a common language for seamless communication across networks. For ships, access is made easy via PC and satellite links. As a multi-functioning tool it allows access to company databases, downloading of data, pictures, voice and ultimately fast full motion video. Access to e-mail services means the ship never disappears over the horizon out of touch. Crews can maintain contact with families. Telemedicine service means greater peace of mind aboard in the case of accidents. The opportunities for the company for the provision of onboard training programs are boundless. Consider the range of other possible services in the operational, maintenance, education and training fields. Network Wizards (2003) claims that the Internet today comprises more than 162 million domain servers or hosts. CyberAtlas (2003) also estimated the number of Internet users at 445 million in March 2002, rising rapidly to 709 million by the end of 2004. The rate of growth speaks for itself.

Communications software companies provide ready made systems to handle ship and shore connections. Can the shipowner afford not to provide these links onboard and ashore? Unfortunately, the spate of consolidations of land earth station operators and software communication developers during 2000 and 2001 produced a rather confusing picture from a training point of view. Digital Ship in its May 2001 edition reported that this process is leading to the emergence of two distinct business models: the one-stop shop and the multi-supplier scenario. Hyundai Line, for example, signed up to EasyLink's store and forward communications package for its 84 ships and 56 offices in 2001. A range of typical services offered is shown in Figure 11.3.

Figure 11.3. Typical IT services to the shipping industry

Where else is technology going? Although many services are only embryonic, technical difficulties are being overcome. Consider Internet voice technology using local call rates for long distance calls, real time 3D graphical systems, video conferencing, video distribution services, intranets or private company networks, for example. Improvements to high-speed data (HSD) services will continue as the volume and complexity of data transmission grows.

In communications the emergence of global satellite telephone systems, such as Inmarsat phone services and the use of hand-held satellite phones by Iridium and Globalstar, possibly joined by Odyssey and New-ICO over the next few years, will find a use onboard also, as they provide complete coverage of all the world's ocean areas. The ongoing lowering of charges for the use of Inmarsat A, B, C or mini-M for voice, fax and data calls, where available, provides increasing encouragement for owners to shift to greater use of these systems. Direct links provide for access to training in the workplace. The operation of new equipment can be mastered onboard quickly through the use of interactive multimedia training programs. Programs dealing with new company operational practices and procedures (e.g. ISM Code) can be downloaded. Skill levels can be monitored.

The use of satellite communications and IT for onboard training using distance learning methods has been discussed before by the author. For the shipowner, the technology opens a window of opportunity to transfer much training to the shipboard environment. The interactive nature of the medium today means that learning does not take place in a vacuum. IT provides scope for an interactive role between training managers, ship personnel, supporting training institutions, approving authorities and program providers.

5. The Future Role of Satellite Communications Systems

Inmarsat Ltd today provides many satellite communication services in addition to its Global Maritime Distress Safety System (GMDSS) obligations. Its range of communication systems A, B, C, Mini M, D/D+, Fleetnet and E, added to by the new Mobile Packet Data Service (MPDS) and FleetF77 in 2002, provides a comprehensive family of voice and data services to the global community. The latest offering, FleetF77, offers general business applications, including secure access to information online, image transfer and video communications. The potential for adoption for onboard education and training purposes is thus extended. An example of how such services can benefit seafarers has been the introduction of pre-paid calling cards that work with cost effective and compact terminals.

The Inmarsat-A or B duplex 64 Kbps high speed data (HSD) service allows for multimedia transmissions (video, voice, data) to be used. While the tariff rate for use is approximately twice that of a satellite telephone call, the use of compressed video provides useful visual links between ship and shore. The potential for using video technology for maintenance support, and delivering training programs onboard from ashore is considerable. However, for full streaming video capability, broadband connectivity needs to be at a much higher level and awaits new generation satellites and services in 2004 and 2005.

In choosing a mode for the transmission of data, consideration must be given to the nature of the material to be sent (text, figures, graphs, still pictures or video), the volume and frequency of exchange and how critical speed of transmission is to the training process, which will influence the cost. In addition, in the case of Inmarsat, the type of terminal facility will have a bearing on the form of transmission. It is an easy process to send and exchange drawings, graphs, sketches and photographs to ships fitted with Inmarsat-A or B equipment and a fax facility. This is not possible with ships fitted only with Inmarsat-C equipment. The new marine service from Inmarsat called Mobile Packet Data Service (MPDS), that started in November 2001, charges only for data packets sent or received, while the continuous Internet connection eliminates dead-time. This should be more cost advantageous to the ship in the longer term.

A possible solution for ship and seafarer communications, and potentially one of the most exciting developments, is the proposed 'Teledesic' system ('Internet in the Sky') that plans to use 30 satellites to roam the Internet worldwide (Teledesic, 2002). Designed to support millions of simultaneous users, it will provide up to 100 Mbps of capacity on the uplink and 720 Mbps on the downlink. The potential to provide access to distance education programs and leisure pursuits from any position in the world could change the face of onboard life as well as the activities of shore based training institutions. The targeted start up date is 2005, and initial satellite building contracts were let in 2002 to get this ambitious project off the ground.

6. Cyberspace and Distance Learning

Technology has created new opportunities for delivering education and training through the medium of computers, software programs or simulators within an institution, at home or on a ship. But we have also seen that the advent of the Internet, the World Wide Web and satellite communications systems extends the possibility of delivering education and training services directly between institution and student anywhere, anytime. It can be synchronous or asynchronous in form. This potential to deliver learning at a distance (distance learning) has led to a global revolution in education. Many institutions are hurrying to get a foothold in the distance learning marketplace, both locally and globally. Two key aspects of distance learning are physical separation of teacher and student, and the use of communication technology to bridge the physical gap. Selection of the best available forms of communication technology, such as e-mail, fax, telephone, tele and video conferencing, Netchat, bulletin boards, and Netmeeting software are important in overcoming any feelings of isolation by the student.

Seafarers, as a result of their environment, have long been denied access to effective education and training opportunities at sea. Many educational institutions now provide a range of courses and programs for delivery to students living outside of their local boundaries, using structured distance education methods. These programs can be developed and be instructionally designed for the workplace. Ashore, access to a tutor is normally provided by fax, telephone, tele-conferencing and attendance at summer schools. Access to a tutor when at sea is difficult. Feedback to the student can be haphazard and take months.

Satellite communication provides a unique link between student at sea and the tutor ashore. Assignments can be transmitted, marked and returned within a very short period of time. Queries can be responded to in a matter of hours by fax, telex or telephone. The student benefits from the early response and feedback and the links developed with the tutor; the teacher benefits from a rapid perception and understanding of the student's difficulties and rate of progress. Examinations may be arranged to be taken onboard, as has been the case with students enrolled on the Graduate Diploma schemes offered in external study mode by the Australian Maritime College. Even at ratings level, distance learning programs onboard are now available.

This could equally apply to a company running its own in-house onboard training program. An owner may require a ship's crew to undertake refresher or upgrading training, covering onboard equipment or operations at regular intervals. Both programs and individuals can be monitored to ensure that onboard safety standards and levels of skill are maintained. 'Train the trainer' programs can be developed for interactive use between company management and the onboard deliverer or between training institution and the onboard trainer.

There is no technical reason why many aspects of education and training could not be carried out on a ship, as well as on shore, through the supportive medium of distance learning. The real constraints are developmental costs of materials, access to computing and communications technology, course fees, availability of learning time and self motivation. The motivational aspect of persuading crew members to use CBT methods to enhance their knowledge and skills needs careful attention. However, distance learning methods combined with IT resources have the potential to extend the regime of learning to both the shipboard environment and the shore based workplace.

Many education institutions are aware of the need to change and are experimenting with new approaches, as discussed earlier. Many are trying multimedia based programs, both on and off campus. Digitized versions of conventional courses are being prepared. Students solve problems in a smaller and more intimate learning environment, instead of sitting in an impersonal passive learning environment in a large lecture hall. In Australia, students can already enrol in postgraduate distance learning programs in port and shipping management utilising instructional material, Internet, e-mail and tele-conferencing, without having to step inside the institution. Video links are now common in the large remote areas of Australia and Northern Sweden, for example. The trend towards the virtual campus is accelerating daily.

As stated earlier, technology will allow much refresher and upgrading training to be carried out onboard, replacing many courses delivered ashore. For the mariner, the opportunity for private study at sea, a service long denied him or her, will also become reality as Internet links become common onboard ship. Such tools could also support some of the onboard training tasks to be found in the trainee's Training Record Book.

The author is of the view that the following three major categories have the greatest potential to provide benefits to both shipowner and seafarer, and should be targeted in any future delivery of education and training via the Internet and IT:

1. Onboard training obligations of ship operators under the revised STCW Convention, ISM Code and other associated quality control measures;

2. New technical or operational skills, where the communications and technology medium can demonstrate its potential to provide more effective training in situ onboard, as against ashore;

3. Access to further education and knowledge by shipboard personnel, whether leading to an accredited award or just for leisure or interest purposes.

Despite the disadvantages arising from the 'tyranny of distance' and lack of direct supervision, distance learning, when used in conjunction with communications technology for personal education purposes or for onboard training, has the potential to open up new avenues of knowledge and skill relevant to changing workplace needs. Why shouldn't the mariner, for example, be able to take an educational award program at sea via an Open Learning University or from a delivering Maritime Cyberspace Education Centre, in future?

7. Marine Simulation at a Distance

In meeting the new requirements for standards of training, competence and quality assurance imposed upon them by the ISM Code and STCW 95, shipowners are increasingly looking for new means to assure themselves that the officers and ratings they hire across the globe do indeed meet required standards. The maritime industry has been using marine simulation in limited ways since the late 1950s, but its acceptability has been somewhat tardy and its use for assessment purposes even less well accepted, a situation still existing in many minds today. Making marine simulator training mandatory for seafarers has always been a troublesome issue. Despite many perceived benefits of simulator training, delegates revising the STCW 1978 Convention (STCW 95) were unwilling to extend the mandatory requirements beyond radar and ARPA training, a situation unchanged in 2003.

Since the advent of STCW 95 there has been clear evidence of a discernible shift in marine simulation technology away from the larger more expensive CGI based 'full mission' systems to smaller less expensive modular PC based systems of so called 'single or multi-task' type. However, technology is advancing so quickly that the modest 'desktop' or 'work station' computer can form the basis of very sophisticated, flexible and realistic training tools, capable of meeting many of the designated functions and tasks specified in the STCW Convention.

As broadband links become available to the ship at sea in the future, so will the opportunity present itself to use such links in the field of marine simulation, a fast growing and well recognized training and skilling medium. The concept of a computer simply moving data and information from place to place, and comparing it according to a set of prescribed rules or algorithms, leans on the computer's major strength of being able to process information very quickly and accurately. This gives the computer the ability to adapt and respond to the learner's needs, difficulties and progress. Simulators offer close-to-reality training for many important safety and operationally related tasks without any physical risk to the ship or trainee.

As a result of advancing broadband technology in the 21st century, sophisticated simulation training programs will be capable of being accessed onboard (and ashore) from servers via a Web Education Management Systems (WEMS). Such single-task or part-task simulator activity could be monitored and recorded by the institution (or company training officer for that matter) in preparation for further advanced training on the simulators ashore.

To illustrate the potential, A.P.Moeller, parent company of Maersk Line, fitted the Force Technology (DMI) developed SIMFLEX PC based onboard simulator to 16 of its ships in 2001-2002 (see Figure 11.4). The system is being used to train cadets in rule of the road and general shiphandling skills. An interesting feature of the software is that the training can be supervised by an instructor ashore over a ship-shore communications link. This development resulted from a European Commission research project on long distance learning called SEAGULL. Other workstation based simulation programs, such as the 'PortSim' shiphandling system could, for example, also be used onboard by officers to develop strategies for pilot boarding and port entry, as part of voyage planning processes.

A future approach could be for MET institutions to create a web server holding various software simulation training programs, access to which could be offered to trainees, students or graduates both ashore and at sea. For example, the growing range of simulator software products available in the areas of safe cargo handling, stability and stress, terminal planning, chartering practice, logistics and fleet management to mention but a few, could be made available on such a web server as pre-study modules or stand alone units. Links would be provided to real-time data, chartering rates for example.

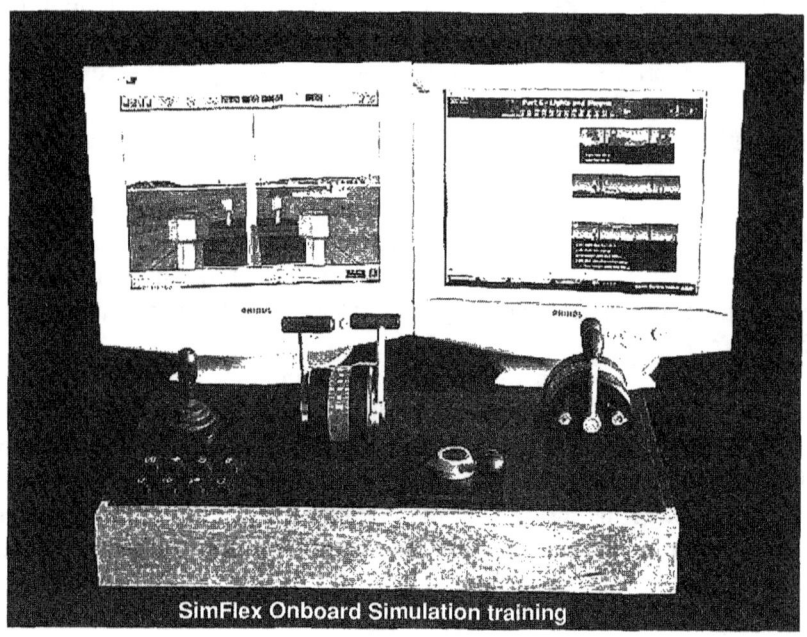

Source: Force Technology 2002

Figure 11.4. Simflex onboard simulation training system

Why undertake simulator training at a distance? What can be gained? Research shows that many officers are not getting the opportunity to acquire key practical skills for good safety and operational reasons. Simulation, if used effectively, provides an alternative medium in which to acquire these operational skills in a risk free environment. The need to narrow the gap between training for knowledge and onboard skill acquisition has become of paramount importance. Many PC based simulation systems today, such as those marketed by Transas, Poseidon, Marinesoft and Sindel, for example, come with very high levels of fidelity that allow meaningful training outcomes to be achieved with many operational functions and tasks. The workstation can be equipped with helm and engine controls allowing for single or part-task training, using the software programs of the full mission simulator (see Figure 11.5).

Figure 11.5. Part-task manoeuvring workstation (Warnemunde, Germany)

The development of marine simulation systems can help to bring maritime training closer to shipboard practices and also allow these facilities to be used to measure trainees' performance in a range of tasks provided certain safeguards are observed. By ensuring that relevant performance standards are followed and training and assessment processes are validated, such forms of simulated training can contribute meaningfully to raising practical safety standards.

The requirement of STCW 95 that seafarers demonstrate their ability to perform tasks and functions safely and effectively in order to ensure competence has been focused on facilities in shore based training establishments. Communications technology is opening up new opportunities to extend the learning and training environment onboard the ship at sea, and simulation tools have the potential to be used just as effectively in the workplace at sea as in a maritime training centre ashore.

8. MET – A Future Technology-rich Training Environment

The technological keys to unlock the system to free students to pursue lifelong learning anywhere, anytime, are rapidly becoming available on a more global basis. Technology is altering all the traditional ground rules. Cyberspace education operates without frontiers, walls or barriers. It is an interactive learning environment, globalized by technology links. It is a concept that can find a ready home at sea, as well, in the future.

Seafarers, as a result of their environment, have long been denied access to effective education and training opportunities at sea. Many educational institutions now provide a range of courses and programs for delivery to students living outside of their local boundaries, using structured distance education methods. These programs can be developed and be instructionally designed for the workplace. Ashore, access to a tutor is normally provided by fax, telephone, tele-conferencing and attendance at summer schools. Access to a tutor when at sea is difficult. Feedback to the student can be haphazard and take months. Access to the Internet, e-mail, video links and satellite phones will mean that the seafarer in future will no longer be disadvantaged in comparison to colleagues ashore. The ship will increasingly become part of normal community life.

New technology, of course, may raise expectations by those working in the related field that such developments will lead to the accruing of advantages, such as increased productivity, greater efficiencies through cost savings, increased employee motivation and job satisfaction, the creation of innovative concepts and ideas, and the sheer excitement of developing new ideas and ways of achieving specific objectives.

Despite the disadvantages arising from the 'tyranny of distance' and lack of direct supervision, distance learning methodologies, when used in conjunction with good communications technology for onboard training or for personal education purposes, has the potential to open up new avenues of knowledge and skill relevant to changing workplace needs.

The earlier mentioned global survey of MET institutions (Muirhead, 2002, p. 60) shows that they range in size from the very small training centre to the large maritime university. Access to capital and recurrent funding also follows very varied patterns in different countries, depending upon the educational and governance structure. The availability of computing and multimedia facilities and supporting expertise varies widely. The author is of the view that many of the smaller, and thus less well resourced, MET institutions would best be advised to create a workable strategic plan prepare themselves for the new technology future.

Table 11.2. A Developmental Technology Matrix for MET Institutions

Continua Institution	Computer Technology	Multimedia Development	Simulation Technology	Delivery Methods	Comms
Training Centre	Computers for staff	Audio-visual Library	PC desktop	Traditional classroom	Basic
Vocational Training Centre	Added accessories	CDR –CD-I Advanced	Single task	Classroom plus limited technology	Low speed links
Small MET academy	Special workstations	Digital technology	Part task	Computer laboratories	Medium speed links
Medium sized MET college	Networks LAN	Web Page site	Full mission	Internet links	High speed links
Large Institute Polytechnic	IT equipped classrooms	Authoring tools	Full mission Internet interactive	Distance learning	High speed links
Maritime University	Interactive PC laboratories	Multimedia studio production	Internet interactive	Web education management system	Satellite links Fibre-optics

Table 11.2 provides a matrix of inter-relationships between size of institution and continuum of development. Development could then be progressed, according to need and capability, based on a series of continua of technology development. Facilities could be then introduced and expanded in a balanced way over a number of years, as learning objectives and market demands dictate.

This does not imply that an institution is constrained in development at its level, but illustrates that technical development should be considered against the key factors of scale of operation, demands of the market place, availability of experienced staff, and funds available. In this way, a progressive and realistic approach to future development can be taken, thereby ensuring that the venture will more likely be assured.

Having determined the learning objectives of the institution and the faculty (the result of a strategic planning exercise), the matrix can be used to establish a starting point (or a continuing point) for institutional technology development. In this way available resources (funding and human) can be matched against agreed developmental needs by ensuring that the most economical and effective pathway is selected. Plans for staff training, both technical and teaching, can also be put in place at the same time. In this way, MET institutions will be technically capable of supporting future demands of the broader maritime community that increasingly is going to be based on a technology-rich learning and training environment.

References

Davies, A., & Parfett, M. (1997). *The Internet - A feasibility Study into its possible role in improving the Welfare and Education of Seafarers*, Report May 1997, SIRC, University of Wales, Cardiff

Hall, B. (2001). *E-Learning - building competitive advantage through people and technology,* Retrieved August 3, 2001 from the World WideWeb: www.Forbes.com/specialsections/elearning/contents.html

How many computer hosts in the Internet, Retrieved January 2 2003 from the World Wide Web: http://www.network.wizards.com

Muirhead, P. M. (1998). *Assessment of the potential in the use of new teaching and training methodologies in MET; distance learning through onboard training*, Work Package 4.4 report, EU Transport Project 'METHAR', WMU, Malmö, Sweden

Muirhead, P.M. (2002). *A study of the impact of new technology and teaching methodologies on global maritime education and training into the 21st century.* Unpublished Ph.D. Thesis, Curtin University, Perth, W.Australia

The world's online population. Retrieved January 2 2003 from the World Wide Web: http://www.cyberatlas.Internet.com

Chapter 12

DESIGNING A WEB-SUPPORTED LEARNING ENVIRONMENT ON COMMUNICATION IN MULTICULTURAL CLASSROOMS[1]

Jan van Tartwijk, Theo Wubbels, Perry den Brok, and Yvonne de Jong
Utrecht University
The Netherlands

Ietje Veldman
Leiden University
The Netherlands

Research has shown that the teacher's interpersonal style is an important factor in the learning environment. Both students' cognitive and affective learning outcomes are related to their teachers' interpersonal style. In The Netherlands, as in many countries, classrooms have become more and more culturally diverse. Perceptions of the interpersonal aspect of behaviour are influenced by the cultural background of the persons involved in communication processes. This implies that teacher education institutes have to prepare their students for communicating with students from various cultural backgrounds. A project was started with the goal of preparing student teachers for the multicultural classroom. A website was used to provide student teachers with both practical and theoretical information on communication processes in multicultural classrooms in The Netherlands. To gather this information, the literature was reviewed, teachers and pupils were interviewed and classrooms videotaped. Workshops were organised in which student teachers and the teachers in schools used the electronic learning environment Blackboard for discussion. Student teachers and teachers also met face-to-face.

---

[1] This chapter is based on work supported by the Dutch Ministry of Education and Science, providing a grant for the project 'A digital learning environment for professional development in intercultural communication'. The Netherlands Organisation for Scientific Research (NWO) also provided funding for this study with a grant of the Foundation for Behavioural and Educational Sciences (411-21-206).

1. Introduction

According to the Central Bureau for Statistics (http://www.cbs.nl), the Dutch population in 2002 was about 16 million. Of these 16 million people, 3 million were either not born in The Netherlands or had parents born outside The Netherlands. About 1.6 million persons have their roots in non-western countries and live primarily in less prosperous areas of major Dutch cities like Amsterdam, Rotterdam, The Hague and Utrecht. Many schools in these cities have classrooms with between 50 and 100% of students from varying non-western backgrounds. Most of these students originated in Morocco, Turkey, Surinam and the Dutch Antilles, and smaller groups have come from countries in Africa (e.g. Nigeria, Ethiopia), Asia (e.g. China, Afghanistan) and the former Yugoslavia, often as refugees. Teachers in schools in the big cities thus have to be prepared for teaching in multicultural classrooms.

Teacher education programs in The Netherlands can hardly rely on results of Dutch research on preparing teachers for multicultural classrooms in secondary education. Internationally conducted research usually focused on other student groups than those present in Dutch classrooms for example on Afro-American and Hispanic students in the USA. Most of the available Dutch research was at the pre-school and elementary level, or was restricted to studies on school careers of minority students, the effects of the government policy on budgets for minority students and all kind of language-related issues. Research groups in The Netherlands only recently have started to investigate other topics that are important for preparing teachers for multicultural classrooms in secondary education. One of these groups is our own at Utrecht University, with a tradition of research on teacher-student communication in the classroom. This research was started mid-way through the 1970s (see e.g. Wubbels & Levy, 1993) and included some studies on American multicultural classrooms (e.g. den Brok, Levy, Rodriguez, & Wubbels, 2002; den Brok, Levy, Wubbels, & Rodriguez, 2003; Levy, den Brok, Wubbels, & Brekelmans, 2003; Levy, Wubbels, Brekelmans, & Morganfield, 1997). Because the multicultural character of the classroom provides an extra challenge for teachers' communicative skills (Ting-Toomey, 1999) we started, in 2000, studies on the specifics of communication in multicultural classrooms in Dutch secondary education. We wanted to extend the available body of knowledge from our research on teacher-student communication to Dutch multicultural classrooms.

In this chapter, we report on a project aiming at this extension of the knowledge base and at the same time wanting to improve the preparation of pre- and in-service teachers. In this project researchers and teacher educators of Utrecht University and the Free University of Amsterdam worked together with teachers of two secondary multicultural schools in two major Dutch cities. The aim of the project was to study multicultural classrooms and design and implement a face-to-face arrangement and an electronic, web-based or *virtual learning environment* (VLE) for student teachers and beginning teachers in multicultural classes. In this learning environment, we wanted to help them further develop their practical knowledge.

This contribution starts with describing the rationale for the simultaneous study of communication in multicultural classrooms and the development of a learning environment for beginning and student teachers. We then discuss the available theoretical ingredients for the development of practical knowledge and pedagogical approach in teacher education. This results in some principles for the design of the environment. The development of the learning environment consisted of four phases: making an inventory of frequently occurring problems, the design process of the environment, testing, and finally evaluation and developing suggestions for further improvement. Each of these four phases is described in this chapter. The chapter concludes with some of the dilemmas that we faced in the design process, as well as some of our plans for future improvement and adjustment of the environment.

2. Rationale

2.1 Developing Practical Knowledge

Through our learning environment we want to help beginning teachers to further develop their practical knowledge. Meijer (1999) refers to teachers' practical knowledge as the cognitions that underlie teachers' actions. Practical knowledge does not stand for a catalogue of empirically verified facts, but rather for all that a person knows or believes to be true, whether or not it is verified as true in some sort of objective or external way. This type of knowledge is described by Korthagen (1998, p. 31) as: 'the eye that one develops for a typical case, based on the perception of particulars'. It is the knowledge enabling a teacher to understand a situation by its particulars and to take appropriate action. Meijer (1999) distinguishes a number of characteristics of teachers' practical knowledge:

- It is personal and to some extend unique.
- It is contextual, meaning it is defined in and adapted to the classroom situation.
- It is based on (reflection on) experience, indicating that it originates in and develops through experiences in teaching.
- It is mainly tacit.
- It underlies teachers' practice.
- It is content related - related to the subject taught.

Citing Fenstermacher (1984), Meijer (1999) distinguishes practical knowledge from formal knowledge or theory. The latter can be characterized as abstract, objective and propositional knowledge, usually the result of a generalization over many situations. We think that it is important that practical knowledge is not only grounded in individual, sometimes idiosyncratic, practical experience, but also in formal knowledge (theory) and experience of other teachers. Theory offers logical explanations based on empirically verified facts for phenomena the teachers come across in their classrooms. Practical knowledge of expert teachers, i.e. expert knowledge, may help student and beginning teachers to overcome the problems they face when starting teaching. Although expert knowledge, theory and research results can inform teacher education, we know that there is often a gap between theory and practice (Wubbels, Korthagen, & Brekelmans, 1997).

In the learning environment, we strive for practical knowledge of teachers that has been productively informed by experts, research and theory. We refer to this kind of practical knowledge as 'theory-rich practical knowledge'.

2.2 Designing a Learning Environment Aimed at Theory-rich Practical Knowledge

In order to be able to ultimately design our learning environment, we need to have answers for three questions (Resnick, 1983; Oost, 1999):

- What is the theory-rich practical knowledge we are aiming for?
- How can this knowledge be acquired?
- What are the specifications for a learning environment enabling teachers and student teachers to acquire this knowledge?

The knowledge base about theories and expert practical knowledge on communication in Dutch multicultural secondary classrooms is not sufficiently extensive to answer the first question and consequently create a solid learning environment for beginning and student teachers. We do not know what theory-rich practical knowledge in this domain would look like. Therefore, we combined in the project, studies of teacher-student communication and experienced teachers knowledge of this communication with the development of a learning environment for (student) teachers. We studied both the literature and experienced teachers' knowledge and their actual communication in multicultural classrooms.

Without an answer for the first, the second and third questions also cannot be answered, but we do have some indications for these answers. We know that an important threat for productive learning in teacher education is the gap between theory and practice. Based on the analysis of this gap we have chosen an inquiry-oriented approach, (Korthagen & Wubbels, 1995; Wubbels et al., 1997), interaction among learners, commuting between theory and practice stimulated by systematic reflection including research-type activities. This combination is what Korthagen (2001) calls a realistic program. He describes as a key principle of such a program that (student) teachers develop their practical knowledge in a process of reflection on practical situations. We add to this principle that expert knowledge and theory should be provided at the moment the teacher has a need for it in order to put his of her individual experiences in schools into a more general perspective.

As a consequence, our learning environment should stimulate reflection on work and learning activities with respect to *teacher-student communication in the multicultural classroom*. Theory and expert knowledge have to be available when the teachers have a need for it: *just in time*. To meet these demands, we developed a web-supported environment with input of experienced teachers, because such a learning environment gives student and beginning teachers involved the opportunity to learn at the time and place that suits them best: usually in-between or after fulfilling their tasks in schools. We now elaborate on the available knowledge base for teaching in multicultural classrooms and the pedagogy for a learning environment.

3. Theories Informing Practical Knowledge

From our previous research, we identified a number of theoretical notions, important in preparing teachers for student-teacher communication. These relate to interpersonal competency, the broader context of teaching, and culture and ethnicity. In addition, we review the scarce literature on strategies for interpersonal behaviour in multicultural classrooms.

3.1 An Interpersonal Perspective on Teaching

The first concern of beginning teachers is whether or not they will be able to cope with discipline problems in the classroom (Veenman, 1984; Wubbels, Créton, & Hooymayers, 1985). Therefore, research findings on the teacher-student relationship in the classroom environment are often perceived as very relevant by beginning teachers. Teachers (and many researchers studying undesirable classroom situations) tend to view misbehaviour as a characteristic of students or a result of poor management strategies of the teacher (Doyle, 1986). In our approach, however, interaction between teacher and students is the focus of attention. We refer to the study of the relational function of the teacher behaviour in this interaction as the *interpersonal perspective on teaching*. This perspective can be distinguished from other relevant viewpoints of describing and studying teaching, such as a learning activities perspective (describing teaching in terms of the learning processes teachers try to elicit and maintain with their students), a moral perspective (describing teaching in terms of the values and norms teachers want their students to pursue), a subject matter perspective (describing teaching in terms of the content of the subject matter) and an organizational perspective (describing teaching in terms of the larger context of the school) (e.g. Brekelmans, Sleegers, & Fraser, 2000; den Brok, 2001).

Our conceptualization of the interpersonal perspective on teaching has been described in Wubbels and Levy (1993) more completely and we only summarize it here. The conceptualization is based on concepts of the so-called *systems approach to communication* (Watzlawick, Beavin,

& Jackson, 1967). Researchers using the systems approach to communication start from the assumption that in communication the behaviours of participants influence each other mutually. The behaviour of the one (the teacher) influences the behaviour of the other (the students) and is in turn influenced by the behaviour of that other. To describe these kinds of processes, the systems approach to communication distinguishes different levels of communication. The lowest level consists of messages: one question, assignment, response, gesture, etc. The intermediate level is that of interactions: chains of several messages. When the interactions show recurrent patterns and some form of regularity, one has arrived at the pattern level. It is this pattern level that is important in describing the rather stable interpersonal relationships that determine the working atmosphere of classrooms.

In the systems approach to communication, the focus is on the effect of communication on the persons involved (the pragmatic aspect). This pragmatic orientation is characterized in our conceptualization of the interpersonal perspective by means of a focus on the *perception of students* of the behaviour of their teacher. The perception of students is mapped and studied with the *Model for Interpersonal Teacher Behaviour* (MITB). This model is based on Leary's research on the interpersonal diagnosis of personality (1957) and its first application to teaching (Wubbels, Créton, & Hooymayers, 1985). The Leary model has been investigated extensively and proven effective in describing human interaction (Foa, 1961; Lonner, 1980). While not conclusive, there is evidence that the Leary model is cross-culturally generalisable (Brown, 1965; Dunkin & Biddle, 1974; Lonner, 1980; Segall et al., 1990). The model describes teacher behaviour along two dimensions: Influence (Dominance – Submission), and Proximity (Cooperation – Opposition). The Influence dimension represents the degree of control or dominance displayed by the teacher, while Proximity describes the level of cooperation or opposition between teacher and students.

Students' perceptions of their teachers´ interpersonal style not only have proven to be related to communication processes in the classroom (e.g. Wubbels, Créton, & Hooymayers, 1985) but also to both cognitive and affective student outcomes. In general, the more the teacher is perceived as dominant, and the more the teacher is perceived as cooperative, the higher the students´ cognitive outcomes (Brekelmans, 1989; den Brok, 2001; Evans, 1998; Goh, 1994; Henderson, 1995;). Studies investigating associations between the teacher-student relationship and affective outcomes find a large and important positive effect of both influence and proximity on affective outcome measures (Brekelmans, 1989; den Brok, 2001; Derksen, 1994; Evans, 1998; Goh, 1994; Henderson, 1995; Rawnsley, 1997; Setz, Bergen, van Amelsvoort, & Lamberigts, 1993; van Amelsvoort, 1993). Furthermore, warm and supportive relationships, rather than corrective classroom management is important in preventing students from dropping out or from displaying disruptive behaviour (Aviles, Guerrero, Howarth, & Thomas, 1999; Jordan, Lara, & McPartland, 1996; Moore, 1994; Sanders & Sanders, 1998). These last findings appear to be particularly true and important for students from minority cultures.

3.2 The Broader Context of Interpersonal Teacher Behaviour

Teacher interpersonal behaviour appears to be co-determined and influenced by a number of other variables, both within and outside the classroom (e.g. den Brok, 2001; Levy, et al., 2003; Wubbels & Levy, 1993). These factors include student characteristics, such as gender, intelligence and socio-economic background, but also class characteristics, including class size, educational type or number of lessons per week, teacher characteristics, such as gender and ethnicity, and school characteristics. Similar factors have been found to co-determine the effects of teachers on student outcomes or drop-out. The literature shows effects of variables such as peer groups, parental involvement and parenting style, extra-curricular activities or ties with the community (e.g. Aviles et al., 1999; Davalos, Chavez, & Guardiola, 1999; Dekkers & Driessen, 1997; House, 1999; Jordan et al., 1996; Sanders & Sanders, 1998; Zea, Reisen, Beil, & Caplan, 1997).

In order to structure the various influences of factors on teaching and its effects, interesting frameworks can be found in the effectiveness literature. Usually, effectiveness researchers theoretically and pragmatically structure relevant factors on teaching and outcomes in terms of clusters or spheres, which are ordered in terms of the 'distance' they have to students' learning. In such models (e.g. Creemers, 1991; Scheerens, 1994; Veenstra, 1999), a distinction is made between *student variables* (or within-class variables), *class variables* (including teaching), *the school* (organization) and the *school-environment* (including parent-school relationships, neighborhood, etc.). We feel that such a distinction may also be valuable and useful to structure the knowledge and strategies of teachers with respect to interpersonal teacher behaviour in multicultural classrooms.

3.3 Culture and Ethnicity

In this chapter, the terms "culture" and "ethnicity" are both used. Following Nieto, (1996, p. 390), we define culture as 'the ever-changing values, traditions, social and political relationships, and world-view created and shared by a group of people bound together by a combination of factors (which can include a common history, geographic location, language, social class, and/or religion), and how these are transformed by those who share them'. We use ethnicity to refer to 'foreign or native population groups' (Pinto, 2000, p. 9). As such, ethnicity can be regarded as one of the indicators that binds people, therefore, one of the many elements that make up culture.

Student, class and teacher background characteristics are linked with students' perceptions of their teacher (e.g. den Brok, 2001; Wubbels & Levy 1993). Cultural membership, as one of those characteristics, influences students' interpretations of their learning environment, including their teacher's interpersonal style. Teaching and learning require perception and communication, both of which are culturally influenced (e.g. Au & Kawakami, 1994; Grossman, 1995; Matsuda, 1989; Nieto, 1996; Nguyen, 1986; Samovar & Porter, 1995; Stefani, 1997). Cultures differ in the type of information perceived, stored and used (Cole & Scribner, 1974; Segall, Dasen, Berry, & Poortinga, 1990; Sturtevant, 1964; Witkin, 1967). As a result, an extensive literature on cultural differences in cognition, conceptualization and knowledge construction has accumulated (for a review, see Gordon, 1995). Culture's role in influencing students' perceptions is also a continuing research theme, with numerous books and journals devoted to it.

A number of studies have investigated the effects of cultural factors on students' perceptions of their teachers' interpersonal behaviour. This research has included a number of ethnic variables such as self-designated ethnicity, country of birth, the numbers of years students have been living in the country of interest and the primary language spoken at home. Studies conducted in multicultural classrooms in the USA reported that Asian-American students viewed their teachers as less dominant and cooperative than students from other ethnic groups, and that Asian-American teachers were seen to be less dominant and cooperative by students than their Hispanic-American, African-American or Caucasian colleagues (den Brok et al.2002; 2003; Levy, et al. 2003; Levy, Wubbels & Brekelmans, 1996). In one study in the USA, primary home language, rather than self-designated ethnic membership, was significant: students speaking mainly English at home perceived the least dominance, and classes with the most predominantly English-speaking students perceived the least dominance of all groups (Levy et al. 1997). Another study found a significant effect for the number of years students had been living in the USA, the longer they lived there, the less dominance they perceived (Levy, et al., 2003). A few studies on the same topic have been initiated in Australia and the Pacific. In contrast to the USA results cited above, an Australian study by Evans and Fisher (2000) found that students born in South Africa perceived more dominance than their Australian counterparts, while Asian born students felt their teachers were more dominant than did their South-African born classmates. Similarly, in a cross-national study it was found that students in Singapore perceived more dominance than Australian students (Fisher, Rickards, Goh, & Wong, 1997). Naturally, context (the country of interest) helps explain the differences in the results.

The associations between student perceptions and student and teacher cultural membership can be explained in various ways. One plausible argument is that teachers treat students from different ethnic backgrounds differently and that this results in variations in students' perceptions. Evidence for this explanation was provided by a series of observation studies conducted in the 1980s and 1990s (e.g. Casteel, 1998; Irvine, 1985; 1986; Simpson & Erickson, 1983). Another explanation is that students perceive the same teacher behaviour differently. Accordingly, such variations in perceptions are the result of differences in interpretation, values, norms, or needs of the students, all influenced by ethnicity. An example can be seen in a recent study by den Brok (2001), who demonstrated a systematic bias in students' perceptions, related to needs and norms for structured support, rejection and autonomy. Further evidence for this explanation was found in another study (den Brok et al., 2003). Both explanations may be valid, and no arguments can be made regarding their relative importance.

Knowledge on the effects of background characteristics can assist teachers in properly affirming the diversity in their classrooms and contribute to the development of culturally-responsive strategies (Nieto, 1996).

3.4 Interpersonal Teacher Behaviour Strategies in Multicultural Classrooms

Research and empirically supported literature on teaching competencies or strategies for effective interpersonal behaviour in multicultural classes as they are found in The Netherlands is scarce. While research on teaching from an interpersonal perspective, educational effectiveness and student drop-out suggests the importance of warm and supportive teacher-student relations, research is vague on how to achieve such relationships in multicultural classes with students from the countries of origin found in The Netherlands. More generic suggestions can be found in the extensive literature on intercultural communication and intercultural conflict management (e.g. Ting-Toomey, 1999). Among the skills suggested are:

- Mindful listening to students;
- Mindful reframing (translate messages of students to their cultural context);
- Adequate face-management (prevent humiliation or loss of face);
- Trust-building;
- Adaptive communication: practising patience, using vocal cues that signal listening attentiveness, being open to stories, proverbs, metaphors, analogies or understatements, encouraging, addressing conflicts to the whole group/class, accepting longer turn-taking or pauses, using head nods that indicate affirmation and listening to relational meaning of messages;
- Use of collaborative dialogue strategies: stimulating verbal assertiveness, using verbal and direct responses, articulating reasons behind responses or statements, using direct and specific questions, targeting questions to specific individuals, engaging in overlap talks and fast turn-taking, using verbal paraphrasing, using perception check questions and listening well to content; and
- Check students' understanding of words, sentences and concepts that are particular difficult for second language users and use teaching strategies for improving understanding of these if necessary.

4. Pedagogy for Developing Practical Knowledge

In the previous section, we presented theoretical notions to be included in a learning environment that wants to help develop teacher practical knowledge on communication in multicultural secondary classrooms. We now turn to the pedagogy of such an environment. Practical knowledge is based primarily on experiences. Teachers mainly develop practical knowledge by teaching and reflecting on their experiences. Without reflection, however, they also may develop practical knowledge, for example, by simple stimulus and response patterns. Practical experiences are thus the starting point for learning in our learning environment. This practical experience refers to teaching in actual classrooms, rather than laboratory or experimental settings. Providing students with the opportunity to teach is a key element in the learning environment.

Hermans et al. (1993; see Wubbels et al. 1997) propose a five-phase procedure to structure student teachers' learning from experiences of activities in teacher education programs. In the first phase, activities that student teachers will perform and that will lead to experiences are *pre-structured through assignments*. The aim of this phase is to assure a reasonable chance that student teachers will go through experiences that might give a need for theoretical notions on the topic under study. The environment should provide students with activities that stimulate them to link practice to theory and the practical knowledge of experienced teachers. This can be done also by including inquiry oriented activities, such as formulating research questions or hypotheses based on student teachers' own practical knowledge, gathering and analyzing data, and discussions with experienced teachers.

In the second phase, they actually *perform the activities* followed by the third phase: *structuring of the experiences*. This third phase can be both an individual act of reflection or a group-reflective activity. Students', often implicit, practical knowledge is elicited and made explicit in this phase. This can be done by (for example) writing logs, making portfolios or learner reports about the experiences and through coaching by supervisors asking questions that stimulate student teachers to elicit their own practical knowledge. In group reflective activities, students can be given opportunities to share their (practical) knowledge with colleagues. Thus student teachers can read about or listen to the explicit practical knowledge of others and can stimulate each other to discuss their own practical knowledge and compare it with practical knowledge of other student teachers who are, or have been, in similar positions or situations.

In the fourth phase, *focusing*, specific aspects of the structured experiences can be studied in more detail (in our case, specifics of communication in multicultural classrooms) using similar procedures as in the third phase. The student teacher can search for recurring patterns, particular behavioural routines, and habits to respond in certain situations. A step towards explanations for what happened can be set. In group activities, they then can search for common patterns and differences between each other. They also can give and receive peer-feedback (with the intention to provide alternative explanations for experiences and alternative methods of action).

In the final phase, *relating to theory*, theoretical notions and expert knowledge can be brought in explicitly and the practical knowledge can be confronted with this theory and expert knowledge. Conclusions can be drawn, for example, about alternative methods of actions. Thus, students can be provoked to broaden their knowledge and teaching repertoire, and make it applicable to a range of situations. Coaching in this phase can stimulate students to formulate methods of action which are in line with the conclusions of discussions, expert knowledge, research and literature reviews. This need not only be done by the teacher educators but also can be based on student teachers reviews of relevant literature, interviews with experienced teachers and comparing such literature and expert knowledge with own findings. 'Just-in-time' availability of theoretical notions and expert knowledge, however, not only applies to the last phase, it also can play a role in structuring and focusing. In these phases, the student teacher is trying to understand why phenomena in the classroom or the school occur in their particular way and what role his or her own behaviour plays in these events. Theory and expert knowledge function as empirically based explanations for phenomena and as a basis for successful intervention, and can help the student to understand what happened and why, and identify alternative plans for action.

5. Developing and Testing the Learning Environment

The aims of the project reported in this chapter were to study teacher-student communication, to explore teacher practical knowledge about this communication and to develop a learning environment that would help student teachers and in-service teachers to prepare themselves for communicating in multicultural classrooms. In this learning environment, teachers should develop theory-rich practical knowledge about this topic. We have chosen a hybrid learning environment consisting of both face-to-face contacts and an electronic part. We chose this combination because it is well known that discussions in electronic environments are more lively and productive when the participants have come to know each other in face-to-face contact, and in order to prevent a feeling of isolation for the student teachers that often is found to hinder electronic learning environments (Lockhorst, Admiraal, Pilot, & Veen, 2002). For the latter reason, we also planned that the students would work in groups with both face-to-face and electronic communication.

In the electronic part of the learning environment, we distinguished a *content area* and a *working area*. The content area, represented in a website, wants to provide teachers easy access to the available body of relevant knowledge inside and outside the institutions participating in the project. The working area, using the virtual learning environment BlackBoard, is the place were students were stimulated to communicate electronically with each other, with the teacher educator and with experienced teachers of the schools that participated in the project, work on assignments and explicitly reflect on their experiences.

In creating the learning environment, we proceeded through four phases.

- Making an inventory of frequently occurring problems in teacher-student interaction in secondary multicultural classrooms;
- Designing a content area, a working area, and opportunities for face-to-face communication and instruction;
- Testing the first version of the learning environment;
- Evaluating and improving the environment.

These phases, of course, displayed some overlap, and sometimes we had to go back and forth between phases, particularly with respect to the first three phases. In the remainder of this section, we report on our experiences in each of the phases.

Phase 1 – Making an inventory of frequently occurring problems
The aim of the activities in this phase was to identify relevant problems and topics that, according to the teachers, should be addressed in the learning environment. We interviewed beginning and experienced

teachers about the problems they encountered with respect to communication in a multicultural class. Teachers were interviewed both individually and in small groups. We frequently made use of stimulated recall techniques (e.g. Beijaard, 1991; Verloop, 1989) using videotaped lessons. We also conducted a literature search on the topic.

One finding in this phase was that according to experienced teachers, one would not be able to fully comprehend the nature of communication processes in multicultural classrooms, without taking into account the way the students lived their lives outside these classrooms. Topics that were mentioned, for instance, were language problems that students had to cope with, shortage of time to do homework or distracting contexts (rooms, houses), stressful situations in the neighborhood, peer group pressure from students within the school or from students of other schools, and communication with parents.

Another finding was that with respect to classroom communication, teachers were able to provide several elements of practical knowledge or examples of practical experience. One example they provided was the observation that students with a non-Western background tend to react in a much more emotional manner than do native-Dutch students. As a consequence, the native-Dutch teachers were inclined to regard the students' interpersonal messages as personally offending or threatening and the potential for conflicts was higher than for conflicts with native-Dutch students. For beginning teachers, it seems important to realise that messages in various cultures are sent in different ways and by means of verbal and nonverbal cues that may signify different meanings from those in their own culture. A second example was that Dutch teachers often were not used to negotiate with students, whereas students with a non-Western background interpreted some behaviours (such as providing independence and responsibility, allowing for discussion) of their teachers as openness to negotiation, while teachers did not mean them to. Teachers acknowledged that gauging the effect of their behaviours in a multi-interpretable environment is a skill that beginning teachers have to acquire in the new context of the multicultural classroom. A third example was that beginning teachers in the multicultural classroom tended to avoid techniques like whole-class discussion and cooperative learning. A first reason was that those techniques might result in the 'street wise' students with a non-western background taking over control (by putting the volume of their messages before the content, for example). A second reason, quite the opposite, was that native-Dutch students have a language advantage and therefore may dominate discussions. A last example was that students with a non-Western background often regarded corrections as personal attacks and humiliation. To avoid lasting damage to the relationship, experienced teachers, immediately after the correction, compensated this by some kind of personal attention and kept corrections as small as possible.

Phase 2 - Designing the elements of the learning environment
In this second phase, the goal was to develop a first version of the content and working area of the electronic part of the learning environment and of the face-to-face part. In developing the content area, the sources to inform the development of practical knowledge mentioned before (the interpersonal perspective on teaching and its broader context, the notions on culture and ethnicity, and the interpersonal strategies for multicultural classrooms) were used. In addition, the inventory of phase 1 played an important role. As a consequence, the scope of the learning environment evolved in to something that went further than teacher-students communication in the multicultural classroom alone. In line with the school effectiveness literature, we decided to structure the content in terms of the 'distance' to students' learning. In line with such models (e.g. Creemers, 1991; Scheerens, 1994; Veenstra, 1999), we distinguished between themes that related to the student, class (including teachers and teaching), school and environment (including parent-school relationships, neighborhood, etc.). This resulted in a structure for the content area as depicted in Figure 12.1.

This structure was used as an 'agenda' for both a literature review and gathering and sampling of video- and audio-fragments of lessons in multicultural classrooms. The literature reviewed was summarized in short paragraphs per topic addressed in the content area. Furthermore, hyperlinks to relevant websites were provided and lists of relevant literature were made available as suggestions for further reading. In the participating schools, videos were made in multicultural classrooms and interviews were held with students, teachers and other workers in the schools. These interviews were audio-taped. In sessions with experienced teacher educators and teachers, fragments out of those video-tapes and interviews were sampled in relation to the problems that were identified in phase 1.

Figure 12. 1. First page of the content area (website) of the learning environment.

(Explanation of the Dutch terms: from right to left the column headings mean: environment, school, classroom, teacher student relationship. The far left column refers to parts of the website that provide general information, literature, websites, video tapes, and an extensive case description of one teacher's teaching in a multicultural classroom)

In developing the working area and the face-to-face part of the learning environment, the pedagogy for the learning environment described before formed the basis. Furthermore, earlier experiences within the teacher education programs of Utrecht University and Free University in Amsterdam were used. Assignments were developed stimulating students to systematically investigate their own experiences and those of others. These assignments were placed in a standard electronic learning environment (BlackBoard). When working on these assignments, student teachers were urged to use the content area of the learning environment (website) and to communicate their findings and reflections with each other, with the teacher educators, and with experienced teachers. Therefore, a discussion area for the whole group of participants and separate areas for the groups working on the same assignment were installed.

During this phase, it became evident that representing video-taped lessons and audio-taped interviews in the website was problematic. Adequately comprehending video-taped lessons required a lot of content information of student teachers which made their use time consuming and puzzling for them. Furthermore, for comfortably playing videotapes on the student teachers local computer, broad-band Internet connections and adequate hardware were required that appeared not sufficiently available to many student teachers at home. With respect to the audio-taped interviews, it appeared that reading transcripts of interviews was easier and less time consuming than listening to samples of interviews. We therefore decided to use descriptions and transcripts of video-taped classroom situations on the website, illustrated with photos.

It also became evident during this phase that developing a comprehensive content area was very time consuming even though we could use the results of the long research tradition at Utrecht University in this field. As a consequence, we were not able to completely cover all the topics in the content area before starting to use the environment in phase 3.

A problem of completely different nature we had to cope with in this phase was that one of the participating schools was forced to close down due to decreasing student numbers. This decrease was an immediate consequence of the overwhelming and growing number of minority students in the school and the dislike of parents of this development. Of course, this had consequences for the available time and effort of teachers and school management for the project. This complicated gathering materials and discussing the structure and content of the learning environment with the expert teachers of this school.

Phase 3 Testing the first version of the learning environment
In this phase, the learning environment was tested even though not all the topics in the content area had been covered. In this trial phase, five expert teachers of the one school remaining in the project participated. Fifteen student teachers of the teacher training department of the Free University of Amsterdam volunteered to participate in a course taught by the Free University teacher educator participating in the project. The student teachers were all interested in the topic of teacher-students communication in multicultural classrooms. They had some experience in teaching, but only a small number of them had taught in multicultural classrooms. The course combined the three elements of the learning

environment that had been designed in the previous phase. It started off with two two-hour face-to-face seminars on the theoretical principles of the interpersonal perspective, on an instrument to collect data on student perceptions of the teacher's interpersonal behaviour, the *Questionnaire on Teacher Interaction* (QTI, Wubbels & Levy, 1993), on the assignments for the student teachers in school and on the use of the electronic BlackBoard working area. The seminars used earlier experiences of the student teachers in their placements for the introduction of the interpersonal perspective.

The assignment for the student teachers was to investigate in their schools, topics relevant to teaching in multicultural classrooms, use their own teaching experience and the available material in the content area as a starting point, discuss their findings with the teachers experienced in the multicultural classroom in the working area, and present the result of their research project to each other and the participating teachers in a third two-hour face-to-face seminar, the plenary closing session of the course. The role of the teacher educator in this phase was to conduct the face-to-face seminars, moderate the discussions in BlackBoard, and grade the presentations and papers of the student teachers' assignments. The experienced teachers were asked to comment on the discussions in the working area and answer any questions explicitly put to them by the student teachers and participate in the third seminar.

Phase 4 Evaluation and improvement
The way we had envisioned the learning environment was one that helped students to communicate in multicultural classrooms based on general notions about teacher-students communication as described in the interpersonal perspective on teacher behaviour. In order to apply this perspective in multicultural classrooms, student teachers need to be rather "fluent in this interpersonal language". It appeared that a lot of time had to be used for student teachers to learn and understand the concepts that are necessary to be able to adequately discuss teacher-student communication in the classroom from an interpersonal perspective. It takes considerable time to learn that language, more than the planned two-hour seminar. Therefore, in future use of the learning environment we think that it should be embedded in a teacher education program that places the interpersonal perspective more central in its approach.

Evaluation of the course with student teacher questionnaires showed that the time consuming effort of understanding the interpersonal perspective, the consequent scarce attention to the specific problems in multicultural classrooms, and the incomplete nature of the content area in this phase had resulted in limited use of this part of the learning environment. The online communication with teachers experienced in multicultural classrooms was appreciated, but occurred infrequently and less than planned. One reason for this might have been that this facility was rather new for the participating student and experienced teachers and in future use we will take care that using a BlackBoard environment is common in the entire teacher education program. The face-to-face seminars and additional face-to-face meetings between student teachers and the experienced teachers were regarded as valuable and certainly not superfluous.

It proved to be difficult to make the experienced teachers' practical knowledge explicit and thereby available to the participating student teachers. The experienced teacher did not feel confident in discussing the ideas of the student teachers and, probably, also were hesitant about the value of their own insights.

The students' research projects were adequate and provided them more insight in the nature of multicultural classes, but the reports were not of high quality among others because the content area of the learning environment was not used as often as planned. There was some tension between the wish to commute between theory and practice and the need of insight in the interpersonal perspective as a basis to work from. The dilemma is that focusing too much on theory without linking it to practical experience does not fit with the concept of a realistic teacher education, but on the other hand some theoretical base is necessary to have discussions of sufficient quality.

As a follow up of the evaluation, a lot of effort has been invested in further 'filling' the content area. This has resulted in a richer but not yet complete coverage of all the topics identified in the agenda. A complication that arose during this phase was that the participating schools for reasons of privacy had second thoughts about putting the photos and quotes of teachers and students open on the Internet. It was therefore decided to make the content area only available to other teacher education institutes and relevant schools, and this only after consultation with the project leaders.

6. Dilemmas

Through working on the development of the learning environment and its evaluation, we have become aware of three dilemmas. We think that these dilemmas are of a general nature and that developers of a computer supported learning environment involving expert teacher practical knowledge will have to cope with these. The dilemmas were related to the design of the content area of the learning environment, in particular its extensiveness and organization, making the experienced teachers' practical knowledge explicit, and the balance between online and face-to-face meetings.

6.1 Extensiveness and Organization of the Content Area

The first dilemma we faced was related to the tension between 'completeness' and 'selectivity' in covering topics and themes for the learning environment related to teaching in multicultural classrooms. When discussing these topics during phase 1, experienced teachers pointed out that only paying attention to the teacher-students communication in the multicultural classroom was not enough. To adequately comprehend these communication processes, one should also be mindful with respect to the context of the school, the neighborhood, home situation and even the countries from where the students or their parents originated. Topics from the field of communication sciences, language studies, cultural anthropology, sociology, and educational studies are relevant in this respect. The dilemma faced is one between cognitive overload or superficiality of information. On one hand, covering the entire context creates too much information for student teachers who are familiarizing themselves with communication in multicultural classrooms because they may easily be overwhelmed by the complexity of the issue; on the other hand, the information might easily be too superficial for students having specific questions and problems

A related dilemma is that of providing relevant information in the content area. Providing particular context cues might prevent the students from looking for this information themselves and we could lose the inquiry oriented learning activities which we thought would be beneficial to the development of their practical knowledge. We had to decide again and again what information we would place on the website ourselves and what would be made available through links or references to further reading or what only would be hinted at.

To solve these dilemmas, we decided to design the content area as a map for topics that, in our opinion and that of the experienced teachers, cover the major areas of interest when studying communication in Dutch secondary multicultural classrooms. For each topic, we aimed to provide a brief introduction based on theory and the materials we had gathered. We also provided suggestions for further reading and hyperlinks to relevant websites. We hoped this would stimulate the students to search for theory themselves, but in the direction we provided. Further experience with the content area will have to prove whether this strategy is successful.

6.2 Experienced Teachers' Practical Knowledge

The practical knowledge of the experienced teachers was an important element in the learning environment from which student teachers could learn. It was a difficult endeavour to make the practical knowledge of the experienced teachers explicit and share it with the student teachers. The teachers found it difficult to answer questions and to participate in discussions. This is in line with other research (e.g. Meijer, 1999) showing difficulties in making implicit practical knowledge explicit and thus available to others. We are convinced of the usefulness of the expert knowledge but in our use of the working area of the learning environment it appeared to be not sufficiently elicited.

There is a dilemma about the energy invested by student teachers in eliciting the experienced teachers practical knowledge and possible controversial outcomes that may be delivered. Practical knowledge can vary a lot between teachers (cf. Meijer, 1999). It need not be based on empirical evidence but can be a result of personal rather idiosyncratic experience which may not always be generalisable across contexts, but often it is very convincing for student teachers. So both a threat and a challenge for using this knowledge in the way we planned (input in the working area) is that knowledge may be introduced that is at odds with the theoretical notions in the content area.

Our experiences have raised some doubts if it is a viable way to have the input of expert teachers knowledge organised primarily in the working area. Another approach that we are investigating now is to gather data on the expert knowledge of many experienced teachers and try to incorporate it in the content area directly connected to the theoretical notions with which it is connected. In doing so, the practical knowledge of the teachers is used to ground formal theory and make it more acceptable to student teachers.

6.3 Face-to-face or Online

When piloting the use of the learning environment it turned out to be difficult to stimulate student teachers and experienced teachers to communicate online. Our hypothesis was that communication within an electronic learning environment would be easier compared to communication in face-to-face meetings, because student teachers and experienced teachers can communicate in an electronic learning environment at a time and place that suits them best. This often heard hypothesis was not confirmed in our situation in which student teachers also met each other at the university and had the option to invite the experienced teachers on campus. The dilemma is that introducing face-to-face contacts may make electronic communication superfluous while on the other hand the face-to-face contact often is mentioned as a prerequisite for productive electronic communication.

7. Conclusion

In the project described in this chapter, we designed a hybrid learning environment consisting of face-to-face meetings, a website as content area and an electronic working environment (BlackBoard). This environment was meant to help student teachers and beginning teachers to acquire theory rich practical knowledge with respect to teacher-students communication in secondary multicultural classrooms. Our conclusions about the success of the project are ambivalent. On the one hand, we were confronted with a number of problems. These involved selecting theory and how to organize and present it, with how to make practical knowledge available to others, with how to provide students with the necessary knowledge base, with balancing online and face-to-face communication, with putting recognizable persons on the Internet, and many more. On the other hand, we are still convinced of the potential of this type of learning environment to organize in a teacher education program the provision of theory and expert knowledge at the time the student teachers need it. We are also convinced that the development and implementation of this kind of learning environment requires substantial investment of resources and development time, something that probably too often is underestimated.

References

Au, K. H., & Kawakami, A. J. (1994). Cultural congruence in instruction. In E. R. Hollins, J. E. King, & W. C. Hayman (Eds.), *Teaching diverse populations: Formulating a knowledge base* (pp. 5-23). Albany: State University of New York Press.

Aviles, R. M. D., Guerrero, M. P., Howarth, H. B., & Thomas, G. (1999). Perceptions of Chicano/Latino students who have dropped out of school. *Journal of Counseling and Development, 77* (4), 465-473.

Beijaard, D. (1990). *Teaching as acting.* Wageningen, The Netherlands: Wageningen Agricultural University.

Brekelmans, M. (1989). *Interpersonal teacher behaviour in the classroom.* In Dutch: Interpersoonlijk gedrag van docenten in de klas. Utrecht: W.C.C.

Brekelmans, M., Sleegers, P., & Fraser, B. (2000). Teaching for active learning. In P. R. J. Simons, J. L. van der Linden, & T. Duffy (Eds.), *New Learning* (pp. 227-242). Dordrecht: Kluwer Academic Publishers.

Brown, R. (1965). *Social psychology.* London: Collier-McMillan.

Casteel, C. A. (1998). Teacher-student interactions and race in integrated classrooms. *Journal of Educational Research, 92,* (2), 115-121.

Cole, M., & Scribner, S. (1974). *Culture and thought: a psychological introduction.* New York: John Wiley & Sons.

Creemers, B. P. M. (1991). *Effectieve instructie. Een empirische bijdrage aan de verbetering van het onderwijs in de klas* [Effective instruction. An empirical contribution to the improvement of education in the classroom]. Den Haag: SVO.

Davalos, D. B., Chavez, E. L., & Guardiola, R. J. (1999). The effects of extracurricular activity, ethnic identification and perception of school on student dropout rates. *Hispanic Journal of Behavioural Sciences, 21,* 1, 61-77.

Dekkers, H., & Driessen, G. (1997). An evaluation of the educational priority policy in relation to early school leaving. *Studies in Educational Evaluation, 23*, 3, 209-230.

den Brok, P. J. (2001). *Teaching and student outcomes: A study on teachers' thoughts and actions from an interpersonal and a learning activities perspective.* Utrecht: W. C. C.

den Brok, P. J., Levy, J., Rodriguez, R., & Wubbels, T. (2002). Perceptions of Asian-American and Hispanic-American teachers and their students on interpersonal communication style. *Teaching and Teacher Education, 18*, 447-467.

den Brok, P. J., Levy, J., Wubbels, T., & Rodriguez, M. (2003). Cultural influences on students' perceptions of videotaped lessons. *International Journal of Intercultural Relations, 27* (3), 268-288.

Derksen, K. (1994). *Between taking over and activating instruction.* In Dutch: Tussen sturen en activeren. Masters thesis. Nijmegen: Vakgroep Onderwijskunde.

Doyle, W. (1986). Classroom organization and management. In M. C. Wittrock (Ed.), *Handbook of research on teaching (third edition)* (pp. 392-431). New York: Macmillan.

Dunkin, M.J., & Biddle, B.J. (1974). *The study of teaching.* New York: Rinehart & Winston.

Evans, H. (1998). *A study on students' cultural background and teacher-student interpersonal behaviour in secondary science classrooms in Australia.* Unpublished doctoral dissertation. Perth: Curtin University of Technology.

Evans, H., & Fisher, D. (2000). Cultural differences in students' perceptions of science teachers' interpersonal behaviour. *Australian Science Teachers Journal, 46*, 9-18.

Fenstermacher, G.D. The knower and the known: the nature of knowledge in research on teaching. *Review of Research on Teaching, 20*, 1-54.

Fisher, D., Rickards, T., Goh, S., & Wong, A. (1997). Perceptions of interpersonal teacher behaviour in secondary science classes in Singapore and Australia. *Journal of Applied Research in Education, 1*, 2-11.

Foa, U. (1961). Convergences in the analysis of the structure of interpersonal behaviour. *Psychological Review, 68*, 341-353.

Goh, S. (1994). *Interpersonal teacher behaviour, classroom climate and student outcomes in primary mathematics classes in Singapore.*

Unpublished doctoral dissertation. Perth: Curtin University of Technology.

Gordon, B. (1995). Knowledge construction, competing critical theories and education. In: J. Banks & C. Banks, (Eds.), *Handbook of Research on Multicultural Education* (pp.184-202). New York: Macmillan.

Grossman, H. (1995). *Teaching a diverse society*. Boston: Allyn & Bacon.

Henderson, D. G. (1995). *A study of the classroom and laboratory environments and student attitude and achievement in senior secondary biology classes*. Unpublished doctoral dissertation. Perth: Curtin University of Technology.

Hermans, J.J., Créton, H. A., & Korthagen, F. A. J. (1993). Reducing the gap between theory and practice in teacher education. In J.T. Voorbach (Ed.), *Teacher Education 9, Research and developments on teacher education in The Netherlands* (pp. 111-120). The Hague: SVO.

House, J. D. (1999). Self-beliefs and background variables as predictors of school withdrawal of adolescent students. *Child Study Journal, 29* (4), 247-265.

Irvine, J. J. (1985). Teacher communication patterns as related to the race and sex of the student. *Journal of Educational Research, 78*, 338-345.

Irvine, J. J. (1986). Teacher-student interactions: effects of student race, sex and grade level. *Journal of Educational Psychology, 78*, 14-21.

Jordan, W. J., Lara, J., & McPartland, J. M. (1996). Exploring the causes of early dropout among race-ethnic and gender groups. *Youth & Society, 28*, 62-94.

Korthagen, F. A. J. (2001). *Linking practise and theory. The pedagogy of realistic teacher education*. Mahwah, NJ: LEA.

Korthagen, F. A. J. & Wubbels, T. (1995). Characteristics of reflective practitioners: towards an operationalization of the concept of reflection. *Teachers and Teaching: Theory and practice 1*(1), 51-72.

Leary, T. (1957). *An interpersonal diagnosis of personality*. New York: Ronald Press Company.

Levy, J., Wubbels, T., & Brekelmans, M. (1996, April). *Cultural factors in students' and teachers' perceptions of the learning environment*. Paper presented at the annual meeting of the American Educational Research Association, San Francisco.

Levy, J., den Brok, P., Wubbels, T., & Brekelmans, M. (2003). Students' perceptions of interpersonal aspects of the learning environment. *Learning Environments Research, 6*, 1, 5-36.

Levy, J., Wubbels, T., Brekelmans, M., & Morganfield, B. (1997). Language and cultural factors in students' perceptions of teacher communication style. *International Journal of Intercultural Relationships, 21*, 1, 29-56.

Lockhorst, D., Admiraal. W., Pilot, A., & Veen, W. (2002). Design elements for a CSCL environment in a teacher training programme. *Education and Information Technologies, 7*, 4, 377-384.

Lonner, W.J. (1980). The search for psychological universals. In H. C. Triandis & W. W. Lambert (Eds.), *Handbook of cross-cultural psychology* (vol. 1, pp.143-204). Boston: Allyn & Bacon.

Matsuda, M. (1989). Working with Asian parents: Some communication strategies. *Topics in Language Disorders, 9*, 45-53.

Meijer, P. (1999) *Teachers'practical knowledge. Teaching reading comprehension in secondary education.* Doctoral dissertation. Leiden, The Netherlands.

Moore, K. J. (1994). Florida seminole school dropouts. *Journal of Multicultural Counseling and Development, 22*, 3, 165-172.

Nguyen, L. (1986). Indochinese cross-cultural adjustment and communication. In M. Dao & H. Grossman (Eds.), *Identifying, instructing and rehabilitating Southeast Asian students with special needs and counseling their parents.* (ERIC Document Reproduction Service No. ED 273 068).

Nieto, S. (1996) *Affirming diversity: The sociopolitical context of multicultural education.* New York: Longman.

Oost, H. (1999). *The quality of research problems in dissertations. An evaluation of the elaboration of formal aspects of research problems (in Dutch).* Doctoral dissertation. Utrecht: WCC.

Pinto, D. (2000). *Intercultural communication: A three-step method for dealing with differences.* Apeldoorn: Garant.

Rawnsley, D. G. (1997). *Associations between classroom learning environments, teacher interpersonal behaviour and student outcomes in Secondary Mathematics classrooms.* Unpublished doctoral dissertation. Perth: Curtin University of Technology.

Resnick, L. B. (1983) Toward a cognitive theory of instruction. In S. G. Paris, G. M. Olsen & H. W. Stevenson (Eds.), *Learning and motivation in the classroom* (pp. 5-38). Hillsdale NJ: Prentice Hall.

Samovar, L. A., & Porter, R. E. (1995). *Communication between cultures* (2nd ed.). Belmont, CA: Wadsworth Publishing Company.

Sanders, J. S. J., & Sanders, R. C. (1998). Anti-dropout interventions. *Education Digest, December*, 1-2.

Scheerens, J. (1994). The school-level context of instructional effectiveness: a comparison between school effectiveness and restructuring models. *Tijdschrift voor Onderwijsresearch, 19*, 26-38.

Segall, M. H., Dasen, P. R., Berry, J. W., & Poortinga, Y. H. (Eds.). (1990). *Human behaviour in global perspective: An introduction to cross-cultural psychology*. New York: Pergamon.

Setz, W., Bergen, Th., van Amelsvoort, J., & Lamberigts, R. (1993). *Perceived and observed behaviour of teachers*. In Dutch: Gepercipieerd en geobserveerd lesgedrag van docenten. Research report. Nijmegen: Katholieke Universiteit Nijmegen/ITS.

Simpson, A. W., & Erickson, M. T. (1983). Teachers' verbal and nonverbal communication patterns as a function of teacher race, student gender and student race. *American Educational Research Journal, 20*, 183-198.

Stefani. L. A. (1997). The influence of culture on classroom communication. In L. A. Samovar & R. E. Porter (Eds.), *Intercultural communication: A reader* (8th ed.) (pp. 196-215). Belmont, CA: Wadsworth Publishing Company.

Sturtevant, W. C. (1964). Studies in ethnoscience. In J.W. Berry & P.R. Dasen, (Eds.), *Culture and cognition: readings in cross-cultural psychology* (pp.39-59). New York: Harper & Row.

Ting-Toomey, S. (1999). *Communicating across cultures: ESL learners in the non-ESL classroom*. New York: Guildford Press Company.

van Amelsvoort, J. (1993). Teachers' behaviour during the lesson as perceived by students. In T. Bergen, J. Van Amelsvoort, K. Derksen, R. Lamberigts, W. Setz, & P. Sleegers (Eds.), *Between taking over and activating instruction* (research report). Nijmegen: VON/ITS.

Veenman, S. (1984). Problems of beginning teachers. *Review of Educational Research, 54*, 143-178.

Veenstra, R. (1999). Leerlingen-klassen-scholen [Students-classes-schools]. Groningen: Groningen Universiteitsdrukkerij.

Verloop, N. (1989). *Interactive cognitions of student-teachers. An intervention study*. Arnhem, The Netherlands: CITO.

Watzlawick, P., Beavin, J.H., & Jackson, D. (1967). *The pragmatics of human communication*, New York: Norton.

Witkin, H. A. (1967). A cognitive-style approach to cross-cultural research. *International Journal of Psychology. 6*, 4-87.

Wubbels, T., Créton, H. A., & Hooymayers, H. P. (1985, April). *Discipline problems of beginning teachers, interactional behaviour mapped out*. Paper presented at the American Educational Research Association annual meeting, Chicago. Abstracted in Resources in Education, 20, 12, p. 153, ERIC document 260040.

Wubbels, T., Korthagen, F., & Brekelmans, M. (1997). Developing theory from practice in teacher education. *Teacher Education Quarterly, 24*, 3, 75-90.

Wubbels, T., & Levy, J. (Eds.). (1993). *Do you know what you look like? Interpersonal relationships in education*. London: The Falmer Press

Zea, M. C., Reisen, C. A., Beil, C., & Caplan, R. D. (1997). Prediction intention to remain in college among ethnic minority and nonminority students. *Journal of Social Psychology, 137*, 2, 149-160.

Chapter 13

EVALUATING E-LEARNING ENVIRONMENTS IN SINGAPORE LOWER SECONDARY SCIENCE CLASSROOMS

Quek Choon Lang and Angela F. L. Wong
Nanyang Technological University
Singapore

The use of Information Technology in teaching and learning has now become a reality in classrooms and across different instructional academic disciplines in Singapore. Due to recent increases in the application of e-learning to the traditional mode of instruction, it is now timely for those examining classroom learning environments to begin focussing their research on the evaluation of e-learning as a viable approach to teaching and learning. However, no comprehensive instrument has been developed to evaluate e-learning environments for secondary school education. Using the context of lower secondary science, this study aims to evaluate the effectiveness of using e-learning in addition to normal face-to-face interaction for learning science. Using the perceptual approach, a modified psycho-social classroom learning environment instrument called the 'E-learning Classroom Environment Questionnaire' (ELCEQ) was administered to obtain the students' perceptions of their e-learning classroom learning environments. The ELCEQ consisted of a 30-item questionnaire, with 5 scales, namely Investigation, Open-endedness, Organisation, Material Environment and Satisfaction. The collected data was analysed quantitatively. The results, implications and suggestions for effective implementation of e-learning in lower secondary science classrooms will be described in the following pages.

1. Introduction

In recent years, the rate of Information Technology use in teaching and learning across different academic disciplines has increased rapidly in Singapore. This increased use of e-learning (technologically-assisted or technologically-driven means of learning delivery) in the curriculum has given the teachers and students opportunities to extend learning beyond the physical classrooms and curriculum hours. Currently, some schools have already incorporated e-learning formally into their curricula as part and parcel of teaching and learning, while others are only beginning to venture into the use of commercially available e-learning platforms for the teaching of English, Mathematics, Sciences, the Humanities and Project Work. As the use of instructional technology becomes more prevalent in schools, the pedagogical knowledge, skills and mindsets of teachers have to change. Teachers need to understand how to incorporate the e-learning teaching approach into current classroom practices, and be better informed of how their students react to the use of e-learning, in order to enhance the learning environment.

As most of the schools in Singapore embark on the use of e-learning teaching, it has become necessary for the stakeholders to understand how the psychological and social aspects of e-learning environments might affect students' learning. By drawing from the students' perceptions of the e-learning environment, this study describes the e-learning environments in two typical secondary schools and evaluates the effectiveness of e-learning in the teaching of lower secondary science in Singapore.

2. Learning Environments and Development of Instruments

Studies on the learning environment started about 30 years ago with the independent development of two widely-used research instruments—the Learning Environment Inventory (LEI) and the Classroom Environment Scale (CES). Both the LEI and the CES became the basis for the development of several other instruments commonly used to assess various learning and teaching environments.

Over the years, the original research instruments were gradually refined to suit specific environments. Moar and Fraser (1996) and Teh and Fraser (1995) drew on existing scales when developing specific-purpose instruments. For the evaluation of geography classrooms, Teh and Fraser (1995) developed a four-scale instrument to assess Gender Equity, Investigation, Innovation and Resource Adequacy and validated it among 671 high school geography students in Singapore. Teh (2001) administered the Internet-based Classroom Environment Inventory (ICEI) to 12 classes of a total of 256 postgraduate diploma-in-education students to assess their perceptions of synchronous Internet-based learning environments. Synchronous Internet-based learning refers to online learning conducted in a real-time mode, and takes the form of on-line mediated conferencing and telecommuting approaches. The

Computer Classroom Environment Inventory (CCEI) (Maor & Fraser, 1996) is among the seminal examples of subject-specific instruments. Moar and Fraser (1996) developed a five-scale classroom environment instrument (assessing Investigation, Open-Endedness, Organisation, Material Environment and Satisfaction) based on the Learning Environment Inventory (LEI) Individualised Classroom Environment Questionnaire (ICEQ) and Science Learning Environment Inventory (SLEI). The CCEI was validated with a sample of 120 Grade 11 students in Australia. This instrument was unique in that it evaluated the extent to which inquiry was supported by the use of technology and how technology could support the inquiry approach in the teaching of secondary school science. Moar(2000) developed a new instrument, Constructivist Multimedia Learning Environment Survey (CMLES) to assess the science teachers' perceptions of their inquiry-based and constructivist-oriented multimedia learning environment. Moar and Fraser (in press) validated CMLES among 221 grade 10 and 11 Australian students and found that CMLES demonstrated a high degree of internal consistency reliability (with alpha reliability coefficients ranging from 0.73 to 0,82) with all the six scales displaying satisfactory factorial and discriminant validity. Research on the on-line environment (Khan, 1997; Palloff & Pratt, 1998, 2001; Tobin, 1998) has shown the increasing trend of on-line teaching and learning in tertiary institutions. In the present context, the term "on-line learning" is also used to refer to e-learning, as well as internet-based and web-based modes of instruction. The purpose of on-line learning environments is to provide greater access to learning for all students who are separated by distance from the instructors. The online learning environment can either supplement or complement a traditional face-to-face learning environment. Alternatively, it may provide a complete learning package that requires little face-to-face interaction. In light of the changing trends in teaching and learning in tertiary institutions, Jegede, Fraser, and Fisher (1998) developed the Distance and Open Learning Environment Scale (DOLES) for university students studying via distance education.

While further research on the nature and evaluation of on-line learning environments is still in progress (Tobin, 1998), it was decided that it would be beneficial to adapt and build on the earlier work of inquiry-based computer-assisted learning by Maor and Fraser (1996) to evaluate the lower secondary school science classroom environments in Singapore. Thus far, there has been no learning environment instrument developed to assess the students' or teachers' perceptions of e-learning classroom environments for secondary schools.

3. Incorporating Technology into Learning Environments

Jonassen, Howland, Moore and Marra (2003) highlighted significant roles of technology in fostering meaningful learning. These roles involve using the computer:

- as a tool for knowledge construction,
- as an information vehicle to support learning by constructing,
- as a context to support learning by doing and conversing,
- as an intellectual partner (Jonassen, 2000).

(adapted from Jonassen et al, 2003,P 12)

In order to fully reap the benefits of the use of technology in teaching and learning, the changing roles of teachers and students must not be overlooked. Jonassen, Howland, Moore and Marra (2003) urged teachers to accept and learn a new model of learning by relinquishing their authoritative role. On the other hand, the students are encouraged to assume an active role in learning by setting their own goals, asking questions, reflecting on their learning and evaluating their learning.

Lynch (2002) noted that learning in the online environment is interactive and that teachers must gain comfort and confidence. The managerial aspect of their role in this environment requires them to use e-mail, set up discussion forums and learning activities to interact with their students. They are expected to be responsive, competent and organized in facilitating the entire learning process. During on-line interaction, teachers ought to foster a sense of community among the learners as well as themselves by creating a non-threatening and friendly environment. They are expected to provide frequent feedback, encourage student participation and acknowledge comments. Within the community of learners, the teachers are to monitor actively the assumption of roles, conceptions of ideas, construction of knowledge and interactions, at the level of the individual learner as well as at intra-group and inter-group levels. During the entire on-line learning process, the teachers' pedagogical knowledge and skills in facilitating, mentoring and managing are crucial in helping the community of learners achieve their learning goals. In other words, the manifold roles of teachers in online learning are challenging: they are expected to plan, re-shape their familiar face-to-face classroom interactions and practices, and interact with the learners in the online environment.

As regards the on-line learning environment, Palloff and Pratt (1998) also stressed that successful on-line learners are those who adopt an active approach to learning. The roles of on-line learners include knowledge generation, collaboration and process management. In on-line learning environments, the learners are expected to actively seek solutions to problems and view problems and questions presented by the teachers and other students. Students are also expected to participate actively and to learn and work collaboratively (Khan, 1997) in order to achieve deeper understanding of the subjects which underlie the learning tasks. Students are also expected to share resources and other materials that they have found with other learners. In the role of process management, students are expected to voice their opinions, interact with one another and participate actively in the discussions.

Many students view on-line learning as an opportunity for them to learn and interact freely in a borderless world (Marlowe & Page, 1998). With the incorporation of on-line learning into teaching and learning, this means that the teachers' pedagogical skills have to be shaped in such a way as to meet the new way of teaching and learning in schools. In most schools, the teachers are comfortable with face-to-face interaction in teaching, but the incorporation of online learning will require them to be better equipped with the necessary skills to facilitate and manage the students' learning in an online environment. Similarly, the students will also be required to understand the purpose and function of online learning environments. With this added dimension to teaching and learning, both the teachers and students will need time to be comfortable in using the tools provided in the online environment.

4. Use of the Perceptual Approach to Evaluate the Learning Environment

Throughout the 1980s and 1990s, the perceptual approach was increasingly used as a quick and effective means of obtaining information about the learning environment. This approach, which focused on the perceptions of individuals working in the environment studied, has several advantages.

First, it is economical. The participants are themselves the observers. Hence, there is no need for an external observer. Less time is needed to discover and evaluate the environment. The relevant quantitative data can be obtained simply by having participants fill out surveys based on their own observations.

Second, it makes use of pooled data. The perceptual approach draws its data from all participants (Fraser, 1984), thus providing a more varied and holistic view of the classroom. In contrast, external observers are limited to their own perspectives and are likely to miss some relevant aspects of the learning environment.

Third, it involves the direct participation of the students. They are likely to be the best judges of a particular environment, because they have encountered many different learning environments and spent sufficient time in each particular environment to form accurate impressions. Even if teachers are somewhat inconsistent in their day-to-day behaviour, a consistent image of their selves is usually projected to their students through classroom interaction over a period of time. In more recent times, the assessment of learning environments and research applications has involved a variety of quantitative and qualitative methods. Qualitative methods have become more prevalent for providing a deeper understanding of learning environments (Tobin, Kahle & Fraser, 1990). Recent accomplishments within the learning environment field have been the productive combination of quantitative and qualitative approaches (Huang, Fraser & Aldridge, 1998; Tobin & Fraser, 1998).

5. Purpose of Study

The study aims to examine how the incorporation of an online learning environment into the existing classroom environment would affect how students learn science. By drawing from the students' perceptions about the learning environment, such information will help the teachers and the school administration evaluate the on-line learning environment in schools.

With the incorporation of e-learning into the science curriculum, the students will be spending part of their curriculum time, as well as time after school hours, using web-based tools to learn science. It is therefore important to investigate how they perceive the e-learning environment that they experience; this information should be of interest to science teachers, school administrators, researchers and technologists.

The objectives of this study are to:

(1) assess the lower secondary science classroom learning environment using the E-learning Classroom Environment Questionnaire (ELCEQ), a modified version of the Computer Classroom Environment Inventory (CCEI),
(2) identify differences in perceptions of the lower secondary science classroom environment between the actual and preferred forms of ELCEQ, and
(3) suggest strategies to address the perceptual differences that exist in the lower secondary science classrooms with the view of introducing e-learning into the science learning environment in Singapore.

5.1 Design and Procedures

The study was conducted with a sample size of 134 students (aged 13-14) who came from four Secondary One classes from two typical co-educational secondary schools in the eastern part of Singapore. These students came from the Express stream (a 4-year secondary school course for more academically inclined students, as opposed to the 5-year Normal stream). They were able to use computers and Microsoft Office applications comfortably.

Table 13.1. Description of the Sample

Schools	Boys	Girls
A	42	20
B	40	32
Total	134	

The science teachers who participated in this study came from these two schools and chose the common e-learning system 'MoreAtOnce' (as shown in Figure 13.1) for teaching lower secondary science.

The students in school A did not experience any difficulty in accessing the e-learning system. However, due to the move to the new premises, students in school B encountered some technical problems such as limitations in the number of computers available and an unstable network connection.

The students who participated in this study were given almost 9 months to use the online learning environment during science lessons as well as after curriculum time. The schools paid for the subscription to the e-learning platform for the students and teachers. At the end of that period, the students' perceptions were assessed using the 30-item E-learning Classroom Environment Questionnaire (ELCEQ) which is an adaptation of the Computer Classroom Environment Inventory (CCEI) (Maor & Fraser, 1996). Both the actual and preferred forms were administered to schools A and B.

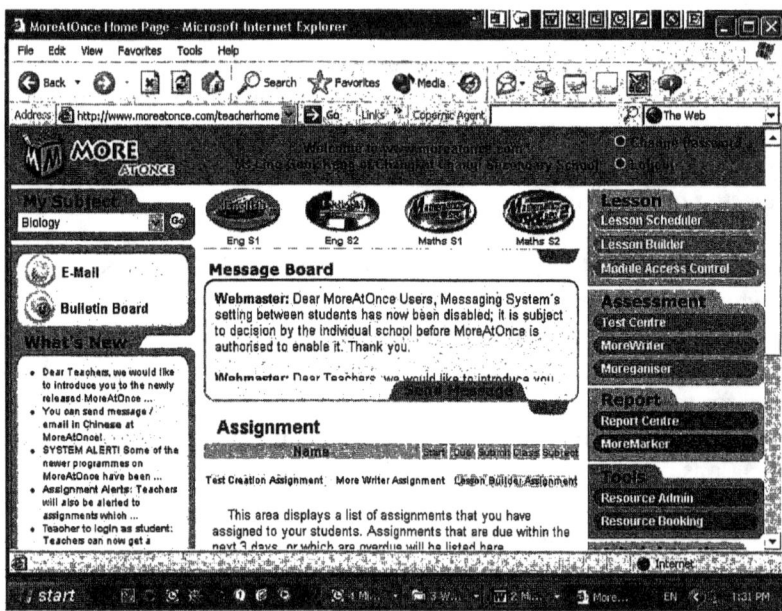

Figure 13.1. A screen capture of an opening screen in the e-learning system (Image courtesy of MoreAtOnce)

5.2 Curriculum Materials

The teachers were provided with training and familiarization with the pedagogical tools built into the 'MoreAtOnce' e-learning system. With their students' learning needs in mind, the teachers designed their e-lessons, enrichment activities and quizzes to motivate their students in learning science. The teachers used the resource bank built into the e-learning system by selecting appropriate multimedia resources and designing e-lessons for their students. In view of the varying ability levels of the students in their classes, the teachers customized the lessons separately for high ability, average ability and low ability students. The teachers also made available the e-lessons taught in class for the students to access after the curriculum hours. Besides face-to-face interaction in the science classrooms, the teachers also used the provided web-based assessment tools to monitor the progress of their students' learning in the e-learning environment.

Using the secondary 1 science textbook (Chan, Lam & Loo, 2001), the following topics were taught in both face-to-face and e-learning modes:

- Science & technology
- Measurements
- Classification of matter
- Elements, compounds & mixtures
- Separating mixtures
- Solutions & Suspensions
- Acids, alkalis & salts
- Classification of living things
- Cells, tissues organs, systems
- Photosynthesis
- Respiration
- Sources & storage of energy
- Heat & its effects
- Transmission of heat
- Force & pressure
- Moment of a force
- Work done by a force
- Abuses of life

Figure 13.2 shows some of the science resources, administrative tools and communication tools in the e-learning environment. (Image courtesy of MoreAtOnce)

The students were also provided with user identification numbers and passwords to access the e-learning materials available in the e-learning system. They were able to access the e-learning materials at any time, both in and out of the classroom. An example of the e-lesson designed by the science teachers is shown in Figure 13.3.

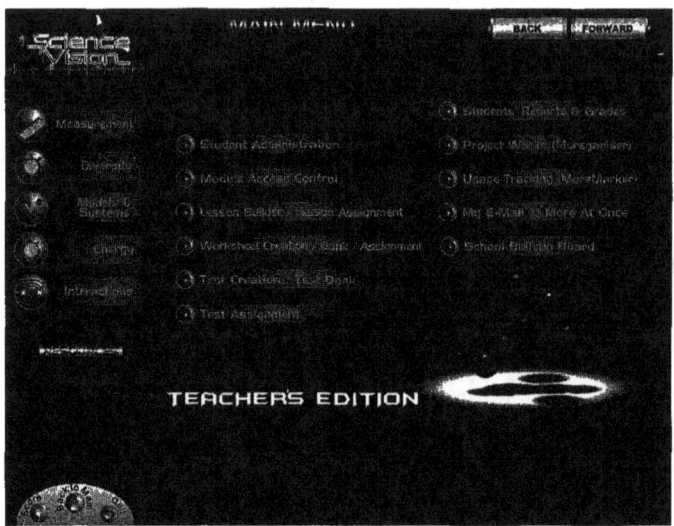

Figure 13.2. A screen capture of the topics, activities and web-based tools available in the e-learning system (Image courtesy of MoreAtOnce)

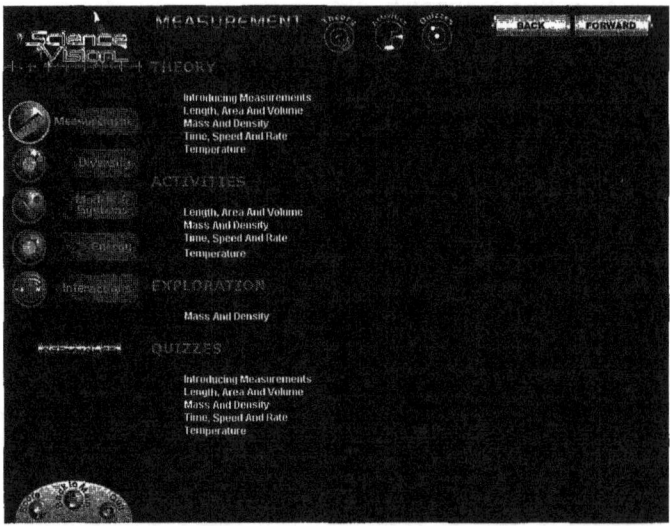

Figure 13.3. A screen capture of the topic on measurement in the e-learning system (Image courtesy of MoreAtOnce)

The students logged on to the e-learning system to either access the resources or communicate with their classmates and teachers. In other words, the teachers' e-lessons were also made available for students to access after curriculum hours. The students used the online features to take self-check quizzes, ask questions concerning the topics taught and share their ideas with their peers. Both the teachers and students communicated via the e-mail platform available in the e-learning system. Further examples of the online resources designed by the teachers are shown in Figures 13.4 and 13.5.

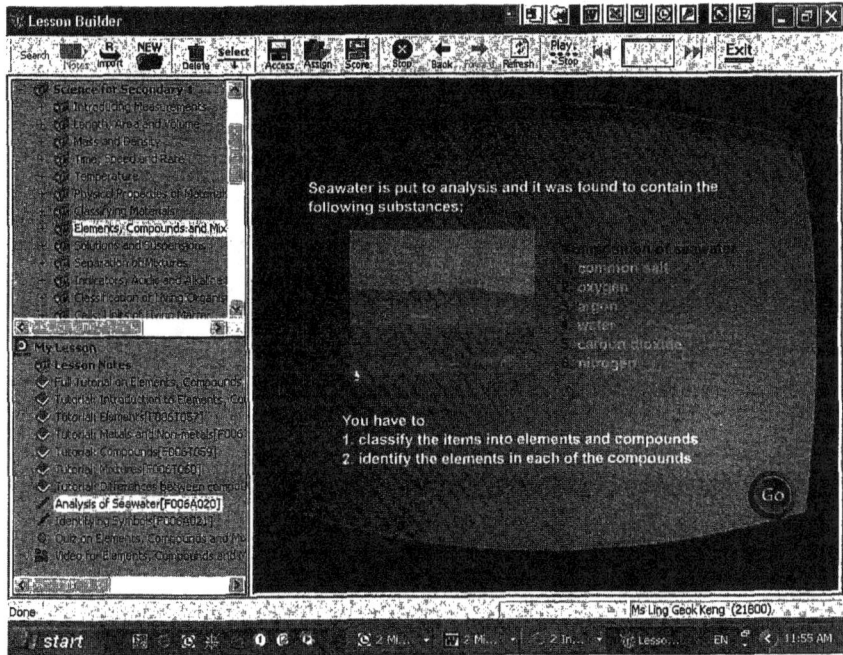

Figure 13.4. A screen capture of the Science topic "Elements, Compounds and Mixtures" in the e-learning system (Image courtesy of MoreAtOnce)

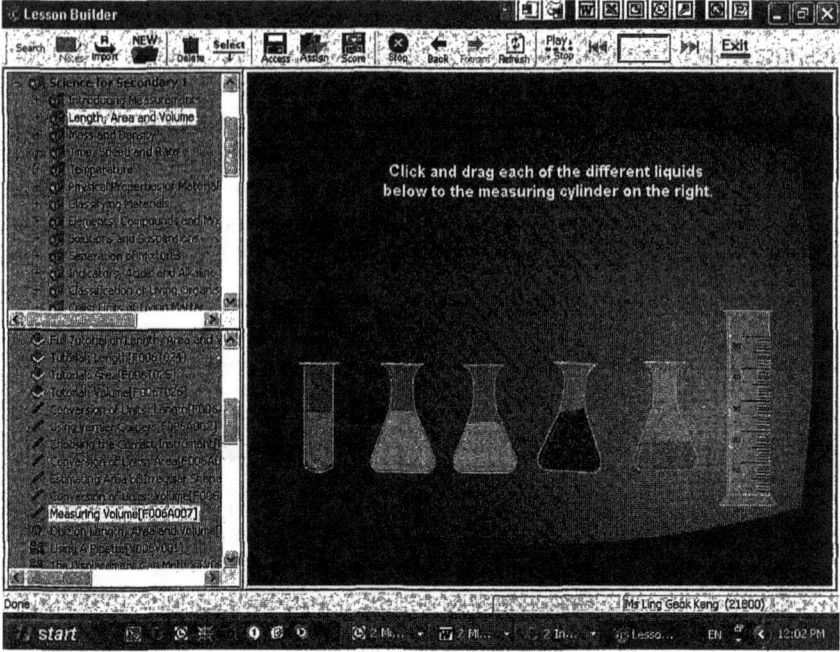

Figure 13.5. A screen capture of the Science topic "Length, Area and Volume", involving the measurement of liquids, in the e-learning system (Image courtesy of MoreAtOnce)

6. The E-learning Classroom Environment Questionnaire (ELCEQ)

Maor and Fraser (1996) observed that the original version of CCEI was developed to assess students' perceptions of the inquiry-based learning environment. The Satisfaction scale was modified from the Learning Environment Inventory (LEI) (Fraser, Anderson, & Walberg, 1982). Investigation was adapted from the Individualised Classroom Environment Questionnaire (ICEQ) (Fraser, 1990), and Open-endedness was adapted from the Science Laboratory Environment Inventory (SLEI) (Fraser, Giddings, & McRobbie, 1993). The initial version of CCEI contained 40 items but with continued validation and refinement, the final 30-item version was used. Table 13.2 shows the description of each scale of the CCEI.

The instrument used a 5-point Likert scale with response options of Almost Never, Seldom, Sometimes, Often, and Almost Always. The students were required to indicate their responses to both the actual and preferred versions of the ELCEQ.

Table 13.2. Description for Each Scale of the Computer Classroom Environment Inventory (CCEI)

Scale name	Items per scale	Description of scale	Moo's scheme
Investigation (IN)	6	Degree to which the skills and processes of inquiry are used in investigation and problem solving	Personal development
Open-endedness (OE)	6	Degree to which the learning activities emphasise an open-ended, divergent approach to experimentation	Personal development
Organisation (OR)	6	Degree to which the learning activities are presented in an organised manner.	Personal development
Material Environment (ME)	6	Degree to which students have access to the equipment and materials.	System maintenance and change
Satisfaction (SA)	6	Degree to which students enjoy learning	Relationship

Adapted from Maor & Fraser (1996)

Table 13.3. Description for Each Scale of the E-learning Classroom Environment Questionnaire (ELCEQ)

Scale name	Item per scale	Item number	Sample item
Investigation (IN)	6	1,6,11,16,21,26	In this module, I use the web-based tools to prove my ideas.
Open-endedness (OE)	6	2,7,12,17,22,27	I pursue my own interests in science in this module
Organisation (OR)	6	3,8,13,18,23,28	I am able to log on to the module website as planned.
Material Environment (ME)	6	4,9,14,19,24,29	I have easy access to computers that are in working condition.
Satisfaction (SA)	6	5,10,15,20,25,30	I feel satisfied with the web-based activities provided by this module.

In view of the incorporation of e-learning into existing face-to-face interactions in the science classroom, the context, the terminology and the descriptions of the statements in CCEI were modified. Without changing the scales in CCEI, the statements were modified by changing the words to better describe the context of e-learning used in this study. For example, 'this class' is changed to 'this module' and 'computers' is changed to 'web-based tools'. A brief description of the items and sample items are provided in Table 13.3.

7. Findings

7.1 Internal Consistency Reliability (Cronbach Alpha Coefficient)

A summary of the internal consistency reliability for the ELCEQ (actual and preferred versions) is presented in Table 13.4. The Cronbach alpha coefficient for each ELCEQ scale was calculated as a measure of internal consistency reliability. The individual was used as the unit of analysis.

Table 13.4. Internal Consistency Reliability (Cronbach Alpha Coefficient) and Item Mean

ELCEQ Scale	No. of items	Form	Alpha reliability	Item mean
Investigation	6	Actual	0.55	3.2
(IN)		Preferred	0.87	3.3
Open-endedness	6	Actual	0.60	3.3
(OE)		Preferred	0.70	3.4
Organisation	6	Actual	0.63	3.0*
(OR)		Preferred	0.70	3.7*
Material Environment	6	Actual	0.60	3.6*
(ME)		Preferred	0.70	4.3*
Satisfaction	6	Actual	0.70	2.8*
(SA)		Preferred	0.83	3.5*

* $p < 0.05$
$N=134$

In Table 13.4, the alpha reliability ranged from 0.55 to 0.70 for the actual version of ELCEQ and 0.70 to 0.87 for the preferred version of ELCEQ. Except for the Investigation scale, all the others reported appropriate alpha reliability values. Table 13.4 showed that all the 5 ELCEQ scales had Cronbach alpha coefficients above 0.6. These 4 scales (Open-endedness, Organization, Material Environment and Satisfaction) had values which were comparable to that for the actual version of CCEI conducted in the previous studies (Maor & Fraser,

1996). The low reliability obtained in Investigation scale could be due to the fact that the item did not measure what it was supposed to. Alternatively, it is possible that the respondents were not familiar with the term or the practice, and this might have led to erroneous responses on their part.

7.2 Comparing the Student Actual and Preferred Perceptions on the ELCEQ

In Table 13.4, the paired t-test (2-tailed) calculated for the actual and preferred ELCEQ showed that significant differences between actual and preferred perceptions emerged for 3 out of 5 scales. They are the Organisation, Material Environment and the Satisfaction scales. Using the individual students as the unit of analysis, the students' actual and preferred means were calculated for each of the scales of ELCEQ. Figure 13.6 shows that the preferred version of the ELCEQ seemed to give to higher means compared to the actual version of ELCEQ for all the scales. This is consistent with findings of previous research – that the preferred scores are always more favourable than the actual scores.

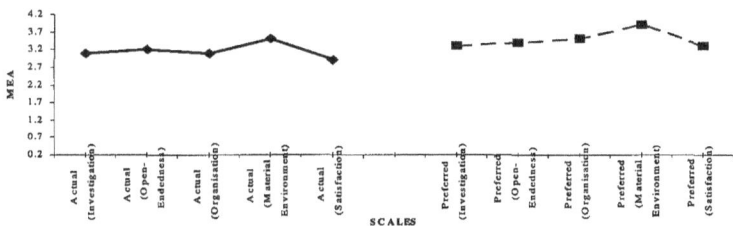

Figure 13.6. Simplified plot of significant variations between students' actual and preferred perceptions in two schools

The Investigation and Open-endedness scales were not significantly indicated and this has caused some concern among the science teachers. According to the science teachers, they observed that their students seemed to 'accept' most of the learning activities passively without asking questions about the concepts presented. They did not seem to be able to conduct investigations by using the web-based tools. They seemed rather reluctant to clarify ideas or challenge ideas with their peers. They also seemed rather passive in receiving feedback only from their teachers.

In the actual version of ELCEQ, a higher mean score was obtained for the Material Environment scale. It may be inferred from this that there was adequate equipment and computers available for students to access the on-line learning resources in school. High mean scores were obtained for all the scales except the investigation scale in their actual (3.2) and preferred (3.3) science classroom learning environment respectively. This could imply that the students would like to learn by on-line learning in addition to existing face-to-face science lessons in the two schools.

Table 13.5 shows the item means obtained in schools A and B for all the scales in the actual and preferred versions of ELCEQ. These mean scores were illustrated in Figure 13.7 which shows the graph of comparisons of differences between students' actual- and preferred-perception mean scores on the ELCEQ of the two schools.

By comparing schools A and B, the students in these two schools perceived almost similarly low mean scores in the actual version of ELCEQ. However, in the preferred ELCEQ, the students in school A perceived higher mean scores for all the scales than the students in school B.

Table 13.5. Description of Item Means of Schools A and B in ELCEQ Scales

ELCEQ Scale	No. of items	Form	Item mean	
			School A	School B
Investigation (IN)	6	Actual	3.2	3.1
		Preferred	3.3	3.3
Open-endedness (OE)	6	Actual	3.3	3.1
		Preferred	3.4	3.4
Organisation (OR)	6	Actual	3.0*	3.1*
		Preferred	3.7*	3.4*
Material Environment (ME)	6	Actual	3.6*	3.5*
		Preferred	4.3*	3.7*
Satisfaction (SA)	6	Actual	2.8*	3.0*
		Preferred	3.5*	3.2*

* $p < 0.05$
N=134

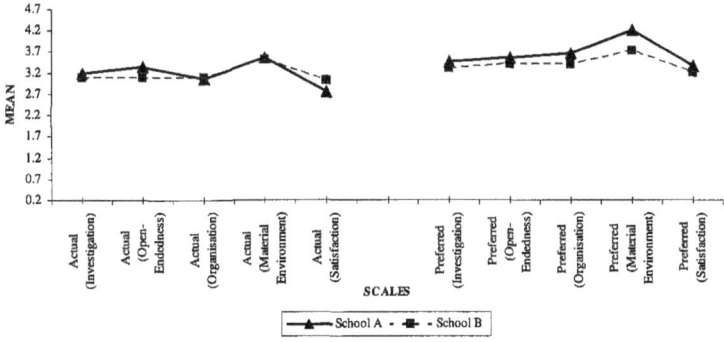

Figure 13.7. Simplified plot of differences between students' actual and preferred perceptions in school A and school B

In the preferred version of ELCEQ, the students from school A perceived the highest mean score (4.3) for the Material Environment scale among other scales. This could mean that either the students in school A had higher expectations of the computer facilities, which were not being met, or the students in school B believed their expectations of the computer facilities, as well as the actual state of said facilities, to be low when in fact both were adequately provided.

Hence, from the trends observed in Figure 13.7, this could explain why these students perceived their e-learning science classroom environment positively. Overall, the mean scores obtained for all the five ELCEQ scales indicated that the lower secondary science e-learning classroom environment was conducive for students to interact and collaborate effectively because it was viewed favourably in terms of levels of investigation, satisfaction, organization, open-endedness and material environment.

8. Conclusion

The significance of this study lies in the fact that there is currently no research conducted at the secondary school level that focuses on the psychosocial aspects of e- learning environments.

This study provides a basic understanding of how e-learning is incorporated into the existing mode of teaching science in Singapore secondary schools. By drawing from the students' perceptions about their science learning environment, the study shows that the students perceived the learning environment with e-learning incorporated into face-to-face interaction to be positive. Using the individual students as the unit of analysis, the students' actual and preferred means were calculated for each of the scales of ELCEQ. The paired t-test (2-tailed), which was calculated for the actual and preferred ELCEQ, showed that significant differences between actual and preferred perceptions were present for three out of five scales. They are the Organisation, Material Environment and the Satisfaction scales. In comparing the actual and preferred versions of the ELCEQ, the three significant differences shown in the Organisation, Material Environment and Satisfaction scales reveal that the existing provision of resources, organisation of activities and the students' feeling about the e-learning environment were important areas for schools to pay attention to and for the future implementation of e-learning in the science curriculum.

The coordination and organisation of teaching resources in the e-learning environment will require teachers to plan and work collaboratively. The teaching resources in the e-learning environment are often shared across many classes and it is important that the teachers involved in e-learning provide feedback to one another. In terms of the material environment, besides the good maintenance of computers and the provision of conducive computer laboratories in schools, the teachers also need to be pro-active in finding out if the students face any difficulty in accessing the e-learning system from home. In order to enjoy the benefits of e-learning, the schools will have to work out schedules to ensure that all the students involved in e-learning have access to the computers. In the process of e-learning, the teachers will need to communicate with the students responsively. E-mail, online discussions and bulletin boards provide the necessary channels of communication that help the teachers and students stay connected. Before embarking on the journey of e-learning in science, it would be advisable for teachers to set aside time to teach communication skills to their students in the e-learning environment. Only when the students are given sufficient time to warm up in the e-learning environment will they be comfortable and confident enough to navigate it, and only then will they be able to fully enjoy learning within such an environment.

Perhaps the teachers could, at this point, address the perceptions of the levels of Investigation and Open-endedness in the learning environment. In the provision of learning activities, the teachers could pay more attention to the design of more open-ended activities, encourage students to ask questions prior to the teaching of the topics and challenge students' understanding of concepts during the teaching. Perhaps some of the topics in secondary one science could be taught by the provision of open-ended discussion forums to allow students to ask questions and find out the possible answers on their own. With the incorporation of online learning into the teaching of science, the teachers are to be more mindful about their roles as they facilitate and mentor students' learning. However, the incorporation of online learning does not rule out the importance of face-to-face interactions in any teaching and learning situation in schools.

References

Chan K. S, Lam, Y. K, Lam P. K, Loo P. L. (2001). *Science adventure for secondary 1 textbook.* Singapore: Times Media Publication.
Fraser, B. J. (1984). Differences between preferred and actual classroom environment as perceived by primary students and teachers. *British Journal of Educational Psychology, 54,* 336-339.
Fraser, B. J. (1990). *Individualised classroom environment questionnaire.* Melbourne, Australia: Australian Council for Educational Research.
Fraser, B. J., Anderson, G. J., & Walberg, H. J. (1982). *Assessment of learning environments: Manual for Learning Environment Inventory (LEI) and My Class Inventory (MCI)* (3rd vers.). Perth, Australia: Western Australian Institute of Technology.
Fraser, B. J., McRobbie C. J., & Giddings, G. J. (1993). Development and cross-national validation of a laboratory classroom environment instrument for senior high school science. *Science Education, 77,* 1-24.

Fraser, B. J. (1994). Research on classroom and school climate. In D. Gabel (Ed.). *Handbook of research on science teaching and learning* (pp. 493 - 541). New York : Macmillan Publishing Co.

Jegede, O., Fraser, B. J., & Fisher, D. (1998). *Development, validation and use of a learning environment instrument for university distance education settings.* Paper presented at the Annual Meeting of the American Educational Research Association, San Diego, CA.

Jonassen, D. H. (2000). *Computers as mindtools for schools: Engaging critical thinking.* New Jersey: Prentice Hall.

Jonassen, D. H., Howland, J., Moore, J., & Marra, R.M. (2003). *Learning to solve problems with technology: A constructivist perspective.* New Jersey : Prentice Hall, Inc.

Hiltz, S. R. (1994). *The virtual classroom: Learning without limits via computer networks.* Norwood, New Jersey : Ablex.

Huang, T.-C. I., Fraser, B. J., & Aldridge, J. M. (1998). *Combining quantitative and qualitative approaches in studying classroom climate in Taiwan and Australia.* Paper presented at the annual meeting of the National Association for Research in Science Teaching, San Diego, CA.

Khan, B. H. (1997). *Web-based instruction.* Englewood Cliffs, New Jersey: Educational Technology Publication, Inc.

Lynch, M. M. (2002). *The online educator:A guide to creating the virtual classroom.* London : Routledge Falmer.

Maor, D., & Fraser, B.J. (1996). Use of classroom environment perceptions in evaluating inquiry-based computer-assisted learning. *International Journal of Science Teaching, 18,* 401-421.

Maor, D. (2000). A teacher professional development program on using a constructivist multimedia learning environment.*Learning Environment Research, 2,* 307-330.

Maor, D., & Fraser, B.J. (in press). An online questionnaire for evaluating students' and teachers' perceptions of constructivist multimedia learning environments. *Research in Science Education.*

Marlowe, B. A., & Page, M.L. (1998). *Creating and sustaining the constructivist classroom.* California : Corwin Press, Inc.

Palloff, R. M., & Pratt, K. (1998). *Effective teaching and learning in the virtual classroom.* World Computer Congress: Teleteaching 98, Vienna/Austria and Budapest/Hungary, August.

Palloff, R. M., & Pratt, K. (2001). *Lessons from the cyberspace classroom : The realities of online teaching.* California : John Wiley & Sons, Inc.

Teh, G.P.L. (2001). *Assessing students' perceptions of synchronous internet-based learning environments.* Paper presented at the annual meeting of Australian Association for Research, Perth, Australia.

Teh, G., & Fraser, B. J. (1994). An evaluation of computer-assisted learning in terms of achievement, attitudes and classroom environment. *Evaluation and Research in Education, 8*, 147-161.

Teh, G., & Fraser, B. (1995). Development and validation of an instrument for assessing the psychosocial environment of computer-assisted learning classrooms. *Journal of Educational Computing Research, 12*, 177-193.

Tobin, K. (1998). Qualitative perceptions of learning environments on the world wide web. In B. J. Fraser & K. G. Tobins (Eds.). *International handbook of science education* (pp. 139-162). United Kingdom : Kluwer Academic Publishers.

Tobin, K. and Fraser, B. J. (1998). Qualitative and Quantitative Landscapes of Classroom Learning Environments. In B. J. Fraser & K. G. Tobins (Eds.). *International Handbook of Science Education* (pp. 623-640). United Kingdom : Kluwer Academic Publishers.

Tobin, K. G., Kahle, J. B., & Fraser, B. J. (Eds.). (1990). *Windows into science classes: Problems associated with higher-level cognitive learning.* London: Falmer Press.

Chapter 14

STUDENTS AS CHANGE AGENTS: THE GENERATION Y MODEL

Dennis Harper
Olympia Washington School District
USA

This chapter looks at the often forgotten stakeholders in our schools — the students. Students make up more than 92% of most K-12 school systems yet they are seldom meaningfully involved in school reform or the professional development of teachers. Recent research in the United States shows that 54% of American schools involve students in the maintenance of computers and network infrastructure, students carry out only 4% of professional development in technology. This chapter looks at both the Generation Y (Gen Y) model, which accounts for most of this 4%, and a comprehensive review of research support for student voice, perspectives, and involvement.

1. The Generation Y Model

The Generation Y (Gen Y) program has been implemented in over 500 schools throughout the USA for students in grades K-12. Begun in 1996 with federal Technology Innovation Challenge Grant (TICG) funds, it has received more than 10 million dollars in funding in its six-plus years of implementation serving both inservice and preservice teachers. While promoting the effective use of technology in schools, Generation Y develops student leadership, and fosters a collaborative, constructivist learning community between student and teacher. Students and partner teachers learn how telecommunications, the Internet, multimedia, and presentation tools can enhance lesson plans and support a standards-based curriculum. Generation Y achieves this by giving students experience with educational technology, communication skills, and information literacy, allowing students to act as responsible partners with their teachers in building new curriculum materials and new teaching and learning practices.

1.1 How Generation Y Works

When Generation Y begins in a school, a group of students become the "Gen Y Class". This class is the central component for training students in grades 3 to 12 to partner with a teacher to produce technology-infused lessons. A "Gen Y teacher" in the school manages the process. Each Generation Y student is paired with a partner teacher, who decides which curriculum unit they will produce together. These technology-infused units are then used in the partner teacher's regular classroom. One Generation Y class can thus impact teaching practices and student engagement for 20 to 30 teachers in a school. Further, to support its inherent scaling-out strategies, the core model enables program graduates of the Generation Y program (Gen Dids) to: (1) work with participating schools of education to improve technology integration into teacher education; (2) work in community-based labs to improve access to networked computers to mentor families and community members; (3) continue work on technology projects with new or former partner teachers, acting as teaching assistants or peer mentors; and (4) provide leadership and technical expertise in other community organizations (Coe & Ault, 2001). Generation Y's model provides individualized support for building effective curricula and can be customized to fit a wide range of content, grade levels, technology infrastructures, scheduling requirements, interests, and skill levels. The "heart" of Generation Y is not technology, but redefining boundaries between teachers and learners in order to improve student achievement, motivation, and lifelong learning skills.

The Expert Panel on Educational Technology, commissioned by the USA Department of Education, reviewed evaluation data on Generation Y. In the summer of 2000, the program was awarded "Exemplary" status by the panel. Only two educational technology models have ever received this distinction.

Generation Y is a program which uses partnerships between students and teachers to integrate modern computer technologies into the classroom. The program promotes the effective use of educational technology in schools, develops opportunities for student leadership, and fosters a collaborative, learning community atmosphere in schools. Rather than teaching technology skills to teachers and hoping they will use these skills to improve their students' learning, Generation Y trains students to form working partnerships with teachers in order to improve teaching and learning in their schools. Students become agents of change, assuming responsibility for helping to improve the educational resources available to themselves and their classmates. Generation Y students learn technology skills with an emphasis on applying these skills to a real world problem: helping teachers use technology to deliver more effective lessons. Students and partner teachers learn how telecommunications tools, the Internet, digital imaging and presentation tools, and other technologies can enhance lesson plans and curriculum units.

Many Generation Y students and partner teachers also learn about their state academic standards and learning goals, and the process of aligning classroom activities with these goals. Each Generation Y student is paired with a partner teacher (or an administrator, librarian, counselor or other educator), who decides what lesson plan, curriculum unit, or other school need will be addressed by a collaborative, technology-enriched curriculum project, which the partner teacher and the Generation Y student produce together. These projects are then used in the partner teacher's regular classroom, or in the library, administrative offices, etc. Through this model, participating educators receive individualized support as they strengthen their use and integration of new technologies. Students learn technology, communication, collaboration, and project management skills in an authentic, personally meaningful context, and many go on to further extend their skills through advanced school or community service projects.

The program was developed in the Olympia, Washington School District, with a five-year award in 1996 from the USA Department of Education's Technology Innovation Challenge Grant program. Numerous state and local grants as well as corporate sponsorships have also supported the development of the instructional model and materials, as well as dissemination of the model to schools outside Olympia.

Data from the nationwide project indicate that the program can be an effective alternative for schools wishing to integrate technology into their regular curriculum and increase their use of project-based, student-centered learning practices. The model provides individualized support for educators who wish to increase their use of technology without becoming distracted from the essence of their jobs of building and delivering effective curriculum units and lesson plans.

Participating teachers and students report that their involvement in Generation Y afforded them an excellent opportunity to improve their basic technology skills, and to develop more advanced abilities to integrate technology in standards-based lessons, projects, and curriculum units. Both teachers and students report that they gained meaningful, authentic experience developing skills in technology use, collaboration, project management, and information literacy, while contributing to the improvement of their schools. Most found the Generation Y model to be an effective professional development strategy for teachers, as well as an effective approach to increasing student engagement, student learning, and student leadership.

Extensive research has provided useful information regarding facilitating conditions, challenges, and keys to success, which should be provide much useful information to schools interested in implementing Generation Y. This information can help schools determine if the program is a good match for their needs, and help them prepare and develop a successful Generation Y program. A number of other challenges, policy issues and recommendations are also highlighted at http://www.genes.org.

1.2 Extensions to the Generation Y Model

The core Generation Y class has been developed for use as a regular class or extracurricular activity that provides immediate benefits for participating students and partner teachers. However, in order to extend the impact of the program, the model is also designed to prepare students for continued growth and service in their schools and communities. Toward this end, a number of additional components have been developed in the Olympia School District and in other participating districts across the country. These extensions provide further opportunities for students to apply their skills in technology applications and collaborative project work.

Four primary types of extensions to the core model have been developed in Olympia. These allow students who have been through the Generation Y course to continue developing and applying their technical, communication and leadership skills. These extensions include:

- Opportunities for Gen Dids (graduates of the program have been nicknamed "Gen Dids.") to work with pre-service teachers at participating institutions of higher education, in order to improve the integration of technology into the education and field experience of pre-service teachers. During 1999, this aspect of the Generation Y project contributed to the development of a proposal by The Evergreen State College, also in Olympia, to the U.S. Department of Education program on *Preparing Tomorrows Teachers to Use Technology*. This project was funded as a Catalyst grant, and has resulted in a three-year effort to build networked learning communities in several states, involving K-12 Generation Y schools and nine colleges of education.

- Opportunities for Gen Dids to work in after-school computer labs or community-based computer labs, to improve access to networked computers and individualized mentoring for students, family members, and community members.

- Opportunities for Gen Dids to continue working on educational technology projects with new or former partner teachers, administrators, or staff in their schools, including opportunities to act as teaching assistants or mentors with other students.

- Opportunities for Gen Dids to provide leadership and technical expertise in other community organizations.

2. Pre-Service Teacher Training

During the first three years of the project, Generation Y graduates in the Olympia, Washington School District served as instructors and facilitators for educational technology classes at preservice teacher education programs in two local institutions of higher education, The Evergreen State College and St. Martins College. In addition to classroom activities and discussions about educational technology, pre-service teachers accompanied these Gen Y students to their elementary, middle, and high schools for demonstrations and hands-on experience with the uses of integrated technology in real educational applications.

This program is currently being further developed through a 1999 award to The Evergreen State College, in partnership with Generation Y, under the *Preparing Tomorrow's Teachers to Use Technology* Catalyst Grant program of the U.S. Department of Education. Through the

Student Teacher Technology Education Partnership (ST2EP), nine participating teacher education institutions are developing networked learning communities, incorporating educational technology and integrating efforts at participating colleges and universities with the Generation Y programs in local middle schools and high schools. Experiences and data from the Generation Y project were used as formative information for the new Evergreen State College project. For more information see the ST2EP web site at http://step.evergreen.edu.

3. Community Computer Labs

Another leadership opportunity for graduates of Generation Y in Olympia has been the development of public access computer labs at schools or community centers. Pre-service teachers have also worked in these labs as an additional experience with educational technology integration. Five such computer labs were developed in Olympia, providing access to networked computer resources for students, their family members, and other individuals. These labs have been open after school hours, staffed by pre-service teachers and Gen Dids, and have provided individualized support to users as well as access to modern software, hardware, and the Internet.

4. Student Leadership in Schools and in the Community

Many individual Generation Y graduates have continued applying their skills in various roles, in their academic settings or in community organizations. The following list conveys some of the opportunities for student leadership that Gen Dids have enjoyed around the United States as extensions of their Generation Y experiences:

- Involvement in local citizen leadership programs
- Presentations at national, state and regional educational technology conferences
- Formal or informal positions as teaching or technical assistants in their schools
- Employment or internships as Webmasters for schools or districts
- Service as student representatives to national and regional educational organizations

- Management of school telecommunications programs
- Employment or internships as educational technology consultants for district or state educational officers
- Participation as expert panel members in online discussions of educational policy
- Providing computer application instruction to state departments of education officials
- Developing local, state, and national education plans and policies

As the number and collective expertise of Generation Y graduates increases, developing further opportunities for continued growth and participation is currently a high priority for the Generation Y program. The majority of Generation Y students are in middle schools or junior high schools. Unfortunately, many of these students move on to high schools in which opportunities to continue applying and developing their leadership and technical skills are limited. It is hoped that more communication and integration will develop between grade levels and school buildings, in order to maximize the effectiveness of these programs.

Diagram shows the how Generation YES works with the Gen Y teacher is a school to train students to provide professional development and support for partner teachers. The Gen Y students become Gen Dids who continue to support teachers and students as they pass through the school system.

5. Summary and Recommendations from Generation Y Research

Over the past five years, the Generation Y curriculum model, materials, training, and online resources have undergone several cycles of development and revision. The award-winning program has been implemented in elementary, middle, and high schools across the United States, and has spurred the development of a teacher-training project through the USA Department of Education's program for Preparing Tomorrows Teachers to Use Technology.

A variety of data has been collected to inform the improvement of the project as well as to document knowledge about the project. Extensive surveying of participating Generation Y teachers, partner teachers, and students has been integrated into the online facilities used by participants. In addition, evaluation studies have included case studies of selected schools, site visits, interviews with teachers and administrators from participating schools, and a quasi-experimental study comparing participating and non-participating teachers in selected sites. Survey data, case studies and interviews have been collected from a wide variety of schools and geographic regions, including rural, suburban, and urban schools with a range of affluence and demographic characteristics.

The Generation Y model is implemented differently in different sites. This variability is intentional, and the resources provided to schools are intended to be adapted to local conditions. One general finding is that it often takes one or more semesters of floundering in order for a particular Generation Y implementation to take hold. During this period, administration and faculty must work to become oriented to the model, and to clear away scheduling problems, infrastructure deficits, or other structural hurdles. Of particular importance is properly introducing the model to the faculty, so that they understand their role in the program.

In schools that have moved through these hurdles and fully implement the model, participants report overwhelmingly positive outcomes. Participating teachers and students report that their involvement in Generation Y afforded them an excellent opportunity to improve their basic technology skills as well as their more advanced abilities to integrate technology in standards-based lessons, projects and curriculum units. Both teachers and students report that they gained meaningful, authentic experience developing skills in technology use, collaboration, project management, and information literacy, while contributing to the improvement of their schools. Most found the Generation Y model to be an effective professional development strategy for teachers, as well as an effective approach to increasing student engagement, student learning and student leadership.

Ongoing problems limit the success of the model in some schools. A large and apparently growing fraction of teachers report that their students do not have adequate network access or user privileges for online educational activities, often due to overly stringent network security procedures in their buildings. Many teachers and partner teachers noted that chronic time constraints made it difficult for them to implement a new and innovative program, particularly one involving projects and partnerships with students that may require activities that do not follow the regimented structure of today's schools. An ongoing struggle for the program is the number of partner teachers who remain unclear about their role in the model.

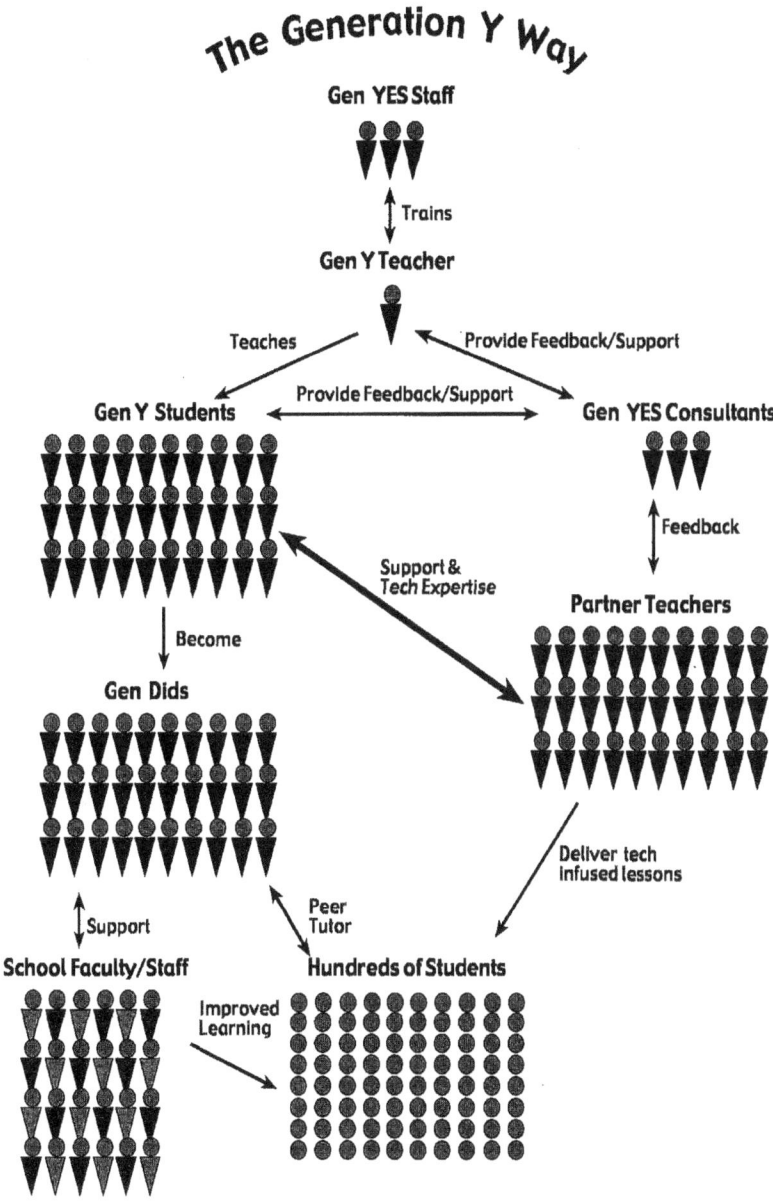

Figure 14.1. The generation Y way

5.1 Research Support for Student Voice, Perspectives, and Involvement in Critical Educational and Public Policy Issues

We now turn our attention to what research says about student involvement in policy issues with an emphasis on technology infusion. Educators rarely consider asking students (of any age) what they think about school and how they would like to learn – in spite of findings from brain research that even young children have the capacity for complex thinking and that their perspectives are valid (e.g., Caine & Caine, 1997; Diamond & Hopson, 1998; Jensen, 1998; Sylwester, 1995; Wolfe & Sorgen, 1990). A variety of sources reveal that today's school-age children – currently referred to as Generation Y – consider themselves to be living in a fearful world, have lost their sense of hope, and feel adults do not respect or listen to them. Yet their voice continues to be ignored – despite the fact that they make up more than 92% of schools, have probably 95% of the technology skills and are 100% of why schools exist. It should be no surprise that today's students report being increasingly alienated and disconnected from schools and from adults who ignore their perspectives.

The importance of meeting basic human needs for control, competence, and belonging is confirmed by motivation experts and educators in research-validated principles of motivation, learning, and development (Deci & Ryan, 1991; Ryan, 1992). When students talk about how they would meet these needs, satisfy their natural curiosity and the need to make sense of things, they provide a blueprint for finding the most effective practices for engaging student voice in the process of learning. By listening to students' voices, educators can learn how schools and classrooms can be more relevant as well as safer and more secure. Research findings reveal there is another payoff when conditions that foster natural motivation to learn are provided. Feelings of anger and rebellion are reduced that otherwise commonly occur under conditions that do not allow student choice, do not respect students' feelings or interests, and do not consider students' perspectives (e.g., McCombs & Whisler, 1997; Rogers & Freiberg, 1994).

5.2 What Is Known About the Needs of Today's Learners

Denver area expert on Generation Y, Eric Chester, reports that this generation of youth is not being challenged in school, things are too easy, and consequently, they easily give up when things get hard. At the same time, Generation Y youth are questioning deep spiritual concerns such as "Why am I here?". "Why go to school – when all I'm going to do is die?" Many youth have friends who died young and want to know why it matters to learn things like algebra. In a recent survey of 825 children aged 11-18 in Colorado, the *Denver Rocky Mountain News* (December 10, 1998) reports that 99% of those surveyed want respect and attention from adults. Regrettably, this survey found that, on the average, adults spend only seven minutes of quality time each day with their children. One third of those surveyed did not feel valued or cared about, 56% of those in grades 5-7 felt adults did not value them, and this increased to 78% in grades 8-12 felt adults did not value them. Compounding these issues, children are dealing with the stress of (a) school (homework, grades, passing, violence), (b) family (fear of losing parents, broken families, worry over health issues such as AIDS), (c) peers (bullies, gangs, fickle friends, vicious teasing, informal initiations into codes of conduct), (d) world (safe air and water, global warming, crime, drive by shootings, terrorism, nuclear war), and (e) the future (kids said they are stressed "about everything"). Research (McCombs, in press) reports that (a) children as young as three years old are suffering from stress-related illnesses, (b) one out of 20 children under the age of 10 suffer from depression, (c) cigarette smoking is now considered a pediatric disease with more than 3,000 children starting to smoke each day, and (d) suicide is now the third most common cause of death among teens

The current Y Generation children born in 1985 and later say they want structure and discipline. Because many have not received discipline, structure, or quality time with adults – too many are angry, disrespectful, and alienated. The youth culture has become their parent and guide. Unfortunately, that youth culture has become increasingly vicious and competitive. The Y Generation is also called the Millennium Generation – they will redefine society in the 21st century as the baby boomers did in the last half of the 20th century (*Denver Post*, December 21, 1998). They will reshape social, political, and economic areas of life for better or for worse. Yet many in this generation are said to have no loyalty, whether to family, corporations, or political parties. In addition, recent data show that this Y generation have been shaped by TV programming to see authority figures as stupid. They report that their parents give them too much materially and not enough in terms of the time spent with them (*Denver Rocky Mountain News*, December 20,

1998). As a result many are desensitized, disenfranchised, and disengaged.

5.3 How Youth Can Contribute to Educational Change

When asked, youth are clear about what defines schools in which they love to learn. Rogers and Freiberg (1994) asked students what motivates them to learn in school. Students consistently reported that they want (a) to be trusted and respected, (b) to be part of a family, (c) their teachers to act as helpers, (d) opportunities to be responsible, (e) freedom, not license, (f) a place where people care, (g) teachers who help them succeed, and (h) to have choices. Current research is increasingly supporting the educational and social benefits of not only listening to youth, but also engaging them in authentic adult partnerships that address key issues of relevance to their lives such as education. In fact, many researchers now argue that it is amazing and, for some, unconscionable that the primary persons served by the educational system are rarely if ever asked how they think the system should be designed and implemented (e.g., Cook-Sather, 2002; Ericson & Ellet, 2002).

Research (McCombs, 2001a, b)clearly shows that it is critical to honor student views in meaningful adult-youth partnerships if schools are to achieve increased motivation, learning, and academic achievement for a much larger number of students, including those who are underachieving, dropping out of school, or suffering a range of negative emotions ranging from alienation to life-threatening despair. At the core of these issues, many experts and students themselves report that youth are in a spiritual crisis of questioning who they are, their purpose, and the meaning of life (Brendtro, 1999; Brendtro, Brokenleg, & Van Bocern, 1992). These issues highlight the need for positive adult-youth relationships and partnerships.

Those looking at youth perspectives on education provide data on the benefits of practices that involve learning partnerships, honoring student voice, and engaging students in personal ownership over their own learning. For example, Mitra (2002) found that while teachers blame students for not being interested in their education or blame uninvolved parents, students point to problems such as instruction not being compatible with their learning styles and the need for additional tutoring and counseling. Such disparities in perspective suggest that a school reform model involving students in reform work might focus efforts on different problems and suggest different solutions for enhancing their motivation and achievement.

Mitra's (2002) research shows that the Student Forum experience is a promising strategy for balancing student and teacher-focused activities. Its success is primarily due to three organizational contexts: (1) its focus on activities does not strike at the core of teacher practice (activities are targeted toward influencing policy and the school reform process rather than directly challenging teacher practice – a less threatening approach); (2) it buffers the forum from external threats and builds bridges with teaching staff (this protects students from school bureaucracy and connects them to opportunities within the school); and (3) it backs up the adults that support the Student Forum (the school reform leader has authority and clout to provide information and funding while also bringing inspiration, emotional support and energy to the group). Mitra's study provides a beginning of needed research on mechanisms for increasing student participation and decision-making in schools.

Ericson and Ellet (2002) argue powerfully that students are central to educational excellence as well as being would-be-beneficiaries of reform, yet have been almost entirely overlooked. By ignoring their views, students have incentives to undercut the intent of reforms. Ericson and Ellet (2002) have conducted theoretical/analytical research (systematic review and thoughtful analysis of a multi-disciplinary literature) regarding this issue. Their findings indicate that when educational systems demonstrate the features of a 'meritocratic' social and economic system, student preferences are guaranteed to result in mediocrity of learning and achievement rather than excellence. Meritocratic goals are based on the ideology that schooling pays social and economic dividends and that social rewards and privileges should go to individuals of talent, intelligence, and industry. In such systems the ideal of teaching subject matter in ways that assist students to develop intrinsic motivation is often thwarted, either toward learning in general or the subject matter in particular. These systems, according to Ericson and Ellet (2002), at best view education as a means to the end of grades, degrees, and careers; at worst the true pursuit of knowledge and understanding is an impediment and is less efficient and coercive than externally motivated self-interest.

As a way to offset this pattern, Calvert (2002) provides evidence from a broad range of school settings supporting the view that students can participate meaningfully as agents of positive change at both the classroom and school levels. He maintains that this fits the current trend in educational research that focuses on school climate, social conditions, and school culture. These are factors important to positive student learning environments and good working conditions for teachers. These trends also support research from educational psychology that increasing student autonomy, membership, and agency leads to higher engagement and academic achievement (e.g., Larson, 2000; McCombs, 2001a). Schools provide a powerful context for youth to become engaged in meaningful and relevant decision-making. For youth to be involved in meaningful decision-making, however, Calvert (2002) argues that they must be infused into ongoing planning and implementation of both policies and programs. Youth must work with adults in equitable partnerships that benefit both youth and the school community as a whole. When this youth infusion occurs, youth bring a sense of mission that positively affects youth and adults. Adults who experience collective action with youth then experience a sense of being more connected and effective in their work with youth and also demonstrate a change in beliefs about both the competence and motivation of youth in general.

In his case study of a large, comprehensive high school, Calvert (2002) studied an action research model for involving youth in school decision-making via a focus on building student-teacher dialogue. This "Communities" program examined whether the action research approach could improve the youth development environment of the school and provides avenues for youth infusion into authentic organizational decision-making. Emerging results indicate that student-staff relations are improving along with changes in the organizational culture. These changes take time since both students and teachers are not habituated to their partnership roles, and supportive structures are needed to scaffold these skills and habits.

Of particular relevance in this research is Calvert's (2002) recognition that structural issues in schools mitigate against allowing students to have significant roles in organizational decision-making. These issues include scheduling and time constraints that make communication among staff and students difficult. Teacher and student roles are generally structured in ways that inhibit reciprocal relationships. In large high schools, teachers see more than 100 students per day and have few opportunities for individual or small-group conversations. As his action research project progressed, however, Calvert found that teachers and students are more personally satisfied with their reciprocal learning opportunities than with traditional educational experiences in the school. As a result, staff and students are questioning current structures and examining schedules that can provide more space for relationship building. These findings are important in identifying issues in the sustainability of partnership interventions that actually change relationships and cultures in schools.

A growing international recognition of the importance of authentically including students as meaningful partners in school reform is occurring, particularly in Great Britain and Australia. This research provides a multicultural view of the importance of student voice in studying the complexity of social settings and various perspectives in understanding learning and instructional phenomena. Fielding (2000, 2001, 2002, in press) provides an international perspective on the importance of student voice in British school reform, while contending that it is sought through the imperatives of accountability rather than a commitment to democratic agency. As an alternative, he offers a transformative approach that includes the voices of students, teachers, and significant others working together in new, empowering ways affecting both process and outcome.

Fielding (2001) describes a four-year student-as-researcher project in which students identified important issues in their daily experience of schooling. Staff, together with students, gathered data, constructed meaning, shared recommendations for change with fellow students and staff, and moved these forward to the governing body of the school. Students began challenging the curriculum, to move it away from a delivery model to a jointly derived meaningful, negotiated curriculum and pedagogy. As the project continued, cultural and structural changes occurred that were student led and sustained by a culture of dialogue. Structural changes followed from the cultural changes in attitudes toward students. As the students demonstrated the quality of their research and ability to identify and articulate insights into curriculum practices, new structures emerged. These resulted in commitment and retention of transformative practices that led to sustainability and robustness over time. Fielding (2001) attributes this to radical collegiality or a professionalism in which the reciprocity of dialogue between and among students and staff helped them learn with and from each other. Reciprocal dialogue and engagement of joint work opened new understandings and insights. These, in turn, generated practical and hopeful possibilities that nurtured a genuine and inclusive sense of community. This model is transformative in its commitment to teaching and learning as a genuinely shared responsibility and a redefinition of what it means to be a student and a teacher.

In his recent work, Fielding (2002) points out the difficulties with the current system and the profound failing of policies that focus on technical solutions to profound human challenges. He argues for a refocusing on the centrality of relationships in the process of education, to provide collaborative learning opportunities where meaning can be collectively derived. A focus on schools as systems can change the status quo and gain institutional support for more transformative views. In order to incorporate student voice in schools as learning communities, systems and structures are needed that allow dialogue to emerge as a central feature. Fielding contends that one of the most interesting challenges is building systems that support and sustain both student and teacher voice. He supports a movement to construct new practices and create new space for teachers and students to "make meaning" together. Schools will then be transformed into learning communities "in which the voices of students, teachers and others are acknowledged as legitimately different and of equal value, the necessary partners in dialogue about how we learn, how we live and the kind of place we wish our community to become" (Fielding, 2002, p. 13).

Clarke (2002) describes the viability of using student voice and learner perspectives not only as an instructional method for enhancing student learning and motivation but also as a way to use complementarily to enhance practice-oriented analytical approaches. These approaches focus on studying learning methods that use learner's perspectives as a strategy for including a wider range of cultural perspectives than has previously been studied. Teachers and students in eighth-grade mathematics classes from nine participating countries, including the US, provided diverse European and Asian perspectives. Clarke's methodology also suggests a way to study a view of learning as emergent individual practice in which individuals choose the nature of their participation in community practice and contribute to and change that practice.

The "Generation Y" program, developed by the author in the Olympia Washington School District, is listening to what kids have to say (Harper, 1998, 2002). The first section of this chapter gives details on this program This approach has led to greater student engagement in learning, and also led to increased school attendance and reduced discipline problems (Coe & Ault, 2001). New positive relationships have been formed between youth and teachers and new school cultures of mutual respect and caring have emerged. Students who would have dropped out of school or been involved in gangs are now making plans to go on to college and/or enter high tech careers. Positive adult-youth relationships are at the center of this change, combined with attention to youth voice in how to engage them in meaningful learning.

This simple idea – listening to kids in meaningful partnerships with adults as a foundation for addressing youth and public policy issues – is central to empowering youth and changing many system inequities and failures. Further, meaningful change and positive growth have consistently been found to derive from supportive and caring relationships between and among youth and adults (e.g., Lambert & McCombs, 1998, McCombs & Whisler, 1997; Rudduck, Day, & Wallace, 1997). In such contexts, Cook-Sather (2002) has argued that students not only have the knowledge and position to shape what counts in education, but they can help change power dynamics and create new forums for learning how to speak out on their own behalf in a variety of arenas and on a range of issues.

5.4 How Youth Can Contribute to Public Policy Areas

Beyond the area of education, attempts to authorize youth perspectives in wider public policy issues have been few. Although youth clearly have a range of issues that are personally relevant to them including health related issues, they are rarely included in policy decisions. At the same time, there are alarming rises in youth suicide, alcohol and drug abuse, school disciplinary problems, school dropout, and delinquent behaviors. In the educational domain, there are few opportunities for insights from youth themselves about how these issues might best be addressed. School system and community responses often run the gamut from fear-based attempts to rid schools and neighborhoods of all youth who are apparent troublemakers. Methods include expulsion, suspension and incarceration, or may incorporate more positive, restorative approaches that build the strengths and assets of even the most troubled youth (e.g., Nissen, 1999; Norris, 1999). In fact, new models of restorative justice within the juvenile justice system are recognizing that it is possibility-oriented relationships that change and heal youth, not programs (Nissen, 1999). There is acknowledgement that people change through hope and strengths and not through shame and humiliation.

Researchers and educators working in the area of living systems and systemic change agree that negative, fear-based approaches will not work (e.g., Wheatley, 1999a, 1999b; Wheatley & Kellner-Rogers, 1996, 1998). They argue for new ways of thinking about human needs and basic functions that are restorative and strength-based, focusing on positive growth and development. This approach centers on understanding that all people are connected and that relationships and networks are the natural form of organization in life, i.e. life can be characterized as interconnected and interdependent webs of relationships. The recommended solution is to deal directly with feelings of alienation and disconnection by designing new kinds of systems that connect rather than isolate individuals, give voice to concerns of all people in the system, and promote positive growth, development of personal and social responsibility, and learning for all.

The research literature is growing in its support of violence prevention strategies that are based on (a) student as well as adult views and perceptions and (b) positive relationships and caring rather than coercive and punitive approaches (e.g., Kenney & Watson, 1999; Larson, 2000; Schaps & Lewis, 1999). As Kenney and Watson (1999) report, students want to be involved in making their schools safe and in taking responsibility for the school environment and when offered the chance, contribute positively to creating new cultures of fairness and caring. Thus, the research supports that giving students voice and ownership not only creates increased personal and social responsibility, but also has positive motivational, academic, and social-cultural benefits. These benefits are particularly important in today's too prevalent school climate and culture of "toxicity" or unnecessarily hard and punitive disciplinary practices (Hyman & Snook, 2000), or zero tolerance policies that treat all children the same without the balance of being strong and fair (Curwin & Mendlar, 1999). As Noguera (1995) has argued, many get-tough approaches to school violence fail to create a safe environment because the strategies interrupt learning and increase mistrust and resistance. For the current generation of school age children – many of whom are already alienated and disconnected from adults and learning – it is particularly important to avoid classroom violence and aggressive behavior, increase personal and social responsibility for school and societal safety, and cultivate empathy and morality.

For Brendtro (1999), the major cause of youth violence and delinquency are the "broken bonds" between adults and youth – caused by adults being too busy to connect with youth and by adults focusing their priorities on the pursuit of wealth and material things. He suggests ways to offset feelings of abandonment and distrust. Trust can be earned by listening to kids, honoring what they say, and focusing on the social climate in schools. Many youth are subjects of "recreational ridicule" and hardcore bullying. In response, they resort to "outcast bonding" with other alienated youth in response to being disconnected and ridiculed (Brendtro, 1999). In the current context of rising youth violence, new systems can be built that are fortified with the understanding of what youth need to feel connected, supported, cared about. Knowing that they respond to having some voice, new systems can be built based on research-validated principles to meet their needs. For example, Brendtro et al. (1992) describe a process for reclaiming at-risk youth that is based on empowering them to care and contribute to the betterment of their families, friends, schools, and communities. In this model, it is not sufficient for adults to care; they must also provide the structure and guidance to instill social responsibility, respect for diversity, and an understanding of our interdependencies. The process is a developmental one, moving from meeting needs for belonging, mastery, and independence towards outcomes of generosity and caring. Brendtro (1999) contends that all people are born to be concerned but that conscience is taught through positive adult modeling.

Wheatley (1999b) has claimed that we are in perilous times and have created a culture of alienation and violence. Her work with a variety of organizations including educational systems confirms that people are disconnected and suffering because of it. It is time to bring the best knowledge, along with hope and courage, to the task of building systems with the connections necessary for the positive growth and learning for all youth as well as development of life-long social responsibility skills for creating new cultures of caring and shared responsibility. Youth, themselves, have recognized that "We need to stop pointing fingers and learn to take responsibility for what we do. If people could do this, things would actually change. I think that some people are frustrated because change is not done as quickly as they want it. It's hard to remember that things take time." (Statements from Colorado teens at MTV forum on reducing youth violence, July 20, 1999, *Denver Rocky Mountain News*).

Acknowledgement

The author would like to thank and acknowledge the work of Dr. Barbara L. McCombs of the Denver Research Institute for her contributions to this section titled *Research Support for Student Voice, Perspectives, and Involvement in Critical Educational and Public Policy Issues.*

References

Brendtro, L. K. (1999, June). *Tools for reclaiming at-risk youth.* Keynote presentation at the 8th Annual Rocky Mountain Regional Conference in Violence Prevention in Schools and Communities, Denver.

Brendtro, L. K., Brokenleg, M., & VanBockern, S. (1992). *Reclaiming youth at risk: Our hope for the future.* Bloomington, IN: National Educational Service.

Caine, G., & Caine, R. N. (1997). *Education on the edge of possibility.* Alexandria, VA: Association for Supervision and Curriculum Development.

Calvert, M. (2002, April). *Raising voices in school: The impact of young decision-makers on schools and youth organizations.* Paper presented at the annual meeting of the American Educational Research Association, New Orleans.

Clarke, D. (2002, April). *Learner's perspective study: Exploiting the potential for complementary analyses.* Paper presented as part of the symposium, "Primary Research, Secondary Research and research Synthesis," at the annual meeting of the American Educational Research Association, New Orleans.

Coe, M. T., & Ault, P. C (2001, September). *Students, teachers, and technology building better schools: Generation Y Project Evaluation.* Portland, Oregon: Northwest Regional Educational Laboratory.

Cook-Sather, A. (2002). Authorizing students' perspectives: Toward trust, dialogue, and change in education. *Educational Researcher, 31*(4), 3-14.

Curwin, R.L. & Mendler, A.N. (1999). Zero tolerance for zero tolerance. *Phi Delta Kappan, 18* (2), 119-120.

Deci, E. L., & Ryan, R. M. (1991). A motivational approach to self: Integration in personality. In R. Dienstbier (Ed.), *Nebraska symposium on motivation. Vol. 38. Perspectives on motivation.* Lincoln, NE: University of Nebraska Press.

Diamond, M., & Hopson, J. (1998). *Magic trees of the mind.* New York: Dutton.

Ericson, D. P., & Ellet, F. S., Jr. (2002, April). *The question of the student in educational reform.* Paper presented at the annual meeting of the American Educational Research Association, New Orleans.

Fielding, M. (2000). The person centred school. *Forum, 42*(2), 51-54.

Fielding, M. (2001). Students as radical agents of change. *Journal of Educational Change, 2*(3), 123-141.

Fielding, M. (2002, April). *Beyond the rhetoric of student voice: New departures or new constraints in the transformation of 21st century schooling?* Paper presented as part of the International Symposium on "Student Voices and Democracy in Schools" at the annual meeting of the American Educational Research Association, New Orleans.

Fielding, M. (in press). Transformative approaches to student voice: Theoretical underpinning, recalcitrant realities. *The McGill Journal of Education.*

Harper, D. (1998, May). *Generation Y: Second annual report.* Washington, DC: U.S. Department of Education.

Harper, D. (2002, March). *Generation Y White Paper. 2.* Olympia, WA: Generation Y Organization.

Hyman, I.A. & Snook, P.A. (2000). Dangerous schools and what you can do about them. *Phi Delta Kappan*, 81(7),489-501.

Jensen, E. (1998). *Teaching with the brain in mind.* Alexandria, VA: Association for Supervision and Curriculum Development.

Kenney, D. J., & Watson, T. S. (1998). *Crime in the Schools: Reducing fear and disorder with student problem solving.* Washington, DC: Police Executive Research Forum.

Lambert, N. & McCombs, B. L. (Eds.) (1998). *How students learn: Reforming schools through learner-centered education.* Washington, DC: APA Books.

Larson, R. W. (2000). Toward a psychology of positive youth development. American Psychologist, 55(1), 170-183.

McCombs, B. L. (2001a). Self-regulated learning and academic achievement: A phenomenological view. In B. J. Zimmerman & D. H. Schunk (Eds.), *Self-Regulated learning and academic achievement: Theory, research, and practice* (2nd. Ed.). Mahwah, NJ: Lawrence Erlbaum Associates, Publishers. (pp. 67-123)

McCombs, B. L. (2001b, September). *The learner-centered framework on teaching and learning as a foundation for electronically networked communities and cultures.* Paper prepared for the PT3 Vision Quest on Assessment in e-Learning Cultures. Denver, CO: University of Denver. Also available at http://www.pt3.org/VQ/

McCombs, B. L. (in press). Applying educational psychology's knowledge base in educational reform: From research to application to policy. In W. M. Reynolds and G. E. Miller (Eds.), *Comprehensive Handbook of Psychology, Volume 7: Educational Psychology.* New York: John Wiley & Sons.

McCombs, B. L., & Whisler, J. S. (1997). *The learner-centered classroom and school: Strategies for increasing student motivation and achievement.* San Francisco: Jossey-Bass.

Mitra, D. L. (2002, April). *Makin' it real: Involving youth in school reform.* Paper presented in the International Symposium on "Student Voices and Democracy in Schools" at the annual meeting of the American Educational Research Association, New Orleans.

Nissen, L. B. (1999, June). *The power of the strength approach.* Keynote presentation at the 8th Annual Rocky Mountain Regional Conference in Violence Prevention in Schools and Communities, Denver.

Noguera, P. A. (1995). Preventing and producing violence: A critical analysis of responses to school violence. *Harvard Educational Review, 65,* 189-212.

Norris, T. (1999, June). *Healthy communities for healthy youth.* Keynote presentation at the 8th Annual Rocky Mountain Regional Conference in Violence Prevention in Schools and Communities, Denver.

Rogers, C., & Freiberg, H. J. (1994). *Freedom to learn* (3rd Ed.). New York: Merrill.

Rudduck, J., Day, J., & Wallace, G. (1997). Student perspectives on school improvement. *1997 ASCD Yearbook: Rethinking educational change with heart and mind.* Alexandria, VA: Association for Supervision and Curriculum Development.

Ryan, R. M. (1992). A systemic view of the role of motivation in development. In R. Dienstbier (Ed.), *Nebraska symposium on motivation: Vol. 40. Developmental perspectives on motivation.* Lincoln, NE: University of Nebraska Press.

Schaps, E., & Lewis, C. (1999). Perils on an essential journey: Building school community, *Phi Delta Kappan, 81,* 215-218.
Senge, P. M. (1990). *The fifth discipline: The art and practice of the learning organization.* New York: Doubleday.
Sylwester, R. (1995). *A celebration of neurons: An educator's guide to the brain.* Alexandria, VA: Association for Supervision and Curriculum Development.
Wheatley, M. J. (1999a). *Leadership and the new science: Discovering order in a chaotic world* (2nd ed.). San Francisco: Berrett-Koehler Publishers.
Wheatley, M. J. (1999b, July). *Reclaiming hope: The new story is ours to tell.* Summer Institute, University of Utah.
Wheatley, M. J., & Kellner-Rogers, M. (1996). *A simpler way.* San Francisco: Berrett-Koehler Publishers, Inc.
Wheatley, M. J., & Kellner-Rogers, M. (1998). Bringing life to organizational change, *Journal of Strategic Performance Measurement,* April-May, 5-13.
Wolfe, P., & Sorgen, M. (1990). *Mind, memory, and learning.* Napa, CA.

Chapter 15

A SYSTEM OF RECIPROCITY: EMPOWERING STAKEHOLDERS TO DO MORE WITH LESS IN EDUCATIONAL TECHNOLOGY

Catherine P. Fulford
Ariana Eichelberger
University of Hawaii
USA

The System of Reciprocity is a way of thinking and working within an existing system to generate resources or services that one does not have, in return for giving resources or services that one does have. The systems approach is commonly taught in educational technology programs, but how often is it used to redesign, recreate and improve the program itself. The System of Reciprocity has been employed by the Educational Technology Department, University of Hawaii, to create a mutually beneficial situation for its students, faculty, the department, the college and the university. A key element of a functional System of Reciprocity is that those involved in the system are aware of their involvement and how it directly benefits them. The synergy created by this faculty-student effort allows both to accomplish far more than either could accomplish alone. A System of Reciprocity acts cyclically and is mutually beneficial to its participants. Students are motivated to get involved because of the value they receive from quality mentoring. It is based on the concept of mentoring and training-the-trainer to integrate technology. In this chapter the geometrical progression produced by this System of Reciprocity, including students of students, will eventually benefit the entire community by producing graduates who are prepared to live and work in this high tech world, is described as a model for use in sustaining technology-rich environments into the future.

1. Introduction

The pace of changing technology has created a climate of frenzy in many institutions. With changes in hardware, upgrades in software, and new inventions occurring daily, it is impossible to keep up. Budgets have shifted to accommodate purchases while technology training needs are frequently overlooked. Systems are short of the human resources required to accommodate growing needs in professional development. Pressure is put on educational technology programs to provide solutions to these growing needs. Often, these programs lack the resources to keep up themselves, much less accommodate everyone else's needs.

A shift in thinking may be required to help solve these complex problems. The systems approach is commonly taught in educational technology programs, but how often is it used to redesign, recreate, and improve the program itself? Harries (1972) said that general systems theory is used as a tool by social scientists "for understanding human behaviour and for increasing the ability of individuals to work creatively and productively with one another" (p. 1). He noted that "an important advantage of a systems approach is flexibility. You can arrange and rearrange the environment any way you want which is consistent with the school's purpose" (p. 7).

In the Educational Technology (ETEC) Program at the University of Hawaii (UH), one faculty member introduced what she termed a "System of Reciprocity" as a way to empower the department to do more with less. The System of Reciprocity is a way of thinking and working within an existing system to generate resources or services that one does not have, in return for giving resources or services that one does have. This type of system is an example of a Win/Win situation described by Covey (1994). "Win/Win means that agreements or solutions are mutually beneficial, mutually satisfying. With a Win/Win solution, all parties feel good about the decision and feel committed to the action plan" (p.117). This concept should work equally well in a university, government agency, or business. The System of Reciprocity has been employed by ETEC to create a mutually beneficial situation for its students, faculty, the department, the college, and the university.

2. History

The system was originally developed in 1988 by an ETEC faculty member when she had worked as a training manager in a government setting. The agency had 6000 employees who needed services, yet there was no budget and the secretary was shared with five units. When brought in to develop the district training program, the training manager applied her experience in instructional systems and team-building. It was in this challenging environment that the System of Reciprocity was originated (see Figure 15.1). The concept was that when services were rendered, the recipient would provide resources to the system, which in turn would allow more services to be provided. Payment for services was not possible, so a subtle system of barter was created. The key to making the system work was to consistently act upon this concept and inform those requiring services of their role in the system.

Concepts were used from research on change theory to create a conducive environment. Havelock (1973) emphasised the importance of involving stakeholders, that is, people in system that have an interest in the outcome. In this case, the orientation for new employees and management training were used as an opportunity to positively "market" the training department. The training manager used the idea of the "primacy effect" and the "recency effect" (Dawson & Medler, 1997) to help employees remember her. These mean that the first thing and the last thing one does are remembered best. The training manager personally handled the orientation, and the beginning and ending management training sessions, and sought to make them memorable experiences. She made a point of acquainting herself with the new employees and management staff, alerting them to her services, and assuring them they could ask for assistance.

System of Reciprocity

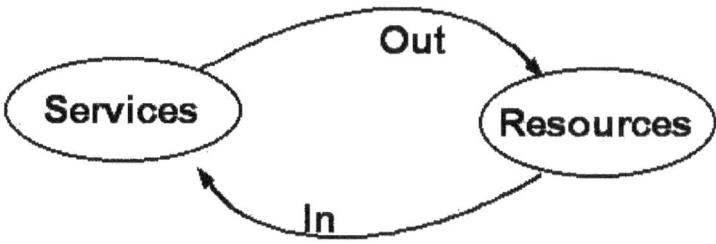

Figure 15.1. *Original System of Reciprocity.*

Another group of stakeholders was the trainers hired to meet specific unit needs. These people operated independently and in isolation. The training manager created events to organise them. This empowered the trainers by giving them an identity and making them an integral part of the training system. They gained a support system and professional development. With this strategy the training manager expanded her sphere of influence and gained access to a pool of qualified trainers.

A key element of a functional System of Reciprocity is that those involved in the system are aware of their involvement and how it benefits them. When the training manager was asked for services, she would give clients a diagram of the system and explain it (see Figure 15.2). For example, consultation was provided to employees who needed it. In exchange for the *consulting*, recipients were asked to verbally *support* the training department by saying positive things about the training department's services to fellow employees. When people heard good things about the department, they came to her for *technical assistance*. The training manager would explain that if the employee's department purchased the materials and the excess *supplies* where kept in the training department, supplies would be available for continued media support for all departments.

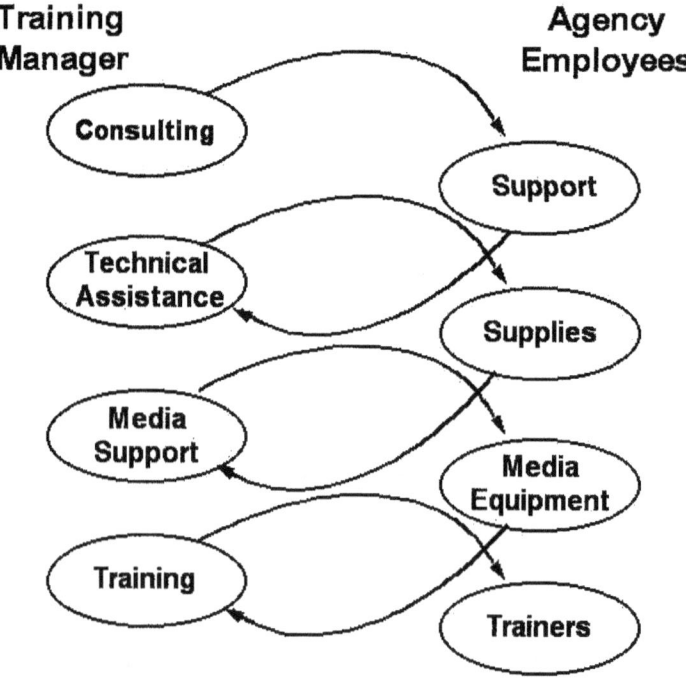

Figure 15.1. Government agency –System of Reciprocity

When providing employees with *media* support, they were asked to remember the training department at the end of the year when they had their budget surplus to spend. This money provided *media equipment* and training materials for the system. With more resources the department was better able to meet the needs of the agency in its primary function -- training. In a district of 6000 employees, one person could not meet the demand for general training. When managers asked for *training* for their department, she would in turn ask if they or someone in their department might be a good trainer. In the training sessions, the training manager would be keenly aware of the people who caught on quickly and were self-assured. She would also recruit these people to conduct training sessions. In this way, she created a network of available *trainers*. Through this process, with no budget and one-fifth of a secretary, the training manager was able to get supplies and equipment and spread her services further than she could do alone. Everyone benefited.

3. Educational Technology Department

The System of Reciprocity has now been successfully transferred to the Educational Technology Department at the University of Hawaii. When the training manager became a professor, she found that the System of Reciprocity worked equally as well in an academic environment (see Figure 15.3). The System of Reciprocity started in the department as a means to help individual faculty members. Since the department had no graduate assistantships to help faculty with research and teaching, the department was convinced to allow the independent-study course and the required internship as a way to recruit help. Previously, the independent-study course generally benefited one student while increasing the workload of the faculty member. Internships were primarily sought outside of the department. The emphases of these courses were changed to allow faculty to recruit and handpick students as teaching and research assistants. The students in turn were allowed to count these credits toward their degree program.

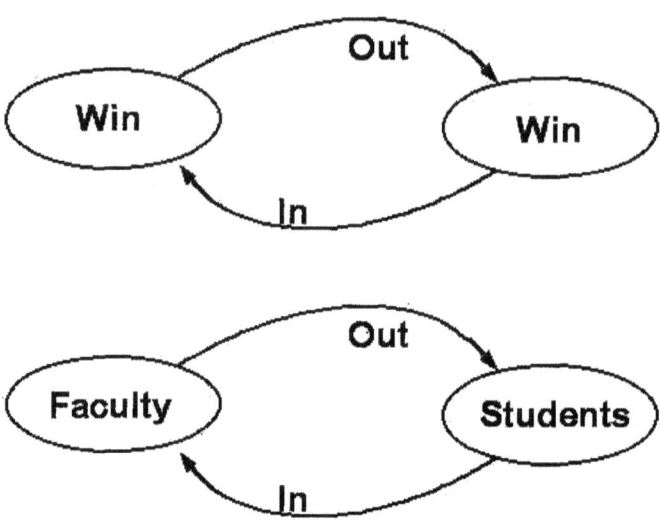

Figure 15.2. Department of Educational Technology System of Reciprocity

ETEC faculty have provided many collaborative and authentic projects for their students. One of the most valuable has been involving students in research, publication, and grant writing. The students receive special attention and mentoring through the process, and most importantly use their newly learned skills to work on real projects or practice teaching. In this Win/Win situation students provide their time and effort to faculty who need publications and good teaching evaluations for tenure and promotion.

The key to making this work is having the student and faculty member ask themselves "what's in it for me?" (WIIFM). Then, the student and faculty member negotiate a plan that is mutually beneficial. As seen in Figure 15.4, the department provides the *opportunity*; the students supply the *time*. The department gives the student credit and the students gain *expertise*. While the department receives *help*, the students gain *real-world experience*. The faculty members receive *recognition* and entries on their vitas for work accomplished, as does the student in improving their *resumes and portfolios*.

A System of Reciprocity 337

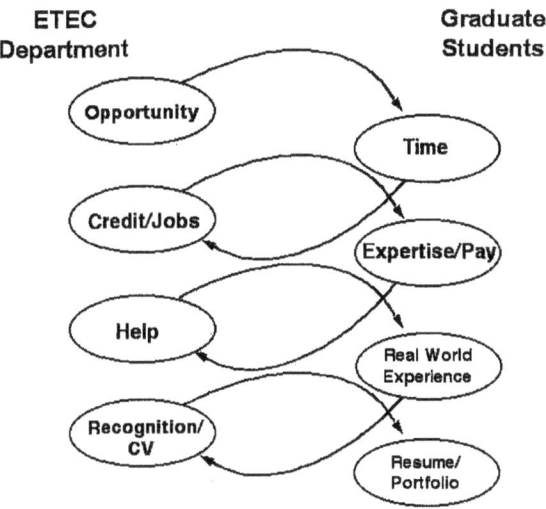

Figure 15.4. ETEC Department – Expanded System of Reciprocity

Knowing this help is available, faculty have sought numerous opportunities to obtain grants providing the additional benefit to students of paid positions. The department now has the equivalent of graduate assistantships without having the budget for them. The professor who introduced the System of Reciprocity has benefited from 22 teaching assistantships, 25 research assistantships, and 45 paid employees for a total of 92 collaborators over a ten-year period.

In addition to helping individual faculty, the System of Reciprocity is also at work on the departmental level. As in the government setting, a yearly orientation and renewal session is provided to instil an environment of co-operation and promote opportunities for working on various projects. As a result, many students choose course and master's projects to develop course materials, create databases, and conduct needs assessments, and research that benefit the department. Students are not required to do these projects, but many find value in projects that have a direct, real-world use.

The System of Reciprocity also contributes much to departmental grant projects. Students' willingness to participate in the system has resulted in ETEC faculty being awarded six grants and matching resources for over $6.3 million to support technology integration in

College of Education (COE) courses. Since the department has not been allotted any graduate assistantships, one of the most important outcomes of grant funding has been to provide relevant employment for ETEC master's students. The recognition and jobs available help a great deal in recruiting additional and quality graduate students into the program. The department through its grant efforts has been able to hire more than 50 students over the last five years for this project. With the assistance of the students, the faculty and staff are able to stretch their time and get more done. As the department is able to do more, it receives recognition, which enhances relationships with the college, university, funding agencies, and professional organisations.

4. Educational Technology Courses

For a number of years the university has been experiencing the most severe budget crisis in its history. While the COE is committed to using technology in the teaching and learning process there were very few technology resources or training sessions made available to students and faculty through university funding. Because of the Educational Technology faculty's technical expertise, the department was often asked to fill this gap by providing informal training and technical assistance to other faculty in the college. While the department provided this help, it took time from the faculty members' already busy schedules and did not provide them with many rewards. At that point, the system was non-reciprocal. The ETEC faculty provided valuable services to the college beyond their job descriptions, and yet they themselves did not directly benefit from it.

Again, the ETEC faculty member who had developed the System of Reciprocity applied it to an ETEC course to reduce the pressure on the department for technology training. A Win/Win situation was created through a required practicum course in which graduate students are provided an authentic setting to apply their new skills by designing and conducting technology workshops for COE faculty. In their first year, students learn to analyse instructional systems, develop needs assessments, apply change theory, design instruction, develop various media, and make high-tech presentations. As a way to apply these skills, ETEC practicum courses are offered every fall to advanced students. They use current needs assessments as a guide to inform them of the topics faculty are interested in learning. They also consider their own

WIIFMs in choosing topics. Based on this knowledge, the students develop a semester-long series of technology workshops for the COE faculty. Students handle all aspects of each workshop including design, delivery, advertising, registration, and evaluation. Past workshops have covered such topics as using layers in Photoshop, online collaboration with Web CT, electronic portfolios in Powerpoint, and editing digital video with iMovie.

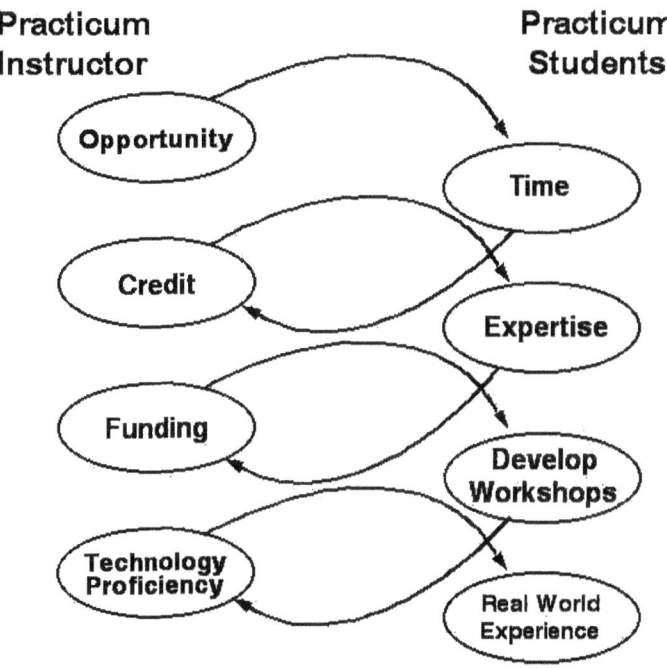

Figure 15.5. Practicum Course – Expanded System of Reciprocity.

The System of Reciprocity in this context works by the instructor first offering the *opportunity* to the ETEC students through teaching the course (see Figure 15.5). In exchange for the opportunity to take the course, the students give their *time* to create the workshops. They receive *credit* for the course in exchange for *expertise*. ETEC students come from a variety of backgrounds and bring in a multitude of skills. Due to the success of the course the department has received grant *funding* to support the course and its efforts. This funding helps the practicum students buy supplies they need to produce professional quality materials for workshop participants. The instructor benefits by increasing the overall *technology proficiency* of COE faculty. The students benefit from a *real-world experience* that provides them with design experience and presentation skills. They are empowered through the role reversal of becoming mentors to the faculty. Every year students have chosen to continue this project. Their reflections of the course in their final report show they value the experience (Fulford & Eichelberger, 2000).

Other course instructors have followed this model. For example, in one course students were involved in developing the Technology Learning Center. They wrote letters to vendors requesting software and hardware donations, organised a database, and set up a computer as a software viewing station. The outcome of this project was a corporate gift that funded graduate students as workers to run the system and the purchase of additional hardware and software. Another course created a photographic database on CD-ROM so that students and faculty could have access to copyright-free local images. The video design course has created several instructional videos used in other ETEC courses.

5. The College and University

Once students were willing participants, the System of Reciprocity was expanded to include both the College of Education and the University of Hawaii faculty through grant funding. Again, a Win/Win situation was created to be able to recruit faculty to participate in the grant projects (see Figure 15.6). The technology workshops developed by the ETEC practicum courses provide *technology training* for the COE/UH faculty. The *attendance and time* spent by the faculty in the workshops allows the department a venue for grant funding. The COE/UH faculty recruited from the workshops agree to participate in the grant project. Their *participation* provides them with *incentives* such as equipment and software to *redesign their courses* to integrate technology. To help them in this process, the most valuable resource provided is one-on-one technology *mentoring* by ETEC graduate students. In turn, the COE/UH faculty's efforts provide the necessary *outcome* of technology integrated courses required by the grant and enhances possibilities for continued grant funding. In this way everyone wins.

A System of Reciprocity

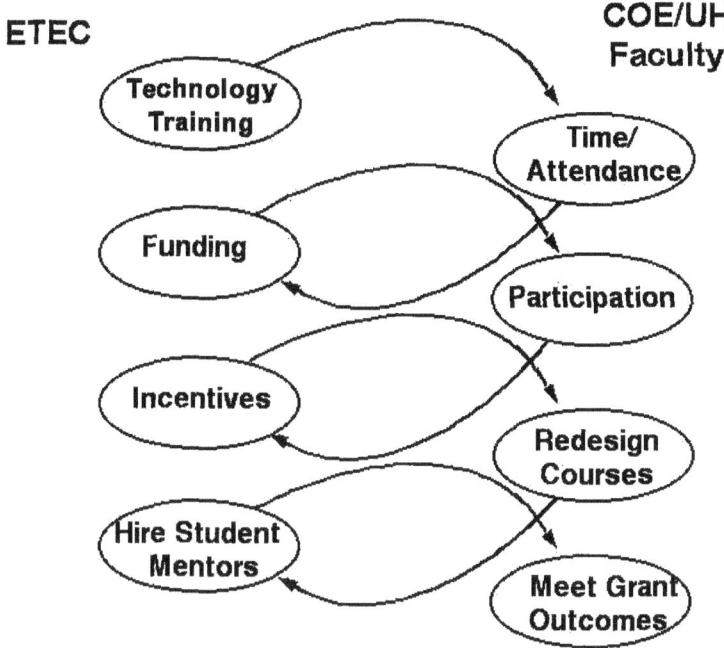

Figure 15.6. College/University Expanded System of Reciprocity.

The $6.3 million in funding has enabled the department to hire a staff of 25 including three new faculty members and enhance the Technology Learning Center that circulates high-tech equipment for faculty and student use. Through these efforts, ETEC graduate students have assisted faculty in revising more than 60 COE and UH courses to be "Technology Intensive." From a pedagogical perspective, this Win/Win relationship empowers the stakeholders -- ETEC, faculty and students -- with more options for effective, innovative, and relevant teaching.

References

Covey, S. R. (1994). *Daily reflections for highly effective people.* New York: Fireside - Simon and Schuster.

Dawson, M., & Medler, D. (1997). *The University of Alberta's Cognitive Science Dictionary.* [http://web.psych.ualberta.ca/~mike/Pearl_Street/Dictionary/dictionary.html] 10.15.2000.

Harries, T. (1972). *The application of general systems theory to instructional development.* Washington, DC: US Office of Education, Bureau of Libraries and Educational Technology & National Special Media Institute.

Havelock, R. (1973). *A change agents guide to innovation.* Englewood Cliffs, New Jersey: Educational Technology Publications.

Fulford, C. P., & Eichelberger, E. (2000, October). Win-Win: Students using instructional design skills to teach faculty to integrate technology in teacher education. *22nd Annual Proceedings of Selected Research and Development Presentations of the 2000 National Convention for the Association for Educational Communications and Technology.* Denver.

Chapter 16

WEB-BASED E-LEARNING ENVIRONMENTS IN TAIWAN: THE IMPACT OF THE ONLINE SCIENCE FLASH PROGRAM ON STUDENTS' LEARNING

Hsiao-Ching She
National Chiao Tung University
Taiwan

Darrell Fisher
Curtin University of Technology
Australia

This chapter reports on a web-based, multimedia, flash science learning program that focuses on helping students develop an understanding of water pressure through online e-learning environment in Taiwan. The study examines the learning environment created during use of this online flash science program in their science classes and also investigates its impact on students' cognitive and affective learning outcomes among different learning styles and grade levels. The results focus on three aspects: how the www flash science program promotes students' science concept learning; how students' feel about their satisfaction with learning with the www flash science program; the type of learning environment created during the use of this online flash science program in science classes; and associations between students' cognitive learning outcomes, satisfaction with web-based learning, web-based computer-assisted learning, and perceptions of science classroom learning environments.

1. Introduction

Web-based e-learning technology has been widely used in many ways in school teaching and learning science. Many studies have reported that technology-assisted instruction helps students develop a conceptual understanding of abstract representations of physical science. The nature of this technology-assisted instruction is that it emphasizes simulation, or visualization, or animation, etc. to enhance students' deeper mental imagery.

Some studies have reported that students whose learning styles are matched with their teachers' approach to teaching result in greater ease of learning (Packer & Bain, 1978) and higher satisfaction (Renninger & Snyder, 1983) than for those whose styles are mismatched. These studies show the importance of understanding how a teacher's approach to science teaching affects the science learning of students with different preferred learning styles.

Therefore, it is of interest to know whether web-based e-learning technology can help all students learn science, regardless of their preferred learning styles and grade levels. Also of interest is how students perceive this web-based e-learning environment.

2. Theoretical Framework

2.1 Web-based E-learning Education

Web-based e-learning technologies offer promise and potential for the delivery of enhanced learning in any topic to as many students as possible without limitation of time, place and language. Advances in information and communication technology are allowing web-based courses to replicate the features of face-to-face instruction through the use of audio, video, and high-speed Internet connections that facilitate synchronous and asynchronous communication. Very often, traditional class instruction has strongly depended on the delivery of knowledge through lecture presentation. However, Bonk and Cummings (1998) have argued that conventional face-to-face learning may not fully satisfy the needs of all learners. In a constructivist learning environment, part of the ownership for learning is shifted from the teacher to the students (Aggarwal & Bento, 2000). The key is to design a web-based e-learning environment that is suitable for the appropriate level of the students. Tetiwat and Igbaria (2000) suggested that at the secondary school level, students can use web-based teaching an aid for developing technology skills. There are obvious advantages in combining web-based learning with traditional face-to-face instruction.

For about two decades science educators have explored how to use the technology-assisted representations to assist students to develop a conceptual understanding of abstract representations of physical science (Gregory, & Stewart, 1997; Monaghan, & Clement, 2000; Steinberg, 2000). Many studies also have shown that students who go through active-engagement computer-based activities do better than students who go through traditional instruction (Beichner, et.al, 1999; Goldberg, 1997). Rieber (1991) investigated two groups of fourth graders learning from using computer simulations that dealt with Newton's law of motion. His results showed that the group of students who saw animated graphics performed better than the group of students who saw static graphics, but also displayed more new misconceptions. He further noted that even if students attend to an animated display, they often failed to notice the information it contained. De Jong (1991) indicated that novices have difficulty with unstructured simulations; he contended that for novices, it is necessary to provide a structure. De Jong and Van Joolingen (1998) recommended scaffolding to enable content learning in simulation environments, while Tao and Gunstone (1999) investigated the use of predict-observe-explain activities with computer simulations of force and motion and found it could affect students conceptual change.

Finke (1989) defined mental imagery as the mental invention or recreation of an experience that in at least some respects resembles the experience of actually perceiving an object or an event, either in conjunction with, or in the absence of, direct sensory stimulation. Oyama and Ichikawa (1990) noted that visualization, kinesthetic movements and eye movements have been associated with mental imagery. Kosslyn (1994) has documented a similar area of brain activation during actual visual perception and during the memory of or imagination of visual stimuli. Clement (1994) noted that the presence of dynamic imagery reports, hand motions, imagery enhancement techniques and the effort put into imagistic simulations all support the view that simulations in this case are very different from descriptive, language-like representations. He further suggested that the subjects are somehow mentally simulating some aspects of the rich flow of perceptions and or motor actions over time that would exist if they were actually viewing and/or causing such events.

Therefore, the design of our web-based flash science program is to provide students with the opportunity to visualize the physics phenomena instead of doing the simulation on their own. The use of flash in designing a world wide web-based science learning program provides students with the opportunity not only to obtain a visual understanding of the science content being presented, but also to develop a clearer understanding of science knowledge and build on their previously conceptual framework of understanding. In our design of the web-based science flash program, we constrained the program to facilitate systematic collection of data on students' cognition before, during and after interaction with our web-based science flash program. So students can quickly know their level of understanding of the topic and then learn the lessons. Each part of the lesson consisted of exercises to help students reorganized their understanding and finally do the post-test. In addition, students can also learn after class and build up a deeper understanding. The web-based course also enhances the flexibility of the learning process and learning time.

2.2 Learning Environment and the Web

International research efforts involving the conceptualization, assessment, and investigation of perceptions of aspects of the classroom environment have firmly established classroom environment as a thriving field of study (Fraser, 1994, 1998a; Fraser & Walberg, 1991). Past research has confirmed the important contribution made by teachers in creating a classroom environment or atmosphere conductive to science learning (Fraser, 1998a, 1998b). Teachers make a major contribution toward creating positive learning environment in science classes, particularly through their interaction or communication with students (She & Fisher, 2000, 2002; Wubbels & Levy). She and Fisher (2000, 2002) have indicated that positive relationships occur between students' perceptions of their teachers' communication behaviors and their attitudes toward science. In addition, they also found that students' perceptions about their teachers' communication behavior also influence their cognitive outcomes.

The web-based learning environment has tried to replicate more seamlessly the features of face-to-face instruction through the use of audio, video, and high-speed Internet connections that facilitate synchronous and asynchronous communication. Therefore, the effectiveness of the web-based learning environment has became more important. There are many useful instruments that have been developed to measure students' perceptions of a variety of aspects of the learning environment and this has extended to computer-based learning environments (e.g., Maor & Fraser, 1996; Teh & Fraser, 1994). Using such questionnaires in learning environment studies may provide us with useful data about how to improve the web-based learning environment.

2.3 Preferred Learning Styles

Studies on student differences have recognized that factors, such as culture, cognition, physical development, socioeconomic status, gender and teacher-student communication patterns are influential in determining student success in the classroom (e.g., Maccoby, 1988; She & Fisher, 2000, 2002; Sternberg, 1997; Wiles & Bondi, 1992). Also, in the last two decades, student learning preferences have received attention as an area to be considered in designing effective instructional practices for a wide variety of students (e.g., Okebukola, 1986; Owens & Barnes, 1982). Sternberg (1997) found that people with different styles tend to use their ability in different ways and so respond in varying ways to the kinds of thinking required in different occupations. Dunn and Dunn (1990) feel that classrooms need to concentrate more on individual learning styles because students tend to learn and remember better, and enjoy learning more, when they are taught through their learning style preferences.

Felder and Silverman (1988) reported that generally the teaching style of most teachers does not match the learning style of most of their students. They also found students learnt better from processes which are sensory, visual, inductive, and active. In another example, Riding and Douglas (1993), using 59 15-16-year-old students, found that a computer presentation of material on motor car braking systems in a text-plus-picture format better facilitated the learning by images, compared with the same content in a text-plus-text version. The visual-spatial aptitude has been strongly linked to academic mastery of several sciences (Trindade, Fiolhais, & Almeida, 2002). The visual-spatial aptitude is the ability to form and control a mental image.

An interesting approach to learning styles was presented by Hermann (1990). This model is based on the physical brain, in which four quadrants of the brain are labeled A, B, C, and D, counterclockwise beginning with the left cerebral quadrant. The thinking modes clustered within each quadrant have similarities and the modes in different quadrants identify distinctly different characteristics or ways of thinking. Quadrant A (the upper left cerebral quadrant, external learning) is logical, factual, analytical, technical, mathematical and critical. These learners prefer to be taught from authority through lectures and textbooks. They do well in the traditional, lecture-based, textbook-driven classrooms, and look to teachers to provide knowledge in answering their questions. Quadrant B (the lower limbic left quadrant, procedural learning) is sequential, structured, organized, planned, and detailed. These learners prefer to learn through a methodical, step-by-step testing of what is being taught, as well as practice and repetition to improve skills. They do well in hands-on activities and use abstract knowledge and commonsense. Quadrant C (the lower limbic right quadrant, interactive learning) is interpersonal, kinesthetic, emotional, sensory, and feeling. These learners prefer to learn through experience, feedback, listening, sharing, experiencing sensory input, and sharing ideas. Quadrant D (the upper right cerebral quadrant, internal learning) is visual, holistic, innovative, imaginative, and conceptual. These learners prefer to learn through visualization, insight, idea synthesis, and sudden understanding of a concept holistically and intuitively. It would be interesting to know which types of learning style students would benefit from the web-based science flash learning program.

3. Purpose

The aims of this chapter are to report a web-based, multimedia, flash science learning program focusing on helping different learning preference students develop understanding of water pressure through an online e-learning environment in Taiwan. It specifically examines the learning environment created when teachers and students used this online flash science program in their science class and also investigated the impact on students' cognitive learning outcomes among different learning styles and different grade levels. Moreover, students' satisfaction toward web-based learning also was examined. The relationships among students' cognitive learning outcomes, satisfaction toward web-based learning, web-based computer assisted learning, and their perceptions of science learning environment also were examined.

4. Methodology

4.1 Sample and Procedures

There were 459 grade 7 to 9 students from 11 middle schools in Taiwan involved in this study. The sample consisted of 65 grade 7 students, 270 grade 8 students, and 124 grade 9 students. All of the students were given a learning preference questionnaire to differentiate them into four different learning styles: QA, QB, QC and QD. Learning environment questionnaires were given during the teachers' and students' use of this online flash science program to assess the learning environment. A satisfaction of web-based learning questionnaire was administered to 459 students after they the use of web-based online flash science program. All of the 459 students were also given a pre-test before getting into the web-based online flash science program and a post-test of water pressure immediately after the web-based online flash science program. The pre-test and post-test were the same test and were given as an online-test. All of the results were analyzed by the SPSS version 10.

4.2 Questionnaires

The *Questionnaire of Learning Preference* (Lumsdaine & Lumsdaine, 1995) differentiates the students into four different learning preference styles based upon Hermann's Quadrants A, B, C, and D. It consists of 60 items which describe a series of learning activities according to Quadrants A, B, C, and D and each quadrant consisted of 15 items. Students were required to circle the learning activity for those items that are easy for them and that they enjoy doing. The total for all the responses was added and the percentage contribution calculated for each quadrant. The students were grouped into the four learning styles in which they had the highest percentage. Cronbach's alpha was computed to estimate the internal consistency of each scale and was found to be 0.73, 0.78, 0.76, and 0.78 for QA, QB, QC and QD learning preference scale, respectively.

The seven scales of the questionnaire entitled *What is Happening in this Class* (WIHIC) (Fraser, 1998; Fraser, Fisher & McRobbie, 1996) were selected to measure the learning environment. Specifically, the scales of Student Cohesiveness, Teacher Support, Involvement, Investigation, Task Orientation, Cooperation, and Equity were used in this study. In addition, the Challenging scale of the *Teacher Communication Behavior Questionnaire* (TCBQ) (She & Fisher, 2000, 2002) was also used in this study. The Differentiation scale from the *Individualized Classroom Environment Questionnaire* (ICEQ) (Fraser, 1990) was also used to add to the description of the learning environment. Another scale used was the Student Self-Efficacy scale based on a scale developed by Jinks and Morgan (1999).

The *Web-based Computer Assisted Learning Questionnaire* (WBCAL) was developed specifically for exploring students' perception of the web-based computer assisted learning environment. This questionnaire included Computer Usage and Web Usage scales adapted from the *Computer Attitude Scale* (CAS) developed by Newhouse (2001). An Attitude to Using Computer scale is based on a scale from the *Test of Science-Related Attitudes* (TOSRA) (Fraser, 1981).

A *Satisfaction of Web-based Learning* (SWBL) questionnaire was developed specifically to examine students' satisfaction toward learning with the web-based science flash program It included three scales Attitude toward WWW Learning, Attitude toward WWW Reasoning, and Attitude toward WWW Challenging. The first of these use selected and modified from the TOSRA (Fraser, 1981). The scales of reasoning and challenging toward www flash scales were developed from the Challenging scale of the TCBQ (She & Fisher, 2000, 2002).

4.3 Water Pressure Pre-test and Post-test

The pre-test and post-test contained the same questions in order to measure students' cognitive learning outcomes. A panel of eight, physical science teachers, scientists, and science educators were responsible for developing the water pressure test. The test specifically focuses on the objectives of the water pressure flash program. The Cronbach alphas of the pre-test and post-test were 0.79 and 0.81, respectively. The test-retest reliability was 0.75.

4.4 Design of the Web-based Online Flash Physical Science Program

In the design of the physical science web-based course, two panels were used. A panel of eight physical science teachers, scientists, and science educators were responsible for designing the presentation of content, thinking questions, and tests of water pressure, air pressure and buoyancy topics. Another panel of five computer engineers, scientists, science educators, and science teachers were responsible for the designing of the web-based system, infrastructure and interface. The flash was used to develop fully animated web-based pages that allowed learners to discover concepts that are not readily accessible on pages in a textbook or on static web pages. The flash includes animations, buttons, pictures, sounds and text. In addition, it also provides students with thinking questions after each section of the flash animation in order to make them think. The content of the flash was also designed mainly in a dyad format to encourage student thinking.

5. Results

5.1 Validation of Scales WIHIC(What is Happening in This Class)

Estimates of the internal consistency of the seven scales of the WIHIC were calculated using Cronbach's alpha coefficient and are shown in Table 16.1. The alpha reliability coefficient for each scale, using the individual as the unit of analysis, ranged between 0.86 and 0.93. The discriminant validity, the extent to which each scale measures a dimension different from that measured by any other scale, was examined using the mean correlation of one scale with the other four scales. These figures ranged from 0.45 to 0.57. The values can be regarded as small enough to confirm the discriminant validity of the WIHIC, indicating that each scale measures a distinct although somewhat overlapping aspect of learning environment.

The ability of a classroom questionnaire like this to differentiate between classes is considered important. Students within a class usually view the classroom learning environment similarly, but differently from students in other classes. The instrument's ability to differentiate in this way was measured using one-way analysis of variance (ANOVA) with class membership as the main effect. The results, depicted in Table 16.1, show that each of the scales did in fact significantly differentiate between classes ($p<0.001$). The amount of variance explained by class membership is reflected in the eta^2 scores which ranged from 0.18 to 0.26.

Estimates of the internal consistency of the Challenging, Differentiation and Student Self-efficacy scales were 0.91, 0.87, and 0.82.

Table 16.1. Internal Consistency (Cronbach Alpha Coefficient), Discriminant Validity (Mean Correlation with Other Scales) and Ability to Differentiate Between Classrooms for WIHIC

Scale	Alpha Reliability	Mean Correlation With Other Scales	ANOVA Results
Student Cohesiveness	0.92	0.49	0.26***
Teacher Support	0.89	0.45	0.22***
Involvement	0.89	0.57	0.23***
Investigation	0.86	0.48	0.18***
Task Orientation	0.91	0.56	0.21***
Cooperation	0.92	0.54	0.18***
Equity	0.93	0.55	0.23***

***$p < 0.0001$, N=396

5.2 WBCAL (Web-based Computer Assisted Learning)

Estimates of the internal consistency of the three scales of the WBCAL, calculated using Cronbach's alpha coefficient and shown in Table 16.2, were found to be generally satisfactory, particularly considering the small sample. The reliability coefficient for each scale, using the individual student as the unit of analysis, ranged between 0.70 to 0.89. The mean correlation of one scale with the other two scales ranged from 0.53 to 0.67. These values can be regarded as small enough to confirm the discriminant validity of the WBCAL indicating that each scale measures a distinct, although somewhat overlapping, aspect of the web-based computer assisted learning. The results, depicted in Table 16.2, show that each of the scales did in fact significantly differentiate between classes ($p<0.001$). The amount of variance explained by class membership is reflected in the eta^2 scores which ranged from 0.19 to 0.22.

Table 16.2. Internal Consistency (Cronbach Alpha Coefficient), Discriminant Validity (Mean Correlation with Other Scales) and Ability to Differentiate Between Classrooms for WEBCAL

Scale	Alpha Reliability	Mean Correlation With Other Scales	ANOVA Results
Attitude to Using Computer	0.70	0.53	0.22***
Computer Usage	0.82	0.65	0.19***
Web Usage	0.89	0.67	0.18***

*** $p < 0.0001$, N=375

5.3 SWBL (Satisfaction of Web-based Learning)

Estimates of the internal consistency of the three scales of the Satisfaction of web-based learning (SWBL), calculated using Cronbach's alpha coefficient and shown in Table 16.3, were found to be generally satisfactory, particularly considering the small sample. The reliability coefficient for each scale, using the individual student as the unit of analysis, ranged between 0.88 to 0.93. The mean correlation of one scale with the other two scales ranged from 0.55 to 0.68. These values can be regarded as small enough to confirm the discriminant validity of the SWBL, indicating that each scale measures a somewhat overlapping, aspect of the SWBL. The eta^2 scores which ranged from 0.08 to 0.15. It shows that the Attitude and Challenging scales did in fact significantly differentiate between classes.

Table 16.3. Internal Consistency (Cronbach Alpha Coefficient), Discriminant Validity (Mean Correlation with Other Scales) and Ability to Differentiate Between Classrooms for SWBL

Scale	Alpha Reliability	Mean Correlation With Other Scales	ANOVA Results
Attitude toward www learning	0.93	0.55	0.15***
Reasoning toward www learning	0.88	0.68	0.08
Challenging toward www learning	0.89	0.68	0.09*

* $p<0.05$, *** $p <0.0001$, N=437

5.4 Descriptive Information of Learning Environment

Table 16.4 presents the general profile of the learning environments. The mean scores and standard deviations scores for each scale of the WIHIC questionnaire, Challenging scale of TCBQ, Differentiation scale of ICEQ, and Student Self-Efficacy scale. In general, students viewed their learning environment positively and these environments were characterized by relatively high levels of student cohesiveness, task orientation, cooperation, equity and differentiation (these mean scores ranged from 3.1 to 3.5). In addition, students perceived their teacher as using more challenging questions. Moreover, the two mean scores of the scales of students' perceptions about web-based computer assisted leaning (WBCL) are favourable. In particular, students' attitudes toward using computer and web usage are quite high with mean scores of 3.1 and 3.5.

After learning from the web-based flash program, the students' satisfaction of web-based learning (SWBL) was quite high on all of the three scales, ranging from 3.81 to 3.91. This indicates that students rated their satisfaction about learning in this web-based science learning program as highly positive.

Table 16.4. Scale Means and Standard Deviations

	N	Item No.	Scale item mean	Scale item SD	Minimum	Maximum
WIHIC Scale						
Student Cohesiveness	395	8	3.92	0.77	3.70	4.06
Teacher Support	396	8	3.04	0.79	2.64	3.58
Involvement	395	8	3.13	0.78	2.82	3.43
Investigation	390	8	3.14	0.83	3.02	3.33
Task Orientation	388	8	3.77	0.74	3.55	3.93
Cooperation	388	8	3.73	0.77	3.53	3.96
Equity	391	8	3.70	0.87	3.48	3.96

Table 16.4. Continued

TCBQ Scale						
Challenging	388	8	3.52	0.75	3.15	3.65
Self-Efficacy Scale						
Student Self-Efficacy	391	8	2.97	0.69	2.64	3.26
ICEQ Scale						
Differentiation	392	8	3.08	0.76	2.38	3.46
WBCL Scale						
Attitude to Using Computer	373	8	3.51	0.62	2.10	4.14
Computer Usage	375	8	2.91	0.83	2.05	3.90
Web Usage	373	8	3.11	0.92	2.68	3.62
SWBL Scale						
Attitude toward WWW Flash	437	8	3.82	0.75	3.61	4.03
Reasoning toward WWW Flash	424	8	3.86	0.63	3.68	4.04
Thinking toward WWW Flash	431	8	3.92	0.64	3.79	4.11

5.5 Cognitive Outcomes

It has found that students of all four different learning styles made statistically significant gains after learning water pressure from the web-based flash program ($p<0.0001$) (see Table 16.5).

Table 16.5. Different Learning Styles' Students' and Cognitive Learning Outcomes

	Pre-test		Post-test		Difference	T test
	Mean	SD	Mean	SD		
QA learning preference	7.96	3.46	10.38	2.68	2.42	9.93***
QB learning preference	7.75	3.34	10.38	2.74	2.62	10.74***
QC learning preference	7.94	3.44	10.51	2.66	2.56	11.53***
QD learning preference	8.62	3.22	10.84	2.39	2.22	9.75***

*** $p<0.0001$, N=459

Students' means on the pre-test ranged from 7.75 to 8.62 while on the post-test they ranged from 10.38 to 10.84.

In addition, it was found that all of the students' made progress after learning water pressure from the web-based flash program regardless of grade level (see Table 16.6). The grades 7, 8 and 9 students' means on pre-test are 8.17, 7.07, and 10.30, and their post-tests are 10.92, 10.02, and 11.69, respectively. The grades 7 and 8 students had not been taught water pressure before while the grade 9 students had been taught it in their eight grade indicating that students who had not been taught water pressure before gained as much as those who had. However, it does shows that students can make further progress even when they had been taught that topic before.

Table 16.6. Students' Cognitive Learning Outcomes Across Grades 7 to 9

Grade level	Pre-test		Post-test		Difference	T test
	Mean	SD	Mean	SD		
Grade 7	8.17	3.27	10.92	2.65	2.75	7.79***
Grade 8	7.07	3.08	10.02	2.81	2.95	17.20***
Grade 9	10.30	2.71	11.69	1.92	1.40	7.14***

*** $p < 0.0001$, N=459

5.6 Association between Scales of WIHIC and WBCAL

Table 16.7 reports associations between the seven WIHIC scales and the three WBCAL scales. Multiple regression analysis involving the whole set of WIHIC scales was conducted, in addition to a simple correlation analysis, to provide a more conservative test of associations between each WIHIC scale and the WBCAL scales when all other WIHIC scales were mutually controlled.

An examination of the simple correlation coefficients in Table 16.7 indicates that there were statistically significant relationships ($p<0.0001$) between students' perceptions of their classroom learning environment for seven of the scales of the WIHIC with all three scales of students' perceptions of web-based computer assisted learning. A weak association was found between the Teacher Support scale and attitude to using computer. That is, students' perception of web-based computer assisted learning scores were higher where they perceived their classroom as having more student cohesiveness, involvement, investigation, task orientation, cooperation, and equity. However, using the more conservative standardized regression coefficient (ß) which measures the association when the effect of the other scales is held constant, the regression coefficients of the Involvement, Investigation, and Cooperation scales retained their significance correlated with two of the WBCAL scales confirming the importance of having more involvement and investigation in the classroom. It is noteworthy that the students' perceptions of their classroom learning environment contributed between 16 and 24 percent of the measured variance in students' perception of their web-based computer assisted learning environment.

Table 16.7. Associations Between WIHIC and WBCAL Scales in Terms of simple (r) and multiple correlations (R)

Scale	Attitude to Using Computer		Computer Usage		Web Usage	
	r	β	r	β	r	β
Student Cohesiveness	0.29***	0.16	0.23***	0.02	0.25***	-0.03
Teacher Support	0.03	-0.24***	0.25***	0.01	0.26***	-0.04
Involvement	0.23***	0.14	0.39***	0.25**	0.44***	0.28***
Investigation	0.20***	0.02	0.35***	0.17*	0.41***	0.18*
Task Orientation	0.32***	0.20*	0.29***	-0.03	0.32***	0.00
Cooperation	0.24***	-0.04	0.32***	0.20***	0.37***	0.20*
Equity	0.27***	0.12	0.21***	-0.12	0.29***	-0.03
Multiple correlation, R	0.40***		0.45**		0.49***	
R^2	0.16		0.20		0.24	

*$p<0.05$, **$p<0.001$, ***$p<0.0001$, N=373

5.7 WIHIC and SWBL Associations

A similar pattern was found between students' perceptions of their learning environment for seven of the scales of the WIHIC with all three scales of satisfaction of web-based learning (SWBL) (see Table 16.8). A weak association was found between the Teacher Support scale and satisfaction of web-based learning, but only at the $p<0.05$ level. However, using the more conservative standardized regression coefficient (ß), the

Investigation scale is the only scale that retained its significance correlated with all three of the SWBL scales confirming the importance of having more investigation in the classroom. It is noteworthy that the students' perceptions of their classroom learning environment contributed between 11 and 16 percent of measured variance in students' attitude toward web-based learning.

Table 16.8. Associations Between WIHIC and SWBL Scales in Terms of Simple (r) and Multiple Correlations (R)

Scale	Attitude toward WWW Flash		Reasoning toward WWW Flash		Challenging toward WWW Flash	
	r	β	r	β	r	β
Student Cohesiveness	0.19***	0.02	0.20***	0.06	0.24***	0.11
Teacher Support	0.13*	-0.02	0.15**	0.03	0.22***	0.07
Involvement	0.23***	-0.00	0.19***	-0.15	0.24***	-0.10
Investigation	0.29***	0.22**	0.31***	0.31***	0.33***	0.26***
Task Orientation	0.26***	0.09	0.28***	0.18	0.32***	0.19
Cooperation	0.27***	0.17	0.21***	0.02	0.22***	-0.06
Equity	0.19***	-0.09	0.19***	-0.06	0.26***	0.20
Multiple correlation, R	0.34***		0.36**		0.40**	
R^2	0.11		0.13		0.16	

*$p<0.05$, **$p<0.001$, ***$p<0.0001$, N=388

5.8 WBCAL and SWBL Associations

An examination of the simple correlation coefficients in Table 16.9 indicates that there were statistically significant relationships between students' perceptions of their perception of web-based computer assisted learning for all three scales of the WBCAL with all three scales of the SWBL. That is, student satisfaction of web-based learning was higher when they had a more positive attitude towards using computers, computer usage and web usage. However, using the more conservative standardized regression coefficient (ß), the Web Usage scale retained its significance with all the SWBL scales confirming the importance of having more web usage in classroom. The students' satisfaction of web-based learning contributed between 8 and 28 percent of measured variance in students' perception of web-based computer assisted learning.

Table 16.9. Associations Between WBCAL and SWBL Scales in Terms of Simple (r) and Multiple Correlations (R)

Scale	Attitude toward WWW Flash		Reasoning toward WWW Flash		Challenging toward WWW Flash	
	r	β	r	β	r	β
Attitude to Using Computers	0.20***	0.06	0.18**	0.06	0.16*	0.02
Computer Usage	0.20***	-0.08	0.18**	-0.09	0.19***	-0.07
Web Usage	0.29***	0.33***	0.27***	0.32***	0.27***	0.33***
Multiple correlation, R	0.31***		0.29***		0.28***	
R^2	0.09		0.28		0.08	

*$p<0.05$, **$p<0.001$, ***$p<0.0001$, N=373

5.9 Association between the WIHIC and Cognitive Outcomes

Associations between students' perceptions of their learning environment and their cognitive outcomes before and after learning water pressure from the web-based flash science program also were analyzed using simple correlation analyses and standardized regression (Table 16.10). The students' scores in the pre-test and post-test were used separately in these analyses. The simple correlation (r) figures reported in Table 16.10 indicate that there were statistically significant ($p<0.001$) associations between students' pre-test scores and three of the scales of the questionnaire, namely, Student Cohesiveness, Investigation, and Equity. There were statistically significant ($p<0.001$) associations between students' post-test scores and five of the scales of the questionnaire, namely, Student Cohesiveness, Investigation, Task Orientation, Cooperation, and Equity. An examination of the standardized regression coefficients shows that the Student Cohesiveness and Investigation scales contribute to students' cognitive outcomes in both the pre-test and post-tests. Thus, having more student cohesiveness and investigation is very important for improving students' cognitive outcomes in web-based flash science learning program. Students' perceptions of their learning environment contributed between 9% and 12% to the measured variance in students' cognitive outcomes.

Table 16.10. Associations Between WIHIC Scales and Students Cognitive Outcomes in Terms of Simple (r) and Multiple Correlations (R)

	Pre-test		Post-test	
Scale	r	β	r	β
Student Cohesiveness	0.18***	0.15*	0.26***	0.15*
Teacher Support	0.10*	-0.04	0.10	-0.03
Involvement	0.17***	-0.03	0.17**	-0.12
Investigation	0.24***	0.19*	0.25***	0.19*
Task Orientation	0.16*	-0.05	0.25***	0.05
Cooperation	0.15*	-0.06	0.26***	0.11
Equity	0.22***	0.16	0.24***	0.05
Multiple correlation, R		0.29***		0.35***
R^2		0.09		0.12

*$p<0.05$, **$p<0.001$, ***$p<0.0001$, N=388

Table 16.11. Associations Between Challenging, Students' Self-Efficacy, and Differentiation Scales and Students Cognitive Outcomes in Terms of Simple (r) and Multiple Correlations (R)

	Pre-test		Post-test	
Scale	r	β	r	β
Challenging	0.22***	0.19**	0.33***	0.34***
Student Self-Efficacy	0.19***	0.13	0.20***	0.11
Differentiation	0.09	-0.05	0.08	-0.09
Multiple correlation, R		0.25***		0.36***
R^2		0.06		0.13

*$p<0.05$, **$p<0.001$, ***$p<0.0001$, N=388

In addition, it was also found that there were statistically significant ($p<0.001$) associations between the Challenging and Students

Self-Efficacy scales and students' pre-test and post-test. That is, students' cognitive achievement scores were higher where students perceived their teacher using more challenging questioning and where the students had a higher feeling of self-efficacy (see Table 16.11). No associations were found with the Differentiation scale.

5.10 SWBL and Cognitive Outcomes

Associations between students' satisfaction of web-based learning and their cognitive outcomes before and after learning water pressure from web-based flash science program also were analyzed using simple correlation analyses and standardized regression (Table 16.12).

Table 16.12. Associations Between SWBL Scales and Students Cognitive Outcomes in Terms of Simple (r) and Multiple Correlations (R)

	Pre-test		Post-test	
	r	β	r	β
Attitude toward WWW Flash	0.04	0.06	0.19***	0.13
Reasoning toward WWW Flash	-0.02	-0.18	0.09	-0.23*
Challenging toward WWW Flash	0.05	0.15	0.18***	0.30***
Multiple correlation, R		0.12		0.24***
R^2		0.01		0.06

*$p<0.05$, **$p<0.001$, ***$p<0.0001$, N=424

The students' scores in the pre-test and post-test again were used separately in these analyses. The simple correlation (r) figures reported in Table 16.12 indicate that there were statistically significant ($p<0.001$) associations between students' post-test scores and two of the scales of the questionnaire, namely, Attitude and Challenging. That is, students' cognitive achievement scores were higher where students had a more favourable attitude toward the program and had more opportunity of think. An examination of the standardized regression coefficients shows that the Challenging scale is the only factor which retains its significance. Thus, having more challenging opportunities is very important for improving students' cognitive outcomes in web-based flash science learning program. Students' satisfaction of web-based leaning contributed about 9% and 12% to the measured variance in students' cognitive outcomes.

6. Discussion

This study attempted to facilitate students' science learning involving the use of a web-based, multimedia, flash science learning program focusing through an online e-learning environment. This study examined the learning environment created during teacher and student use of this program in their science class and also investigated its impact on students' cognitive and affective learning outcomes among different learning styles and different grade levels. The WIHIC, WBCAL, and SWBL questionnaires, Challenging scale, Differentiation scale, and Students' Self-Efficacy scale were used in this study. The validation data provided in the study have confirmed the reliability and validity of the questionnaires for use in Taiwan.

During the use of this program, students perceived their learning environment as having high levels of student cohesiveness, task orientation, cooperation, equity and differentiation. They also perceived their teacher as using more challenging questions. In addition, the students' attitude toward using computer and web usage were positive.

Students' satisfaction with the web-based online science flash learning program was also quite high on the three scales of Attitude, Reasoning, and Challenging. Thus, students were very positive satisfaction about learning in this web-based flash science learning program. In particular, they perceived that the program is very interesting, satisfying, promoting their ability to reason, and challenging their thinking and problem solving ability.

Students' cognitive outcomes also increased dramatically after learning science through the program, regardless their type of learning preference. This supports the Felder and Silverman (1988) study where they noted that the teaching style of most teachers does not match the learning style of most students in general, but, they found students learn better from processes which are sensory, visual, inductive, and active. In addition, students from different grade levels all made a significant cognitive improvement after learning from the program.

Strong and consistent relationships were found between students' perception about their classroom environment (WIHIC) and their perception of Web-based computer assisted learning (WBCAL). Simple correlations showed that students' perception of web-based computer assisted learning scores were higher where they perceived their classroom as having more student cohesiveness, involvement, investigation, task orientation, cooperation, and equity. The more conservative multiple regression analysis indicated that between 16 and 24 percent of measured variance in students' perception of web-based computer assisted learning could be attributed to their perceptions of classroom learning environment. If teachers wish to develop better perceptions in their web-based computer assisted learning, then they should allow more involvement, investigation, and cooperation.

Strong and consistent relationships also were found between students' perception about their classroom (WIHIC) and their perception of satisfaction of web-based learning (SWBL). Simple correlations showed that students' perception of satisfaction of web-based learning scores were higher where they perceived their classroom as having more student cohesiveness, teacher support, involvement, investigation, task orientation, cooperation, and equity. The more conservative multiple regression analysis indicated that between 11 and 16 percent of measured variance in students' perception of satisfaction of web-based learning could be attributed to their perception of learning environment. If teachers wish to develop better satisfaction toward web-based learning, then they should allow more time for investigation.

Strong and consistent relationships also were found between students' perception of web-based computer assisted learning (WBCAL) and their perception of satisfaction of web-based learning (SWBL). Simple correlations showed that students' perception of satisfaction of web-based learning scores were higher where they perceived as having more positive attitude to using computers, computer usage and web usage. The more conservative multiple regression analysis indicated that between 08 and 28 percent of measured variance in students' perception of satisfaction of web-based learning could be attributed to their perception of web-based computer assisted learning. If we wish to promote students' better satisfaction toward web-based learning, then we might need to enhance students' perception of web-based computer assisted learning.

Associations with students' cognitive outcomes were also found and were higher when students perceived more student cohesiveness, investigation, equity, self-efficacy, and the teacher used more challenging questioning. Having more of these aspects in the classroom is very important for improving students' cognitive outcomes in web-based flash science learning program. It supports the Fraser (1994) study between student cognitive and affective outcomes and the learning environment, which indicated that classroom environment perceptions can influence students' outcomes. Moreover, it again supports She and Fisher's previous studies (2000, 2002) that the use of challenging questions can increase students' science learning outcomes.

7. Conclusions and Summary

The work presented in this chapter provides a significant contribution to science learning involving the use of a web-based, multimedia, flash science learning program using an online e-learning environment. Results show that students perceived their learning environment created during the use of this online flash science program is their science class as having high levels of students' cohesiveness, task orientation, cooperation, equity, differentiation, and their teachers using more challenging questions. Students' attitudes toward using computers and web usage are very favourable. Students were satisfied with the program and their cognitive outcomes increased dramatically after learning science this way, regardless of any types of learning preference or grade levels. In particular, students' cognitive outcomes were also found to be higher when students perceived more student cohesiveness, investigation, equity, self-efficacy, and more teacher use of challenging questions. These results are very encouraging and shed some light on how to successfully promote students' science learning through the use of a web-based online physical science learning program.

References

Aggarwal, A. K., & Bento, R. (2000). Web-based education. In A. Aggarwal (Ed.), *Web-based learning and teaching technologies: opportunities and challenges.* London, UK. IDEA Group Publishing.

Beichner, L .B., Bernold, E. B., Dail, P., Felder, R, Gastineau, M. G., & Risley, J. (1999). Case study of the physics component of an integrated curriculum. *American Journal of Physics, 67,* 16-24.

Bonk, C. J., & Cummings, J. A. (1998). A dozen recommendations for placing the student at the center of web-based learning. *Educational Media International, 35* (2), 82-89.

Clement, J. (1994). Imagistic simulation and physical intuition in expert problem solving. In the *Proceedings of the sixteenth Annual conference of the cognitive science society* (pp. 146-156). Hillsdale, New Jersey: Lawrence Erlbaum,

De Jong, T. (1991). Leanring and instruction with computer simulations. *Education and Computing, 6,* 217-229.

De Jong, T., & Van Joolingen, W. R. (1998). Scientific discovery learning with computer simulations of conceptual domains. *Review of Educational Research, 68,* 179-201.

Dunn, R., & Dunn, K (1990). Understanding the Dunn and Dunn learning styles model and the need for individual diagnosis and prescription. *Reading, Writing, and Learning Disabilities, 6,* 223-247.

Felder R., & Silverman, L. (1988). Learning and teaching styles in engineering education. *Journal of Engineering Education, 78,* 674-681.

Finke, R.A. (1989). *Principles of mental imagery.* Cambridge, MA: MIT Press.

Fraser, B. J. (1981). *Test of Science-Related Attitudes handbook (TOSRA).* Melbourne, Australia: Australian Council for Educational Research.

Fraser, B. J. (1990). *Individualised Classroom Environment Questionnaire: Handbook and test master set.* Melbourne: The Australian Council for Educational Research.

Fraser, B.J. (1994). Research on classroom and school climate. In D. Gabel (Ed.), *Handbook of research on science teaching and learning* (pp. 493-541). New York: Macmillan.

Fraser, B. J. (1998a). Science learning environments: Assessment, effects and determinants. In B.J. Fraser & K.G. Tobin (Eds.), *The international handbook of science education* (pp. 527-564). Dordrecht, The Netherlands: Kluwer.

Fraser, B. J. (1998b). Classroom environment instruments: development, validity and applications. *Learning Environments Research: An International Journal, 1,* 7-33.

Fraser, B. J., McRobbie, C. J., & Fisher, D. L. (1996, April). *Development, validation and use of personal and class forms of a new classroom environment instrument.* Paper presented at the annual meeting of the American Educational Research Association, New York.

Fraser, B. J., & Walberg, H. J. (Eds.), (1991). *Educational environments: Evaluation, antecedents and consequences.* Oxford, England: Pergamon Press.

Goldberg, F. (1997). *Constructing physics understanding in a computer-supported learning environment.* AIP conf. Proc., 399, 903-911.

Gregory, J. R., & Stewart, M. F. (1997). Production of a multimedia CAL package in basic physics. *Physics Education, 32* (5), 332-39.

Hermann, N. (1988). *The creative brain.* Lake Lure, NC: Brain Books.

Jinks, J. L., & Morgan, V. (1999). Children's perceived academic self-efficacy: An inventory scale. *Clearing House, 72,* 224-230.

Kosslyn, S. M. (1994). *Image and brain: The resolution of the imagery debate.* Cambridge, MA: MIT Press,

Lumsdaine, E., & Lumsdaine, M. (1995). *Creative problem solving.* New York, NY: McGraw-Hill, Inc.

Maor, D., & Fraser, B. J. (1996). Use of classroom environment perceptions in evaluating inquiry-based computer assisted learning. *International Journal of Science Education, 18,* 401-421.

Maccoby, E. E. (1990). The role of gender identity and gender constancy in sex-differentiated development. *New Directions for Child Development, 47,* 5-20.

Monaghan, J. M., & Clement, J. (2000). Algorithms, visualization, and mental models: high school students' interaction with a relative motion simulation. *Journal of Science Education and Technology, 9*(4), 311-325.

Newhouse, C. P. (2001). Development and use of an instrument for computer-supported learning environments. *Learning Environment Research: An International Journal, 4,* 115-138.

Okebukola, P. A. (1986). The influence of preferred learning styles on cooperative learning in science. *Science Education, 70* (5), 509-17.

Owens, L., & Barnes, J. (1982). The relationships between cooperative, competitive, and individualized learning preferences and students' perceptions of classroom learning atmosphere. *American Educational Research Journal, 19* (2) 182-200.

Oyama, T., & Ichikawa, S. (1990). Some experimental studies on imagery in Japan. *Journal of Mental Imagery, 14,* 185-195.

Packer. J., & Bain, J. D. (1978). Cognitive style and teacher-student compatibility. *Journal of Educational Psychology, 70*, 864-871

Renninger, K. A., Snyder, S. S., (1983). Effects of cognitive style on perceived satisfaction and performance among students and teachers. *Journal of Educational Psychology,75* (5), 668-676.

Riding, R. J., & Douglas, G. (1993). The effect of cognitive style and mode of presentation on learning performance. *British Journal of Education Psychology, 63*, 297-307.

Rieber, L. P. (1991). Animation, incidental learning, and continuing motivation. *Journal of Educational Psychology, 83*, 318-328.

She, H.C., & Fisher, D. (2000). The development of a questionnaire to describe science teacher communication behavior in Taiwan and Australia. *Science Education, 84*(6), 706-26.

She, H. C., & Fisher, D. (2002). Teacher communication behavior and Its association with students' cognitive and attitudinal outcomes in science in Taiwan. *Journal of Research in Science Teaching, 39*(1), 63-78.

Steinberg, R. (2000). Computers in teaching science: to stimulate or not to stimulate. *American Journal of Physics, 68*(7), 37-41.

Sternberg, R. (1997). *Thinking styles.* New York: Cambridge University press.

Tao, P. K., & Gunstone, R.F. (1999). The process of conceptual change in force and motion during computer-supported physics instruction. *Journal of Research in Science Teaching, 36* (7), 859-82.

Teh, G., & Fraser, B.J. (1994). An evaluation of computer-assisted learning in terms of achievement, attitudes and classroom environment. *Evaluation and Research in Education, 8*, 401-421.

Tetiwat, O., & Igbaria, M. (2000). Opportunities in web-based teaching: The future of education. In A. Aggarwal (Ed.) *Web-based learning and teaching technologies: opportunities and challenges.* London, UK: IDEA Group Publishing.

Trindade, J., Fiolhais, C., & Almeida, L. (2002). Science learning in virtual environments: a descriptive study. *British Journal of Educational Technology, 33* (4), 471-488.

Wiles, J. & Bondi, J. (1993). *The essential middle school (Second Edition).* New York, NY: Macmillan Publishing, Co.

Wubbels, T., & Levy, J. (Eds.). (1993). *Do you know what you look like? Interpersonal relationships in education.* London, England: Falmer Press.

Chapter 17

STUDENTS' AND TEACHERS' PERCEPTIONS OF ACTUAL AND PREFERRED CLASSROOM ENVIRONMENTS IN JAPANESE JUNIOR HIGH SCHOOL: THE POTENTIAL OF PSYCHOLOGICAL MEASURES IN THE CLASSROOM

Sonomi Hirata
Hakuoh University Women's College
Japan

Darrell Fisher
Curtin University of Technology
Australia

For the last few decades, classroom environment research has been prominently developed with paper and pencil perceptual measures. A distinctive feature of these psychological scales is that they have not only a form to measure perceptions of actual but also a form to measure perceptions of preferred classroom environment. The practical implication of these findings is that student achievement could be enhanced by attempting to change the actual classroom environment in ways that make it more congruent with that preferred by the students. A Japanese junior high school modification of the Classroom Environment Scale (Moos, 1974) was developed and factor analysis revealed five factors: (1) Teacher Control, (2) Sense of Isolation, (3) Task Difficulty, (4) Order, and (5) Discipline. As comparisons between teachers' and students' perceptions of their actual classroom environments, it was observed that students felt stronger control and discipline by teachers, and more difficult class work than the teachers expected. The findings of this study also suggested the fruitful possibility that researchers and educators in school management could collaborate using these perceptual approaches in technology-rich classrooms in Japan.

1. Introduction

Numerous attempts have been made by educational researchers to construct methods of studying and assessing personality and leaning environment since Lewin (1936) and Murray (1938) wrote about the interaction between the learning environment and individual personality in human decision making. Both Lewin's well-known formula; Human behavior = f (Personality, Environment), and Murray's need-press theory directed attention to the interaction of human factors and environment. For many years the study of learning environments remained superficial, however, over the last three decades research on classroom environment has flourished, and has concerned teachers' and students' perceptions.

During this time, a number of instruments have been developed to measure classroom environment. In reviews, Fraser (1994, 1998) indicated that the earlier *Learning Environment Inventory* (LEI; Anderson & Walberg, 1974; Fraser, Anderson, & Walberg, 1982) and *Classroom Environment Scale* (CES; Trickett & Moos, 1973) had been used most extensively to assess classroom environment, and had provided models for the development of a range of instruments. Additional instruments have been developed for specific classroom contexts such as individualized classrooms (Rentoul & Fraser, 1979), constructivist classrooms (Taylor, Fraser & Fisher, 1997), computer-assisted instructional settings (Teh & Fraser, 1994), science laboratories (Fraser, Giddings, & McRobbie, 1991), primary school classrooms (Fraser & O'Brien, 1985) and higher education classrooms (Fraser, Treagust, & Dennis, 1986).

A distinctive feature of many classroom environment questionnaires is that they have not only a form to measure perceptions of actual classroom environment but also a form to measure perceptions of preferred classroom environment. The preferred, or ideal, form is concerned with goals and value orientations and measures perceptions of the classroom environment ideally liked or preferred. Learning environment research which adopted a person-environment fit perspective (Hunt, 1975) revealed that a similarity between the actual environment and that preferred by students leads to improved student achievement and attitudes (e.g., Fisher & Fraser, 1981; Fraser & Fisher, 1983). The practical implication of these findings is that student achievement could be enhanced by attempting to change the actual classroom environment in ways that make it more congruent with that preferred by the students.

The wealth of information obtained from secondary school studies suggests that it could be of value for teachers to gain a fuller understanding of students' perceptions of their learning environments. If teachers have a clear understanding of students' preferred learning environments, they can implement changes to achieve more positive environments and thus foster better learning.

Though a great deal of effort has been made on student perceptions of actual and preferred environment, what seems to be lacking is enough feedback on these outcomes to educators in classrooms and school management. This present study arose from the commissioning of one school administrator to investigate the psychological environment of his school as perceived as by students. The study adds to the discussion on how psychological researchers can work in conjunction with school teachers, and finally on the potential use of psychological measures in the future classroom.

2. Method

2.1 Sample

The sample consisted of representative group of 20 classes, each with a different teacher, from first to third grade in a junior high school in Japan,. The school, in which this study was conducted, is a public junior high school in a provincial insular region in Japan. The total number of students providing data was 669. There were approximately equal numbers of boys and girls in the sample.

2.2 Administrator's Story

Both students' academic achievement and conduct are on a par with the national standard and the school could be considered as relatively conventional. There had been no particular pressing question for years at this school, however, the administrator happened to hear that teachers felt there was something unusual about communicating with the second grade students of the school in one particular year. The teachers perceived that most classes in the second grade had no sense of solidarity, and it was difficult to understand the students' feelings about the class. What made the teachers feel the way they did? Were there any differences between the second grade students and the students in the other grades? What was going on amongst these students?

The administrator's commission was to try to clarify the particular classroom climates, of the teachers. This study is not only his story, but it compares the teachers' views with the results of psychological assessment and this could be a good cue to introduce these measures to teachers in classrooms in Japan.

2.3 The Learning Environment Measure

The original scale consisted of 50 items. Twenty-two items were derived from the Classroom Environment Scale (Trickett & Moos, 1973) and nine items were taken from the CES-J (Hirata & Sako, 1999). The remaining 19 items were written and added to the questionnaire. In a previous study, where the CES was introduced to Japanese junior high schools (Hirata, Watanabe, & Souma, 1998; Hirata, Kanno, & Koizumi, 1999), such sub-scales in Moos' Personal growth dimension as Task Orientation and Competition were not revealed via factor analysis. However, it must be noted that this did not mean that students in Japan were free from pressures of grades and recognition in their classroom. It is obvious that they have serious competition in the examination for entrance to higher education. Therefore, in this study, 19 items of the Task Orientation and Competition scales were rewritten and made more suitable for the Japanese context. For example, three new items were, "Student' grades will be lowered if they won't prepare and review their lessons independently", "Students have to do a lot of extra study if they want to go on to the school of their first choice", and "Students do the higher level studies at a cramming school rather than in this class".

The resulting 50 items were administered to 669 junior high school students. Before administering the questionnaire, the teacher informed all students that they could answer anonymously. Also, the teacher instructed students to choose just one of the five choices: 1 = "strongly agree", 2 = "agree", 3 = "neither agree nor disagree", 4 = "disagree", or 5= "strongly disagree". Each student responded to the actual and preferred form of this version of the Classroom Environment Scale. The teachers also responded to both forms of the Classroom Environment Scale.

3. Results

3.1 Developing the Scales

A principal components factor analysis with varimax rotation revealed five factors from the 50 items. These factors were given the scale names of: (1) Teacher Control, (2) Sense of Isolation, (3) Task Difficulty, (4) Order, and (5) Discipline and the questionnaire was referred to as the CES-J.II.

The Teacher Control scale consists of six items. For example, "Some teachers will be partial toward some students", "Whether or not students can get away with something will depend on how the teacher is feeling that day.", and "The teacher will be consistent in dealing with students who break the rules".

The Sense of Isolation scale consists of six items, including, "I cannot get along with classmates", "At this school, I feel like a stranger", and "In this class, I feel nobody will accept me".

The Task Difficulty scale consisted of five items which included, "If a students misses class for a couple of days, it will take some effort to catch up", "Students will try hard not to get a lower grade", and "A student's grade will be lowered if she/he won't prepare and review her/his lesson independently".

The Order scale consisted of two items, "This class will often be in an uproar" and "It is easier to get into trouble here than in a lot of other classes".

The Discipline scale consisted of three items, "Most of the students in this class will really pay attention to what the teacher is saying", and "Students will not interrupt the teacher when he's talking".

The use of Cronbach's alpha reliability coefficient on these five scales showed that the CES-J.II has an acceptable internal consistency for students' responses about their classroom environments ranging from 0.59 to 0.82 for the actual form and from 0.60 to 0.89 for the preferred form (see Table 17.1).

The data were then analyzed using a two-way Analysis of Variance (ANOVA) with the two forms of the CES-J.II as the dependent variables and the groups of teachers and students as the independent variables. As no statistically significant gender difference was found for any scale, male and female data were pooled.

Table 17.1. Factor Structure of the Classroom Environment Scale (CES-J.II)

No.	ITEM	I	II	III	IV	V
I. Teacher Control						
Q9	Some teachers will be partial to some students.	**0.7850**	0.0850	0.0560	-0.0070	-0.0360
Q12	Some teachers are dishonest.	**0.7330**	0.0910	-0.0370	-0.0080	-0.0760
Q21 *	The teacher will be consistent in dealing with students who break the rules.	**0.7300**	-0.0100	0.0670	0.0510	0.0300
Q27	The teacher will be consistent in dealing with students who break the rules.	**-0.6280**	-0.0360	0.0260	0.0450	0.1550
Q8 *	Assignments will often be inconsistent among teachers.	**0.6170**	0.0160	-0.0170	0.0830	-0.0640
Q18 *	Sometimes the teacher will embarrass students for not knowing the right answer.	**0.5840**	0.0510	0.0240	0.2920	-0.0840
II. Sense of Isolation						
Q13	I cannot get along with classmates.	0.0140	**0.8590**	-0.0070	0.0280	-0.1020
Q10	In this class, I feel nobody will accept me.	0.0930	**0.8120**	0.1080	0.0840	-0.0190
Q11	I feel I have no friends in this class.	0.0420	**0.7940**	0.0410	0.0350	0.0050
Q20	Most of my classmates are my friends.	0.0450	**-0.7720**	0.0510	0.0690	0.0710
Q17	At this school, I feel like a stranger.	0.0920	**0.7040**	0.1270	0.1350	0.0090
Q7	I guess I cannot fit into the class.	0.0290	**0.5910**	-0.0090	-0.0240	0.0490
III. Task Difficulty						
Q31 *	If a student misses class for a couple of days, it will take some effort to catch up.	-0.0070	-0.0050	**0.6520**	0.0690	0.1270
Q33	Students will get the lower grade if he is lazy.	0.0400	0.0630	**0.6350**	-0.0360	-0.0410
Q44	A student's grade will be lowered if he won't prepare and review his lesson independently.	0.0010	0.0530	**0.6300**	0.0550	0.1500
Q30	Students will try hard not to get the lower grade.	-0.0650	0.0850	**0.4620**	-0.0070	0.1370
Q48	It is quite easy to get the better grade here.	0.0400	-0.0960	**-0.4150**	0.3120	0.0920
VI. Order						
Q5 *	This class will often be in an uproar.	0.0700	0.0320	0.0530	**0.8120**	-0.1310
Q23 *	It will be easier to get into trouble here than in a lot of other classes.	0.1040	0.0720	-0.0080	**0.8090**	-0.0710
V. Discipline						
Q26 *	Most students in this class will really pay attention to what the teacher is saying.	-0.1740	-0.0990	0.0580	-0.0890	**0.6810**
Q40	Students won't interrupt the teacher when he's talking.	-0.0330	0.0050	0.0840	-0.0290	**0.6550**
Q35	Students won't interrupt the teacher when he's teaching.	-0.1050	0.0060	0.0560	-0.1580	**0.6530**
Eigenvalue		6.67	3.55	2.86	2.07	1.87
Variance		13.33	7.10	5.70	4.10	3.70
Cumulative variance		13.33	20.43	26.13	30.23	33.93
Cronbach's — coefficients (Actual)		0.80	0.82	0.59	0.78	0.60
Cronbach's — coefficients (Preferred)		0.89	0.81	0.82	0.60	0.69

* Items are quoted from CES (Trickett & Moos, 1974).
** Factor loadings with absolute values of <.40 are not presented for the sake of clarity.

3.2 Actual and Preferred Classroom Environment for Teachers

Table 17.2 shows that no statistically significant differences were found among teachers for the actual and preferred forms on the scales of Sense of Isolation, Task Difficulty, and Order. Both on Teacher Control and Discipline, however, teachers preferred to control and discipline their students much more strongly than they do in their actual classrooms.

Table 17.2. Validation data (Mean, Standard Deviation, ANOVA Results for each scale of CES-J.II

Scale	Form	No. of Itesms	Teacher (n=29)			Students (n=669)			Interaction
					Actual vs.Pref. Simple main effect			Actual vs.Pref. Simple main effect	Form vs.Group
			Mean	SD	F	Mean	SD	F	F
I. Teacher Contro	Actual	6	13.76	3.43	13.74 **	17.16	4.07	4.74 **	17.33 **
	Prefered		16.24	2.03		15.71	2.61		
II. Sense of Isolati	Actual	6	12.21	2.65	n.s.	10.11	4.07	n.s.	n.s.
	Prefered		11.38	2.21		10.46	2.58		
III. Task Difficulty	Actual	5	11.76	2.13	n.s.	14.23	3.06	28.23 **	14.52 **
	Prefered		11.79	1.88		11.81	3.22		
IV. Order	Actual	2	4.00	1.69	n.s.	4.50	1.85	17.13 **	6.58 *
	Prefered		3.86	1.75		3.38	1.73		
V. Discipline	Actual	3	7.07	1.28	13.77 **	6.11	1.76	33.80 **	n.s.
	Prefered		8.45	1.70		8.27	2.53		

*$p<.05$, **$p<.01$.

3.3 Actual and Preferred Classroom Environments

The difference between students' perceptions of actual and preferred Teacher Control for students in the classrooms was statistically significant. The interaction between form and group was also statistically significant (see Table 17.2). Though teachers preferred stronger control in class, conversely students preferred less teacher control than the present situation. Teachers and students showed a complete opposite view on this scale. No statistically significant difference among students was found for the Sense of Isolation scale.

Statistically significant differences were found between students' perceptions of actual and preferred environment on Task Difficulty. The interaction between form and group was also statistically significant. Students preferred much less difficulty in their study than perceived in the actual learning environment. In contrast, the teachers' perceptions on the two forms were similar. This difference between students and teachers on the two forms of their learning environments may give us suggestions about the tense situation students are in regarding academic achievement.

The interaction between form and group was also statistically significant on the Order scale. Though teachers showed no discrepancy between actual and preferred classroom perceptions, the difference of students ideal and actual perceptions was statistically significant. Students preferred a more organized classroom than they actual perceived.

On the Discipline scale, it was shown that the ideal classroom for students was more disciplined than the actual classroom. This was also true for teachers.

3.4 Teacher and Student Perceptions of Actual Classrooms

Statistically significant differences were found between teachers and students on actual Teacher Control. The students' mean score on this scale was higher than the mean score for teachers. It showed that the students felt more intense Teacher Control in the classroom than teachers did.

Regarding the Sense of Isolation scale, the difference between students' and teachers' perceptions was statistically significant in that students felt less sense of isolation in the classroom than the teachers believed was present.

With Task Difficulty, the students' mean scale score was significantly higher than for teachers. Thus, students felt the tasks they had to do in the classrooms were more difficulty on than did the teachers.

No statistically significant difference between teachers and students was found on the Order scale for their actual classroom perceptions. However, a statistically significant difference also was found on the Discipline scale. The students considered they received more disciplined than the teachers thought they were giving.

3.5 Teacher and Student Preferred Classrooms

The following results were obtained when comparing teacher and student perceptions of the preferred classroom environment. Table 17.3 shows that no statistically significant differences were found between teachers and students on any of the scales. The preferred classroom environments of students and teachers are similar.

Table 17.3. Simple main effect for Group at Actual and Preferred

Scale	No.of Items	Actual	Preferred
		Simple effect Teacher vs. Students. F	Simple effect Teacher vs. Students. F
I. Teacher Control	6	27.98 **	n.s.
II. Sense of Isolation	6	10.76 **	n.s.
III. Task Difficulty	5	17.64 **	n.s.
IV. Order	2	n.s.	n.s.
V. Discipline	3	5.51 *	n.s.

$**p < .01$.

3.6 Actual and Preferred Classroom Environments for Students in Three Grades

Table 17.4 shows the results of an ANOVA, and Table 17.5 summarizes the results of the simple main effect for grade. A statistically significant difference was seen for Teacher Control between the second grade students and the other students. The second grade students perceived stronger Teacher Control than the first and the third students.

There was a statistically significant difference between the third grade students and the others on the Sense of Isolation scale. The third grade students felt a higher sense of isolation in the actual classroom. The peculiar feature among the second grade students was the discrepancy between the actual and the preferred classrooms. Although the actual-preferred classroom environments of both the first and third grade students are consistent, the second grade students apparently prefer to isolate themselves from peers in the classroom.

Statistically significant differences were found among the grades on the Order scale. It was clear that the lower the grade, the less order there was in the classroom.

No statistically significant differences among three grades were found on the Task Difficulty or Discipline scales for their actual classroom perceptions.

Table 17.4. Validation Data (Mean, Standard Deviation, ANOVA Results) for Each Scales of CES-J.II

Scale	Form	No. of Items	Students (n=669)									Interaction Form vs. Group
			1 (n=238)			2 (N=197)			3 (n=233)			
			Mean	SD	Simple main effect Actual vs. Pref. F	Mean	SD	Simple main effect Actual vs. Pref. F	Mean	SD	Simple main effect Actual vs. Pref. F	F
I. Teacher Control	Actual	6	17.42	4.05	16.23 **	16.56	4.23	37.78 **	17.41	3.90	18.98 **	n.s.
	Preferred		16.19	2.48		14.69	2.25		16.08	2.52		
II. Sense of Isolation	Actual	6	9.81	3.96	n.s.	9.71	3.64	12.10 **	10.73	4.46	n.s.	9.68 **
	Preferred		10.16	2.49		11.00	2.69		10.33	2.51		
III. Task Difficulty	Actual	5	14.29	3.09	50.56 **	13.82	3.01	29.36 **	14.50	3.04	58.53 **	3.60 *
	Preferred		11.78	3.20		11.90	3.02		11.79	3.39		
IV. Order	Actual	2	5.44	1.67	129.22 **	4.41	1.86	4.08 *	3.61	1.53	14.29 **	54.49 **
	Preferred		3.32	1.71		4.03	1.89		2.90	1.40		
V. Discipline	Actual	3	5.95	1.73	157.58 **	5.95	1.73	26.46 **	6.40	1.79	128.74 **	21.11 **
	Preferred		8.68	2.35		7.07	2.56		8.86	2.36		

*$p<.05$, **$p<.01$.

Table 17.5. Simple Main Effect for Grade at Actual and Preferred

Scale	No. of Items	Actual Simple main effect for Grade F		Preferred Simple main effect for Grade F	
I. Teacher Control	6	5.17 **	2 > 1, 3	15.04 **	2 > 1, 3
II. Sense of Isolation	6	4.67 **	3 > 1, 2	n.s.	
III. Task Difficulty	5	n.s.		n.s.	
IV. Order	2	48.86 **	1 > 2 > 3	18.76 **	2 > 1 > 3
V. Discipline	3	n.s.		41.15 **	1, 3 > 2

**$p < .01$.

The differences between the second and the other grade students for their preferred learning environments was statistically significant on the Teacher Control scale. The second grade students preferred less Teacher Control than the first and the third grade students.

On the Order scale, a statistically significant difference was found between grades. The mean scale score for second grade students for the preferred classroom was higher than for the first and third grade students. The second grade students preferred more order than the other grade students.

Also with Discipline, statistically significant differences were found between the second grade students and the others. The second grade students preferred the least discipline.

No statistically significant differences among the preferences of the three grades were found on the Sense of Isolation and Task Difficulty scales.

4. Discussion

For the last few decades, classroom environment research has been prominently developed with paper and pencil perceptual measures. It was of significance that assessing students' and teachers' perceptions has become an influential research method of learning environment research, in addition to systematic observation and case study. Fraser (1982) pointed out that educators to that date had paid surprisingly little attention to the potentially useful approach of having actual-preferred forms of learning environment instruments. Having these two forms of data can make it possible to alert educators to the discrepancies not only between actual and preferred perceptions of students, but also among teachers' actual, teachers' preferred, students' actual, and students' preferred perceptions.

The findings of this study might also be informative to educators. As comparisons between teachers' and students' perceptions of their actual classroom environments resulted in some noteworthy discrepancies on the scales of Teacher Control, Sense of Isolation, Task Difficulty, and Discipline. It was observed that students felt stronger control and discipline by teachers, and more difficult class work than the teachers expected. Conversely, on the scale of Sense of Isolation, the students were less friendly in the classroom than teachers were concerned about. In spite of these discrepancies in perceptions of the actual environment, it must be noted that statistically significant differences between teachers' and students' preferred classroom environment perceptions were not found for any scales. These results make it clear that while students and teachers did not agree about their perceptions of actual conditions, they do agree about their ideal learning environments.

These findings might give teachers some confidence to continue their educational endeavours at classroom management. Let us return to the administrator's story. Could one say that this present study made teachers' intuitions clear? What was the characteristics of the second grade students? In the analyses focusing on the effect of grades, the following results were shown. The second grade students felt stronger teacher control in the actual classroom but preferred less teacher control and discipline than the other students. They also wished for more order in the classroom. They also showed a notable discrepancy on the Sense of Isolation scale. Students in second grade preferred to isolate themselves from classmates. We cannot say whether teachers' strong control and discipline had produced the particular classroom climate in the second grade, or the other way around. However, we can inform teachers what the students' perceptions are and that perhaps they should begin classroom management of the second grade students not as an academic issue but rather one of relationships among students.

While this present study suggested a possibility that the actual and preferred forms of these assessments could help teachers to understand student perceptions, there remain some problems to be solved. These perceptual measures must be adapted to fit the psychosocial context of each learning environment. The reason could be explained by the factor analysis results of the CES-J.II. In previous studies (Hirata & Sako, 1998; Hirata, Watanabe, & Souma, 1998), the original CES scales such as Task Orientation and Competition were not extracted via factor analysis. It does not mean that students in Japan are free from any pressures of grades and recognition in their classroom. It is obvious that they have serious competition in the exam for entrance to higher education. Actually, in the CES-J.II, with item corrections for the Japanese context, Task Difficulty was revealed as one of the scales with good reliability. This finding might be derived from the conceptual differences between different societies. These cultural differences are of concern for researchers, but at the same time they are useful knowledge for scale constructions. The findings here also suggested the fruitful possibility that teachers and researchers could collaborate using these perceptual approaches. The results of the present study were consistent with teachers' intuitive impressions, but made these intuitions clear. This study might be a cue to introduce these useful measures to more educators in Japan and thus provide more feedback to both researchers and teachers in the classrooms.

5. The Potential of Psychological Measures in Future Classes

Finally, this chapter discusses the potential use of these psychological instruments to improve teaching and learning. Nowadays, new educational technologies, such as computer-assisted instruction (CAI), electronic teaching materials, for example, using presentation software with a projector as a substitute for writing on the blackboard, open schooling, team-teaching, and so on, have been tried in Japan. But it might be not be sufficient in these new situations just to assess the rate of pupil's attendance, academic achievement and behaviour as determinants of effectiveness. For example, Hirata (2003) reported on the relationship among students' perceptions of their psychological environment in higher education and their achievement and LOC tendency (Locus of Control; Nowick & Strickland, 1973). Statistically, it was shown that the high-achieving students felt more satisfaction toward their classes than the low-achievers, and that students with a more internal LOC reported greater satisfaction in the classroom.

These results suggest that student perceptions of their classes are clearly relevant to individual student characteristics. If this kind of class assessment were to be used in classrooms generally, it would be of considerable benefit to teachers not only in classroom management, but also in determining the effectiveness of new teaching materials. The use of such student perceptual measures would be less time consuming for a teacher than talking with all the pupils in his/her class, and easier, especially for Japanese boys and girls than talking directly to a teacher. The perceptual measures will be very useful tools for teachers and pupils in technology-rich future classrooms in Japan.

Innovation, of course, means the use of new technology in classrooms, and students' perceptions of teacher involvement with students in these new environments will be important components of classes in order to increase students' satisfaction. In Japan, teachers using these psychological measures, teachers can obtain with ease information about what is happening in their classrooms whenever they would like to know. Psychological measures assessing learning environment, therefore, have abundant uses in future classrooms where various new technologies will be used to enrich teaching and learning.

References

Anderson, C. J., & Walberg H. J. (1974). Learning Environments. In H.J.Walberg (Eds.), *Evaluating educational performance: A source book of methods, instruments, and examples.* Berkeley, California: McCutchan.

Fisher, D. L. & Fraser, B. J. (1981). Validity and use of My Class Inventory. *Science Education, 65,* 145-156.

Fraser, B.J. (1982). Differences between students and teacher perceptions of actual and preferred classroom learning environment. *Educational Evaluation and Policy Analysis. 4* (4). 511-519.

Fraser, B. J. (1994). Research on classroom and school climate. In D. Gabel (Ed.), *Handbook of research on science teaching and learning.* (pp. 493-541). New York. Macmillan.

Fraser, B. J. (1998). Science learning environment: Assessment, effect and determinations. In Fraser, B. J. and Tobin, K. G. (Eds.), *International handbook of science education.* (pp. 527-564). Dordrecht, The Netherlands: Kluwer.

Fraser, B. J., Anderson, C. J., & Walberg H. J. (1982). *Assessment of learning environment: Manual for Learning Environment Inventory (LEI) and My Class Inventory (MCI) (third version).* Perth: Western Australian Institute of Technology.

Fraser, B. J., & Fisher, D. L. (1983). Use of actual and preferred classroom environment scales in person-environment fit research. *Journal of Educational Psychology, 75* (2), 303-313.

Fraser, B. J., Giddings, G. J., & McRobbie, G. J. (1991, April). *Science laboratory classroom environments: A cross-national perspective.* Paper presented at annual meeting of American Educational Research Association, Chicago.

Fraser, B. J. & O'Brien, P. (1985). Student and teacher perceptions of the environment of elementary school classrooms. *The Elementary School Journal, 85* (5), 567-580.

Fraser, B. J., Treagust, D. F. & Dennis, N. C. (1986) Development of an instrument for assessing classroom psychological environment in universities and college. *Studies in Higher Education. 11,* 43-54.

Hirata, S. (2003). Class assessment by university and junior college students: relations between CUCEI (College & University Classroom Environment Inventory) measures, student achievement, and Locus of Control. Journal of Hakuoh University Women's College, 27 (1), 105-121.(in Japanese).

Hirata, S., Kanno, J., & Koizumi, E. (1999). Some characteristics of non-attendant students' cognition toward their school environment. Japanese *Journal of Counseling Science*, *32*, 124-133 (in Japanese).

Hirata, S., & Sako, T. (1999). Perceptions of school environment among Japanese junior high school, non-attendant, and juvenile delinquent students. *Learning Environment Research: An International Journal*, *1*(3), 321-331.

Hirata,S., Watanabe, T., & Souma, I. (1998). Perceptions of school environment and locus of control among Japanese juvenile delinquents. *Japanese Journal of Crime Psychology*, *36* (2), 1-18 (in Japanese).

Hunt, D. E. (1975). Person-environment interaction: A challenge found wanting before it was tried. *Review of Educational Research*, *45*, 209-230.

Lewin, K. (1936). *Principles of topological psychology*. New York: McGraw-Hill.

Murray, H.A. (1938). *Explorations in personality*. New York: Oxford University Press.

Nowicki, S. Jr. & Strickland, B.R. (1973). A locus of control scale for children. *Journal of Consulting and Clinical Psychology*. *40*, 148-154.

Rentoul, A. J., & Fraser B. J. (1979). Conceptualization of enquiry-based or open classrooms learning environments. *Journal of Curriculum Studies*, *11*, 223-245.

Taylor, P. C., Fraser, B J., & Fisher D. L. (1997). Monitoring constructivist classroom learning environments. *International Journal of Educational Research*, *27*, 293-302.

Teh, G., & Fraser, B. J. (1994). An evaluation of computer-assisted learning in term of achievement attitude and classroom environment. *Evaluation and Research in Education*, *8*, 147-161.

Trickett, E. J., & Moos, R.H. (1973). Social environment of junior high and high school classrooms. *Journal of Educational Psychology*, *65* (1), 93-102.

Chapter 18

DESIGN PRINCIPLES FOR WEB-BASED LEARNING: BALANCING INDIVIDUAL AND SOCIAL PERSPECTIVES IN TECHNOLOGY-RICH LEARNING ENVIRONMENTS

David Hung
Tan Seng Chee
Nanyang Technological University
Singapore

The purpose of this paper is to describe more recent conceptions of learning which differ from traditional conceptions of individualised thinking to a more collaborative and social approach towards learning. However, we recognize the merits of both individual and social levels of learning and cognition, and attempt to provide a balanced perspective. In this regard, we proposed four models of e-learning which are web-based and subsequently discuss design principles which can be generalized. We recognize that technology-rich learning environments require these design principles in order to facilitate the learning process.

1. Introduction

In the last two decades, interesting debates have arisen among proponents of individualised and social orientations to learning and cognition. The individualised orientations fall mostly within the constructivist school of thought; whereas the social orientations to learning spring from social cultural and more recently the situated perspective to learning and cognition. The two perspectives differ significantly; whereas, the former emphasizes qualitative change in how knowledge is constructed by individuals as a result of his or her interaction with the world; the latter is characterized by social participation, the setting of activities, and the important dimension of historical change over time within social communities and individuals. Although there can be heated differences over the epistemologies of the two camps, Hiebert et al. (1996) stressed that constructivism has a functional objective of "what students take with them from the classroom" (p. 17); whereas social cultural perspectives focus on a structural dimension of "the activity of the classroom" (p. 17). The synthesis is an important agenda in educational research (Greeno, 1997).

Constructivism holds that there is a real world that we experience, however, that experience is mediated by meanings imposed by our interpretation (or meaning-making) of the world. There are many ways to structure and interpret the world, and there are many meanings and perspectives for any event or concept. Hence, the constructivist view is opposed to the one correct objectivist meaning that we strive for (Duffy & Jonassen, 1992). In current literature, there are many interpretations of constructivism – from the radical views of individualised cognition to the other side of the continuum where mind is simply social in orientation. Constructivist perspectives attend to very individualised orientations to cognition (e.g., Piagetian psychology) whereas social-cultural views are placed within a broader social, cultural, and contextual-environmental milieu (e.g., Vygotskian psychology). The social perspective to the mind will be explained in the following sections. Based on Vygotskian (1978) understanding, higher mental functions in the individual are derived from social life (Wertsch, 1998). There is no activity that is not situated (Lave & Wenger, 1991). Learning is thus active and is accomplished through the process of co-participation and cognition is socially shared. Central to the concept of situated learning is the emphasis that Vygotsky (1978) placed on activity, person-in-activity, as well as on mediation through socio-cultural tools such as language.

In essence, we argue for a balanced and pragmatic view of the mind bridging both the individual and social levels of cognition – balancing between Vygotskian and Piagetian views. From such a perspective, we propose the design of e-learning environments where both personalization of learning (individual) and affiliations to the community of learners (social) are complemented. Both a collective and individual understanding of knowledge and meanings are important.

2. Balancing the Individual and Social Perspectives

The two dominant roots of constructivism are the radical constructivist and the social-cultural views. Arising from Piaget (1972) and von Glasersfeld is the radical constructivist view where learning is defined as a predominantly individual self-organization of the mind – an active cognitive reorganization through processes such as assimilation, accommodation, and equilibrium. These views are highly influenced by Descartes and Immanuel Kant where experience of the world is objective (rather than interpretative) and that the mind is influenced by sensory impressions, this man experiences the world. Thus the constructivist view places 'great' emphasis on the individual mind – *a cognito* – and other factors of culture are minimal. Knowledge is regarded as objectifying the world and certain (subjected to singular truths) and that such knowledge becomes learning when transferred into the individual mind.

The social-cultural view, on the other hand, argues that mind is a by-product of external culturally organized phenomena such as practices in the context of artifacts, tools, and language. Such a view is attributed to Vygotsky, Leont'ev and other Marxist orientations. Recent notions such as cognitive apprenticeship, legitimate peripheral participation, or the negotiation of meaning in stipulated construction zones are notions arising from the social-cultural perspective. Understanding and learning is developed through continued and situated use and application within communities of learning (e.g., schools) and practice (e.g., scientific communities). Learning involves picking up the jargon, behavior, and norms of a social community; adopting the belief systems of a group such as a school, and being members of that community. Through this process, learners develop not only the knowledge and skills, but a way of seeing knowledge (interpretation of meanings) or identity.

> [L]earning and development are viewed as progress along trajectories of participation and growth of identity. ... In these practices, students develop patterns of participation that contribute to their identities as learners, which include the ways in which they take initiative and responsibility for their learning and function actively in the formulation of goals and criteria for their success. (Greeno, 1997, p. 8)

It is important to realize that proponents of the above two views did not deny the presence of either the social or individual dimensions. For example, although von Glasersfeld defines learning as self-organization, he attributes this constructive activity as the cognizing individual who interacts with other members of the community (Cobb, 1994). Von Glasersfeld elaborates that *knowledge* refers to "conceptual structures that epistemic agents, given the range of present experience within their tradition of thought and language, consider *viable*" (1992, p. 381); and contents that "the most frequent source of perturbations for the developing cognitive subject is interaction with others" (1989, p. 136).

In the same vein, the social-cultural view as dominated by the Vygotskian perspective also did not deny the individual view. The oft-quoted Vygotskian cultural law of development emphasizes the view of *internalization* from the social intermental to the individual intramental level. However, there still remains much research on how this internalization process from then social to individual occurs. The Vygotskian view claims that cognition begins at the social level – social interactions, situated contextual practices, signs, tools, etc. – yet there is now ample evidence from Piagetian and neo-Piagetian studies that young children work out a substantial knowledge of the physical world, well before they could have gained much of it from the surrounding culture (Carey & Gelman, 1991). In other words, social learning plays a significant role, but it cannot be said that all of conceptualization and learning must originate from the social plane.

Stripped to their essentials, constructivism tells us to pay close attention to the active learner's mental activities (organization of his / her mind) and social-culturalism tells us to pay close attention to the cultural practices of the learner's milieu. Except for the practical difficulty of doing both at once, there is nothing incompatible in these two proposals. Neither one rejects the other. Thus, from a pragmatic point of view, we should consider what the two perspectives have to offer. *Learning should be a process of active individual construction and a process of enculturation into the practices of the social society*, of which, the immediate wider society of our trainee-teachers is the teaching community. In other words, learning for school students is a process in which students actively reorganize their ways of thinking and participating in classroom practices – which includes the concepts and knowledge required of them to learn (Cobb & Bowers, 1999).

Brown and Duguid (2000) elegantly describe learning as demand driven, a social act, and an identity formation. By demand-driven, the learning context should create the active need for reorganization of cognitive processes; by social act, learning is embedded in the larger community beyond the individual; and by identify formation, learning creates the personality of the learner affiliated to the community of practice – for example, the teaching community – through internalization and appropriation of knowledge, skills, beliefs, and norms. These terms are similar to the emphases on attitudes, skills, and knowledge. Attitudes are acquired through appropriation of exemplary behaviors, and skills through the internalization and application of knowledge.

Finally, in comparing the two views, it can be noted that the social-cultural view as enculturation via guided participation (for example within the Vygotskian notion of the Zone of Proximal Development) assumes an active constructing learner. Conversely, the constructivist view of learning as cognitive self-organization implicitly assumes that the learner is participating in cultural practices. In effect, active individual construction constitutes the background against which guided participation in cultural practices comes to the fore for the social-cultural view, and this participation is the background against which self-organization comes to the fore for the radical constructivist view.

Each of the two perspectives tells us what we should do in our instructional and learning 'story' and they can be used to complement each other. For example, a young newly-trained teacher gets enculturated in the school practice and acquires all the rules of the cultural practice as he or she progresses from a novice learner to a mature teacher-practitioner – the strengths of legitimate peripheral participation through observations and guided participation. On the other hand, the newly trained teacher reflects upon what he or she had learned and encounters self-reorganization – refining her theoretical knowledge in relation to his/her practical experiences. In this regard, there is a need for a similar culture in terms of norms and practices (for example the constructivist practice) between institutions and schools. Otherwise, we may not be fostering the creation of a teacher-identify in real practice. As a dynamic consequence of activities and demands of the real-world practice, the actions of teachers and practitioners are again 'fed-back' to the social context and milieu – a classroom or school for example – changing the social cultural setting and influencing the policies and practices over time. In other words, everything is dynamic – the social context, the teacher, the student, and the interactions among them. Such an authentic and dynamic process is the consequence of both social and individual processes being active and dynamic. As Hanks (1996) puts it: "we realize ourselves; effect changes in our worlds; connect with other people; experience beauty, rage, and tenderness; exercise authority; refuse; and pursue our interests" (p. 236). Hanks's expressions infuse both the individual and social dimensions and intricacies of cognition, emotions, and behavior.

In the next section of this chapter, we illustrate a practical approach to this complement of the individual and social perspective of constructivism through the design of three models of e-learning. The first model is the traditional instructional/learning approach where we complement the best use of media to facilitate both the individual and social process; and the second approach is a newer and more exciting direction of e-learning environments focusing on personalization (individual) and its relationships to the larger community of practitioners (social).

3. E-Learning – Complementing the Individual and Social Perspectives

Model 1

In the first approach for e-learning (Model 1), we fundamentally compare the strengths and weakness of different media types (for example, the Internet, the text book, the classroom, etc.) and ask ourselves how we can deliver instruction in the most effective manner complementing the use of the different media for the learner. How do we use the different media types to ensure that self-organization and appropriation of knowledge from social others' occur?

We use an example from an *Instructional Technology* module for teacher preparation conducted at the *National Institute of Education* in Singapore. We combined a text-book/web site (*Blackboard CourseInfo* system) approach where we recognized that the text-book readings (no mass lectures) provided the knowledge content for instructional technologies integration into subject curriculum. The Blackboard website provides online activities (which can be updated according to different cohorts) in complement with the text-book readings (the best way we envisage to engage in reading text). These on-line activities,

Design Principles for Web-based Learning 391

such as quizzes and tasks to be accomplished, assist in the internalization of knowledge resulting in integration skills for the training-teachers. A large component of the on-line activities involves on-line discussions where students socially interact and discuss on issues relating to the readings from the text-book. In essence, the students discuss pertinent issues relating to IT integration in the context of the school culture and practice (see Figure 18.1).

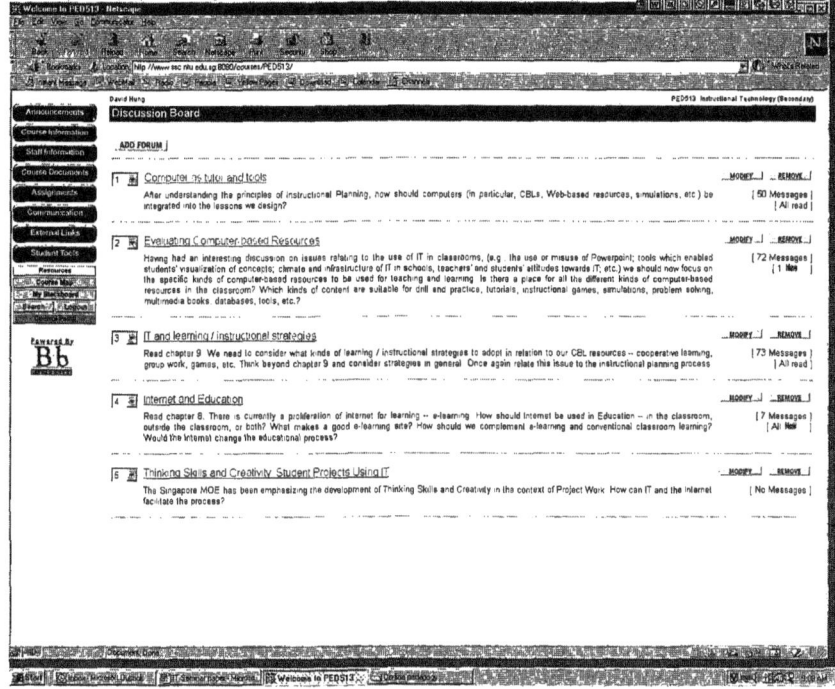

Figure 18.1. Discussion forums.

These on-line activities are to be seen in the context of two larger projects that must be accomplished by the students. These two projects are done out-of-class time and within tutorial consultation sessions. The students work in pairs for their projects and in the facilitation of the online discussions. In essence, the projects attempt to also foster a social collaborative process where the tasks given to the students would be of relevance to the larger school community, and through the collaboration, actual practical integration and creation of IT resources would facilitate the internalization of skills and knowledge. Fundamentally, we felt that since the web is dynamic and updating of information and activities are facilitated we put information and materials which were "fluid" on the web, for example, what students needed to do each week (see Figure 18.2).

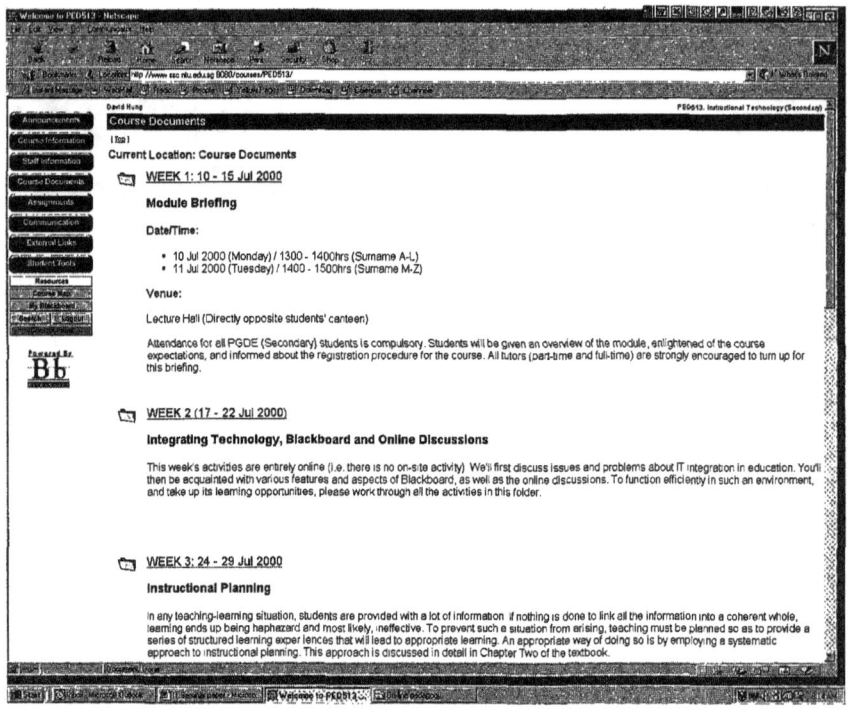

Figure 18.2. Weekly activities

These weekly activities which students must work on individually and in pairs reinforce the kinds of ideas and formulations possibly derived from social discourse and interactions. Model 1 is a relatively primitive conceptualization of how social and individual dimensions of learning and cognition can be complemented. To reiterate, social-cultural structures are set up via online and face-to-face discussions, but ultimately what trainee-teachers 'bring home' is set by the kinds of learning they can transfer from social-instructional activities to individual-paired projects/activities.

Model 2

Alternatively as in Model 2, students can be presented with a conceptual issue, for example, physics concepts such as motion, force, velocity, acceleration, etc. in frictional and non-frictional concepts. Here, students can be presented with simulations of physical phenomena (where students are also able to play around with the variables involved). Different models of theoretical constructs can be presented to the learners through which they can discuss and build theories of which construct approximate most closely to the physical phenomena experimented. Students can discuss these issues through more sophisticated platforms such as Knowledge Forum (see Figure 18.3). These platforms allow facilitate students' thinking via the use of scaffolds encouraging theory building, conjecturing, and the defending of these propositions.

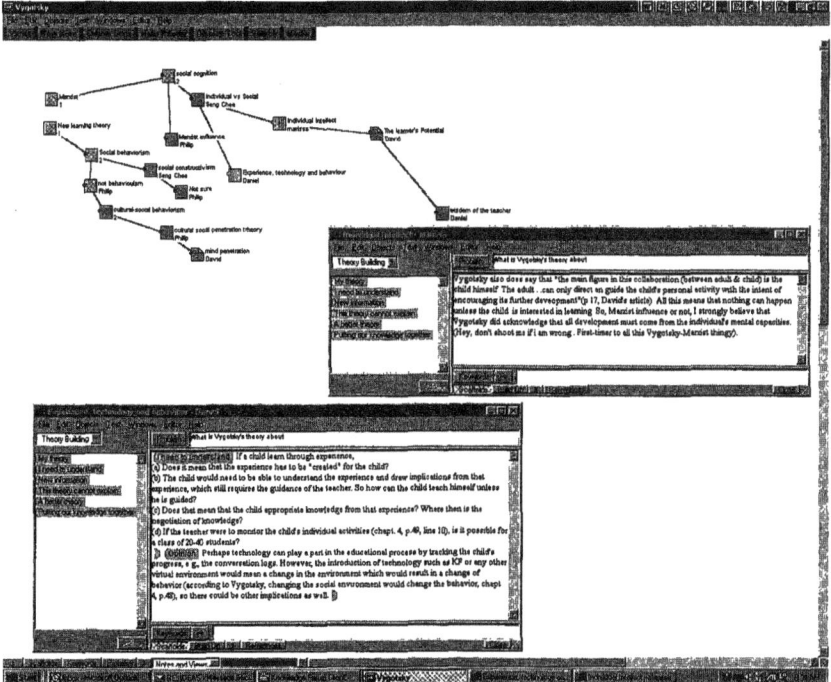

Figure 18.3. Collective representations of knowledge

As in Figure 18.2, the platform allows for a collective representation of ideas and knowledge discourse. Chen & Hung (2002) also argue for a personalized knowledge representation function in online discussions. Personalized representations are one's own conceptualizations which may be in-progress and these conceptualizations can be superimposed upon collective representations in order to make comparisons with collective understandings.

In this Model 2 approach, it is important to scaffold students' understanding by challenging them to prove or defend their theories of questions, issues, and ideas formulated. For example, students may wish to provide a reason for a historical event and why certain decisions had taken place in our history. Usually, no precise right or wrong solutions hold in these instances, but the qualitative manner in which arguments are presented and tentatively accepted are critical to students' learning. Teachers may wish to present three or more views on the interpretation of events and students formulate personal and group accounts about to which view they would preferably ascribe. In these efforts, students are seen to labour through the reasonings behind theories and perspectives, and such a study or research gradually enculturates our students towards knowledge pursuits and theory building. Importantly, teachers need to guide students away from 'heretical thinking' (views and conclusions drawn which may deviate from the parameters of interpretation of historical facts and accounts) and lead thinking towards critical formulations of personal and collective understandings.

Model 3

In the third approach to e-learning (Model 3), we build on the concept of *personalization* as it is being used in e-commerce models, and try to map it onto an e-learning model. Personalization as a means of catering to individual consumer's needs and wants, has long been touted as one of key benefits of the Web (Stellin, 2000). Because of its wide acceptance as a powerful marketing tool, it is alternatively described in some circles as "one-to-one marketing", or "targeted merchandizing". But this concept of personalization also exhibits some of the characteristics of key learning issues raised by the perspectives of Jean Lave, Etienne Wenger, John Seely Brown, Paul Duguid, Donald Norman, etc. In this approach, we hope to distill some of these characteristics and incorporate them into an e-learning model.

Any of us, who has visited websites like Amazon.com (www.amazon.com) and CDNow (www.cdnow.com), or more so, who have bought some products from these sites, would immediately recognize a type of personalization at play. This type of personalization, which is usually referred to as "recommendation systems" by these sites, works something like this: If customer one bought items A, B C and D, and customer two bought items A, B and C; then it is quite probable that customer two might like item D also. If this is the case, then the personalization engine recommends item D to customer two. But this is as easy as it gets. Personalization engines are built around complex mathematical algorithms that scan through thousands of customers buying and browsing habits, and then try to match them up with a particular customer's profile. As these complex algorithms are called "collaborative filters", this type of personalization also known as "collaborative filtering-based" personalization.

In another type of personalization, known as "rule-based" personalization, customers are required to make their likes and dislikes known beforehand, by filling up a certain "profile-forms". When, for example, a customer specifies that he/she would like to get health news or financial news, then the website satisfies this customer's need by providing content and services related to health and finance only.

Analyzing the above two methods, one cannot fail to recognize the similarities with the social (collaborative filtering) and individual (rule-based) characteristics of learning that were discussed above. Collaborative filtering-based personalization systems help to expose an individual to a related community. For example, it may not have been possible for a customer to know about certain books in Amazon.com if it were not been recommended in the first place. By recommending book titles read by a particular community or group, the recommendation system tries to suggest a community or group to which an individual might belong. And when a customer discovers his/her affinity to a particular community or group, then he/she can indulge in similar reading habits of other members of the community. In Lave & Wenger's terms, the customer received an opportunity to get enculturated with the practices of his/her community (Lave & Wenger, 1991). It is this ability to enable enculturation that makes personalization a promising candidate for inclusion in learning environments—be it corporate learning environment, or a university environment.

But before we can describe personalization's role in such environments, we have to clarify an important point. The reason why personalization is so effective in sites like Amazon.com or CDNow, is because these companies carry thousands or even millions of products, or in other words, they have huge selections. It does not make sense for a company to use personalization systems when it sells just ten products. Thus, for personalization to be effective, having a big selection is a necessity.

But having a selection is not a concern for schools and universities. Information is in abundant supply in the form of articles, lecture notes, presentations, archived thesis and dissertations, etc. More importantly, information in universities is being accumulated all the time. If all these sources of information are present and made available in electronic forms, as a part of a large database, it will create a very favourable environment through which the benefits of personalization can be leveraged. If such were to be the case, we can paint the following scenario.

Students log onto the university network. Information relating to the courses they wish to take, their previous experiences, their modes of learning, etc. is gathered and their personal profile is created. Rule-based personalization can then be used to target instructional content and media to specific individuals based on their profile. For example, students at the Singapore *National Institute of Education* logging into the system will have personalized views according to their course profiles such as Bachelor and Masters' students, and others. Rule-based personalization can go many levels deeper by tracking the students' content area expertise, the kinds of information sites usually accessed, the assignments undertaken, the lecturers from various disciplines consulted, etc. By keeping a history of the students' activities, the e-learning environment would be able to recommend timely and appropriate resources and materials for the students' learning. It would also be able to recommend directions for the students, for example, possible projects or assignments where the student would most likely be able to be interested in. This can be achieved by the system searching databases both locally and internationally. It could also recommend research areas of interest and associate these areas to special interests groups, which is related to the collaborative filtering-based personalization.

Collaborative filtering-based personalization can be used to guide specific individuals to their most related community or communities by exposing the modules, articles, media that others in the community are viewing or reading. By being able to trace the students' preferences, the e-learning environment is able to associate or affiliate the student to people in the community, such as school teachers, university professors, special interest groups, etc. who have similar preferences. Gradually, an identity with this community is formed. This collaborative-filtering method basically tries to associate the targeted student to other related educators and collaborators.

Thus, we envisage personalization-based systems to capitalize on the abundant information and knowledge held in universities to target specific individuals with appropriate instructional content and media, as well as enable specific individuals to get encultured with communities to which they display the strongest affinities.

Model 4

The predominance of handheld devices can be seen in the wallet-size handheld devices used by professionals and even many students to keep track of schedules and appointments. The wireless and mobile technologies with the accompanying portable devices in the classroom can qualitatively enhance the classroom interactions because of their flexibility and mobility. No longer do we need to 'go to the computer lab' where tables and chairs are 'rooted' to the positions in a rigid manner. With no wires and heavy computers that cannot be shifted easily, teachers in the traditional set-ups of computers labs have not been able to adopt alternative modes of learner-centred pedagogies. Classroom interactions were also merely confined to the classroom, whereas now mobile and Internet technologies can bridge students to learning situations or project work with experts outside the classroom. These technologies need not only connect students to experts, but can assist in peer-tutoring or collaborative situations with other students outside the boundaries of the classroom and school. In essence, the wireless and mobile technologies enhance flexibility of instructions within a classroom, and afford the ability to transcend the physical boundaries by effectively linking the classrooms and the external resources. Let us illustrate using the SimCalc Project (http://www.simcalc.umassd.edu) where the e-learning of calculus is only made possible by technology. For SimCalc, a key technology is directly editable graphs of piecewise functions, connected to simulations of motion. From the research done, learners were able to explore concepts, apply their understanding, and subsequently reflect on their conceptualisations (see http://www.cilt.org).

Students have been confined to classrooms and experimental laboratories for a large part of their schooling life. Now students are able to extend their learning experiences to field trips and study groups outside the traditional classrooms. Imagine students using data-loggers attached to their hand-held devices where they can collect data of water samples and collate the data on the spot with spreadsheets. The data are immediately sent back to the teacher or other groups of students in the school-classroom through mobile telecommunications technologies. Consider another scenario – the 'control tower' approach. Take the tablet PCs which are becoming popular in the personal computer market. Students can take along these tablet PCs and record data of phenomena and they are able to communicate with experts at any location (in the world) or with supervisors at the local universities through Internet technologies, either through the traditional emailing features or through synchronous means accompanied with a talk-head video facility. Instead of waiting to return to their schools or classrooms, students can communicate with experts 'on the fly' because real-time information is needed before students can proceed with their next steps in their discovery and experimentation in the field. The supervisors at the local universities are acting like air-traffic controllers, providing real-time advice to the several groups of students. These 'control tower' supervisors can even collate data from different field sites and transmit the data back to students so that they can compare and contrast the data and decide on further actions (Figure 18.4).

Groups of students may be working at two different locations of the campus, for example, one group at the library and the other group at the science laboratory. The groups may access a common collaborative workspace, and share information with each other synchronously. The group at the library sends scanned images from books and magazines (using their hand-held scanners or web-cams) while the other group collates incoming data captured from their science experiments and internet resources accessible from the laboratory. The supervisor interacts with the groups accordingly by providing advice and timely feedback on the data that were collected.

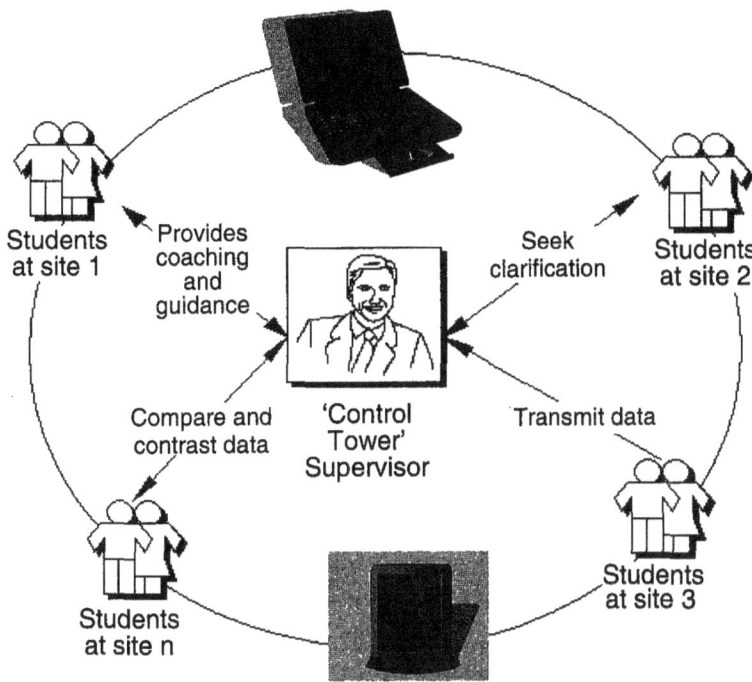

Figure 18.4. 'Control Tower' supervisor advising and connecting students working at different sites with mobile and wireless technologies

4. Discussion

From the perspective of both an individual and social constructivist view, we recognize that individual and collective knowledge construction and understanding is important. Certain learning community-based environments primarily emphasize the collective goal of knowledge building, where the objective is to advance corporate understanding. We are advocating that unless the collective understanding is appropriated or internalized by the individuals in the community, there is only a collective identity formed but not an individual identity. Learning should ultimately occur in the learner's head, and not just at the social level.

In a learning community, where individuals count, there must be a process of learning where diverse expertise and perspectives are mutually complemented and valued. In other words, there is a mutual dependency on one another's expertise. Sharing and respect for each other's views are also part of the rules of the community. When knowledge is socially constructed, there are the notions of negotiation and discourse. Learners are encouraged to dig deeply into concepts, overcoming misconceptions and queries for understanding. In such communities, the goals and objectives are clear – learning knowledge and learning how to learn.

In summarizing and making explicit our conceptualizations above, we distill principles through which practitioners can 'handle' concretely. From these principles, we draw design principles for e-learning environments. From a balanced view of both constructivism and social cultural perspectives, the following principles can be derived.

- **Learning is demand driven or problem centrered** – This principle is both social and individual in orientation. In many instances, demands of projects, problems are derived from social settings such as schools and these demands are translated into individual cognition in terms of tasks to be learned and achieved. Learning in this sense can be personalized and at the convenience of the learner.
- **Learning is a social act/construction mediated between social beings through language, signs, genres, and tools** – This principle is inclined more towards the social end of the 'continuum' (if we could use this term), as it suggests that the activities which work around projects are mediated by language and other signs, for example, the discourse by students and teachers around scientific concepts.
- **Learning is an identity formation** – This principle is both a social and individual phenomena as it suggests that although identity or one's character is individualistic in nature, it is socially influenced. An identity formation is a construction within an individual of a "way of seeing" the world, for example, mathematicians see the world through a lens of patterns and number sensing.
- **Learning is reflective and metacognitive** – This principle is individualistic in orientation suggesting the importance of reflection and understanding the way in which we learn and think.

- **Learning is embedded in rich cultural and social contexts** – This principle suggests that cognition is socially influenced by the rich cultural and situational/social contexts which imbue meaning to the world around us.
- **Learning is interdisciplinary or multidisciplinary** – It is important to recognize that domains of problems and knowledge overlap in real life authentic situations. For learning to be meaningful, contexts for learning should be thus enriched from multiple perspectives.
- **Learning is socially distributed between persons, rules, and tools** – As with the earlier principle that learning is mediated by language and other signs, here learning is distributed in other individuals and tools. Just as it is everyday phenomena to see individuals use calculators, hand-phones, PDAs, we recognize that these tools are an extension of human-minds. Similarly, human knowledge is also 'distributed' or shared among other individuals.
- **Learning is to transfer knowledge from situations to situations discovering relational and associated meanings in concepts** – An important individualistic principle here is that cognition within the constructivist orientation emphasizes the element of transfer of meanings of the generalization of knowledge (somewhat lacking in social cultural perspectives).

Table 18.1 draws some design considerations for web-based e-learning environments for the above learning principles. Because the web fosters a wealth of learning both socially and individually, we draw the following design principles as a conclusion to this chapter.

Table 18.1. Design Principles for Web-based e-learning

Individual and Social Cognition Balanced	Design considerations for e-learning through web-based environments
Learning is demand driven or problem centered	1. Web-based learning environments should have personalized content for the learner with tasks and projects embedded in a meaningful activity context. 2. Web-based learning content should be personalized to learners on a must-know and need-to-know basis, customizing and prioritizing the information.

Table 18.1. Continued

	3.	Web-based learning can be made available in portable devices so that learners can communicate and gather resources.
Learning is a social act/construction mediated between social beings through language, signs, genres, and tools.	4.	Web-based learning environments can track the learner's history, profile, and progress and tailor personalized strategies and content.
	5.	Web-based learning environments should capitalize on the social communicative and collaborative dimensions allowing mediated discourse.
	6.	Web-based learning environments should have scaffolding structures which contain the genres and common expressions used by the community, e.g., "My hypothesis is …".
	7.	Web-based learning environments should be embedded with facilitating tools for the engagement of tasks, e.g., concept maps and other mind-tools for working out problems, emphasizing depth of knowledge construction.
Learning is an identity formation	8.	Web-based learning environments should create a 'structural-dependency' between individuals where novices need more capable peers capitalizing on the zone of proximal development.
	9.	Web-based learning environments should create a situation where there is continual growth and interaction through the tools embedded in the environment.
	10.	Web-based learning environments should be designed to capitalize on the diverse expertise in the community.
Learning is reflective and metacognitive	11.	Web-based learning environments can facilitate reflection and metacognitive actions through the provision of facilitation cues or questions.
	12.	Web-based learning environments can focus on depth over breadth, thus enabling learners to analyze communicative 'speech acts'.
	13.	Web-based learning environments can focus on tasks and projects, thus enabling learning through doing and refection in action.

Table 18.1. Continued

Learning is embedded in rich cultural and social contexts	14. Web-based learning environments should be Internet or web-based so that with such a common networked platform, learners can access the learning environment in their embedded contexts.
	15. Web-based learning environments should be portable as far as possible so that they can be used in the context.
	16. Web-based learning environments should complement other forms of interaction, e.g., face-to-face, allowing tacit knowledge to emerge.
Learning is interdisciplinary or multidisciplinary	17. Web-based learning environments should capitalized on the wealth of interdisciplinary and multi-disciplinary resources such that learners can play roles and functions from various disciplinary perspectives.
	18. Web-based learning should capitalized on the availability of the communicative technologies to enable learners to engaged in interdisciplinary problems.
	19. Web-based learning environments should enable learners to be connected to experts in multiple disciplines.
Learning is socially distributed between persons, rules, and tools.	20. Web-based learning environments need not contain time-critical knowledge where the human skill is most valued.
	21. Web-based learning environments should contain knowledge that can 'stay in the world' where tools are available in locating the knowledge.
	22. Web-based learning environments should have tools which can optimize human performance.
Learning is to transfer knowledge from situations to situations discovering relational and associated meanings in concepts.	23. Web-based learning environments can challenge learners to reflect on concept principles that can be applied to other contexts Alternative solutions, views, and approaches challenging the learner's views can be presented.

Table 18.1. Continued

24.	Web-based learning environments can facilitate learning through observations of visual representations patterns or stable variables.
25.	Web-based learning environments can organize information to allow the leaner to engage in further analysis.

5. Conclusion

Finally, we conclude by emphasizing that a balanced view to learning and cognition provides a firmer basis for the design of learning environments for learning and cognition. E-learning must be grounded in the theoretical foundations of the learning sciences. The recent emphasis of exposing learners to authentic problems and projects lends itself well to the meaningful use of learning technologies within the e-learning context. The future of technology-rich environments entails media-rich authentic problems, tools which support the problem solving process, timely and personalized resources, social collaborative platforms, and portable devices where the learner can work and learn anytime and anywhere. The distinctions between working and learning are fast fading and we see the advances of technology playing a crucial role in blurring this distinction.

The way ahead can be exciting if these e-learning technologies can be perceived with optimism. Technology hiccups will abound. But educators should see how these technologies can add value to the learning and instructional process, rather than demean the advantages technology can bring to our lives. Just as if a doctor who died a 100 years ago could be resurrected and see the surgical rooms in our hospitals today, she/he would be quite lost; we hope that in a similar vein, a teacher of a 100 years ago would enter today's classrooms and 'be quite lost', albeit in a meaningful perspective.

References

Brown, J. S., & Duguid, P. (2000). *The social life of information.* Cambridge, MA: Harvard Business School.

Carey, S., & Gelman, R. (1991). *The epigenesis of mind: Essays on biology and cognition.* Hillsdale, NJ: Lawrence Erlbaum Associates.

Cobb, P. (1994). Where is the mind? Constructivist and sociocultural perspectives on mathematical development. *Educational Researcher, 23*(7), 13-20.

Cobb, P., & Bowers, J. (1999). Cognitive and situated learning perspectives in theory and practice. *Educational Researcher, 28*(2), 4-15.

Chen, D-T, & Hung, D. (2002). Personalised knowledge representations: The missing half of online discussions. *British Journal of Educational Technology, 33*(3), 279-290.

Duffy, T., & Jonassen, D. (Eds.). (1992). *Constructivism and the technology of instruction: A conversation.* Hillsdale, NJ: Lawrence Erlbaum Associates.

Greeno, J. (1997). On claims that answer the wrong questions. *Educational Researcher, 26*(1), 5-17.

Hanks, W. F. (1996). *Language and communicative practices.* Boulder, CO: Westview.

Hiebert, J., Carpenter, T. P., Fennema, E., Fusion, K., Human, P., Murray, H., Oliver, A, & Wearne, D. (1996). Problem solving as a basis for reform in curriculum and instruction. The case of mathematics. *Educational Researcher, 25*(4), 12-21.

Lave, J., & Wenger, E. (1991). *Situated learning: Legitimate peripheral participation.* Cambridge: Cambridge University Press.

Piaget, J. (1972). *The principles of genetic epistemology* (W. Mays, Trans.). New York: Basic Books.

Stellin, S. (2000, August 28). *Internet Companies Lean How to Personalize Service,* [World Wide Web]. The New York Times on the Web. Available: http://www.nytimes.com/library/tech/00/08/cyber/commerce/28commerce.html [2000, August 30].

von Glasersfeld, E. (1992). Constructivism reconstructed: A reply to Suchting. *Science and Education, 1,* 379-384.

von Glasersfeld, E. (1989). Cognition, construction of knowledge, and teaching. *Synthese, 80,* 121-140.
Wertsch, J. (1998). Mind in action. Cambridge, MA: Cambridge University Press.
Vygotsky, L. S. (1978). *Mind in society: The development of higher psychological processes.* Cambridge, MA: Harvard University Press.

Selected Bibliography

Abad, V.J. (1999). Hebdo-Chim, a Web application to support learning in a chemistry methods pre-service course. *Journal of Science Education and Technology, 8,* 283 - 290.

Aggarwal, A. K., & Bento, R. (2000). Web-based education. In A. Aggarwal (Ed.), *Web-based learning and teaching technologies: opportunities and challenges.* London, UK. IDEA Group Publishing.

Albon, R. & Trinidad, S. (2002). Building learning communities through technology. In K. Appleton, C. Macpherson, & D. Orr (Eds.), *International Lifelong Learning Conference: Refereed papers from the 2nd International Lifelong Learning Conference,* (pp. 50-56) Yeppoon, Central Queensland, Australia.

Albon, R., & Trinidad, S. (2001). Tapping out new rhythms in the journey of learning. In A. Herrmann and M.M. Kulski (Eds), *Expanding Horizons in Teaching and Learning.* Proceedings of the 10th Annual Teaching Learning Forum, 7-9 February 2001. Perth: Curtin University of Technology. [verified 10 Jan 2003]. http://cleo.murdoch.edu.au/confs/tlf/tlf2001/trinidad.html

Aldridge, J. M., & Fraser, B. J. (2000). A cross-cultural study of classroom learning environments in Australia and Taiwan. *Learning Environment Research: An International Journal, 3,* 101-134.

Aldridge, J. M., Fraser, B. J., & Huang, I. T.-C. (1999). Investigating classroom environments in Taiwan and Australia with multiple research methods. *Journal of Educational Research, 93,* 48-62.

Aldridge, J. M., Fraser, B. J., Taylor, P. C., & Chen, C.-C. (2000). Constructivist learning environments in a cross-national study in Taiwan and Australia. *International Journal of Science Education, 22,* 37-55.

Alister, B. F. (1999). Colleges should tap the pedagogical potential of the World Wide Web. *Chronicle of Higher Education. 48,* 8.

Anderson, C. J., & Walberg H. J. (1974). Learning Environments. In H.J.Walberg (Eds.), *Evaluating educational performance: A source book of methods, instruments, and examples.* Berkeley, California: McCutchan.

Bain, D., McNaught, C., Mills, C., & Leuckenhausen, G. (1998). Describing computer facilitated learning environments in higher education, *Learning Environments Research, 1,* 163-180.

Bannan, B., & Milheim, W. D. (1997). Existing Web-Based instruction courses and their design In B. H. Khan (Ed.), *Web-based instruction* (pp. 381-387). Englewood Cliffs, New Jersey: Educational Technology Publication, Inc.

Barnea, N., & Dori, Y. J. (1999). High-school chemistry students' performance and gender differences in a computerized molecular modeling learning environment. *Journal of Science Education and Technology, 8,* 4, 257-271.

Barnes, S. (2003). *Computer-mediated communication: Human-to-human communication across the internet.* Boston: Allyn & Bacon.

Bitter, G., & Pierson, M. (2002). *Using technology in the classroom.* Boston: Allyn & Bacon.

Bonk, C. J., & Cummings, J. A. (1998). A dozen recommendations for placing the student at the center of web-based learning. *Educational Media International, 35* (2), 82-89.

Breck, J. (2002). *How we will learn in the 21st Century.* Oxford: The Scarecrow Press.

Brekelmans, M. (1989). *Interpersonal teacher behaviour in the classroom.* In Dutch: Interpersoonlijk gedrag van docenten in de klas. Utrecht: W.C.C.

Brekelmans, M., Sleegers, P., & Fraser, B. (2000). Teaching for active learning. In P. R. J. Simons, J. L. van der Linden, & T. Duffy (Eds.), *New Learning* (pp. 227-242). Dordrecht: Kluwer Academic Publishers.

Brown, J. S., & Duguid, P. (2000). *The social life of information.* Cambridge, MA: Harvard Business School.

Brown, J. S., Collins, A., & Duguid, P. (1989). Situated cognition and the culture of learning. *Educational Researcher, 18,* 32-41.

Carpi, A. (2001). Improvements in undergraduate science education using web-based instructional modules. *Journal of Chemical Education, 78,* 1709-1712.

Chen, D-T, & Hung, D. (2002). Personalised knowledge representations: The missing half of online discussions. *British Journal of Educational Technology,* 33(3), 279-290.

Churchland, P. S. (1996). Toward a neurobiology of the mind In R. Lilnas & P. S. Churchland (Eds.), *The mind brain continuum* (pp. 281–303). Cambridge, MA: MIT Press

Clayton, J. (2000, December). *Does online teaching add value to the teaching of science?* Paper presented at the Science in Nursing Education Conference, Hamilton.

Cobb, P. (1994). Where is the mind? Constructivist and sociocultural perspectives on mathematical development. *Educational Researcher, 23*(7), 13-20.

Cobb, P., & Bowers, J. (1999). Cognitive and situated learning perspectives in theory and practice. *Educational Researcher, 28*(2), 4-15.

Commonwealth Department of Education, Science and Training, (2001). *Making better connections: Models of teacher professional development for the integration of information and communication technology into classroom practice.* [Online] Available: http://www.dest.gov.au/schools/publications/2002/professional.htm

Covey, S. R. (1994). *Daily reflections for highly effective people.* New York: Fireside - Simon and Schuster.

Davalos, D. B., Chavez, E. L., & Guardiola, R. J. (1999). The effects of extracurricular activity, ethnic identification and perception of school on student dropout rates. *Hispanic Journal of Behavioural Sciences, 21,* 1, 61-77.

Davies, A., & Parfett, M. (1997). *The Internet - A feasibility Study into its possible role in improving the Welfare and Education of Seafarers,* Report May 1997, SIRC, University of Wales, Cardiff

den Brok, P. J. (2001). *Teaching and student outcomes: A study on teachers' thoughts and actions from an interpersonal and a learning activities perspective.* Utrecht: W. C. C.

den Brok, P. J., Levy, J., Rodriguez, R., & Wubbels, T. (2002). Perceptions of Asian-American and Hispanic-American teachers and their students on interpersonal communication style. *Teaching and Teacher Education, 18,* 447-467.

den Brok, P. J., Levy, J., Wubbels, T., & Rodriguez, M. (2003). Cultural influences on students' perceptions of videotaped lessons. *International Journal of Intercultural Relations, 27* (3), 268-288.

Derksen, K. (1994). *Between taking over and activating instruction.* In Dutch: Tussen sturen en activeren. Masters thesis. Nijmegen: Vakgroep Onderwijskunde.

Dorman, J. P. (1998) The development and validation of an instrument to assess institutional-level environments in universities, *Learning Environments Research, 2*, 79-98.

Dorman, J. P. (2001). Associations between classroom environment and academic efficacy. *Learning Environment Research: An International Journal, 4*, 243-257.

Dorman, J. P., Adams, J. E., & Ferguson, J. M. (in press). Confirmatory factor analysis of the 'What is Happening in this Class' questionnaire and its structural invariance across groups. *Journal of Classroom Interaction.*

Evans, H., & Fisher, D. (2000). Cultural differences in students' perceptions of science teachers' interpersonal behaviour. *Australian Science Teachers Journal, 46*, 9-18.

Fisher, D. L. & Fraser, B. J. (1981). Validity and use of My Class Inventory. *Science Education, 65*, 145-156.

Forgasz. H. J. & Leder, G. C. (2000). Perceptions of the tertiary learning environment: is mathematics worth the effort? *International Journal of Mathematics Education in Science and Technology, 31*, 37-42.

Fraser, B. (1998). Science learning environments: Assessment, effects and determinants. In B. Fraser & K. Tobin (Eds.), *International handbook of science education* (pp. 527-564). Dordrecht, The Netherlands: Kluwer.

Fraser, B. J. (1984). Differences between preferred and actual classroom environment as perceived by primary students and teachers. *British Journal of Educational Psychology, 54*, 336-339.

Fraser, B. J. (1991). Two decades of classroom environments research, in B. J. Fraser and H. J. Walberg (eds.), *Educational environments: Antecedents, consequences and evaluation,* Pergamon Press, London.

Fraser, B. J. (1994). Research on classroom and school climate. In D. Gabel (Ed.), *Handbook of research on science teaching and learning* (pp. 493-541). New York: MacMillan.

Fraser, B. J. (1998). Science learning environments: Assessment, effect and determinants. In B. J. Fraser & K. G. Tobin (Eds.), *International handbook of science education* (pp. 527-564). Dordrecht: Kluwer Academic Publishers.

Fraser, B. J. (1998). Classroom environment instruments: Development, validity and applications. *Learning Environment Research: An International Journal, 1*, 7-33.

Fraser, B. J. (1998). The birth of a new journal: Editor's introduction. *Learning Environments Research, 1,* 1-5.

Fraser, B. J. (1999). "Grain sizes" in learning environment research: Combining qualitative and quantitative methods. In H. C. Waxman & H. J. Walberg (Eds.), *New directions for teaching practice and research* (pp. 285-296). Berkeley, CA: McCutchan.

Fraser, B. J., Giddings, G. J., & McRobbie, C. J. (1993). Development and cross-national validation of a laboratory classroom environment instrument for senior high school science. *Science Education, 77,* 1-24.

Gagen, M. (2001). The molecular world: a new, integrated, multimedia-rich course from the UK Open University. In A, F. Cachapuz (Ed.), *Proceedings of the 2nd European Conference on Chemical Education.* Aveiro, Portugal, University of Aveiro.

Gordon, B. (1995). Knowledge construction, competing critical theories and education. In: J. Banks & C. Banks, (Eds.), *Handbook of Research on Multicultural Education* (pp.184-202). New York: Macmillan.

Grandjean, E. (1988). *Ergonomics in computerized offices.* London: Taylor and Francis.

Hall, B. (2001). E-Learning - building competitive advantage through people and technology, Retrieved August 3, 2001 from the World WideWeb: www.Forbes.com/specialsections/elearning/contents.html

Harper, D. (2002, March). *Generation Y White Paper.2.* Olympia, WA: Generation Y Organization.

Havelock, R. (1973). *A change agents guide to innovation.* Englewood Cliffs, New Jersey: Educational Technology Publications.

Hiltz, S. R. (1994). *The virtual classroom: Learning without limits via computer networks.* Norwood, New Jersey : Ablex.

Hirata, S., & Sako, T. (1999). Perceptions of school environment among Japanese junior high school, non-attendant, and juvenile delinquent students. *Learning Environment Research: An International Journal, 1*(3), 321-331.

Hirata, S., Kanno, J., & Koizumi, E. (1999). Some characteristics of non-attendant students' cognition toward their school environment. Japanese *Journal of Counseling Science, 32,* 124-133 (in Japanese).

Hofstein, A., & Kempa, R. F. (1985). Motivating aspects in science education: An attempt at an analysis. *European Journal of Science Education, 7,* 221-229.

Hofstein, A., & Walberg H, J. (1995). Instructional strategies. In B. J. Fraser & H. J. Walberg (Eds.), *Improving Science Education. The NSSE Yearbook.* Chicago, IL: The International Academy of Education.

House, J. D. (1999). Self-beliefs and background variables as predictors of school withdrawal of adolescent students. *Child Study Journal, 29* (4), 247-265.

Hyman, I.A. & Snook, P.A. (2000). Dangerous schools and what you can do about them. *Phi Delta Kappan,* 81(7),489-501.

ImpaCT2. (2001). ImpaCT2:Pupils and teachers perceptions of ICT in the home, school and community. Department for Education and Skills (DfES) and BectaICT Research. [verified 10 Jan 2003] http://www.becta.org.uk/research/reports/docs/ImpaCT2_strand_2_report.pdf

Jackson, R. (2002). Weblearning resources. [verified 10 Jan 2003] http://www.knowledgeability.biz/weblearning/#Different%20Shades%20of%20Online

Jensen, E. (1998). *Teaching with the brain in mind.* Alexandria, VA: Association for Supervision and Curriculum Development.

Jonassen, D. H. (2000). *Computers as mindtools for schools: Engaging critical thinking.* New Jersey: Prentice Hall.

Jonassen, D. H., Howland, J., Moore, J., & Marra, R.M. (2003). *Learning to solve problems with technology: A constructivist perspective.* New Jersey : Prentice Hall, Inc.

Jonassen, D.H (2000). *Computers as mindtools for schools: Engaging critical thinking.* Columbus, Ohio: Merrill.

Kesner, M., Hofstein, A., & Ben-Zvi, R. (1997). The development and implementation of two industrial chemistry case studies for the Israeli high school chemistry curriculum. *International Journal of Science Education, 19* (5), 565-576.

Kesner, M., Hofstein, A., & Ben-Zvi, R. (1997). Student and teacher perceptions of industrial chemistry case studies. *International Journal of Science Education, 19* (6), 725-738.

Khan, B. H. (1997). *Web-based instruction.* Englewood Cliffs, New Jersey: Educational Technology Publication, Inc.

Khine, M. S. & Fisher D.L. (2001, December). *Classroom environment and teachers' cultural background in secondary science classes in an Asian context,* Paper presented at the annual conference of the

Australian Association for Research in Education, Fremantle, Western Australia.

Khine, M. S. & Goh, S. C. (2001). Students' perceptions of the university learning environment in Singapore. *Journal of Applied Research in Education,* 5(1), 45-51.

Khine, M. S., & Fisher, D. L. (2001). *Classroom environment and teachers' cultural background in secondary science classes in an Asian context.* Paper presented at the annual conference of the Australian Association for Research in Education, Fremantle, Western Australia.

Laurillard, D. (1993). *Rethinking university teaching: A framework for the effective use of educational technology.* London: Routledge.

Lave, J., & Wenger, E. (1991). *Situated learning: Legitimate peripheral participation.* Cambridge: Cambridge University Pres.

Law, N., Yuen, H.K., Ki, W.W., Li, S.C., Lee, Y. & Chow, Y. (2000). (Eds.) *Changing Classrooms & Changing Schools: A Study of Good Practices in Using ICT in Hong Kong Schools.* Hong Kong: Centre for IT in School and Teacher Education, The University of Hong Kong.

Lever-Duffy, J., McDonald, J., & Mizell. (2003). *Teaching and learning with technology.* Boston: Allyn & Bacon.

Levy, J., den Brok, P., Wubbels, T., & Brekelmans, M. (2003). Students' perceptions of interpersonal aspects of the learning environment. *Learning Environments Research,* 6, 1, 5-36.

Lizzio, A., Wilson, K., & Simons, R. (2002). University students' perceptions of the learning environment and academic outcomes: implication for theory and practice, *Studies in Higher Education,* 27, 27-52.

Lynch, M. M. (2002). *The online educator: A guide to creating the virtual classroom.* London : Routledge Falmer.

Maor, D. (2000). A teacher professional development program on using a constructivist multimedia learning environment. *Learning Environment Research,* 2, 307-330.

Margianti, E. S. (2002). Learning environment research in Indonesia. In S.C. Goh & M. S. Khine (Eds.). *Studies in educational learning environments: An international perspective* (pp 153-167). Singapore: World Scientific.

Mayer, R. (2001). *Multimedia learning.* Cambridge: Cambridge University Press.

Moos, R. H. (1974). *The Social Climate Scales: An overview.* Palo Alto, CA: Consulting Psychologists Press.

Muirhead, P. M. (1998). *Assessment of the potential in the use of new teaching and training methodologies in MET; distance learning through onboard training,* Work Package 4.4 report, EU Transport Project 'METHAR', WMU, Malmö, Sweden

Newby M., & Fisher D. L. (1997). An instrument for assessing the learning environment of a computer laboratory, *Journal of Educational Computing Research 16* (2), 179-197.

Newby M., & Fisher D. L. (1998, April). *Associations between university computer laboratory environments and student outcomes.* Paper presented at the American Educational Research Association Annual Meeting, San Diego, CA.

Newby, M., & Fisher, D. L. (2000). A model of the relationship between computer laboratory environment and student outcomes in university courses. *Learning Environments Research, 3*(1), 51-66.

Newhouse, C. P. (2001). Development and use of an instrument for computer-supported learning environments. *Learning Environment Research: An International Journal, 4,* 115-138.

Nunnally, J. (1967). *Psychometric theory.* New York: McGraw-Hill.

Palloff, R. M., & Pratt, K. (2001). *Lessons from the cyberspace classroom : The realities of online teaching.* California : John Wiley & Sons, Inc.

Reeves, T. C., & Reeves, P. M. (1997). Effective dimensions of interactive learning on the WWW In B. H. Khan (Ed.), *Web-Based Instruction* (pp. 59-66). Englewood Cliffs, New Jersey: Educational Technology Publication, Inc.

Relan, A., & Gillani, B. B. (1997). Web-Based instruction and the traditional classroom: Similarities and differences. In B. H. Khan (Ed.), *Web-Based Instruction* (pp. 41-46). Englewood Cliffs, New Jersey: Educational Technology Publication, Inc.

Resta, P. (1998). *Collaborative technologies as a catalyst for changing teacher practices.* Washington: US Department of Education.

Rice, M, & Wilson, E. (1999). How technology aids constructivism in the social studies classroom. *Social Studies, 90,* 28-34.

Rogers, C., & Freiberg, H. J. (1994). *Freedom to learn* (3rd Ed.). New York: Merrill.

Senge, P. M. (1990). *The fifth discipline: The art and practice of the learning organization.* New York: Doubleday.

Sharp, V. (2002). *Computer education for teachers: Integrating technology into classroom teaching.* New York: McGraw-Hill.
She, H. C., & Fisher, D. (2002). Teacher communication behavior and Its association with students' cognitive and attitudinal outcomes in science in Taiwan. *Journal of Research in Science Teaching, 39*(1), 63-78.
She, H.C., & Fisher, D. (2000). The development of a questionnaire to describe science teacher communication behavior in Taiwan and Australia. *Science Education, 84*(6), 706-26.
Sherry, L., & Wilson, B. (1997). Transformation communication as a stimulus to Web innovations In B. H. Khan (Ed.), *Web-Based Instruction* (pp. 67-73). Englewood Cliffs, New Jersey: Educational Technology Publication, Inc.
Solomon, G. (1999). Collaborative learning with technology. *Technology and Learning,* 19(5), 51-53.
Steinberg, R. (2000). Computers in teaching science: to stimulate or not to stimulate. *American Journal of Physics, 68*(7), 37-41.
Stern, G. G. (1970). *People in context: Measuring person-environment congruence in education and industry.* New York: Wiley.
Sternberg, R. (1997). *Thinking styles.* New York: Cambridge University press.
Straker, L., Harris C., & Zandvliet, D. (2000, Aug.). *Scarring a generation of school children through poor introduction of IT in schools.* Paper presented at the triennial meeting of the International Ergonomics Association.
Tobin, K. (1998). Qualitative Perceptions of Learning Environments on the World Wide Web. In B. J. Fraser and K. G. Tobin (eds.). *International Handbook of Science Education* (pp. 139-162). Dordrecht: Kluwer Academic Publishers.
Tobin, K., & Fraser, B. (1998). Qualitative and quantitative landscapes of classroom learning environments. In B. J. Fraser & K. G. Tobin (Eds.), *The international handbook of science education* (pp. 623-640). Dordrecht, The Netherlands: Kluwer.
Tobin, K., & Fraser, B. J. (1998). Qualitative and quantitative landscapes of classroom learning environments In B. J. Fraser & K. G. Tobin (Eds.), *International Handbook of Science Education* (pp. 623-640). Dordrecht: Kluwer Academic Publishers.
Trinidad, S. & Albon, R. (2002). Using the potential of technology to reconceptualise assessment. Paper presented at the *Ninth*

International Literacy and Education Research Network Conference on Learning, July 16th – 20th Beijing: Peoples Republic of China.

Trinidad, S. & Albon, R. (2003). Building a community of elearners. Paper presented at *South Africa 2003 - 3rd International Conference on Science, Maths and Technology Education*, January 15th-18th, East London: Rhodes University.

Trinidad, S., Macnish, J., Aldridge, J., Fraser, B., & Wood, D. (2001). Integrating ICT into the learning environment at Sevenoaks Senior College: How teachers and students use educational technology in teaching and learning. Paper presented at *Australian Association for Research in Education AARE2001 Conference*, December 2nd-5th Fremantle: Notre Dame University.

UNESCO Report (n. d.) ICT and Teacher Education: Global Context and Framework. [verified 10 Jan 2003] http://www.gcu-uec.org/UNESCOreport-chap1.rtf

Vygotsky, L. S. (1978). *Mind in society: The development of higher psychological processes.* Cambridge, MA: Harvard University Press.

Walberg, H. J. (1981). A psychological theory of educational productivity. In F. Farley & N. J. Gordon (Eds.), *Psychology and education: The state of the union* (pp. 81-108). Berkeley, CA: McCutchan.

Walberg, H. J. (Ed.). (1979). *Educational environments and effects: Evaluation, policy and productivity.* Berkeley, CA: McCutchan.

Weigel, V. (2002). *Deep learning for digital age: Technology's untapped potential to enrich higher education.* San Francisco: Jossey-Bass.

Wertsch, J. (1998). Mind in action. Cambridge, MA: Cambridge University Press.

Wheatley, M. J. (1999a). *Leadership and the new science: Discovering order in a chaotic world* (2nd ed.). San Francisco: Berrett-Koehler Publishers.

Wheatley, M. J. (1999b, July). *Reclaiming hope: The new story is ours to tell.* Summer Institute, University of Utah.

Wilson, B. (1996). *Constructivist learning environments: Case studies in instructional design.* New Jersey: Educational Technology Publications.

Wilson, B., and Lowry, M. (2000). Constructivist learning on the Web. In E. Burge (Ed.) *The strategic use of learning technologies.* (pp 79-88). San Francisco: Jossey-Bass.

Wilson, B.G. (Ed.). (1996). *Constructivist learning environments: Case studies in instructional design*. Englewood Cliffs, NJ: Educational Technology.

Wubbels, T., & Levy, J. (Eds.). (1993). *Do you know what you look like? Interpersonal relationships in education* (1st ed.). London, England: The Falmer Press.

Yaron, D., Freeland, R., Lang D., & Milton J. (2000). *Using simulations to transform the nature of chemistry homework*. A progress report, Department of Chemistry, Carnegie Mellon University, Pittsburgh, PA.

Zandvliet, D., & Fraser, B.J. (1998, April). *The physical and psychosocial environment associated with classrooms using new information technologies*. Paper presented at the annual meeting of the American Educational Research Association, San Diego, CA.

Zandvliet D.B. and Straker L. (2001, July). Physical and psychosocial ergonomic aspects of the learning environment in information technology rich classrooms. *Ergonomics, 449*, 838-857.

Index

academic efficacy, 41, 42, 44, 56, 62, 63, 64, 66, 168, 180
ACCC, 194, 197, 201
access, 1, 7, 9, 11, 12, 15–17, 22, 23, 26, 99, 101, 105, 108, 111, 115–125, 128–131, 134, 150, 187, 188, 191, 192, 197, 213, 237, 241, 242, 244–247, 249, 252, 268, 287, 293, 295, 297, 300, 302, 308, 311, 312, 314, 334, 340, 398, 403
actual, 41, 44, 46, 47, 50, 57, 59, 62– 64, 71, 72, 74, 76, 78, 79, 81, 85, 87, 88, 89, 91–93, 95, 141, 146, 147, 155, 161, 175, 222, 259, 266, 291, 292, 297, 298–303, 345, 369–373, 375–377, 379, 380, 382, 391
actual classroom, 71, 74, 85, 266, 303, 369, 370, 376, 377, 379, 380

CCEI, 146, 147, 149, 169, 171, 173, 287, 291, 292, 296, 297, 298
CES-J.II, 373, 380
chemistry education, 213, 221, 226
classroom management, 21, 23, 25, 29, 30, 37, 38, 262, 380, 381
CLEI, 167, 194, 195, 197, 200
closed laboratories, 187, 188, 191, 193, 194, 195, 201, 203, 204, 206, 207
collaboration, 5, 9, 23, 99, 100, 105, 106, 109, 167, 174, 289, 309, 310, 314, 339, 391

computer class, 71, 151
computer laboratories, 187, 188, 189, 192, 193, 196, 200, 202, 204, 253, 302
computer-mediated, 18, 23, 38
computers in education, 113, 162, 184
constructivist learning environment, 100, 105, 137, 344
constructivist learning, 21, 38, 39, 65, 100, 105, 132, 137, 307, 344

delivery of education, 247
discussion forums, 288, 303, 391

educational technology, 18–20, 39, 112, 118, 132, 155, 182, 205, 207, 304, 307, 308, 311–313, 331, 332, 367, 405
effective teaching, 20, 38, 115, 118, 119, 125, 131, 304
ELCEQ, 285, 291, 292, 296, 297, 298, 299, 300, 301, 302
e-Learning, 97, 99, 100, 107–110, 180, 182, 254, 285–288, 290–297, 301, 302, 328, 362, 385, 386, 390, 394, 396, 397, 400, 401, 404
e-learning projects, 97
ergonomic checklist, 138, 142
ethnicity, 260, 262, 263, 264, 270
evaluation, 2, 29, 67, 68, 94, 99, 108, 132, 133, 135, 137, 142, 170, 185, 205, 225, 240, 273, 274, 279, 285–287, 305, 308, 313, 339, 366, 367, 382, 383

expert knowledge, 125, 258, 259, 267, 276, 277

flash science learning, 343, 348, 359, 362, 364

Generation Y Model, 307, 310, 314
global links, 235

higher education, 1, 2, 3, 39, 72, 74, 93–95, 112, 179, 180, 185, 226, 310, 311, 370, 372, 380, 381, 382

ICT, 21, 22, 25, 38, 41, 42, 43, 44, 46, 53, 63, 65, 104, 111, 112, 113, 116, 118, 119, 126, 127, 128, 134, 136, 137, 138, 151
ICT-rich, 42
interaction, 1, 3, 4, 9, 11, 12, 14, 15, 17–19, 21, 26, 37, 42, 74, 96, 98, 130, 152, 158, 160, 161, 164, 167–169, 182, 191, 196, 218, 224, 259, 260, 261, 268, 285, 287–290, 293, 302, 346, 366, 370, 375, 376, 383, 385, 388, 402, 403
interactive learning, 20, 100, 103, 110, 252, 348
Internet Learning Environment, 209

junior high school, 313, 369, 371, 372, 383

Learning communities, 23, 38, 111, 311, 312, 322
learning environment, 1–4, 8, 11–13, 15, 17, 19, 21, 24, 29, 37, 38, 41, 42, 44, 45, 47, 53, 54, 56, 57, 58, 61, 63, 64, 66–68, 71–79, 81, 83–85, 87, 89, 91–96, 102, 103, 105, 107, 112, 118, 119, 121, 122, 125, 133, 134, 136–144, 146–149, 152–154, 156–158, 161, 162, 164, 167, 172, 174, 175, 178–180, 183, 184, 187, 188, 193, 194, 200, 202, 206, 207, 212–216, 223–226, 247, 255, 257–259, 263, 266–268, 270–277, 280, 281, 285–287, 289–291, 293, 296, 300, 302–304, 370, 375, 379, 380–382, 395, 403
learning environments, 1, 2, 5, 9, 18, 20, 22, 25, 39, 41–44, 46, 57, 61–63, 65–68, 72, 75, 93, 97–100, 106, 109, 110, 115, 116, 118–122, 124, 126, 129–132, 136–140, 145, 148, 152–155, 161, 162, 171, 179, 181, 183, 185, 193, 206, 207, 214, 222, 281, 285–287, 289, 290, 302–305, 320, 343, 347, 354, 365, 366, 370, 371, 375, 378, 380, 383, 385, 386, 390, 395, 400–404
learning styles, 10, 41, 96, 215, 220, 318, 343, 344, 347, 348, 349, 355, 362, 365, 366

maritime education, 235, 236, 254
multicultural classrooms, 255, 256, 257, 259, 260, 263, 267, 268, 269, 270, 272, 273, 274, 275, 276, 277
multimedia, 21, 24, 25, 37, 67, 135, 150, 184, 189, 193, 206, 213, 226, 227, 236, 237, 238, 244, 247, 252, 287, 307, 343, 348, 362, 364, 366

networked communities, 97, 328

online learning, 1, 2, 3, 4, 5, 8, 15, 17, 157, 158, 159, 160, 161,

162, 164, 172, 173, 178, 179, 180, 182, 185, 236, 286, 287, 289, 290, 292, 303
open laboratories, 187, 188, 191, 198, 200, 201, 202, 203, 204
outcomes-focus, 41, 42

pedagogy, 6, 100, 118, 119, 126, 135, 180, 183, 209, 210, 221, 225, 260, 266, 271, 280, 321
perceptual measures, 162, 173, 369, 379, 380, 381
personalization, 386, 390, 394, 395, 396, 397
Practical Knowledge, 257, 258, 260, 266, 276
preferred, 41, 44, 46, 47, 57, 62, 63, 71, 72, 74, 76, 78, 79, 85, 87, 88, 90, 91, 92, 93, 95, 155, 291, 292, 297, 298, 299, 300, 301, 302, 303, 344, 366, 369, 370, 371, 372, 373, 375, 376, 377, 378, 379, 380, 382
preferred classroom, 41, 44, 62, 63, 71, 85, 93, 95, 155, 369, 370, 376, 377, 379, 382
professional development, 134, 136, 154, 210, 220, 221, 255, 304, 307, 310, 313, 314, 332, 334
psychological measures, 369, 371, 381
psychosocial learning environments, 133, 139

reciprocity, 321, 331, 332, 333, 334, 335, 336, 337, 338, 339, 340, 341

satellite communication, 235, 238, 244

satellite communications, 236, 244, 245
scaffolding, 23, 37, 100, 104, 105, 108, 345, 402
social-cultural, 108, 324, 386, 387, 388, 389, 392
strategies, 8, 22, 24, 26, 93, 97, 102, 108–110, 157, 158, 172, 178, 185, 193, 210, 212, 217, 226, 249, 260, 263–265, 270, 281, 291, 328, 402
student achievement, 42, 53, 56, 63, 64, 84, 92, 136, 137, 162, 168, 308, 369, 370, 383
student attitude, 52, 54, 83
student attitudes, 54, 57, 137, 139, 194, 204
student involvement, 316
Student perspectives, 328
student voice, 307, 316, 318, 321, 322, 327
students' perceptions, 2, 9, 29, 31, 41, 44, 50, 54, 56, 57, 62, 71, 73, 78, 79, 83–85, 87, 92, 94, 95, 167, 187, 188, 203, 205, 261, 281, 286, 290, 292, 296, 302, 305, 346, 354, 356, 357, 359, 371
student-teacher communication, 260
SWBL, 350, 353, 354, 355, 357, 358, 359, 361, 362, 363
systems approach, 260, 261, 331, 332

teacher competencies, , 24 128
technology-rich, 21, 29, 37, 41–44, 57, 62, 63, 65, 97, 99, 102, 103, 109, 110, 111, 115–122, 124, 129, 131, 133, 157, 158, 178, 252, 331, 369, 381, 385, 404
technology-rich learning, 21, 29, 37, 97, 100, 103, 109, 110, 115,

116, 120, 121, 122, 124, 129, 131, 254, 385, 385
tertiary education, 73
TOSRA, 45, 66, 78, 143, 144, 350, 365
training, 43, 65, 101, 112, 118, 123, 126, 127, 131, 134, 179, 180, 188, 192, 218, 225, 235–252, 254, 272, 281, 292, 308, 313, 331–335, 338, 340, 391
TROFLEI, 44, 45, 46, 47, 48, 50, 51, 54, 55, 56, 57, 58, 59, 60, 61, 62, 63, 64, 65

WBCAL, 350, 352, 356, 357, 358, 359, 362, 363

web-based learning, 1, 3, 6, 9, 11, 13, 158, 171, 214, 343, 344, 346, 348, 349, 353, 354, 357, 358, 361, 363, 365, 385, 401, 402, 403, 404
Web-Capable Classrooms, 133
WEBLEI, 1, 8, 9, 10, 11, 12, 13, 14, 15, 16, 17, 171, 173
web-supported learning environment, 255
WIHIC, 45, 46, 47, 65, 71, 76, 77, 78, 79, 81, 82, 83, 84, 85, 86, 87, 88, 89, 90, 91, 92, 133, 136, 141, 143, 144, 145, 146, 149, 349, 351, 352, 354, 356, 357, 358, 359, 360, 362, 363

www.ingramcontent.com/pod-product-compliance
Lightning Source LLC
Chambersburg PA
CBHW052010290426
44112CB00014B/2184